INDIA NOW AND IN TRANSITION

INDIA NOW AND IN TRANSITION

edited by
Atul K. Thakur

with a foreword by
SUNIL KHILNANI

NIYOGI BOOKS

Published by

NIYOGI BOOKS

D-78, Okhla Industrial Area, Phase-I
New Delhi-110 020, INDIA
Tel: 91-11-26816301, 49327000
Fax: 91-11-26810483, 26813830
email: niyogibooks@gmail.com
website: www.niyogibooksindia.com

Editor: K.E. Priyamvada
Design: Shashi Bhushan Prasad
Cover Design: Misha Oberoi
Cover Image: Naintara Jain

ISBN: 978-93-85285-63-9
Publication: 2017
Reprint: 2025

Printed at: Niyogi Offset Pvt. Ltd., New Delhi, India

To the journalist and great human being—late B.G. Verghese,
my paternal grandparents late Upendra Thakur and late Gita Thakur,
and maternal grandfather late Bimlendra Lal Mishra.

Contents

ECONOMICS AND DEVELOPMENT

SECURITY AND FOREIGN POLICY

SOCIETY AND CULTURE

LANGUAGE AND LITERATURE

Foreword

That India is in the throes of unprecedented historical change is a cliché of the age. The transition from an agrarian to an urban society, the shift in demographic balance to a youthful society, the expansion of economic growth alongside the concentration of wealth and capital, the decimation of environmental conditions and the uneven—often conflictual—cultural and political effects of such changes, are apparent to all of us. Yet the nature of changes, their scale, qualities and implications, remain under-investigated and under-interpreted.

We are moving headlong into new circumstances, but with little sense of what that may mean. Perhaps it was always, and necessarily, thus: the owl of Minerva takes wing at dusk, historical understanding is always retrospective. But in a world where journalism and the social sciences are developed, professional, fields designed above all to improve our judgement and choices, it behoves practitioners in those fields to offer us some illumination along the way.

This collection of 37 essays is remarkable in its breadth: covering a range of topics from party politics to economic trends and forms of urbanisation, considerations on the media, literature, sports, studies of foreign policy, domestic inequality and strife, the natural environment and cyberspace. The diverse set of writers include some of our sharpest and most engaged public commentators and analysts. By bringing so many of them together into a single volume, the editor, Atul K. Thakur deserves our compliments.

He deserves our thanks too: for he has managed to orchestrate the variety of subjects covered, and plurality of approaches adopted, into an engaging, illuminating and fast-paced tour of our jagged contemporary landscape. We should read these essays carefully, as well as urgently: for they take us to parts of the country and raise issues which our academic social sciences have in recent decades tended to avoid, with their tendency to drift into a more rarified scholasticism.

The man to whom this volume is dedicated, B. George Verghese, was one of the exemplary journalists of his generation: not least because, even as he traded in the business of daily events and news, he kept with him a historical perspective on current events. An editor and journalist, he was also a writer of books that tackled some of the long-running yet often marginalised conflicts of our republic: the North East, for instance, as well as our insouciant attitude towards that most basic of life resources, water.

If I can be forgiven for a moment a personal memory: I recall going to meet Mr Verghese back in the mid-1980s, when I was a student trying to decide between pursuing further academic research or plunging into the 'real world'—journalism seemed the best example of that. Seated at his desk at *The Indian Express*, he exuded calm authority: I could sense him assessing me, and though he expressed himself in the politest and most subtle ways, I could also sense him suggesting, over measured sips of tea, that I, perhaps, might be better off in the academic world than in the hurly-burly of journalism. India, he drilled home to me, was in the midst of big changes, and whether one chose to be a journalist or an academic, every young Indian had to engage with these epochal changes, had to understand them, and had to try as best they could to shape them in creative directions.

In the decades since, the pace of change has accelerated hugely. We are going to need all the intelligence, hard shoe-leather reporting, courageous investigation and shrewd judgement in order to try to make sense of the world we are creating for ourselves, and will leave for future Indians. Collections such as this one serve as useful springboards: urging us to dig deeper and think harder about our disoriented world—and hopefully, to start to imagine it better.

Sunil Khilnani

Introduction

My first edited work, *India Since 1947: Looking Back at a Modern Nation* (2013) was a collection of essays on a nation that was still trying to come into its own. If we consider the state of our nation today, in certain aspects India has come a long way, while in many others it has a challenging journey and many tough transitions ahead.

This sequel, *India Now and in Transition,* is based on how 'India' is being shaped through contemporary political events and other key determinants. What this book intends is not a prognosis (which is often confused with prediction), but, rather, an inquiry into futures based on current happenings. This necessarily entails deconstructions of the past, as in the previous volume. A causal linearity is maintained, so that the futures proposed will be the likeliest. To that end, the exegesis is rigorously researched, referenced and argued. The book is not intended to be a mere warehouse of opinions. Together, the two volumes cover India's continuum from a nascent nation-state to a mature one.

Since 1947, India as a nation has made significant strides. However, those were not enough. The realisation is growing stronger, as democracy is deepening every day. Despite having followed a 'reluctant revivalist' tendency for close to seven decades, now, in an increasingly technocratic situation, the overall 'governance discourse' is gaining ground to charter something as desired by the people and emerging directly out of compelling necessities. In the early years of this decade it was perceived that 'policy paralysis' and lack of reform impetus in macroeconomic policies led to a downward spiral in business and mass sentiments, which eventually resulted in an alarming level of deceleration in economic growth. The UPA-II regime was blamed for that, which was justified to an extent too, but somewhere there is a need to see the real stumbling blocks. Those stumbling blocks still exist under the new government is at the centre, which was voted to power with an absolute majority in eventful Parliamentary elections of 2014.

It has to be admitted that India's administrative system has become largely non-functional and unresponsive to the interest of the masses. This book focuses on this crux of the problem through 37 essays from some of India's leading policy practitioners, scholars and young writers. Several of the essays seek to trace different aspects of India's political trajectory, from the time of its birth to the modern day. At the heart of the book is the idea that India is struggling to establish a deeper, more definitive democracy. The book captures the centrist tendency in Indian politics, particularly at the national level. The book puts forward the case of political reforms, besides economic and administrative reforms—to bring in structural changes otherwise marred through surviving inconsistencies. Indeed, without a reformed culture of politics, it is naive dreaming of the fruits of economic reforms and that too with equity. Many of the essays from this book have a focus on the interface between politics and economics in India, which actually determines the path of progress for the country.

The essays also offer possible solutions to end the menace of corruption and for achieving inclusive growth—this comes while discussing among others, the pressing issues related to governance, the rise of new politics (through civic activism), growing inequality, alienation, the contradiction between identity politics and development. In the states, identities of various sorts still rule the course of political actions and outcomes. India is presently at a stage wherein the expectations of the electorate are quite diverse, apropos of how the system and its representatives respond to them. Without the freedom movement, India's nationhood would have been inconceivable, which means democracy too would've been inconceivable. This book and the previous volume, focus especially on the consolidation of national democracy after 1947, calling it the next remarkable event after India's independence—where the decisive leadership of Nehru played a major role.

While examining all these changes, the book also indicates the next course of development as far as democracy in India is concerned. In my own view, Indian democracy is the sort that becomes more progressive the more unsettling changes it comes across. After all, time and again, all kinds of political hiccups in India have been solemnised—although with varying degrees of success. Then again, the stakes are much higher at the moment, and forward-looking Indians can no longer trust a government that offers less than a two percent job growth rate, for example. Now is the time for political parties to be as prompt in terms of their actions as their electorates are with their expectations. Overlooking that would be detrimental for success in the political fray as other countries in South Asia have evidenced.

India Now and in Transition offers fresh insights into several crucial areas, elements that have shaped India into what it is today, whether that be the complex set of relations under the country's federal system, the challenges of territorial/cultural diversities, and the contradictory outcomes of economic reforms, among others. This book looks diligently at the successes and failures of India's tryst with democracy, which—despite having many flaws—is charting its course ahead.

The essays in the book are classified into five sections. The first section 'Politics and Governance' has 12 essays beginning with Ramachandra Guha who reflects on the differing perceptions of the Indian *aam aadmi* and the expert in choosing who among us was the greatest Indian, in 'Indians Great, Greater, Greatest?'. As the government and political parties commemorate the 126th birth anniversary of Dr Babasaheb Bhimrao Ramji Ambedkar in 2017, it would be a pity if the life of this extraordinary Indian were reduced to one issue—his championship of the Dalit cause—just as much as it would be wrong to gloss over his path-breaking role in that monumental endeavour. Shashi Tharoor looks beyond the imagined frontier in his piece 'The Enduring Legacy of Dr. Ambedkar'. Chandrahas Choudhury's 'Mr. Modi Wins in Varanasi' assesses the 'paradox of Modi's rise' and the test of Indian democracy's maturity and judgment, in the wake of his landslide victory from Banaras. Rasheed Kidwai makes it clear in the 'Congress and its Ideological Dilemmas' that India's oldest political party is facing many challenges. Wajahat Habibullah's 'Kashmir Today and the Way to the Future' will be remembered as one of the most balanced analytical pieces on Kashmir. India's Northeast is a land distant from the national consciousness and is commonly viewed as a region on the fringe, simmering with trouble, Rajeev Bhattacharyya highlights the issues of the region in 'What Ails the Northeast?' while Rajiv Jayaram's 'Federalism Frenzy: India's Halting Centre-State Relations' is on the derisive treatment given to federalism by the central government since India's

Independence. Robin Jeffrey brings to light the neglected issue of land reform in 'What Happened To "Land Reform"?'. T.S.R. Subramanian's 'Can India Afford not to Eliminate Corruption?' reminds us of the urgency with which the different forms of corruption need to be handled. Manu Bhagavan provides insights into Constitutional history in 'The Hand and the Fist: Human Rights and State Power in India'. Sukanya Natarajan's 'Debating Judicial Reforms in India' and Abinash Chaudhary's 'Governing the Ungoverned: Challenges from Below' are timely reminders of crucial issues.

In the second section 'Economics and Development', economist Jayati Ghosh's 'Indian Economy: Looking Back to Go Forward Differently' is a detailed macroeconomic enquiry, which clears the fog from the 'expectation-reality gap'. Sandeep Dikshit, here more a human development expert than a politician, throws light on 'Human Development: Conceptual Foundations and Practice in India'. No study can be called complete on post-1991 India without having talked about the impact of economic reforms. Here Jaithirth Rao does the needful with his essay 'Whither India's Economic Reforms?'. 'Black Money' is often talked about as flaw in the monetary system by the common people and the political classes. Vivek Kaul's 'Black Money: We Won't Get it Back' is quite educative on the fundamental wrongs of the financial system. Reetika Khera's 'India's Employment Guarantee Act: In a Nutshell' recalls the merit of a flagship programme of UPA, earlier despised but now endorsed by the ruling NDA government. Vinod Rai's 'Audit, Good Governance and Sustainable Development' is written with his first-hand experience of knowing the system and its ailing components in his previous role as a senior bureaucrat known for his integrity. Manu Joseph takes a pragmatic stand on India's growing need for food, and the required ways to accomplish it in 'Falling for the Village Romantics'. My piece discusses 'radical dissent' and the challenges surrounding it in the socio-economic sphere and beyond, in 'The "Real Other" of the World's Largest Democracy'.

India's resources today are greater than at any time in its history, and it no longer confronts existential threats. But while the country may now be less vulnerable, it will have to confront different, and sometimes unprecedented, challenges. In the first piece of the third section 'Security and Foreign Policy', Dhruva Jaishankar takes this thought forward in 'Indian Strategy in a Non-strategic Age'. India's security is a loosely defined term that allows a great deal of misunderstanding. For example, the term 'national security' is not defined in any legislation in India. Omair Ahmad spots this lacuna and elaborates further in his piece 'Indian Internal Security: Are we Sacrificing the Security of our Citizens at the Altar of the Security of the State?'. Samir Saran and Mahima Kaul's 'India's Imminent Prominence in Cyber Oceans' explores India's nuanced stand on Internet governance, and why the world should reciprocate it. Northeast India, has been in the news for long, not for its picturesque landscape and colourful ethnic diversity, not for the rivers that wind down its blue mountains, not for the sound of the hornbills that fly up to the turquoise sky, but for armed violence. Namrata Goswami has written at length on it in 'Insurgency and Statehood: The Drive for Legitimacy in Northeast India'. The latest trend and theoretical propositions of India's foreign policy is well-covered in Rajeev Ranjan Chaturvedy's 'India's Foreign Policy: Asian Dynamics'.

What we have already ended up with are not secular and reliable data analytics with regard to news, mediums of news consumption, rates of news consumption, and real-world prognostics for the future, but with regurgitated bezoars of factoids and bunches of unreconstructed and often tweaked data. Kajal Basu analyses this in 'The Indian News media: The Future of the Numbers Game', the first piece of the fourth section, 'Society and Culture'. Environmental conditions in India ask very political questions of the planners and managers of the government. These problems cannot be solved by having a special day in the calendar dedicated to them. If we have a World Sewage Day, or a World Flooding Day, we will not create a better world. The only way is to study the problem and show readiness to take difficult decisions. Because when it comes to environmental matters, the low-hanging fruits are all gone. Sopan Joshi makes this clear in his piece 'Environmentalism Today'. In the competitive cacophony of the 24/7 news cycle, the Dalit voice is often dismissed in the brief columns of inside pages in mainstream daily newspapers. Daipayan Halder counts the dangers of such a tendency in his 'Hindu India and the Subaltern Voice'. As social changes occur across India, they bring about changes in the social texture of rural India. Abhay Mohan Jha tells this story in 'New Time in Mofussil India'. 'Indianness' is perceived differently by different sets of Indians and their perceptions are moulded by their religious, regional, linguistic and other identities. Abdullah Khan's essay 'The Alchemy of Multiple Identities' discusses the issues of Indian identities in the modern context from the points of view of two major religious communities, Hindus and Muslims, who make up almost 94 per cent of the total population. It also gives hints at how Indians will look at various aspects of their identities in the near future and how the issue of multiple identities will decide the fate of the republic of India. Pallavi Rebbapragada discusses how Indian cinema is 'Forever in Search of its Golden Era' in her piece, while the young writers Aditya Mani Jha and Rini Barman express their views on the tendency of state censorship in 'Wielding the Scissors: Indian Censors and the Silencing of a Generation'. As advertising increasingly impacts our lives, industry insider Anuraag shares his thoughts on the 'Real Market for Dreams: Advertising and the Economics of a Good Deal', while the state of sports is covered in Shamya Dasgupta's 'Money and Mindsets: Sports in India'.

In the fifth and last section 'Language and Literature', Udaya Narayana Singh and Rajarshi Singh's 'View from Below: Utopia and Change' dwells on the lessons from the 'Landscaping of Culture and Education'.Tabish Khair assesses 'Indian Poetry in English', while Namrata Rathore Mahanta and Banibrata Mahanta focus on 'The Indian Novel Today: Existing and Emerging Paradigms'.

The book should be of interest to anyone who has an interest in policy matters and knowing about the fast-changing forms of politics, society, governance and economic processes in India. There is so much happening in India on the policy front that a single book can only provide so much informed analysis and opinion. Given this backdrop, *India Now and in Transition* is an addition to policy studies and has comprehensive insights for general readers, who are curious to know more about their country's ongoing 'tryst with destiny'.

Atul K. Thakur

POLITICS AND GOVERNANCE

Indians—Great, Greater, Greatest?

Ramachandra Guha

Choosing the 'Greatest Indian After Gandhi' is difficult when the present exerts such a strong pull over our view of the past and there is a wide variation between how the 'greatness' of an individual is assessed by the aam aadmi *and by the expert.*

Nations need heroes, but the construction of a national pantheon is rarely straightforward or uncontested. Consider the debate in the United States about which faces should adorn the national currency. The founding figures of American Independence—Jefferson, Washington, Hamilton, Madison, and Franklin—are all represented on the dollar bill, albeit on different denominations. So are the 19th century presidents Andrew Jackson, Abraham Lincoln, and Ulysses S. Grant.

In recent years, right-wing Americans have campaigned for their hero, Ronald Reagan, to be represented on the national currency. This, it is said, is necessary to bring it in line with contemporary sentiments. Among 20th century American presidents, Franklin Delano Roosevelt is represented on the dime, and John F. Kennedy on the dollar. Both were Democrats. Republicans now demand that the pantheon feature one of their ilk. In 2010, a congressman from North Carolina, Patrick McHenry, canvassed for a law mandating that Ulysses S. Grant be replaced on the 50 dollar bill by Ronald Reagan. 'Every generation needs its own heroes', said McHenry. The American hero he was anointing for our times was Reagan, 'a modern day statesman, whose presidency transformed our nation's political and economic thinking'.

Turn now to that other large, complex, cacophonous, democracy—our own. After India became independent, the national pantheon offered to its citizens was massively dominated by leaders of the Congress party. Mahatma Gandhi was positioned first, with Jawaharlal Nehru only a short distance behind. Both had played important roles in the freeing of the country from colonial rule. Both were truly great Indians. That said, the popular perception of both was helped by the fact that the party to which they belonged was in power for the crucial decades after Independence. Newspapers, the radio, and school textbooks all played their role in the construction of a narrative in which Gandhi was the Father of the Nation and Nehru its Guide and Mentor in the first, formative years of the Republic's existence.

Until the 1960s, the dominance of Nehru and Gandhi in the national imagination was colossal. When, in that decade, the American scholar Eleanor Zelliot wrote a brilliant dissertation on B.R. Ambedkar and the Mahar movement in Maharashtra, she was unable to find a publisher. But then the Congress started to lose power in the States. In 1977 it lost power for the first time at the Centre. The rise of new political parties led naturally to revisionist interpretations of the past. New heroes began to be offered for inclusion in the nation's pantheon, their virtues extolled (and sometimes magnified) in print, in parliament, and, in time, in school textbooks as well.

The Indian who, in subsequent decades, has benefited most from this revaluation is B.R. Ambedkar. A scholar, legal expert, institution builder, and agitator, Ambedkar played a heroic (the word is inescapable) role in bringing the problems of the untouchable castes to wider attention. He forced Gandhi to take a more serious, focused, interest in the plight of the depressed classes, and himself started schools, colleges, and a political party to advance their interests.

Ambedkar died in December 1956, a political failure. The party he founded scarcely made a dent in Congress hegemony, and he was unable to win a Lok Sabha seat himself. But his memory was revived in the 1970s and beyond. His works began to be read more widely. He was the central, sometimes sole, inspiration for a new generation of Dalit activists and scholars. Obscure at the time of his death in 1956, condescended to by the academic community until the 1980s (at least), Ambedkar is today the only genuinely all-India political figure, worshipped in Dalit homes across the land. Notably, he is not a Dalit hero alone, his achievements are recognised among large sections of the Indian middle class. No one now seeking to write a book on Ambedkar would have a problem finding a publisher.

The (belated) incorporation of Ambedkar into the national pantheon is a consequence largely of the political rise of the subaltern classes. Meanwhile, the pantheon has been expanded from the right by the inclusion of Vallabhbhai Patel. Paradoxically, while Patel was himself a lifelong Congressman, the case for his greatness has been made most vigorously by the Bharatiya Janata Party (BJP). BJP leaders and ideologues speak of Patel as the Other, in all respects, of Jawaharlal Nehru. They claim that if Patel had become Prime Minister, Kashmir would have been fully integrated into India. Under Patel the country would have followed a more pragmatic (i.e. market-oriented) economic policy, while standing shoulder-to-shoulder with Western democracies against godless Communism. Nor, if Patel had been in charge, would there have been (it is claimed) any appeasement of the minorities.

The BJP reading of history is tendentious, not least because Patel and Nehru were, in practice, collaborators and colleagues rather than rivals or adversaries. To be sure, they had their disagreements, but, to their everlasting credit, they submerged these differences in the greater task of national consolidation. Theirs was a willed, deliberate, division of labour and responsibilities. Nehru knew that Patel, and not he, had the patience and acumen to supervise the integration of the princely states and build up administrative capacity. On the other side, as Rajmohan Gandhi demonstrates in his biography of Patel, the man had no intention or desire to become Prime Minister. For Patel knew that only Nehru had the character and personality to take the Congress credo to women, minorities, and the South, and to represent India to the world.

That the BJP has to make the case for Patel is a consequence of the Congress's capture by a single family determined to inflate its own contributions to the nation's past, present, and future. Sonia Gandhi's Congress Party recognises that a pantheon cannot consist of only two names; however, in their bid to make it more capacious, Congressmen place Indira and Rajiv alongside Nehru and Mahatma Gandhi. Thus the ubiquitous and apparently never-ending naming of *sarkari* schemes, airports, buildings, and stadia, after the one or the other.

The preceding discussion makes clear that political parties and social movements play a crucial role in how the national past is conveyed to citizens in the present. Indians admired by parties and movements, such as Ambedkar and Patel, have had their achievements more widely recognised than might otherwise have been the case. By the same token, great Indians whose lives are incapable of capture by special interests or sects have suffered from the enormous condescension of posterity.

Consider, in this regard, the current invisibility from the national discourse of Kamaladevi Chattopadhyay. Married to a man chosen by her family, she was widowed early, and then married a left-wing actor from another part of India. She joined the freedom movement, persuading Gandhi to allow women to court arrest during the Salt March and after.

After coming out of jail, Kamaladevi became active in trade union work, and travelled to the United States, where she explained the relevance of civil disobedience to black activists (her turn in the South is compellingly described in Nico Slate's recent book *Colored Cosmopolitanism*).[1] After Independence and Partition, Kamaladevi supervised the resettlement of refugees; still later, she set up an all-India network of artisanal cooperatives, and established a national crafts museum as well as a national academy for music and dance. Tragically, because her work cannot be seen through an exclusively political lens, and because her versatility cannot be captured by a sect or special interest, Kamaladevi is an almost forgotten figure today. Yet, from this historian's point of view, she has strong claims of being regarded as the greatest Indian woman of modern times.

»»»»»

Earlier this year, I was invited to be part of a jury to select the 'Greatest Indian Since Gandhi'. The organisers did me the favour of showing me a list of 100 names beforehand. Many of the names were unexceptionable, but some strongly reflected the perceptions (and prejudices) of the present. For example, Kiran Bedi was in this list, but Kamaladevi Chattopadhyay wasn't, a reflection only of the fact that the latter did not live in an age of television. There was also a regional bias: compiled in Delhi, the preliminary list did not include such extraordinary modern Indians as Shivarama Karanth, C. Rajagopalachari, and E.V. Ramasamy 'Periyar'. There was also a marked urban bias: not one Indian who came from a farming background was represented, not even the former prime minister Charan Singh or the former agriculture minister (and Green Revolution architect) C. Subramaniam. Nor was a single Adivasi on the list, not even the Jharkhand leader Jaipal Singh.

Since this was a provisional list, the organisers were gracious enough to accommodate some of these names at my request. The revised list was then offered to a jury composed of actors, writers, sportspersons and entrepreneurs, men and women of moderate (in some cases, considerable) distinction in their field. Based on the jury's recommendations, the 100 names were then brought down to 50.

The names of these 50 'great' Indians were then further reduced to 10, in a three-way process in which the votes of the jury were given equal weightage with views canvassed via an online poll and a market survey respectively. The results revealed two striking (and interconnected) features: the strong imprint of the present in how we view the past, and the wide variation between how the 'greatness' of an individual is assessed by the *aam aadmi* and by the expert.

Here are some illustrations of this divergence. In the jury vote, B.R. Ambedkar and Jawaharlal Nehru tied for 1st place; each had 21 votes. The online poll also placed Ambedkar in 1st place, but ranked Nehru as low as 15th, lower than Vallabhbhai Patel, Indira Gandhi, and Atal Bihari Vajpayee. Even Sachin Tendulkar, A.R. Rahman, and Rajnikanth were ranked higher than Nehru by online voters.

In the jury vote, the industrialist J.R.D. Tata and the social worker Mother Teresa were ranked immediately below Ambedkar and Nehru. Vallabhbhai Patel was ranked 5th by the jury, but an impressive 3rd by online voters. This suggests that like Ambedkar, Patel has a strong appeal among the young, albeit among a different section, those driven by the desire to see a strong state rather than the wish to achieve social justice. Nehru, on the other hand, is a figure of disinterest and derision in India today, his reputation damaged in good part by the misdeeds of his genealogical successors.

The most remarkable, not to say bizarre, discrepancy between the expert and the *aam aadmi* was revealed in the case of the former President of India, A.P.J. Abdul Kalam. Only two (out of 28) jury members voted for Kalam to be one of the shortlist of 10. On the other hand, Kalam was ranked 1st by those surveyed by market research, and second in the online polls.

What explains this massive variation in perception? The jury was motivated perhaps by the facts—the hard, undeniable, if not so widely advertised facts—that Kalam has not made any original contributions to scientific or scholarly research. Homi Bhabha, M.S. Swaminathan and Amartya Sen, who have, were thus ranked far higher than the former

President. Nor has Kalam done important technological work—recognising this, the jury ranked the Delhi Metro and Konkan Railway pioneer E. Sreedharan above him.

In the popular imagination, Kalam has been credited both with overseeing our space programme and the nuclear tests of 1998. In truth, Vikram Sarabhai, Satish Dhawan, U.R. Rao and K. Kasturirangan did far more to advance India's journey into space. Kalam was an excellent and industrious manager; a devoted organisation man who was rewarded by being made the scientific adviser to the Government of India. It was in this capacity that he was captured in military uniform at Pokhran, despite not being a nuclear specialist of any kind.

A key reason for Abdul Kalam's rise in public esteem is that he is perceived as a Muslim who stands by his motherland. In the 1990s, as there was a polarisation of religious sentiment across India, Kalam was seen by many Hindus as the 'Other' of the mafia don Dawood Ibrahim. Dawood was the 'Bad Muslim' who took refuge in Pakistan and planned the bombing of his native Bombay; Kalam the 'Good Muslim' who stood by India and swore to bomb Pakistan if circumstances so demanded.

This was the context in which Kalam was picked up and elevated to the highest office of the land by the Bharatiya Janata Party (BJP). The BJP wanted, even if symbolically, to reach out to the minorities they had long mistrusted (and sometimes persecuted). In this rebranding exercise, the fisherman's son from Rameswaram proved willing and able.

A second reason that Kalam is so admired is that he was an upright and accessible public servant in an age characterised by arrogant and corrupt politicians. As President, Kalam stayed admirably non-partisan while reaching out to a wide crosssection of society. He made a particular point of interacting with the young, speaking in schools and colleges across the land, and impressing upon the students the role technology could play in building a more prosperous and secure India.

A.P.J. Abdul Kalam was a decent man, a man of integrity. He was undeniably a good Indian, but not a great Indian, still less (as the popular vote would have us believe) the second-greatest Indian since Gandhi. Notably, the online voters who ranked Kalam 2nd also ranked Kamaladevi Chattopadhyay 50th, or last. At the risk of sounding elitist, I have to say that in both cases the *aam aadmi* got it spectacularly wrong.

»»»»»

A nation's pantheon is inevitably dominated by men and women in public affairs, those who fought for independence against colonial rule, and thereafter ran governments and crafted new laws that reshaped society. One of the appealing things about the exercise I was part of was that it did not choose only to honour politicians. The longlist of 50 had actors, singers, sportspersons, scientists, and social workers on it. Commendably, in their own selection of '10 Great Indians since Gandhi', expert as well as *aam admi* sought to have a variety of fields represented.

Collating the votes, a final list of 10 was arrived at, which, in alphabetical order of surnames reads: B.R. Ambedkar; Indira Gandhi; A.P.J. Abdul Kalam; Lata Mangeshkar; Jawaharlal Nehru; Vallabhbhai Patel; J.R.D. Tata; Sachin Tendulkar; Mother Teresa; A.B. Vajpayee.

Reacting both as citizen and historian, I have to say that 6 of these 10 choices should be relatively uncontroversial. Ambedkar, Nehru, and Patel are the 3 towering figures of our modern political history. J.R.D. Tata was that rare Indian capitalist who promoted technological innovation and generously funded initiatives in the arts. Although in sporting terms Viswanathan Anand is as great as Sachin Tendulkar, given the mass popularity of cricket, the latter has had to carry a far heavier social burden. Likewise, although a case can be made for M.S. Subbulakshmi, Satyajit Ray, or Pandit Ravi Shankar to represent the field of 'culture', given what Hindi films mean to us as a nation, Lata had to be given the nod ahead of them.

It is with the remaining 4 names that I must issue a dissenting note. Taken in the round, Kamaladevi Chattopadhyay's achievements are of more lasting value than Indira Gandhi's. If one wanted a non-Congress political figure apart from Ambedkar, then Jayaprakash Narayan or C. Rajagopalachari must be considered more original thinkers than A.B. Vajpayee. Mr. Vajpayee's long association with sectarian politics must also be a disqualification (likewise Indira Gandhi's promulgation of the Emergency).

As for Mother Teresa, she was a noble, saintly, figure, but I would rather have chosen a social worker—such as Ela Bhatt—who enabled and emancipated Indians from disadvantaged backgrounds rather than simply dispensed charity. My caveats about Abdul Kalam have been entered already. In the intellectual/ scientist category, strong arguments can be made in favour of the physicist

Homi Bhabha and the agricultural scientist M.S. Swaminathan. Although I wouldn't object to either name, there is also Amartya Sen, acknowledged by his peers as one of the world's great economists and economic philosophers, and who despite his extended residence abroad has contributed creatively to public debates in his homeland.

To choose 50 and then 10 Great Indians was an educative exercise. One was forced to consider the comparative value of different professions, and the claims and pressures of different generations and interest groups. However, I was less comfortable with the further call to choose a single Greatest Indian. For it is only in autocracies—such as Mao's China, Stalin's Russia, Kim Il-sung's North Korea and Bashar al-Assad's Syria—that One Supreme Leader is said to embody the collective will of the nation and its people.

This anointing of the Singular and Unique goes against the plural ethos of a democratic Republic. To be sure, one may accept that politics is more important than sports. Sachin Tendulkar may be the Greatest Indian Cricketer but he cannot ever be the Greatest Indian. But how does one judge Ambedkar's work for the Dalits and his piloting of the Indian Constitution against Nehru's promotion of multiparty democracy based on adult franchise and his determination not to make India a Hindu Pakistan? And would there have been an India at all if Patel had not made the princes and nawabs join the Union?

In his famous last speech to the Constituent Assembly, Ambedkar warned of the dangers of hero-worship in politics. In a lesser-known passage from that same speech he allowed that a nation must have its heroes. That is to say, one can appreciate and admire those who nurtured Indian democracy and nationhood without venerating them like gods. In that spirit, one might choose 100 great Indians, or 50, or 10, or even, as I have ended by doing here, 3. But not just 1.

This piece was earlier published in The Hindu. *It is reproduced here with the author's permission.*

Endnotes

1 Nico Slate, *Colored Cosmopolitanism: The Shared Struggle for Freedom in the United States and India* (Cambridge, MA: Harvard University Press, 2012).

The Enduring Legacy of Dr Ambedkar

Shashi Tharoor

As the government and political parties commemorated the 125th birth anniversary of Dr Babasaheb Bhimrao Ramji Ambedkar in 2016, it would be a pity if the life of this extraordinary Indian were reduced to one issue—his championship of the Dalit cause—just as much as it would be wrong to gloss over his path-breaking role in that monumental endeavour.

Dr Ambedkar is such an icon today that we fail to fully appreciate the remarkable scale of what he accomplished. To be born into what was called an 'untouchable' family in 1891, and that too as the 14th and last child of a poor Mahar subedar in an Army cantonment, would normally have guaranteed a life of neglect, poverty, and discrimination. Not only did Dr Ambedkar rise above the circumstances of his birth, but he achieved a level of success that would have been spectacular for a child of privilege.

One of the first Dalits ever to enter an Indian college, he became a professor (at the prestigious Sydenham College) and a principal (of no less an institution than Bombay's Government Law College). One of the earliest Indian students in the United States, he earned multiple doctorates from Columbia University and the University of London, in economics, politics, and law. An heir to millennia of discrimination, he was admitted to the bar in London and became one of India's founding fathers as the Chair of the Constitution Drafting Committee. The son of illiterates, he wrote a remarkable number of books, whose content and range testify to an eclectic mind and a sharp, if provocative, intellect.

That was not all: by the age of 40 he was speaking as one of India's recognised leaders at the Round Table Conference in London, and his convictions made him a political giant to be reckoned with in the fight for freedom. An insignificant infant scrabbling in the dust of Mhow in 1891 became the first law minister of a free India, in the most impressive cabinet ever assembled in New Delhi. When he died, aged only 65, he had accumulated a set of distinctions few have matched; only one remained. In belated recognition of that omission, he was conferred posthumously in 1990 the highest award his country has to offer—the Bharat Ratna.

Dr Ambedkar's greatness cannot be reduced to any one of these accomplishments, because all were equally extraordinary. Think of what he was born into and who he became, and even this bare outline of his life should take one's breath away.

Dr Ambedkar was a self-made man in the profoundest sense of that term. Even his name was his own creation, for he was born a Sakpal, but decided to take a name based on that of his village (Ambavade) as Maharashtrian Brahmins did. (And he married a Brahmin.) It was part of his self-made style that he wore Western suits—not, as some nationalists alleged, in slavish imitation of the colonial rulers, but in rejection of the traditional trappings of a society that had for so long enslaved his people.

It was he who forced India to confront the reality of discrimination by facing up to the reality of caste oppression. And he did so bluntly, in a manner which youngsters today would call 'in your face'. Not for him the mealy-mouthed platitudes of the well-meaning: he was prepared to rage against the injustice of social discrimination, and to do so in every forum available to him. It was an attitude that Indian society was not prepared for, but at a time when Indians were fighting for their freedom from foreign rule, it was both appropriate and necessary that Indians should fight equally against domestic oppression.

Dr Ambedkar rejected what he saw as the patronising indulgence of the Gandhian approach to untouchability. The Mahatma called them 'Harijans'—children of God. Dr Ambedkar rejected the word—after all, he argued, aren't we all children of God? He used, instead, the Marathi and Hindi words for the 'excluded' (Bahishkrit), the 'oppressed' (Dalit), and the 'silent' (Muka) to define the outcastes.

So even while fighting British rule, Dr Ambedkar was a tireless and courageous advocate of the Dalit cause, an enemy of cant and superstition, and an iconoclast who had contempt for traditions that he felt deserved no sanctity.

As a nationalist, he was sensitive to the charge that he was dividing Indians at a time when they needed to be united against the British. His critics forget that Gandhiji himself acknowledged Dr Ambedkar's 'sterling patriotism', brilliantly displayed in the first Round Table Conference. Yet when Dr Ambedkar demanded separate electorates for his people, Mahatma Gandhi undertook a fast unto death until an unconvinced Dr Ambedkar, fearing mass reprisals if the Mahatma died, caved in. Gandhiji, who abhorred untouchability, believed that the answer lay in the social awakening of caste Hindus rather than in building walls of separation.

Dr Ambedkar, who lived with the daily reality of caste discrimination, was not convinced that the entrenched practices of traditional Hinduism could ever disappear. In the end, he found a Constitutional solution to remedy the injustices he fought against all his life.

His faith in democracy, which he shared with Jawaharlal Nehru, is also one of his proud legacies to our country. Whereas some saw Ambedkar, with his three-piece suit and formal English, as a westernised exponent of occidental constitutional systems, he was inspired far more by the democratic practices of ancient India, in particular the Buddhist sanghas.

Ambedkar saw in the institutions of Indian democracy that he was helping to create, the best guarantee for the future development and welfare of his own people, the oppressed and marginalised of India. He fought hard to introduce into the Constitution fundamental protections and guarantees of civil liberties for individual citizens.

Ambedkar also convinced the Constituent Assembly that it was not enough to abolish untouchability: what was needed to undo millennia of discrimination and exploitation was a system of affirmative action to uplift the oppressed, including reservations of jobs in the civil services, schools, and universities. This gave India the world's oldest and farthest-reaching affirmative action programme, which guarantees not only equality of opportunity but of outcome, with seats reserved for Dalits in government jobs, universities, and even in Parliament.

Through his role Dr Ambedkar ushered in momentous change into Indian society and politics, but to him it had not come fast enough. He saw the entrenched practices of Hindu society as something he had to reject. 'I am born a Hindu,' Dr Ambedkar declared in 1936, 'but I swear I will not die a Hindu.' Twenty years later he died a Buddhist, months after converting with hundreds of thousands of his followers at a public ceremony.

As a political leader, Dr Ambedkar was better at articulating powerful ideas than in creating the structures to see them through. None of the three parties he founded ever acquired the following or the permanence that his ideas deserved. But the Constitution of which he was the principal author remains the best instrument for pursuing his ideas. The leader and spokesman of a community left his greatest gift to all communities—a legacy that belongs to all of us, and one of which we are yet to prove ourselves wholly worthy. Let us hope that this 125th anniversary year is not spent entirely in platitudes, but in an honest recognition of the life and the message of one of the greatest sons of India.

»»»»»

Dr Ambedkar's legacy continues to resonate in a recent judgement of the supreme court of India. In all the understandable attention paid to the supreme court's judgement on Section 66A, the media and the commentariat have overlooked another supreme court decision at roughly the same time, which is potentially even more far-reaching and significant for our democracy.

In a 64-page judgment, a Bench of Justices Ranjan Gogoi and Rohinton Nariman (who also wrote the 66A judgement, though this one is mainly Justice Gogoi's work) struck down the United Progressive Alliance (UPA) Government's notification including Jats in the Central list of Other Backward Classes (OBCs). Equally significant was the rationale the justices provided: they observed that the state should not go by the 'perception of the self-proclaimed socially backward class or advanced classes' on whether they deserved to be categorised among the 'less fortunates'. New formulae, the court averred, have to be found to determine backwardness.

Most significantly, the supreme court held that caste, while acknowledged to be a prominent cause of injustice in the country historically, could not be the sole determinant of the backwardness of a class. 'Owing to historical conditions, particularly in Hindu society, recognition of backwardness has been associated with caste. Social groups who would be most deserving must necessarily be a matter of continuous evolution. New practices, methods and yardsticks have to be continuously evolved moving away from caste-centric definition of backwardness,' the court argued in its judgment.

The court ruled that the state should maintain a high level of vigilance to uncover emerging forms of backwardness in a continually evolving society. 'The gates would be opened only to permit entry of the most distressed. Any other inclusions would be a serious abdication of the constitutional duty of the State,' the court warned.

The Central Government had claimed that the inclusion of the Jats on the OBC list was based on the 'compelling factor' that the Centre is obliged to 'work in tandem and not at cross purposes' with the states, which had already included Jats in many state OBC lists over a decade ago. The court rejected that reasoning, observing that such 'grave and important' decisions in reference to Articles 14 and 16 of the Constitution must be made on the basis of 'contemporaneous inputs', which were not available. (The statistical data on which the government had based its decision was more than 10 years old and the court felt that it was already 'outdated and antiquated' for the purpose).

Most striking are the court's observations on what constitutes 'social backwardness'. It says that educational backwardness, which the government referred to, isn't enough; neither is purely economic backwardness, though both may contribute to social backwardness. 'But social backwardness', the court observes, 'is a distinct concept that emerges from multiple circumstances ranging from the social and cultural, to economic, educational and even political.'

What about caste, since Jats are, after all, a caste in nine northern Indian states? The court concedes that caste may be a prominent factor for 'easy determination of backwardness', but the judgment discourages 'the identification of a group as backward solely on the basis of caste' and calls for 'new practices, methods and yardsticks' to be evolved. It adds the observation that class may be a factor too, since a class is 'an identifiable section of society', but again it may not be enough to justify reservations. Citing its own decision to recognise transgenders as a distinct community with justiciable rights, the court pats itself on the back for identifying a form of social backwardness that has nothing to do with caste or class. Its judgement points to the shifting definitions of various groups in determining their eligibility for government benefits.

This is fascinating philosophically, but it opens up a proverbial can of worms for government policy-makers. The most contentious element of the court's judgement is, of course, its proposition that caste, and the need to right historical wrongs, is no longer sufficient grounds for government benefits. Nor is the self-perception of a caste that it's backward; not even the perception by other castes that a caste is backward is good enough. New methods, the judgement insists, have to be developed to identify the backwardness of a group of people.

The court, drawing a somewhat fuzzy line between 'past' and 'emerging' forms of backwardness, advances the presumption of the 'progressive advancement of all citizens on all fronts, i.e., social, economic and educational' that makes history an insufficient guide. You can't keep citing historical wrongs and propose reservations as a solution to redressing them, the court says. What it doesn't do, though, is to take the logic of its own reasoning one step farther, by challenging caste-based reservations altogether.

Still, it has set off a conceptual bomb under the complacent edifice of the reservation system. We have long accepted the logic of reservations in our country as a means of making up for millennia of discrimination based on birth. This is why the Constitution inaugurated the world's oldest and farthest-reaching affirmative action programme, guaranteeing Scheduled Castes and Tribes not only equality of opportunity, but guaranteed outcomes, with reserved places in educational institutions, government jobs, and even seats in parliament and the state assemblies. These reservations were granted to groups listed in schedules of the Constitution on the basis of their (presumably immutable) caste identities. The addition of the OBC category —after the acceptance by the VP Singh Government of the recommendations of the Mandal Commission—added more people to the numbers benefiting from reservations, but it didn't change the basis on which they benefited: despite the 'C' in 'OBC' referring to 'classes', the OBC lists contained castes and sub-castes.

So we witnessed the unedifying (and unwittingly hilarious) spectacle of castes fighting with each other to be declared backward: the competitive zeal of the Meenas and the Gujjars in Rajasthan to be deemed more backward than each other would have been funny if both sides weren't so deadly serious. As an uncle of mine sagely observed, 'In our country now, you can't go forward unless you're a backward.'

The transgender judgement, and the latest one disqualifying Jats, opens the floodgates to far-reaching questions. If caste isn't a good enough basis, and class isn't either, and now lack of education or income doesn't suffice, but the condition of being born transgender does, then how do we determine who deserves reservations in our society? The supreme court says historical wrongs are passe; the government needs to establish that a group of potential beneficiaries is suffering backwardness right now. But it doesn't tell us what criteria to apply.

This leaves open all further government classifications to future court challenge. That may be what the court wanted, but they should beware the doctrine of unintended consequences. What if someone goes to the supreme court saying that following this decision, the entire existing system of reservations—and every established list of SCs, STs, and OBCs—should be reviewed, since they were all based on historical wrongs and 'antiquated' data? Why should only Jat claims be dismissed on that basis, and why not everyone else's? And if that happens, doesn't it open the court to the logical follow-up question: since the very basis for deciding them has been demolished by the court, are reservations themselves unconstitutional?

The shadow of Pandora now hovers over the supreme court—but her notorious box may already have been opened by this dramatic, and surprisingly under-reported, judgement.

This essay previously appeared as two articles by the author on ndtv.com. *It is reproduced here with the author's permission.*

Mr Modi Wins in Varanasi

Chandrahas Choudhury

At dusk on a sweltering day in May 2014, late in India's five-week long, nine-phase national elections, I found myself drawn into the serpentine alleys of Bengali Tola in Varanasi in northern India.

The city, also known as 'Kashi' or the City of Light, and in the first Western chronicles of the subcontinent as 'Banaras', lies at the heart of the great plain of north India on one bank of the river Ganga, where, devout Hindus believe, all sins are washed away. Varanasi is one of the oldest continuously inhabited cities in the world, and is therefore susceptible to thinking of itself as an entire civilisation, distinct from the more transient political regime—sometimes a Hindu king, sometimes the Mughals, sometimes the British, sometimes a democracy run from Delhi—in which it has been successively embedded. For as long as anyone can recall, it has been considered by Hindus as the home on earth of the god Shiva, the fierce, austere, and enigmatic head of the Hindu pantheon. Fact and legend, linear time and cyclical time, the earthly and the heavenly, are inextricably intertwined in the stories of Varanasi's past told by its proud, if often impoverished residents, who have, therefore, a skeptical view of the institutions of fresh-faced secular time, such as governments and elections—or indeed the idea of history and the hubris of historiography.

All this gave the present week, leading up to polling day on 12 May 2014, a particularly tense atmosphere. The previous month it had become clear that the city might elect not just the usual legislator to India's 543-member parliament, but India's next prime minister. Narendra Modi, the chief minister of Gujarat and the Bharatiya Janata Party's (BJP) candidate for prime minister, had announced that he would contest the election from Varanasi.

»»»»»

Bengali Tola abuts Dashashwamedh Ghat, one of nearly a hundred ghats that give Varanasi its storied waterfront, never to be forgotten once it has first been seen at its evening crescendo of religious chanting, communion, commerce, and cremation. (Two central ghats are reserved exclusively for the purpose of cremating the dead and raising them into the next world.) Like most other neighbourhoods by the river, Bengali Tola is densely built up and emanates a vigorous shabbiness. No cars have ever invaded its thin, cobbled, cowpat-strewn paths, threading and forking interminably between the river and modern Varanasi's central thoroughfare. Pedestrians, often walking barefoot, and cows divide up the street between them, parted by the odd bicycle or motorbike. The shops still represent the city's ancient trades—ornament-making, weaving, astrology, milk-based confectionery. Seated at small tea and snack stalls, their glasses chipped, the utensils black with use, locals watch with an indulgent eye the human traffic of the restaurants and travel agencies that have mushroomed to serve the tourists who come to Varanasi ever year to experience, not unreasonably, the real India, the eternal India.

It was at one such shop this evening, as I was eating a freshly fried samosa, that I heard the chant of children, growing louder by the moment. What kind of procession was this?

Then around the bend they came, a small swarm of flushed, beaming boys, none more than 12 years old. The motley look of their many-coloured shirts and shorts was unified by boat-shaped caps in saffron. All day long, the streets had been full of campaign sounds. But even so it was a surprise to see children canvass, evidently of their own will—perhaps it's the daily exposure to the reality of death and cremation, but the children of Varanasi grow up early—for a candidate.

The pint-sized parade went marching past, shouting, *'Jab tak sooraj-chand rahega, Modiji ka naam rahega* (till the sun and moon keep their place, Modi's name shall ring through time and space).

»»»»»

May was that sort of month in India. Across the subcontinent (even in neighbouring Pakistan and in Bangladesh, as I discovered, while watching the election results two weeks later, from Dhaka) all mouths repeated—in pride or disgust, fear or elation—the word'Modi', even as the challenger himself, a barrel-chested, imperious 64-year-old, traversed the country at astonishing speed, addressing several rallies each day. The Indian media, buoyed (if not exactly bought over, as some later alleged) by the vast sums raised by the Modi campaign for an advertising blitzkrieg, diagnosed a 'Modi wave' sweeping the country, bringing to the world's largest-ever election a surge of excitement and optimism about the future, and to a fragmented polity—India has had coalition governments since 1989—the first sign in a generation of a genuinely popular, if polarising, choice.

In choosing to contest the election from Varanasi, Modi himself had played a political masterstroke. For one, the city lies in the state of Uttar Pradesh, India's most populous state (about 200 million) and one that contributes 80 MPs to the 543-member Lok Sabha, or lower house of parliament. No party without a presence in the state could hope to win the nation; in the previous election the BJP had won just nine of these seats. By moving into this deeply consequential field, instead of merely coasting in the warm, welcoming, political waters of his home state, Gujarat, (where he had been chief minister since 2002) Modi was drawing voters from the whole of Uttar Pradesh into a grand new political project centred in Varanasi.

It is a quirk of Varanasi's history that the city has always been a fount of religious power without ever being a major political capital. The names of the god Shiva and the goddess Ganga overmaster all others in the city of light; their legends trump any narratives of human dynasties or royal valour. Now, by choosing to contest from Varanasi, the frontrunner for Prime Minister was laying claim to the city's sacred power and grace as no previous Prime Ministerial candidate ever had. Filing his nomination papers in the city late in April, Modi had even declared that it was the call of the Ganga herself that had brought him to the city. The implication was that Varanasi and the Ganga deserved to be the crowning jewel not just of the Hindu faith but of Indian democracy, at 67 a mere cherub when compared to the might and memory of the god Shiva, the river Ganga, and the ancient city.

»»»»»

When the poll results were declared on Friday, 16 May 2014 it turned out even the term 'Modi wave' had been something of an understatement. The

BJP had gone past the crucial halfway mark of 272 seats in Parliament, giving it a power not enjoyed by anyone since the political neophyte Rajiv Gandhi, son of the assassinated Prime Minister Indira Gandhi, riding a 'sympathy wave' in 1984. And in Uttar Pradesh, the BJP had not just won but swept an extremely challenging terrain, taking 71 of the state's 80 seats—the most decisive advance of the entire election.

That evening, Modi did what any good Indian son does, and thanked his mother for his victory. This time, though, there were two mothers: his biological mother Heerabai, 92, and mother Ganga, exact age unknown. On Friday he went to visit the first at her home in Gujarat's capital, Gandhinagar, and on Saturday he appeared on the west bank of the Dashashwamedh Ghat, flanked by party workers and priests, at the centre of a Ganga *aarti* (or mass prayer in honour of the river Ganga) to mark his victory. He'd come to the event straight from a puja, or prayer service, at a great Varanasi temple in honour of the Lord Shiva.

To millions of Hindus among Indian citizens, there was something glorious, natural, unselfconscious, about this commingling of secular and sacred power, as though a world artificially divided by the categories of modern politics had finally been bound back into a whole. To millions of others, however, non-Hindus and Hindus both, the spectacle of the newly elected Prime Minister of a secular democracy thanking a deity and a river for his victory in a public ceremony was deeply disturbing.

To them, it portended a future in which the values of Varanasi, enduring and legitimate in their own sphere, might by a slow creep supersede the more secular and liberal values of New Delhi, painstakingly enshrined in the Indian constitution in the aftermath of decolonisation and the religious bloodbath of Partition in 1947. In this new chapter for the Indian republic, perhaps the grand old trinity Gandhi, Nehru, and Ambedkar would now fade into the back rows, like middle-level dignitaries at an Indian function who mistakenly take the best seats. In their place would enter the new trinity of Shiva, Ganga, and perhaps Modiji himself.

»»»»»

On that startling electoral-Gangetic weekend in May, it could not, however, be the case even of Modi's harshest critics that he had won the battle to shape the future of one-fifth of humanity solely by way of an appeal to majoritarian sentiment.

After all, as the unselfconscious victory celebrations of Modi and his partymen in Varanasi proved, the tension between an secular state and the Hinduism of India's majority has been latent from the very beginnings of the Indian republic. And while the appeal to Hindu sentiment—a mixture of pride in India's ancient Hindu past and paranoia about the modern Hindu's marginalisation in his or her natural habitat—had always been the main enabling force of the BJP in the past, it also constituted the main stumbling block for the party on the road to power in a society as diverse as India's.

This is where 'the Modi effect' comes in: the singular power of the most talented and streetwise politician to appear in India since Indira Gandhi. Even to the casual observer, it's immediately visible that Modi has many avatars. He can play the demagogue, but—as he did increasingly in the year leading up to the elections—also the newly appointed Chief Executive Officer (CEO) bringing a new culture of team-work and discipline into the slack work culture of Indian democracy. (Indeed, the highest praise that thousands of middle-class people from the world of India's new corporate capitalism could bestow upon Modi was to say that he ran his campaign, and would presumably run the country, 'just like a CEO'.) He enjoys the approbation of the captains of Indian business and of large sections of the Indian youth, just as much as he does that of those who dream of a Hindu state. He visits his mother frequently to seek her blessings, but abandoned his wife when still in his teens to dedicate himself of a Hindu nationalist organization. He has written a book of poems—a fascinating book in which the lyric speaker sees himself as an Indian version of Nietzsche's overman—and also a book about climate change.

Modi's ability to combine, for the first time in modern India, the languages of administrative ambition—unusually for an Indian statesman he seems to hold, as Hamilton did in the *Federalist Papers*, that 'energy in the executive is a leading character in the definition of good government'—and Hindu pride and power, explains the decisive five per cent margin between his election returns in May and those of his party, even at its best, in previous elections.

Warming to crowds and warming them in turn, Modi is by all accounts curiously cold in person: very much the classic patriarch of the undivided Hindu family, who represses his affections as a way of grounding his authority.

He seems to possess a fine awareness—perhaps he learnt this from the *Arthashastra*—that although the successful ruler must be loved, he must also be feared. He appeals not just to the Indian voter's more benign desires for stability, leadership, and progress, but also to his or her more fugitive urges for disruption, violence, retribution, and clamour. When we look at his past, we see that he expresses both the burgeoning aspirations and the moral blind spots of India, perhaps even more revealingly than he wishes to.

»»»»»

Late in February 2002, in the early months of Modi's tenure as the chief minister of Gujarat (at 51, his first-ever appointment as a representative of government, rather than his own party), a mass of *karsevaks*, or Hindu religious agitators, from Gujarat were returning home from the north Indian town of Ayodhya.

They'd been participating in an agitation for a cause long on the rage-and-resentment side of the BJP's agenda. This was the demand—one that had brought the BJP rich electoral gains in the 1980s and 1990s—for the construction of a temple in honour of Lord Rama, the hero of the *Ramayana* and to many Hindus a figure as real as any figure from modern history. The problem this posed was twofold. Not only did it mean the blurring of history and legend, as the proposed temple would also be on the site of a mosque in Ayodhya—the city considered the birthplace of Rama—built in the 16th century upon the ruins of a sacked temple by the Central Asian invader Babur, who was to put down roots in India and become the first of the great Mughals, but also this mosque had itself been brought down in 1992 by raging *karsevaks*, with many prominent BJP leaders present on the scene. This single provocative act of arson triggered religious violence all over India and precipitated, at the time, the biggest crisis in the life of the Indian republic.

Now, a decade later, those passions were inflamed again when a train, the Sabarmati Express, carrying the *karsevaks* was suddenly halted at Godhra station in Gujarat, minutes after a bust-up between the *karsevaks* and Muslim vendors on the platform. Some of its coaches were locked from the outside and set on fire by miscreants. More than 50 Hindus in the train were burnt alive. In a state long known as a tinderbox of communal passions, the reprisals were swift. Over the next week, more than a 1,000 people, most of them

Muslims, were killed, mostly by well-prepared Hindu mobs confident that they had carte blanche from the state. Modi framed the Hindu backlash as a 'reaction' to the provocation of Godhra, a narrative that still enjoys wide currency in middle-class drawing rooms across the country, where Godhra has taken its place on a long list of slights and injuries visited across the centuries by the Muslims upon the Hindus.

India's first ever widely televised riots were a grievous blow for the country's standing in the world and the legitimacy of the BJP government then in power at the centre. The Prime Minister, Atal Bihari Vajpayee, dithered over whether to fire Modi. Finally he gave way to influential voices in the party who insisted that asking Modi to stand down would amount to an admission of culpability for the riots.

Had Vajpayee had his way at the time, Modi's political career would have lasted just a few months. Instead, the chief minister's hand was strengthened by the support of his party, and in state elections later that year he embarked on a program of majoritarian consolidation that would ensure that his future political invincibility, at least in Gujarat. (The thought of making a run for prime minister apparently did not occur to him for several years to come).

»»»»»

The extremely convincing case for Modi's culpability in the Gujarat violence is not limited just to the events of the terrible violence of 2002, but also to their aftermath. In the decade after 2002, the Modi government did all that it could, by both legal and extra-legal means, to ensure that the widespread social sanction for the violence in Gujarat—the unspoken consensus that the Muslims of Gujarat 'had it coming' after the massacre of Hindus in Godhra—ensued in a second shortchanging of justice in the very act of fixing responsibility for the first.

In the decade after 2002, as detailed by the journalist Manoj Mitta in his book *The Fiction of Fact-Finding in Gujarat*, a combination of witness intimidation, slack evidence-gathering by the state police, and ham-fisted and partisan work by public prosecutors and the lower judiciary resulted in hundreds of criminal cases related to the riots being closed for want of sufficient evidence.[1] It eventually required India's supreme court to recognise the scale of obstruction at work and transfer some of the more serious cases of mass murder and arson to the neighbouring state of Maharashtra, resulting in a number of high-profile convictions.

But in this sordid story of the collusion of the state, society, and the law in perpetrating violence and injustice at many levels, there is a warming element. For over a decade now, a small army of dedicated people—journalists, human-rights activists, social workers, even high court and supreme court judges—not amounting to any alliance but making up in aggregate a dogged opposition of sorts, have ensured that Gujarat 2002 has not been retired as a burning issue in Indian politics, as Modi would have liked. Their persistence in flagging continuing breaches of the law in Gujarat have been a source of unending embarrassment for Modi, and one that he and his party have had to counter with the most tenuous political syllogisms.

Modi's rise, then, represents a particularly provocative challenge to the equation of democracy with the political good, and free and fair elections as the litmus test of a politician's right to enjoy office. For much of his fairly short political career, he has used a majoritarian and often mendacious agenda to work himself into a position from which he can afford to recast himself as a sagacious, visionary statesman.

And yet it would be dishonest, and even defeatist, to see Modi always as the agent, and India, democracy, and Muslims always as the acted-upon. Modi has been schooled and disciplined by Indian democracy too, and lives every day in the knowledge that he is not yet beyond the pale of the Indian justice system (new charges filed in 2009 in Gujarat led to a life sentence in 2012 for Maya Kodnani, one of his ministers in the Gujarat government). If he cannot bring himself to apologise to the Muslims of Gujarat, it is partly because those citizens of his state have themselves adjusted to the permanency of the rift, and partly because his political capital in many other parts of the country rests on his being staunchly unrepentant—in effect, the CEO who never bends down to a mutiny by disaffected workers, and instead speaks of how a positive balance sheet improves the lives of all.

»»»»»

Two conclusions.

The paradox of Modi's rise is that his humble origins—he is the son of a tea seller, and never went to university—make his appointment as prime minister in May in some ways the embodiment of all that India's founding fathers aspired to when they shifted the bases of political power at the dawn of the new republic, enfranchising all adults and for the first time in Indian history giving traditionally marginalised groups a chance to win power through the ballot box.

And in so orchestrating the currents of time, politics, and society—the timidity and mediocrity of the opposition in the 2014 election, the flowering of Modi's own career at a safe temporal remove from Gujarat 2002, the coming of age of nearly a hundred million first-time voters who want an assertive new prime minister, the falling away of other, more moderate candidates from his own party—to bring about a victory for Narendra Modi in the May 2014 elections, Lord Shiva and Goddess Ganga have, in their apparently infinite wisdom, set up the biggest ever test of Indian democracy's maturity and judgment.

Endnotes

1 Manoj Mitta, *The Fiction of Fact Finding: Modi and Godhra* (New Delhi: Harper Collins India, 2014).

Congress and its Ideological Dilemmas

Rasheed Kidwai

When the grand old party celebrated its 131st foundation day on 28 December 2016, the internal debate in the Congress was how and why the party is falling between two stools on emotive issues. But for some inexplicit reasons, both Sonia and Rahul Gandhi seem reluctant to hold a no-holds barred, in-house debate so far.

While warming opposition benches in the Lok Sabha till 2019, the Congress has reacted cautiously to the contentious issue of religious conversions. When the ABP TV news channel ran a story on the rise of beef exports during the first six months of the Narendra Modi government, the Congress dithered commenting on it. Privately, some leaders said a comment on beef exports had the potential of upsetting the Hindu or Muslim community. In Madhya Pradesh, the state Congress unit has started keeping idols of Lord Ganesh at the party office, ostensibly, to pronounce its 'Hindu identity' but the move did not find approval with the central high command.

Even during the last phase of UPA around 2010–14, the Congress witnessed a subtle but significant battle of wits between conservative sections of the party and radicals who wanted to revert to the Nehruvian position that majority communalism is more dangerous than minority communalism.

Secularism has been an integral part of the Congress ideology, implying separation of religion from politics. In the Indian context, the Congress' definition of secularism meant equal respect for all faiths and protection of the security, identity, and interests of all religious minorities. The concept of equal respect for all religions was first highlighted in the Nehru report of 1928 and by Mahatma Gandhi at the Second Round Table Conference in London in 1931, where he showcased the Congress as India's most national and secular organisation. Successive Congress resolutions kept proclaiming that the Congress would translate the guarantees given in the Indian Constitution into reality.

In September 1951, Jawaharlal Nehru using Mahatma Gandhi's tactics at Haripura (when Subhash Chandra Bose was made to resign) got all the CWC members of P.D. Tandon's team to resign, thus obliging Tandon, a right-wing Congress president himself to resign. It may have been a mere coincidence that in the same month the Bharatiya Jana Sangh was formally launched with both Atal Bihari Vajpayee and L.K. Advani being present. Nehru, who had become the Congress president after Tandon's resignation, pronounced the bottom line of the party's secular creed at a meeting in the Ram Lila grounds on Gandhi Jayanti in 1951: 'If any man raises his hand against another in the name of religion, I shall fight him till the last breath of my life, whether from within the government or outside.'

However, the demolition of the Babri Masjid and successive events cast a shadow on the Congress' commitment towards the minorities. While the Muslim leadership and religious clergy dubbed the Narasimha Rao–led Congress as furthering narrow 'majoritarianism', a group within the Congress began calling for the need to review the concept of secularism.

V.N. Gadgil (who passed away in 2011), and served as All India Congress Committee (AICC) spokesperson during the regimes of Narasimha Rao and Sitaram Kesri, had told Congressmen at a seven-day training camp in Kurla, Maharashtra that he disapproved of the Congress leadership's policy of appeasing Muslims. At the training camp to select 'future Congress leaders', Gadgil launched a scathing frontal attack on Congress policymakers. He observed:

> Every time the Shahi Imam makes a statement, the party reacts as if God himself has spoken. Do minorities mean only Muslims? What about Buddhists, Sikhs, and others? When thirty-six Sikhs were killed in Kashmir, not a single Congressman condoled their deaths. In Jammu and Kashmir, there is not a single Buddhist working in the state secretariat. The only Buddhist who was selected through the state public service commission had to convert to Islam to secure a government job…The Congress is silent on this.

'While appeasing Muslims, we should not forget Hindus, who are a majority in this state,' Gadgil said, pointing at an article published in *The Economist*, which stated that 'Islam and democracy do not go together'. Quoting from the article, Gadgil said a province in China, which had a substantial Muslim population, wanted to break away and form a separate nation. When Gadgil was asked why he was saying all this, he said: 'I have said this earlier. Muslims constitute only 18 per cent of the vote share. Even if all of them vote for the Congress, the party will not return to power. We cannot go on ignoring the sentiments of the other 82 per cent.'

Sonia responded to Gadgil's call equating secular ideals with Hinduism, both as a philosophy and a way of life. At the Ramakrishna Mission, on the occasion of Vivekananda's anniversary in 1999, she said India was secular primarily because Hinduism 'has been based on what our ancients said: Truth is one'. The CWC too met at 24 Akbar Road and adopted a resolution on 16 January 1999, articulating the Congress' definition of secularism. It said,

> The CWC endorses the views of the Congress president, Sonia Gandhi, in her speech on the anniversary of Swami Vivekananda, where she had said, 'India is secular primarily because of Hindus, both as a philosophy and as a way of life based on what our ancients said, *Ekam satyam, vipraha bahudha vadanti* (The truth is one, the wise pursue it variously)'.

Following the rise of Narendra Modi and the BJP on the national scene since 16 May 2014, many Congress leaders like A.K. Antony, Ghulam Nabi Azad, and Janardhan Dwivedi want Sonia and Rahul to showcase the party's pro-Hindu image but there are many within the Congress who feel such a measure would boomerang. Unable to take a call, Sonia and Rahul decided to follow the path of least resistance and skirt the issue, a strategy that has dismayed many. After all, the Congress survival kit for the past 130 years has been continuity with change. Both the Nehruvian and Indira Congress understood that dogmatic or indoctrinated ideology would not yield the party any long-term benefits in a multicultural, multiplural society like India. The Congress, therefore, kept reinventing itself, avoiding confrontations and sharp divisions in society.

Describing the Congress at the Avadi session 1955, U.N. Dhebar, the then AICC chief has stated with a poet's flair,

> What is the Congress? It is a tear, fallen from the sufferings and agonised heart of humanity in bondage, coming to life. India has seen better days, but some of her weaknesses had become prey to the most subtle forms of exploitation—foreign and domestic. The more she tried to shake off the bondage, the faster, closer and tighter grew the bonds around her, till the agony of her heart and aches and pains of her body emaciated and famished for want of nourishment, both physical and cultural, could hardly bear them any longer. The tear was destined to become a stream, the stream a river and the river a mighty Ganga or a Brahmaputra, which was to wash off its sins and weaknesses of ages, to weld her people together, breathe new life and new spirit into their heart, and carry them afloat, united, purified and strengthened by their cherished goal. It was to be a force unparalleled in the history of the world. Its unarmed and unsophisticated armies were to spread the message and undertake a mission the world has heard and worked for only on rare occasions.

From its inception, the Congress functioned as an amorphous organisation. The party constitution articles 1 and 2 said the objective of the Indian National Congress was the well-being and advancement of the people of India and the establishment in India, by peaceful and constitutional means, of a socialist state based on parliamentary democracy in which there was equality of opportunity and of political, economic, and social rights, and which aimed at world peace and fellowship. The second part of its core statement bore faith and allegiance to the Constitution of India and to the principles of socialism, secularism, and democracy, which would uphold the sovereignty, unity, and integrity of the nation.

Bhogaraju Pattabhi Sitaramayya, who had lost the party president's poll to Subhas Chandra Bose in 1939, equated the Congress ideology closely with the Indian nation. He told AICC delegates at the Jaipur plenary in 1948,

> The Congress is the service station of the life giving ideology of the nation. The life sustaining doctrines are pumped through the arteries of the government of the nation, where they become somewhat sullied in implementation and are returned to the Congress for purification. The ideology constantly discussed by the populace and constantly

> renovated as public opinion, is once again canalised by the Congress through the government in a renovated form, that is how the Congress and the government act and react upon each other...The Congress is really the philosopher, while the government is the politician. The latter has power and the former has influence.

According to Nehru, the Congress was always something more than a party and capable of drawing allegiance from millions who were not formally with the party. Speaking in New Delhi at the 1951 AICC session, Nehru said,

> We have to retain something of that wider aspect of the Congress, but this should not lead to floppiness and loose thinking and an accommodation of all kinds of contrary opinions within its fold. In regard to principles—social, economic and political—this must be clear. There should be no room for reactionaries in the Congress fold. Nor should there be any room in it for those who seek, through its medium, personal advancement and profit at the cost of the public good. We have to pull ourselves up from the narrow grooves of thought and action, from factions, from mutual recrimination, from tolerance of evil in public life and in our social structure, and become again fighters for a cause and upholders of high principles.

In subsequent party sessions and position papers, the Congress clarified and explained that its concept of socialism was not dogmatic or indoctrinary. In 1972, under Indira, the election manifesto prepared for the assembly polls read, 'Poverty must go. Disparity must diminish. Injustice must end'. Earlier, at the Mumbai AICC session, Jagjivan Ram moved a resolution saying, 'Modern man is the inheritor of all that is noble and good in human thought. And thus our democratic socialism is a synthesis of all that is best in the thinking of the East and the West and provides an ideology superior to other sectarian ideologies which are communalistic or communitarian.'

In terms of 'science of ideas' or ideology, the Congress' strength lies in the absence of ideological clarity. Senior Congress leader Shriman Narayan Agarwal (he dropped his caste surname, Agarwal) used to insist that the Congress ideology should not be interpreted in any rigid set of ideas whose acceptance was obligatory to all Congressmen. The culture of having a powerful, dominant leader and the tendency to change from time to time as per the political situation kept giving the Congress fresh ideological frames. These were more matters of policy than faith. Such a compromise between various interest groups helped in the sharing of power and the doctrinal pluralism of its leaders.

By the time the Congress under Sonia met at Pachmarhi (1997), Shimla (2003), and Hyderabad (2006), the party had formally accepted the need for coalitions with parties of varying ideology. The political resolution in Hyderabad said, 'At present, coalition of political forces and opinion is inevitable. Each political epoch needs a leader and a visionary who changes the traditional paradigm of society to face contemporary challenges.'

As the venue of most of the meetings of the Congress Working Committee (CWC), 24 Akbar Road has seen the party making its key political, social, economic, and international policy pronouncements. Considered to be the highest decision-making body of the party, the CWC has held different levels of power in the organisation at different times. In the period prior to independence in 1947, the CWC was the centre of power and often seen as more active than the Congress president. In the period after 1969, when the Congress party split for the first time between factions loyal to Indira Gandhi and those led by the syndicate of regional bosses, including K. Kamaraj and Morarji Desai, the power of the CWC declined. Indira's triumph in 1971 marked the return of centralised power, making the CWC once again the paramount decision-making body of the party. In fact, the centralised nature of the CWC has prompted many party leaders, particularly those from the states, to describe its instructions as coming from the 'High Command'.

The Indira era saw the radicalisation of Congress policies, programmes, and leadership, followed by its fall. The relationship between the philosopher and the politician saw many highs and lows with the philosopher losing considerable ground during the regimes of Indira, Rajiv, Narasimha Rao, and Sitaram Kesri.

During the Nehru era, Nehru was the supreme decision maker, no matter what post he occupied. Socialist leaders such as Jayaprakash Narayan, Acharya Narendra Dev, and Ram Manohar Lohia left the Congress in 1948. Nehru's biographer, S. Gopal, felt these socialists had an important role to play as a responsible opposition. Critics such as Gopal felt that even during the Nehru era, the real aim of the Congress was not so much to implement its declared policies and see that the Constitution of India was carried forward in letter and spirit than to live in power. For this objective, the Congress under Nehru, Indira, Rajiv, and Sonia accommodated men of different hues even at the expense of the stated social and economic commitment to the country.

Indira inherited many of these powerful factions that continuously put pressure on her to make adjustments and accommodate them. She deftly dealt with the old guard represented by Desai, Chavan, Patil, and Nijalingappa on the one hand, and the 'young Turks' or the 'verandah boys' (young socialist leaders such as Chandrashekhar, Mohan Dharia, Krishna Kant, C. Subramaniam, Chandrajeet Yadav, and others) on the other. The young Turks inspired the entire new generation of that era when they successfully blocked the entry of Raja Kamakhya Narain Singh of Ramgarh in the Bihar cabinet through the offices of the then chief minister, Harihar Singh, in violation of an earlier decision that feudal lords who were not part of the Congress should not be inducted in party ruled states as ministers. C. Subramaniam, who was then Tamil Nadu Congress chief, resigned from the CWC. On 14 May 1969, the CWC asked Subramaniam to withdraw his resignation and the Bihar government to remove Raja Kamakhya from the Bihar ministry. Thus, Subramaniam won the day.

From 1967 to 1972, Indira displayed her extraordinary political acumen and sense of realpolitik. She kept pitting one Congress leader against the other to deal a body blow to the conservatives during the bank nationalisation, abolition of the Privy Purse and the presidential polls that pitted Neelam Sanjiva Reddy against V.V. Giri. Chandrashekhar and others took on the high and mighty on the basis of her 'stray thoughts' at the stormy AICC meets in Bangalore, Mumbai, and Faridabad. On 28 May 1970, Indira went public, chiding Chandrashekhar at a mini AICC session in New Delhi for his 'armchair criticism'. Indira said the party (Congress) was free to change its leadership (Indira) if it felt that it could not deliver the goods. The subsequent developments saw the systemic exit of dissent from the Congress.

Gone were the days when Neelam Sanjiva Reddy told party colleagues at the Bhavnagar session of the AICC (1961),

> I would, therefore, suggest for consideration that people who have been in power, say for a period of ten years, voluntarily relinquish their offices and take up organizational work. Their wisdom, backed

> by a decade of administrative experience, should be available for the Congress organization so that they can lead the organization into better channels.

Instead, by 1972, Indira and her party were asking for a 'committed bureaucracy', rather than a neutral, professional workforce. Airing Indira's thoughts, Shankar Dayal Sharma told the Kolkata AICC session in 1972, 'The training, the background and the mental make-up of the entire bureaucracy may have served the purpose of colonial rulers, but surely, it does not inspire confidence in India today.'

Gradually, the Congress developed a culture of the 'supreme leader', in which loyalty to an individual leader became critical for survival. The presence of Sanjay Gandhi as an extra-constitutional authority further squeezed inner party democracy and the right to dissent. Lloyd I. Rudolph and Susanne H. Rudolph, who authored *In Pursuit of Lakshmi: The Political Economy of the Indian State*, said that by the time Sanjay died in June 1980, the process of deinstitutionalisation of the party system was complete.

> He (Sanjay) died as he lived: daring, impetuous, contemptuous of the rules, a danger to himself and others...the effect of Sanjay's leadership on the Congress was to deinstitutionalize it further by increasing its patrimonial features. By the time of his death, the party had become his and his mother's bailiwick.

Along with the cult of sycophancy, the pace of political corruption also quickened. The names of two Congress chief ministers, A.R. Antulay and Arjun Singh, were associated with 'scandals'. These leaders earned legal reprieves and went on to become towering leaders in their respective way, but the incidents led to the rise of those who showed little respect for parliamentary conventions or probity in public life.

One of the aspects of the deinstitutionalisation taking place was the lack of inner party democracy. The annual AICC sessions and the democratic elections of office bearers and the CWC became a thing of the past. In fact, after Nehru's death in 1964, while Kamaraj was the party chief, the trend of authoritarianism had already reared its head with elections of office bearers and state party chiefs being postponed on one pretext or the other. After its

1969 split, the Congress began to depend more heavily on Indira, who used trusted lieutenants such as Jagjivan Ram, S.D. Sharma, and D.K. Barooah as party chiefs.

Once the party shifted its office to 24 Akbar Road, inner party democracy was truly dead and gone. Rajiv Gandhi did try to effect some changes, but his preoccupation with Bofors and other controversies gave him no time to meet the goals he had spelt out at the Mumbai plenary session in 1985. It was ironical that both Narasimha Rao and Sitaram Kesri, despite their leadership limitations, tried in their own ways to usher in inner party democracy. Today's party leaders and in-house historians have little or scant regard for those democrats. Sonia Gandhi did try to streamline the party's functioning, but she too functioned with ad hocism and expediency in spite of emerging as the supreme leader of the party. AICC sessions were not held regularly and, for some inexplicable reasons, Sonia avoided constituting the party's all powerful Central Parliamentary Board (CPB). As per the Congress constitution, the powers to grant tickets for the state assemblies, Lok Sabha, and Rajya Sabha lie with the CPB, but successive party presidents from Rao to Sonia and Rahul, have usurped these powers without constituting the apex body.

It is said that once the conqueror Timur the Lame held a discourse with the famous historian and sociologist Ibn Khaldun about the fate of dynasties. Khaldun propounded that the glory of a dynasty seldom lasted beyond four generations. The first generation is inclined towards conquest, the second towards administration. The third generation, being free from the necessity to conquer or administer, is left with the pleasurable task of spending the wealth of its ancestors on cultural pursuits. Consequently, by the fourth generation, a dynasty has usually spent its wealth as well as human energy. Hence, the downfall of each royal house is embedded in the very process of its rising. According to Khaldun, it was a natural phenomenon and couldn't be avoided.

Set in a democratic world of contemporary Indian history, the rise and fall of the great Nehru-Gandhi family seems to be indicating the soundness of Ibn Khaldun's formulation. Jawaharlal Nehru was the architect, his daughter Indira Gandhi expanded, and emerging as one of the 20th century's most powerful personalities, Indira's son Sanjay was groomed as heir apparent but was killed in an air crash just when his political career was about to take off. His brother Rajiv Gandhi too became prime minister of India, experimented a lot and paid heavily. The fourth generation of the Nehru-Gandhi family represented currently by Rahul Gandhi perhaps has good intentions but things are not clicking at all for him, though he is projected by Congressmen as the party's youth leader.

Post the 2014 general elections defeat, the Congress remains a demoralised political force with its leadership refusing to fine-tune its socio-economic and ideological thinking. It has worked out a tacit understanding with the Left parties for the Bengal legislative assembly polls without explaining a rationale or telling the party cadre why it broke ties with the Left in 2008, which was providing crucial support to the UPA regime. For the first time in the history of the Congress, members of the Nehru-Gandhi family i.e. Rahul, Sonia Gandhi, Priyanka and Robert Vadra have became hopelessly dependent upon the party which had a habit of looking up to them for leadership. When the Augusta Westland bribery charges were raised against Sonia, the party came to the streets alleging democracy was under threat. This is certainly a testing time for the nation's oldest political party.

Bibliography

Abbas, K.A. *That Woman: Indira Gandhi's Seven Years in Power*. New Delhi: Indian Book Company, 1973.

Adams, Jad, and Philip Whitehead. *The Dynasty: The Nehru-Gandhi Story.* London: Penguin Books/BBC Books, 1997.

Bijukumar, V. *Reinventing the Congress: Economic Policies and Strategies since 1991.* Jaipur: Rawat Publications. 2006.

Brass, Paul. *The Politics of India since Independence.* Cambridge: Cambridge University Press, 1994.

Chand, Attar. *Congress Party: Politics and New Challenges.* Delhi: UDH Publishers, 1985.

Gill, S.S. *The Dynasty. A Political Biography of the Premier Ruling Family of Modern India.* New Delhi: HarperCollins India, 1996.

Johari, J.C. *Indian National Congress since Independence.* Lotus Press. New Delhi. 2006.

Moraes, Dom. *Mrs. Gandhi.* London: Jonathan Cape 1980.

Nehru, B.K. *Nice Guys Finish Second.* New Delhi: Penguin Books India, 1997.

Nugent, Nicholas. *Rajiv Gandhi: Son of a Dynasty.* London: BBC Books, 1990.

Rao, P.V. Narasimha. *Insider.* New Delhi: Penguin Books India, 1998.

———. *Ayodhya 6 December 1992.* New Delhi: Penguin Books, 2006

Rudolph, Lloyd I, and Susanne H. Rudolph. *In Pursuit of Lakshmi: The Political Economy of the Indian State.* Orient Longman: Hyderabad 1987.

Sarvepalli, Gopal. *Jawaharlal Nehru: A Biography.* New Delhi: Oxford University Press, 1975.

Singh, Dr Govind Narain. *Socialist Ideology in Congress.* New Delhi: Shikha Publications, 1985.

Thakur, Janardhan. *All the Janata Men.* New Delhi: Vikas Publishing House, 1977.

Tully, Mark, and Zareer Masani. *From Raj to Rajiv: Forty Years of Indian Independence.* London: BBC Books, 1988.

Ved, Mahendra. *Times of India* (New Delhi), 3 February 1998.

Vasudev, Uma. *Indira Gandhi: Revolution and Restraint.* New Delhi: Vikas, 1973.

Wolpert, Stanley. *A New History of India.* New York: Oxford University Press, 1989.

Kashmir Today and the Way to the Future

Wajahat Habibullah

And yet he roams in distant vales,
New wine he seeks!
If he comes not, the jasmine pales,
And I, and all!

—Habba Khatoon, 16th-century Kashmiri poet
(Translated by Nilla Cram Cook)

The concept of nationhood and the movement towards building nations across the world owes its origins to the extinction of empires in World War I, whereafter the leader of the nation set to become the world's mightiest power, Woodrow Wilson, President of the US, a staunch Presbyterian, insisted that the ensuing settlement, partly for this reason, was to become 'a peace to end all peace', which must respect the concept of nation state. This hitherto exclusively European idea was steeped in its own history of constant religious conflict. And so it was that in the tranquil backwaters—even though locally volatile Arab domains—of the Ottoman Empire, and across Central Asia, 'nations' were carved out where none existed. India's own former Viceroy, Lord Curzon, as England's Foreign Minister, sought to cast the nations of Central Asia including Iran into this mould, in order to confront the Bolsheviks in the Great Game being played out in Afghanistan. Our world continues to pay the price.

Nandita Haksar, who hails from among the most distinguished Kashmiri Pandit (KP) families and herself a leading lawyer, reminds us in her book *The Many Faces of Kashmiri Nationalism*[1] of the origins of this concept in

Kashmir, with the dissemination in the 1920s of modern education among young Kashmiri Muslims and the birth of a political movement in the state in 1931 under the leadership of the charismatic young Sheikh Abdullah, who returned with a degree in chemistry from Aligarh Muslim University. Although the original movement was nationalist Kashmiri in its outlook it had a religious identity—it went by the name of Muslim Conference. Since the initial target was the repressed Kashmiri peasantry, entirely Muslim, amongst whom was to subsist an abiding following for Sheikh Abdullah, the party's primary objective was the acquisition of civil rights by the Kashmiris, a majority of whom were Muslims. But this made it necessary for the party to seek inclusion of the Pandits; hence the philosophy of *Kashmiriyat*. Yet the underlying philosophy of this movement remained ambivalent on the issue of the extent of its religious moorings, and sought finally to settle this with the renaming of the Muslim Conference as the National Conference in 1937, and the adoption of the manifesto of Naya Kashmir in 1941, with a decidedly secular character. But the much touted idea of Kashmiriyat never fully captured the mind of the Kashmiri—Pandit or Muslim. So, what was the trajectory that movement was to take, and how far did it chart a roadmap for the birth of a Kashmiri nation?

With Independence came India's partition. Although the Maharaja, on the advice of Pandit Ram Chandra Kak, his prime minister from June 1945 to 11 August 1947, did toy with possibilities of seeking independence, such independence would clearly not bring the state under Dogra rule. That possibility had already been extinguished by Kashmir's own freedom movement, which had assertively rejected Kak's endeavour at rapprochement. What then was the choice before Sheikh Abdullah, the undisputed leader of Kashmir's national movement, in prison at the time of India's birth, whence he was released only under pressure from India's PM Nehru at the close of September 1947? It was Abdullah's leadership that made Kashmir the only major princely state that acceded to India enforced by the will of its people. And India had stood true to her history of giving refuge to the oppressed, be they Jews or Parsees. But have the Kashmiris looked upon themselves as Indians—as do Malayalis, Bengalis, Gujaratis or Punjabis?

In September 1948, as the first war between India and Pakistan over Kashmir drew to a close, Sheikh Mohammed Abdullah spoke to Josef Korbel, first Chairman of the UN Commission for India and Pakistan, of his conviction that Kashmiris would be better off with India, and of his dilemma, as undisputed leader of the Kashmiri section of a multi-ethnic state, on the choices before Kashmir:

> I have meditated about four possible solutions to our problem. First or second—accession to India or Pakistan through a plebiscite. This could not take place in less than three years, because of the destruction of the country and the dislocation of its population. Even then it would be difficult to ascertain impartially the wishes of the people scattered over large areas and possibly subjected to intimidation. Would such a plebiscite be democratic, and would India or Pakistan accept the verdict?
>
> Third, there is a possibility of independence under the joint guarantee of India, Pakistan, Afghanistan, China and the Soviet Union. I would be willing to meet the leader of Azad Kashmir, Ghulam Abbas, with whom I was once tied by bonds of friendship and a common struggle. We had been together in prison and often had discussed the future of our country.
>
> But even should Kashmir's powerful neighbours agree to give us a guarantee of independence, I doubt that it could last for long. There is in my opinion, therefore, only one solution open. That is the division of the country. If it is not achieved, the fighting will continue; India and Pakistan will prolong the quarrel indefinitely, and our people's suffering will go on.[2]

This has remained the stuff of the Kashmir debate since. And that 'suffering' has never really ended. But the aspiration to freedom (*azadi*) never waned. A week before the SAARC summit of January 2004 in Islamabad, Yasin Malik, Chair of the Jammu Kashmir Liberation Front (JKLF), then part of the All Parties Hurriyat Conference (APHC), that had spearheaded the insurrection of 1989–90, wrote a joint letter to India's Prime Minister A.B. Vajpayee and Pakistan's President Pervez Musharraf echoing the Sheikh:

> We have organized protests and strikes whenever Indian and Pakistani leaders have held talks portending to cover Kashmir. However, we have decided not to protest at this time with an eye towards giving peace

a chance and in hopes of encouraging an opening between India and Pakistan for a broader peace process. Instead, I would like to convey a message of earnest support and convey my earnest request that you meet and resolve to undertake a peace process that will also effectively and meaningfully involve the people of Kashmir in finding an agreeable solution to all parties.

It is my firm belief that the principle of the inclusion of the people of Kashmir is the missing ingredient for a complete vision for a workable peace process. If a peace process is to be just and sustainable, it must be accepted that Kashmir is not a territorial dispute; it is about the future and aspirations of living people in Kashmir. It is the reality of loss and injustice faced by the Kashmiri population and the very deep and real Kashmiri aspiration for freedom and justice that encompass the major substantive component of the Kashmir dispute. Being the real victims and subjects of this dispute, the Kashmiris have a rightful, necessary, and constructive role to play in the peace process.

No solution on Kashmir will be lasting unless it is legitimate in the eyes of the people of Kashmir. Quite simply, I submit that the key to finding an agreeable middle-ground that will be a win-win-win solution for India, Pakistan and the people of Kashmir is to involve the credible and legitimate representatives of the people of Kashmir in the peace process.

This is not simply my own request; it is the expectation of millions of my fellow Kashmiris who strongly share this yearning that Kashmiris should be involved in the process to develop a shared vision for a peaceful and just future.

This letter had been preceded in 2003 by a massive signature campaign in support of *azadi*, in which 800,000 signatures had been secured from Malik's 'fellow Kashmiris' in the very first month, and copies of which had been sent to Prime Minister Vajpayee and President Musharraf. In 2007 Malik was to undertake a *safar-i-azadi* across the Kashmir Valley addressing more than 600 public meetings heavily attended by men, women, and children, his cavalcade decorated with symbols of unity of the Kashmiris—Muslim, Pandit, and Sikh—pleading primarily that the Kashmiris be allowed to participate in any decision concerning their future. Nandita Haksar has described the public response, based on the eyewitness account of Kashmiri Pandit Sampat Prakash, a leftist leader of trade unions of government employees, who proudly sat side by side with Malik in the caravan:

> The villages reverberated with pro-*azadi* slogans shouted as vociferously by women and children as by the JKLF activists and the youth. The women also burst into song and sang traditional Kashmiri ballads to welcome the caravan. The children danced with joy while the youth were thrilled to get an opportunity to shake hands with the chairman of the JKLF Yasin Malik.

In the mohallas of Srinagar the cavalcade was showered with petals, almonds, and sweets, as is a *barat*. This *safar*, the massive celebratory response to which in villages and Srinagar's mohallas was studiedly ignored by the national media, masked a darker side. Most Pandits, even where present were silent observers, not active participants.

The *safar* was planned for Jammu after the month of Ramadan. Although pro-Pakistan elements led by the still-formidable Hizb-ul-Mujahideen had signally failed to stall it in the valley despite a fitful effort, it was aborted at Doda by the police. Nandita Haksar is of the view that the *safar* was allowed by authorities in Kashmir simply to assess the public response. They had no use for such a *safar* in Jammu.[3]

Today with the widespread alienation of Kashmir's youth it might be disputed that any element of the Hurriyat leadership can legitimately claim to be speaking for all Kashmiri Muslims. But the aspirations voiced in Malik's letter and the cry of his widely attended *safar* still hold. And in Kashmir today's generation of young Kashmiris typified by IAS officers Shah Faesal and Syed Abid Rasheed Shah, Hizb-ul-Mujahideen commander Burhan Wani, and entrepreneur horticulturist Khurram are modern, well-educated representatives of a new generation of Kashmiris, consummate in social media, brought up in an environment steeped in violence. Each of them chose a path by which they felt they could serve their people best. Many had returned to Kashmir from comfortable occupations or businesses, in the hope of a promised opportunity. And with the waning of the separatist appeal, this described well the surge of Kashmiri nationalism—'*azadi*' that grips young Kashmiris.

In my conversations with Kashmiris, including the separatist leadership, what emerges is a continuing thirst for freedom. Never spoken except in one-on-one conversation it is agreed that political independence, which is acceptable neither to India nor to Pakistan, nevertheless does not imply freedom—for reasons recalling Abdullah's comment to Korbel. The alternative then must be self-rule within existing national boundaries. Is this dreaming of *azadi* not then simply, at least in the case of India, wherein Kashmir, the font of the insurrection is located, the free and open practice of democracy? And if that were conceded, surely it should be possible for India and Pakistan, both functioning democracies, one the world's largest, with wide experience in pluralist decentralisation and the other having won democracy through struggle and suffering, to accommodate such aspiration? Instead Pakistan has taken advantage, even exacerbated challenges before us with every means at its command. This came to a head in the turmoil of 2016. We need not have doubted that it would, given Pakistan's violent birth and the wars that followed.

Why then was Kashmir the Achilles heel? The events that followed the Accession, the policies pursued, and most of all the relationship of the Kashmiris with remaining Indians ensured that the Kashmiris might accept, even among some sections develop affection for, but never consider themselves Indian. And as the events of the summer of 2016 played out in the Indian media or in drawing rooms, the casualties among Kashmiris were never referred as the death and injury of Indians.

There have been efforts at peacemaking at least since Prime Minister Narasimha Rao's 'Burkina Faso Declaration' (1995)—part menace and part olive branch—sought to set the tone, after clouds of war between India and Pakistan had lowered in the 1990s. With violence a daily occurrence, both India and Pakistan sought real dialogue at Islamabad's South Asian Association for Regional Cooperation (SAARC) Summit in 2004. This happened perhaps for the first time since the early 1960s, when Prime Minister Nehru and President Ayub Khan of Pakistan—urged on by US Assistant Secretary of State for Far Eastern Affairs Averell Harriman and UK's Minister of Commonwealth Relations Duncan Sandys in the wake of India's China debacle—had announced their agreement to renew efforts to resolve outstanding differences between the two countries in November 1962. However, in 1963 the talks between the then foreign ministers, India's Sardar Swaran Singh and Pakistan's Zulfikar Ali Bhutto collapsed, with each side accusing the other of duplicity and worse.

The thaw of 2004 surprised many as the tone moved by degrees from cynical to merely sceptical and then to hopeful—only to be dashed by the terrorist outrage of 26 November 2008 in Mumbai which has gone down in history as 26/11, when 173 people were killed and at least 308 wounded, both Indian and foreign citizens. But the ceasefire, although increasingly disrupted in the decade to come, has been shown through field studies to have brought tangible relief to residents on both sides of the Line of Control (LoC), particularly on the banks of the Kishenganga in the valleys of the Kazinag mountain range, who had been primary victims of the crossfire. Even as violations peaked in 2014–15 residents have returned to their villages, rebuilt destroyed homes, and resettled despite disruption. For them the ceasefire is of vital interest.

In the meantime, unnoticed outside the Valley, an important but seldom-mentioned undercurrent had begun swirling within Kashmir around the two principal religious trends that have characterised India's Islam. One is catholic and inclusive, while the other is puritanical and exclusive. With the receding of the Sufi ambience, Islam in Kashmir is faced with a choice. On one side is the inclusive tradition of convergence and growth, characterised by Kashmir's own religious evolution. On the other side is the pan-Islamic tradition best characterised in its extreme by the rise of al-Qaeda and the Islamic State in Iraq and Syria (ISIS) in Iraq—the retreat into exclusivism in the belief that insularity will protect and purify. The rudiments of that philosophy underpinned the thinking that had led to the partition of India—a road that Kashmir had decisively refused to take in 1947. What road will Kashmiris choose into their future?

In 1905 Maulvi Rasool Shah the Mirwaiz of Kashmir (a Kashmiri concept of a position akin to a high priest), founded the *Anjuman-i-Nusrat-ul-Islam* in Srinagar to improve the education of Kashmir's Muslims and ensure the dissemination of a pristine Islamic doctrine. Mohammed Yusuf Shah, who became Mirwaiz in March 1931, had been patron of the young Sheikh Mohammed Abdullah. Both served terms in the Maharaja's prisons. In 1932 they together helped found the All Jammu and Kashmir Muslim Conference, which became the main platform for opposition to the Maharaja. But by mid-1932, the conference was divided by an active, sometimes violent political rivalry between supporters of Sheikh Abdullah, who became known as the *sher*, or lions, and the followers of Mirwaiz Mohammed Yusuf Shah, known as *bakre*, or goats (after the beards sported by their supporting clergy). The spiritual fulcrum of the Mirwaiz was Kashmir's Jami Masjid. That of the Sheikh was Hazratbal Shrine, which housed a relic of the Prophet, placing it at the heart of Kashmir's Sufi tradition.

The political expression of this divide was that in 1939 the Muslim Conference was formally dissolved. The Jammu and Kashmir National Conference (JKNC) that replaced it was more concerned with social and political issues, such as land reform, than with matters of theology. In 1941 Maulvi Yusuf Shah, with other conservatives, revived the Muslim Conference, of which he became founding president. Mirwaiz Yusuf Shah opposed Abdullah's 'Quit Kashmir' movement against the Maharaja in 1946 and finally supported accession to Pakistan, to which country, at India's Independence, he was exiled; the Muslim Conference was banned in what remained of the princely state in India.

It was replaced by the Awami Action Committee representing the more orthodox element of Kashmir's Islam, founded in 1963 by Mirwaiz Mohammed Farooq, nephew and successor of Yusuf Shah, in direct consequence of the Hazratbal crisis of 1963, when the holy relic was purportedly stolen from the precincts of the *dargah*. The juxtaposition of the thread of inclusive Sufi tradition with that of the relatively orthodox doctrine of the Mirwaiz camouflaged a disturbing trend that, by 2003, had set into Kashmiri Muslim thought. This trend is manifest in the rise of the Ahl-i-Hadeeth, or Wahabi, school of Islamic theology. The school, originating in 18th-century Arabia as a defensive reaction to misconceived European assaults on Arab tradition, and actively encouraged by sections of the British leadership in the 20th century as a means of controlling Muslim populations across their empire, had developed a following all over India, but until the 1970s the movement was significant only in the Jammu region of Kashmir, most notably the mountainous areas straddling the LoC, south of Muzaffarabad. But by the close of the 20th century, against the backdrop of the failing insurgency, a number of Ahl-i-Hadeeth mosques had sprung up in and around Srinagar as well as in smaller towns. According to the local press on 24 January 2004, there were 94 Jamia Ahl-i-Hadeeth (JAH) mosques in Srinagar alone. This number had grown in Kashmir to 660 by 2010.

These mosques do not conform to the local architectural tradition, which the imperial Mughal had respected. Srinagar's Jami Masjid, rebuilt after a devastating fire by the Emperor Aurangzeb, is the finest example of that tradition—the structure has a single central spire, reminiscent of the Buddhist gompa of the Himalayan region. The new mosques are designed with domes (or imitation domes) and minarets in what has become the standard 'Muslim' design across the subcontinent. The Ahl-i-Hadeeth mosques, and the Madrassas that are usually attached to them, receive their endowments from Saudi Arabia, where the Wahabi school is the ruling theology.

The Wahabi school has admittedly developed only a limited following in Kashmir, but it continues to proliferate because of its superior facilities and its appeal to the youth. By the first decade of the 21st century its leadership sought to distance the school from politics, espousing a gentler theology. But there continued to be a countermovement from within, which sought to impose upon the grouping a more radical agenda. And because it was not perceived as a threat by established Indian authority, this development has not been addressed by the state, nor has its impact on the tattered social fabric of the state been studied. The tragic consequence was the assassination in April 2011 of Maulana Showkat Ahmad Shah—president, JAH, and the man responsible for this moderation—suspected to have been committed by extremists supporting Jama'at-i-Islami, as he entered the local mosque at Maisuma Bazaar to lead the Friday congregation. And in July-August 2016 the Ahl-i-Hadeeth mosques refused to call the populace to arms.

Kashmir's once-vibrant Sufi tradition weakened since the civil breakdown of 1989 and the more conservative yet eclectic school led by the Mirwaiz together continue to command a larger following than the more staid Wahabi, particularly in Srinagar. By 2009 the separatist leadership had become alive to the challenge. Because emotions, politics, and world view are so inextricably bound to religion in Kashmir, much about the region's future will be determined as its Muslims choose between these paths.

India's government on its part, although rejecting reversion to the constitutional status of 1953 when Sheikh Abdullah was rudely supplanted, in Rao's Burkina Faso Declaration made the Indira–Sheikh Accord of 1975 the benchmark for any future settlement. This accord had brought to a close an era of illusory democracy initiated with the assembly election of 1950 by none other than the Sheikh as prime minister. That election was won by the JKNC uncontested. Thereafter Kashmir's administration had developed such skills in rigging of polls as to elevate it into a fine art, a practice finally cracked only in 1977 with the sweeping victory in the assembly elections of a government led by Abdullah, the first after his restoration in 1975. With the return of popular government to Jammu and Kashmir (J&K) in the election of October 1996, the relationship between the Indian Union and Kashmir was again addressed, by the JKNC government.

A State Autonomy Committee was appointed in November 1996 to recommend measures for restoring internal autonomy to the state. The committee's sketchy final report of March 2000 was politically revivalist. It took no account of developments since 1953, entirely ignoring the Indira–Sheikh Accord. The chapter on internal autonomy, claiming to be recommendations, was no more than an introductory note on the subject by the eminent political philosopher of J&K, Balraj Puri, who had been dropped from the committee midway. In words that encapsulate the troubled India-Kashmir relationship, Chief Minister Farooq Abdullah pleaded that hatred had led to the partition of India and created a separate state of Pakistan. 'Don't push us to the wall. We won't push you to the wall,' he told the opposition, constituted primarily of Jammu-based parties, including the Bharatiya Janata Party (BJP) that refused to countenance greater autonomy for the state, advocating instead a closer integration with the rest of India. Shortly after passage in the state assembly, the resolution was rejected out of hand by the National Democratic Alliance (NDA) government ruling at the Centre, of which the JKNC was supposedly part. Today, the BJP is in alliance with the local Jammu and Kashmir People's Democratic Party (PDP) in governing the state.

In 1997 Prime Minister Gujral had offered to discuss relations, including Kashmir, with Pakistan. The following year, Prime Minister Vajpayee, who journeyed to Lahore, inaugurating a bus service between Delhi and Lahore, renewed this offer. In early 1999 the Lahore Declaration put Kashmir on the agenda for discussion between the two countries. But the situation that developed that very year in Kargil put paid to India's incipient rapprochement with Pakistan. The Vajpayee government turned to establishing direct communication with the separatist Kashmiri leadership. That leadership had engaged constructively with the administration in bringing a peaceful resolution to the crisis in Hazratbal in 1993. In March 1999 R.K. Mishra, eminent leftist intellectual and former editor of *Patriot*, a leading leftist newspaper, had become Prime Minister Vajpayee's point man for back-channel talks with Niaz Naik, Pakistan's former foreign secretary, as Prime Minister

Sharif's emissary. When this effort foundered on the bloody reef of Kargil, Mishra focused on engaging the separatist leadership in Kashmir. Outside the glare of media publicity, Mishra was able to establish communication with the separatist leadership because they believed he was fully backed by the prime minister's office.

In early 2000, at the behest of Avtar Singh (Bubbles) Dulat, adviser in Prime Minister Vajpayee's office, I spoke extensively to each of the separatist leaders. At the time, although I was in government (head of the state's Lakes and Waterways Development Authority), because of my relations with separatist leaders, developed during the years of their repeated incarcerations, and cemented with the successful negotiation at Hazratbal in 1993, I was often called upon to play the role of unofficial negotiator. I had in fact been first asked to engage with the separatists by Bubbles Dulat, then serving in Kashmir with India's Intelligence Bureau, when I was secretary in the Rajiv Gandhi Foundation (1991–93) in New Delhi. I regularly met the separatists, including Abdul Ghani Lone, Shabbir Shah, and Yasin Malik—who had spent the longest period in custody—at various times when they were held in arrest, in and around Delhi. To Yasin Malik I had presented the works of Mahatma Gandhi. Upon his release in 1994, he remained committed to Gandhi's thought, although he was to lament that the present government of India could not endure protest against it, even when the form was satyagraha fashioned by the father of the nation.

I also met Syed Ali Shah Geelani, then chairman of the APHC; Mirwaiz Omar Farooq, the first chairman of the APHC; Professor A.G. Bhat, a former professor of Physics at Sopore Degree College, who would take over the APHC chair from Geelani in 2000; Maulvi Abbas Ansari, the Shia cleric who was to be the last chairman of a unified APHC when it broke up in 2003; and Javed Mir, who went by the name of Javed Nalka and was a dreaded militant at the time the entire JKLF leadership was incarcerated in 1990. The JKLF's relationship with the APHC has remained—as it was then—ambivalent. But there was unanimity in the view that there was no alternative to a dialogue; only Geelani expressed doubts about the government's sincerity in seeking a resolution. Geelani believed that the threat of infiltration was grossly exaggerated to create an excuse for allowing excesses by the security forces. Bhat, on the other hand, explained that though the constitution of the APHC calls for settlement in terms of UN resolutions or by negotiation, talks must have a defined purpose, necessary to the interest of peace and stability in South Asia. So, albeit there were differing views on Pakistan's role, everyone agreed that there could be no resolution independent of Pakistan.

This urge for resolution by dialogue, even though the ascendancy of the Hurriyat in Kashmir's present political thinking is open to question, continued to be shared by the bulk of the Kashmiri populace. The dignity and self-respect of the Kashmiri is a key factor, and there is a growing conviction that thus far no party had been sincere in pursuit of such dialogue. There were no clearly defined parameters among the separatist leadership regarding what might be the subject of the dialogue, with the exception of Ali Shah Geelani, who broke with the APHC in 2003 to form an increasingly belligerent splinter group, cashing in on the cleavages within Pakistan's own political leadership on the issue of Kashmir. These cleavages stemmed from the rivalry between elements represented by President Musharraf, who sought to cut loose from the tutelage of extremists in matters concerning Kashmir, and elements that believed in opposing any shift from established Pakistan policy and sought to activate their carefully cultivated resources inside Kashmir to derail any such move. Geelani, a man of much dignity, who formed his own splinter group of the Hurriyat in 2003, is of affable demeanour that has masked a rigid ideology. He was to emerge as the supreme icon of agitators in the summer of 2010.He has always believed that Kashmir's best interest lay with Pakistan. Although in his early years he had contested and won elections in Sopore, by the beginning of the 21st century—afflicted with ill health that has made survival a struggle—his attitudes became increasingly rigid.

In December 2001 a terrorist attack on India's parliament led to mobilisation of the armed forces, and dialogue on Kashmir receded in the face of Operation Parakram. War was avoided, but the situation was further confused. In July 2001 a revived attempt at dialogue with Pakistan in Agra failed. In a bid to win the separatists back to his flagging effort at outreach, in April 2003 Prime Minister Vajpayee, speaking in Srinagar, turned once more to the internal Kashmiri leadership, inviting all with grievances within Kashmir to a dialogue with the government. He declared, with his famed poetic resonance long-recalled by Kashmiris, mainstream and separatist, that a resolution must be found on grounds of *insaniyat*, or humanism. This was the term the Mirwaiz cited as a basis for dialogue in his own overtures to Prime Minister Modi as the latter campaigned for election to the state assembly in 2014.

Elections to the state assembly were held in October 2002 as scheduled. No party was barred from the contest. Given the questionable authenticity of earlier elections and its own objection to accepting India's Constitution, the APHC stayed away, although I had sought to persuade them to put their case before the people of India through participation in elections. They consequently appointed Yasin Malik to establish their own election commission, in which Kashmiris might place their trust. Dr Karan Singh was invited to chair a group of eminent citizens of the State. This move was aborted by the arrest of Yasin Malik on obviously trumped up charges, on the orders of Farooq Abdullah's government.

I had in the meantime met India's Chief Election Commissioner J.M. Lyngdoh, at his request. I had urged that the Election Commission not only be fair, as it has long been seen the world over to have conducted itself, but also appear to be so to mistrusting Kashmiris, who looked upon the Commission as simply an agency of India's government. Although separatists were not agreeable to participating, such a message was necessary for the public, particularly the youth, many of whom were potential rebels. This advice he took, not hesitating to criticise the leadership of the sitting government, even when, in my personal view, this was not necessarily warranted. In the result, for the first time in the state's history, a sitting government was unseated through an electoral defeat. Never again was the state accused of widespread rigging in Kashmir, whether to the assembly, or even to municipality and panchayat. Among the separatists Sajjad Lone, son of the assassinated A.G. Lone, set up his own political party and participated, going on to win his seat in 2014 assisted by the active campaigning of his Pakistani wife Asma, and was appointed minister in the Mufti Sayeed government.

Yet, any claim to democratic governance would remain in question, with heavy infiltration of terrorists from across the LoC and violence endemic in all parts of the state, together with widespread arrest and heavy deployment of security forces. Citizens, few of whom belonged to the security forces, although this number has slowly increased through determined effort, particularly by the army, have long felt as if they were in occupied territory, living with doubts, suspicions, and fear of settlement of scores between organisations and individuals using 'security interest' as an excuse. Despite the army's efforts since 1993 to reach out to the people by providing schools and medical services through their operation 'Sadbhavana', human rights continued to suffer collateral damage because of a misplaced 'security interest'. Among a people characterised until recently by non-violence—which outsiders had often contemptuously dismissed as mere cowardice—violence became an accepted fact of life for a generation raised in an environment infused with bloodshed, so that the cataclysmic earthquake that struck the state in 2005 and made headlines across the world, created hardly a ripple in Srinagar, which went about business as usual. Violence was now commonplace.

There has then been a restoration of democratic rule, at least since 2002, through elections replicated through Panchayat and municipal elections with increasing public participation. But with different groups jousting for dominance in the countryside, using their influence with politicians unsure of their public support, with the police and the security services to bully and cajole and, if necessary, suppress even the mildest assertion of an interest considered contrary to that of the local *kharpainch*,[4] violence has continuously lurked, exploding in 2008 and even more disastrously in 2010, always lowering even when peace prevails. For instance, during Prime Minister Modi's visit to Srinagar in November 2015 to announce a series of development measures, police firing on an agitated mob, killed a Kashmiri youth.

Until each citizen can live free from fear, democracy can only be notional, no matter how elections are conducted or who participates. The people of Jammu and Kashmir, like any other people, aspire to a peaceful, healthy life for themselves and their children. The situation in the state by the close of the first decade of the century had seen gross abuse of human rights both by security forces and by the foreign-based militant organisations, whose leadership, drawn from the cadre of international terrorists, cared little for the people whom they were purportedly there to help. Remedies were available within the system, but the mechanisms were wanting. The situation of the Kashmiri Pandit community illustrates this fatal shortcoming.

There has been talk of the return of Kashmiri 'migrants' to their homes in the Valley since the elected government took office in the state in 1996. The close of the 1980s saw Kashmir spiral into a tailspin of violence, suspicion, and dread. What had begun as an ethnic conflict was given a religious colour by Pakistan's Inter-Services Intelligence (ISI). The Kashmiri Pandits, a minuscule minority of Hindus in the Kashmir Valley, became targets of terrorists from both the JKLF—even though the party's manifesto had sought to build on the original secular foundations of Naya Kashmir—and the Hizb-ul-Mujahideen, supporter of secession to Pakistan, sparking massive emigration. By 2008, the Pandit population in the Valley, assessed by their Kashmiri Pandit Sangharsh Samiti (KPSS) as having numbered 75,343 families on 1 January 1990, was reduced to 651 families. Nearly 70,000 families had fled in the turmoil of 1990–92. But the bulk of the migration thereafter—over 3,000 families—took place when violence had been brought increasingly under control.

By early 1990, when I was Special Commissioner Anantnag, in South Kashmir, the public had ceased visiting government offices. But in early March, a crowd of several hundred from Nai Basti neighbourhood gathered before the Special Commissioner's office in Khannabal demanding to see me. I had set up office (and residence, due to the disturbed circumstances) in the Dak Bungalow in the district headquarters. Mohammad Syed Shah, generally known as Syed Shah, brother of separatist leader Shabbir Shah and Muslim United Front (MUF) member of the dissolved state assembly, demanded to know why Pandits were leaving and why the administration was doing nothing to stop the exodus. Shah accused the administration in all seriousness of encouraging the migration, so that the army would be left free to unleash its heavy artillery on all habitations.

When I asked the delegation if they believed that I, a Muslim like them, would actually be party to such a plan, their response was that I had been kept in the dark and that they were privy to 'secret' information. I told them quite clearly that it was hardly surprising that Pandits were apprehensive. Places of worship of the majority were continually used, at least since 19 January 1990 to blare strident threats to them over loudspeakers—as every mosque in Anantnag, where I could hear them, was being used at the time—and prominent members of their community had been murdered. (I learned later that these inflammatory sermons and their reverberating public applause were audio recordings circulated to mosques to be played over loudspeakers at prayer time.) Local Muslims needed to reassure the Pandits of their safety. The administration would readily provide security whenever a threat to the Pandits was anticipated, but its effectiveness would be doubtful without public support, given that the residences of the Pandits were scattered. The gathering concurred and dispersed quietly.

I did request Governor Jagmohan that he telecast an appeal to Pandits that they stay in Kashmir, assuring their safety on the basis of the assurance of the Nai Basti residents. Unfortunately, there was only an announcement that to ensure the security of Pandits, 'refugee' camps were being set up in every district of the Valley, and Pandits who felt threatened could move to these camps rather than leave the Valley. Those Pandits in service who felt threatened were free to leave their stations; they would continue to be paid salary. I relate this tale because the flurry of allegations upon the announcement of a fresh scheme of resettlement in 2015 carries a strange sense of déjà vu.

Leaders of the separatist movement, such as Mirwaiz Omar Farooq and Shabbir Shah have repeatedly called for the return of Kashmiri migrants. But every time the issue was raised at the national level, Kashmiri Pandits in the Valley were subjected to attack, even massacre, forcing the issue to be dropped. By 2003 the community remaining in the valley was scattered in 270 neighbourhoods in towns and villages. They summoned the courage to form an NGO, the Hindu Welfare Society, which attempted to document information regarding the location and requirements of the community. This society successfully discouraged the exodus of Pandits from the Kashmir Valley after the massacre of 23 innocent Pandits in the village of Nadimarg earlier that year. A similar massacre in the village of Wandhama in 1998 had resulted in the emigration of 10,000 Pandits. The demands of the Valley's Pandits at the time were simple: residence in a secure locality and jobs for 500 men and women. They did not complain of hostility from the Muslim public—in fact, they were grateful for Muslim support, the principal, and perhaps only, reason for their continued determination to stay, apart from the need to earn a living. But although the chief secretary of the state in 2005–06, Vijay Bakaya, himself a Pandit, was willing to lend them a patient ear, the state administration remained unresponsive.

On a visit to Srinagar on 21 June 2008 I met three large groups of Kashmiri Pandits who had stayed in the Valley, two of whom belonged to two groups of the Hindu Welfare Society, Kashmir, which had by this time splintered and the third from the KPSS. On the basis of my meeting I submitted my recommendations, which centred on the initiation of a programme, to implement which a monitoring committee of non-migrant KPs be set up by Chief Secretary S.S. Kapur, suggesting names and telephone numbers. I called upon India's then home minister Shivraj Patil in July

2008 at his home to hand him a proposal, offering to assist if and whenever required. I was never asked.

There was an interim census report prepared by the KPSS, financed by members of the KP diaspora, covering 62 mohallas of Anantnag, Bandipore, Baramulla, Budgam, Ganderbal, Kulgam, Kupwara, Pulwama, Shopian, and Srinagar. There was also a consolidated survey of land attempted by the KPSS. The conclusions arrived at—although subject to re-verification—were alarming. According to these the number of KPs residing in the Valley was reduced to merely 3,000. And although there was some record of buildings occupied by the security forces—mainly houses for which owners were receiving rent—there was then no consolidated record of land and property of this group, which was of justiciable 'munsif' quality. There was, besides, no record of the properties attached to temples, those encroached upon and those leased out, or under occupation. Different groups had different figures of unemployed youths. Their employment was an issue of the gravest common concern to the community. I learned that there were about 150 families in outlying areas reduced to destitution that lived on charity. These numbers were not an unduly cumbersome figure for potential employment in the state services in the Valley.

In answer to a parliament question in 2015, Minister of State for Home Affairs Kiren Rijiju stated that a comprehensive package worth Rs 1,618.40 crores was announced by the Centre in 2008 for return and rehabilitation of migrant Kashmiri families through grant of financial assistance for purchase or construction of houses, renovation of damaged or dilapidated houses, construction of transit accommodation, continuation of cash relief and employment, among others. 'The package is being implemented by the Jammu and Kashmir government and till now, one family has returned to the valley availing the benefit of Rs 7.5 lakh for construction of house,' Rijiju conveyed in a written reply.

Further, as many as 1,474 state government jobs had been provided to newly appointed migrant youths who have been kept in 1,010 newly constructed transit accommodation in south, east, and north Kashmir. In reply to another question, he said that at present 60,452 families of Kashmiri migrants were registered in the country out of which 38,119 were in Jammu, 19,338 in Delhi and 1,995 families in other states. Migrants mainly comprised Kashmiri Pandits and Sikhs.

This then is the culmination of the prime minister's successive packages for the rehabilitation of Kashmiri Pandits, announced in 2004 and 2008, which, through the issue of ID cards had given the migrants much-needed recognition. In terms of their resettlement, it requires no imagination to realise that apart from the danger of ghettoisation that would result from separate townships, it would render the Pandit community vulnerable, given its history of assault and complaint of administrative indifference since the 1990s. But the NDA initiative of 2015, while building on the previous, seems to have been arrived at without consultation with the community, a course that could readily have been undertaken in this age of information technology.

Even in the highly unlikely event of the Pandits resolving to return en masse to Kashmir, the numbers disclosed by Rijiju would scarcely overwhelm the valley. The beauty of Kashmir is a powerful allure to any visitor. But what of earning a livelihood? As Chairman National Institute of Technology, Srinagar, I visited Jammu in 2012, to request migrant teachers and staff to return to Srinagar, where the NIT was headed by a Pandit. All of them refused to forgo their lives built in Jammu.

What I had advised my Kashmiri interlocutors from Nai Basti, Anantnag in 1990 still stands. The ground situation in the valley may not reflect a threat to returning Kashmiri Pandits. But it is the responsibility of Kashmiris within the Valley to reassure those returning of their welcome, instead of contumacious quibbling, which will only raise misgivings in an already tremulous community.

Besides, the state required to be opened up to FDI accompanied with the development of the much talked-of smart cities, an imaginative flagship programme of the Modi government elected in 2014, which could become the new townships. This would encourage young Kashmiris, Pandit, Muslim, Sikh, or Christian, many of whom have achieved excellence in their chosen technologies, to invest and return to settle in Kashmir, providing livelihood and living space to others. As peace returned increasingly to Kashmir, it appeared to be time that it joined the rest of the country in marching ahead in bringing the economic revolution that all Indians looked forward to?

Sadly, the relationship between the two principal communities of the state as a whole is under grave threat. The Amarnath Shrine Board of the state administers the annual pilgrimage to the mountain cave in Amarnath, dedicated to Lord Shiva, a year in advance. In 2008, in consequence of the lease of forest land in the mountain plateau of Baltal being made to the board, an agitation broke out in Kashmir. In attempting to bring it under control by repeated police firing, 40 Kashmiri lives were lost including that of APHC leader Sheikh Abdul Aziz. Then, in violent retaliation for the revocation of the lease order in July 2008, the Hindu-majority areas of Jammu erupted, seeking to impose an economic blockade on the Valley by stopping all transport on the only link road, the Srinagar–Jammu highway. In response to this provocation, the Kashmir Fruit Growers Association issued a 24-hour ultimatum to the government to open the road to Muzaffarabad for trade, failing which they would march to that town across the LoC. That march brought more than 200,000 Kashmiris onto the road to Muzaffarabad. In an impassioned speech to parliament, of which he was then a member, Omar Abdullah cried out:

> You people [meaning the BJP] talk Amarnath…show me one place where any Kashmiri has spoken against the *yatra*…where they have attacked Amarnath *yatris*. It was an issue concerning our land. We fought for our land and will continue to fight for our land till our dying breath.[5]

Omar Abdullah became chief minister after the elections that followed the fall of the Indian National Congress (INC)-led government headed by Ghulam Nabi Azad in 2009, in consequence of what has come to be known as the Amarnath agitation. In his article laced with deep regret in the *Outlook* of 31 August 2008, plaintively titled 'How India Lost the Kashmiris', Prem Shankar Jha, a perceptive observer of Kashmiri developments, at a time that Kashmir was under a blanket curfew noted:

> The 'fruit' march to Muzaffarabad was a result of…part anger at a betrayal, part a desperate attempt to break an economic stranglehold and part political opportunism. But the resulting 40 deaths completed the delegitimisation of Indian rule in Kashmir. But all was even then not lost. For the governor's determination, shared by the prime minister, that there must not be any more deaths in Kashmir, and the consequent restraint, had begun to mend fences once more.

The breach in the relationship between Kashmiri Muslim and Jammu Hindu was dramatically manifested in the results of the 2015 elections to the state assembly, when Jammu and Kashmir made diametrically different choices resulting in a government of opposites. And the communal situation in the state has only deteriorated since. Sameer Arshad Khatlani in his article 'Kashmir is sitting on powder keg again' in *The Times of India* of November 6, 2015, in writing of a lynching by a mob on October 9 in an attack on a truck driven by Kashmiris in Udhampur near Jammu describes an 'atmosphere where any form of protest is brutally muzzled in Kashmir while Hindutva forces enjoy impunity in Jammu.'

In tandem with the need for reconciliation between communities must be the building of confidence between the now ubiquitous security forces and the Kashmiris. But to be an effective instrument of law enforcement, members of the armed forces must also remain protected from mischievous or frivolous complaints. In Kashmir since 1995, the local police have increasingly resumed responsibility for maintenance of law and order.

In 1991 I had inquired into a complaint of mass rape in the villages of Kunan–Poshpura, which has been much discussed at home and abroad.[6] My report concluded:

> While the veracity of the complaint is highly doubtful, it still needs to be determined why such a complaint was made at all. The people of the village are simple folk and by the Army's own admission have been generally helpful and even careful of security of the Army's officers... Unlike Brig. Sharma I found many of the village women genuinely angry...It is recommended that the level of investigation be upgraded to that of a gazetted police officer.

Because of the widespread media attention that resulted from the report and protests by Justice Bahauddin (a Kashmiri and former judge of the High Court of Jammu and Kashmir), the report was investigated in July 1991 by the Press Council of India, led by the redoubtable B.George Verghese.

The Varghese Committee, appointed in an effort at damage control rather than because of any sincere interest in reaching the truth, concluded that the complaint was 'invented'.[7] George Verghese's report concluded that 'unless far better evidence is forthcoming the Kunan rape story stands totally unproven and completely untrue, a dirty trick to frame the army and get it to lay off Kunan Poshpura.'[8] This effectively ended any further pursuit of the investigation and led to an abiding resentment among the villagers in the area, particularly women. The lack of an effective way to redress their grievances continued to blight the lives of the women of Kunan–Poshpura, well into the 21st century, with many failing to find husbands. Even though the protection of human rights is institutionalised at both the state and national levels, this mechanism's effectiveness in ensuring that the public receives protection is questionable. This is where the role of the civil administration becomes critical.

At the heart of the issue lies the continuing application of the Armed Forces Special Powers Act (AFSPA) to the state of Jammu & Kashmir. Then Chief Minister Omar Abdullah's announcement during the United Progressive Alliance's government at the Centre, which he repeated on the second accession of the NDA in 2014 on withdrawal of the application of the law in certain areas, had the army stoutly arguing in favour of continuance of the status quo, which only exacerbated Kashmiris' suspicions of the country's intent. No guideline instructions or even rules have been issued by government regarding implementation of AFSPA in J&K albeit in 1997, the supreme court had decreed a number of dos and don'ts for the enforcement of the law. According to the supreme court guidelines, any person arrested and taken into custody in exercise of the powers under Section 4(c) of the Central Act should be handed over to the officer-in-charge of the nearest police station with the least possible delay, so that he might be produced before the nearest magistrate within 24 hours of such arrest, excluding the time taken for journey from the place of arrest to the court of the magistrate; the property or the arms, ammunition etc., seized during the course of a search conducted under Section 4 (d) of the Central Act must also be handed over to the officer-in-charge of the nearest police station, together with a report of the circumstances occasioning such search and seizure.

The other major guideline says that the provisions of the Criminal Procedure Code (CrPC) governing search and seizure have to be followed during the course of search and seizure conducted in exercise of the power conferred under Section 4 (d) of the AFSPA; and a complaint containing an allegation about misuse or abuse of the powers conferred under the Central Act shall be thoroughly inquired into. None of this has in fact been the practice.

Under the law a member of the army can shoot to kill under Section 4 (a), for the commission or even suspicion of any of a broad spectrum of what are deemed 'offenses'. To justify the invocation of this provision, the officer need only be '*of the opinion that it is necessary to do so for the maintenance of public order*' and only give '*such due warning as he may consider necessary*'. The army is allowed to destroy property if it is an arms dump, a fortified position, or shelter from where armed attacks are even suspected of being made, if the structure is used as a training camp or as a hide-out by armed gangs or absconders. Besides, the army can arrest anyone—without a warrant under the same section 4—who has committed, is suspected of having committed, or even of being about to commit, a cognisable offense and use any amount of force '*necessary to effect the arrest*'.

The army can enter any premises and search without a warrant, to make an arrest or to recover any property, arms, ammunition, or explosives which are believed to be unlawfully kept on the premises. This section also allows the use of force necessary for the search. This means that the AFSPA can be held to be actually in violation of the Constitution of India, of the very right to life, basic to the Fundamental Rights, and to any claim to functioning within a democratic order. Hence the apex court's concern that when the armed forces personnel act in aid of civil power; it should be clarified that they may not act with broader power than the police and that these troops must receive specific training in criminal procedure.

While explicating the AFSPA bill in the Lok Sabha in 1958, the then Union Home Minister stated that the Act was subject to the provisions of the Constitution and the CrPC. If the government truly meant to have the armed forces comply with criminal procedure, then the AFSPA should surely have had a specific clause enunciating this compliance. Contrary to Chapter X of the CrPC, which sets out the conditions under which the armed forces may be called in to disperse an assembly and provides more safeguards than the AFSPA, clearly specifying the ranks which can disperse an unlawful assembly, the act grants the power to use maximum force even to non-commissioned officers. The CrPC does not allow for the use of force to the extent of causing death to be used to disperse any assembly, however unlawful.

Chapter V of the CrPC sets out exactly how arrests are to be made, which does not give the officer the right to cause the death of the persons, unless they are accused of an offence punishable by death or life imprisonment. This power is already too broad. It allows the police to use more force than stipulated in the UN Code of Conduct for Law Enforcement Officials. Yet the AFSPA goes further, allowing the armed forces to kill a person who is not suspected of so grave an offence. And although it cannot be so construed legally, the public is convinced that this has allowed the army to overlook custodial killing of the atrocious kind perpetrated in Macchil in 2010, triggering the widespread agitation that engulfed both the Kashmir Valley and parts of Jammu.

The changing situation of J&K as 2014 dawned, would, in the opinion of many an outsider, also merit the complete revocation of the AFSPA. However, the J&K state government has continued to persist with its own Public Safety Act, 1978 (PSA), a law of more universal application than AFSPA. This PSA is also the most draconian of its kind in India, although there have been amendments by the Omar Abdullah government in April 2012 to debar its application to minors, a method universally used against children by that very government in the violent demonstrations of 2010. And these arrested minors were exposed fully to the blandishments of extremists with whom they were housed in Srinagar's Central Jail.

Even so, it can hardly be denied that given the concentration of security forces on both sides of the Line of Control, continuing infiltration—even though diminished—and an increasing military presence of the Chinese Peoples' Liberation Army in the northern areas of J&K, there could be a case for continuation of the application of the AFSPA, if the military—the agency tasked with ensuring security—so judged. Nevertheless, if it is decided that the operation of the law must continue, it is essential that the process to be followed in applying that law must be spelt out, as in any other law, with details of how the powers conferred by the law are to be exercised. Although the army may have instructions or general orders on how powers must be exercised, these can hardly be a substitute for statutory rules, enforceable by courts of law in a country which prides itself on the rule of law.

The Army's legal branch has worked on formulating rules notified by the law, in order to conform to the Constitution. On the other hand, just as it is the responsibility of the state government to withdraw its own laws that contravene the principles of democracy, it will also be necessary for the Union Ministry of Home Affairs to review its own functioning in relation to the prosecutions permissible under the AFSPA. To file a suit against a member of the armed forces for abuses under the AFSPA, permission must be sought first from the Central Government, which is the Ministry of Home Affairs. Such permission was never given. More recently there has been a lessening of such rigidity. In what former Chief Minister Omar Abdullah described as a 'watershed moment' the Army on 13 November 2013 sentenced five of its personnel, including two officers, to life imprisonment for the murder of three young Kashmiris in April 2010. Muhammad Shafi Lone, Shehzad Ahmed, and Riyaz Ahmed were killed in what was claimed to have been an armed encounter with terrorists in Macchil, a township snuggled in the crags across the Kazinag Mountains, close to the LoC. The preliminary finding of the police identified an Indian army major as instrumental in the killing of the three, all innocent, in what was found to indeed have been a fake encounter; the young men having been lured with promise of employment as labour. All three boys, far from being 'infiltrators' were residents of Nadihal, in the vale of the spectacular but blood-soaked Lolab valley. The officers reported sentenced were Commanding Officer 4 Rajput Colonel Dinesh Pathania, Captain Upendra Singh, Havildar Davender, Lance Naik Lakhmi, and Lance Naik Arun Kumar.

But Macchil was not the first encounter of its kind, and police investigations had been ordered before in cases of suspected fake encounters, as early as the 1993 killing of civilians in Border Security Force (BSF) firing in Bijbehara, the first case of which the then nascent National Human Rights Commission had taken cognisance, and more recently in the killing of innocent civilians by the police in response to the murder of 35 Sikhs in Chattisinghpora in the district of Anantnag in March 2000. On 5 February 2010 Zahid Farooq Sheikh, a 17-year-old schoolboy, had been shot dead by a BSF trooper in the state capital, triggering public outrage and protest across the Valley. The police arrested BSF trooper Lakhwinder Kumar, who admitted to having shot at the youth, but insisted that he did so on the orders of his commanding officer R.K. Birdi, who became the highest officer of the paramilitary forces to have been arrested in Kashmir and remanded to 10 days judicial custody in the high-security central jail, by the chief judicial magistrate in Srinagar. Yet, to this day, both Lakhwinder Singh and R.K. Birdi walk free. So such action can be no substitute to statutory rules.

The weight of the argument then must be that the armed forces be convinced by government and representatives of the public of the arguments to rescind the act, given the protection already extended to them by the existing law, and the challenges now faced in ensuring the security of the state. But there is an alternative. The deployment of the army extensively in civilian areas in Kashmir is a hangover broadly frozen along the demands of the war of 1947–48. Clearly, the premier threat today of war between two nuclear armed states is no longer a military assault along the highway from the Punjab on the state capitals Jammu or Srinagar; it is infiltration. If nothing else, that is the lesson of Kargil. For this purpose the army would do well to consider redeployment along the more vulnerable areas on the LoC, in areas with a scattered population comprised mainly of Gujjars migrating seasonally to the highland pastures, with whom military relations have been increasingly cordial, whereas elsewhere civilians look upon the army as an occupation force, despite laboured efforts by military authorities to dispel such an image.

Such redeployment will indeed require heavy financial investment. But surely the need for allowing India's citizens in J&K the exercise of fullest constitutional freedoms must be the paramount consideration, as it is the view of this writer that there is no other means of bringing the conflict in the state to closure. A passing reference to any Kashmiri blog on Facebook will substantiate this.[9] New construction could then generate employment for Kashmir's masons, carpenters and a host of skilled workers at presently languishing under a regime of high unemployment. And the relinquished military structures can be put to good use for providing public facilities—schools, hospitals, panchayat offices. The Kashmiri diaspora, which is now a prosperous community in the US, the Middle East, and South East Asia, could be invited to invest. If such a plan were implemented there would be no need to withdraw the AFSPA, which would cease to apply in areas which are without an army presence, except when the army is required to be called in. Notwithstanding, the law, for as long as it might subsist, must be in the fullest conformity with the freedoms of every Indian citizen guaranteed to them by no less than the Constitution of India.

Despite the FIR in the Macchil case, by 3 June 2010, Syed Ali Shah Geelani, in a speech in Baramulla, called upon the people to protest what he claimed was an effort at cover-up. And there was then a massive response to that call by the young people of Srinagar where, on 11 June, 17-year-old Tufail Mattoo, returning from tuition, was shot dead by the J&K police, obviously mistaking the child as a stone-pelter from among those with whom they had jousted all day, triggering a state-wide agitation convulsing city and countryside. In none of the cases of death by firing from Sopore to Anantnag to Poonch in Jammu Division has there been any sentence handed down to any accused police or paramilitary personnel. The Macchil decision then indeed turned a new leaf. But what the civilian government failed to perceive was the widespread anger among the Kashmiri youth, 123 of whom had died in police firing in the agitation. Burhan Wani was at the time the younger brother of one such victim of an 'encounter.' Instead, they were herded into prison despite the provisions of the Juvenile Justice Act, and exposed to the admonitions of seasoned convicted terrorists.

In his 'State of Transition', *Indian Express*, November 7, 2014 (Opinion) Lt Gen Syed Ata Hasnain describes what he calls the 'unfortunate' killing of two young boys and injury to two others, who had been shot in their Maruti 800 car as they sped through mobile vehicle check-posts (MVCPs) a few kilometres south of Srinagar without stopping, arguing that 'for the past few years, the situation in J&K has been transiting from a typical public order environment to a law and order one'. My own experience and repeated visits to Kashmir and interaction with a cross section of its people, tells me that such 'transition' has long been complete. There was hope that the Macchil decision and the decisive response of the Army headquarters in J&K in the latter tragedy—after an initial goof up, when it was claimed that a shot had been fired by a non-existent gun in the Maruti—amounts to a recognition, however tacit, of this reality. And the events of 2016, which left a crying need for a restoration of public confidence, indicated an urgent review of repressive laws like the AFSPA.

A silver lining to this environment of gloom is that, despite outbreaks of civil unrest, India's civil society has also begun to come to terms with Kashmir's tragedy. These were admittedly only modest efforts but NGOs have worked to mend ruptures in Kashmir's social fabric. The floods of 2014, unprecedented in their fury compounded by a failure of governance, were a shining example wherein NGOs, national, international and local, worked together to save lives and ensure ready delivery of relief materials, including medicines, so that loss of human life in the Valley was limited to double digits. But education will be critical to the future mindset of Kashmiris. This is where NGOs can continue to contribute. Even at the outset of the outbreak of 2016, NGOs were active in seeking to encourage its local support base to promote resolution by dialogue. Nevertheless, to sustain any such effort, a vibrant economy, with its promise of a brighter future for all constituents, is essential, as is prevailing peace.

The history of peace initiatives between India and Pakistan is clouded, as is the process initiated in Islamabad in 2004, by many false starts. After the arrest of Sheikh Abdullah in August 1953, Mohammed Ali Bogra, Prime Minister of Pakistan, visited Delhi and secured from Prime Minister Nehru an agreement to hold a plebiscite in Kashmir. This plan foundered within months, ostensibly because Pakistan entered the US's Baghdad Pact, later the Central Treaty Organization (CENTO), and accepted military aid from the United States. After the stalled talks between the foreign ministers of India and Pakistan in the wake of the India–China War of 1962, there was hope for a resolution in 1963–64, when Sheikh Abdullah visited Pakistan, but that glimmer faded away with the death of Prime Minister Nehru. The Simla Agreement of 1972 was perhaps the most promising development. In the view of many, it had brought India and Pakistan close to resolution of the entire Kashmir dispute—a resolution prevented only by the overthrow of Prime Minister Zulfikar Ali Bhutto in a coup d'état in 1977. But the agreement had languished and finally collapsed under the pressure of the Kashmir insurgency, when all the pre-Simla phantoms were resurrected—most notably, the internationalisation of the issue. Thus, doubts prevail about whether a continuing détente is viable. Stephen Cohen of the Brookings Institution has been one of the most perceptive US students of this precarious relationship. He believed after the dramatic progress at the SAARC summit 2004, prophetically as it would turn out, that it would be wise to wait at least six months before arriving at any conclusions regarding the fresh initiatives in Islamabad. 'On past evidence,' he pointed out in an article in the *Financial Times* on 16 January 2004, 'the thaw will not last.' Cohen was to be shown to be wrong only in his projection of a time frame.

By the dawn of 2016, Kashmir looked relatively peaceful, but widespread public disaffection persisted. Pakistan's appeal and that of separatists is on the ebb, but this has by no means been supplanted by any support for India. It was only in March of this year that I had travelled to South Kashmir on the invitation of the then popular CPI (M) MLA Tarigami to address officials of Kulgam district on Right to Information (RTI), under the District Development Commissioner, a dynamic young Kashmiri Dr Syed Abid Rasheed Shah, one of several young Kashmiri officers who have successfully qualified for the IAS to serve their people through governance. RTI had captured the imagination of many a young Kashmiri, within government service and without.

I drove to Kulgam and back in a taxi, unaccompanied by any security, and took a train ride to Baramulla in the shabby Srinagar-Baramulla train, lamenting the unplanned expansion of palatial residences into prime agricultural land, but at total peace. In this travel I wandered unaccompanied through village and bazaar in Kulengam, Sopore, Anantnag and Baramulla among Kashmiris milling about or laughing and chattering in couples or small groups along backstreet or graveyard in village and town and in the train compartment. Although I was scolded by young Abid for ignoring security, I had at least since 1982 never felt so at peace in Kashmir. But on that visit I had for the first time heard murmurings of the rising charisma of this young Hizb-ul-Mujahideen Commander from Tral, Burhan Wani. And on July 8 and its aftermath we irretrievably lost the chance of winning the people of Kashmir.

Instead the youth of Kashmir, raised and educated in a free India, are consumed with hatred. *Kashmiriyat* is now only a sad memory for some. India is indeed seen as a land of opportunity, where the youth might seek to earn a living, but is seen by Kashmiris as a nation of which no Muslim would wish to be a part. This stands exacerbated by the sinister undercurrent of hostility between the state's Hindu and Muslim communities.

The challenge for the state government elected in 2015 was primarily that communal polarisation in J&K is a matter of concern since the Amarnath land controversy of 2008 that felled the INC-led coalition, bringing on the 2008 election. This was only exacerbated by the 2010 disturbance following the encounter, now established in a court martial to have been staged by some soldiers in the frontier township of Macchil. The election results serve to deepen such concern. There is not a single Hindu candidate winning from Kashmir, with Moti Kaul of the BJP contesting in Habbakadal of Srinagar being the only runner-up, and although the party leading in the Kashmir valley, the PDP, had fielded candidates in Jammu division, the only seats that it has taken are in Muslim-dominated constituencies in Jammu division: Darhal, Rajouri, and Poonch. Of the three winning contenders in the Valley, the PDP, the JKNC and the INC, it is only the JKNC which has won seats in Hindu-dominated areas in Jammu division.

On the other hand the BJP, the second largest party in the Assembly, has fielded and won with both Hindu and Muslim candidates in Jammu, including in the hitherto Congress fastness in Muslim-dominated Chenab valley, but has taken not a single seat in Kashmir or in Ladakh, a constituency that it holds in the Lok Sabha. Besides, the BJP's share in the Kashmir Valley, set against the 28.7 per cent of the vote taken by it state-wide, is only 1per cent. The increase in the BJP presence is indeed the foremost feature of these elections, rising from a mere 12.6 per cent of the vote share to the present, edging the INC into 4th place. But this stemmed almost entirely from its dramatic gains in only the Jammu division. This was possibly an issue flagged in the process of what Mehbooba Mufti described as cobbling together a coalition but was never addressed.

There can be no question of change of boundaries as clarified by Mahmud Ali Kasuri, former Foreign Minister of Pakistan, the state hitherto seeking such change as having been agreed upon in the heady days when Musharraf and Manmohan Singh had come close to an agreement[10] and acknowledged by all parties, including the Kashmiris. But *azadi*, the theme song of Kashmir's political trajectory, is winnable. India is indeed the land of *azadi* of which all sections will benefit by being part; hence my plea that the future lies in the state being allowed the full and unfettered exercise of democracy to all its citizens, India's greatest asset and the sinew that has bound India into a nation unparalleled in the world in the extent of its diversities in language, culture, caste, and creed held together simply by an idea, the idea of India, a name which has no Indian origin. This may be placed in the context of the decentralisation now mandated by the Constitution of India, wherein it makes every village a self-governing unit: Section 243 (d) of the Constitution of India reads: 'Panchayat' means an *institution (by whatever name called) of self-government*[11] constituted under article 243B, for the rural areas. The objective of Prime Minister Rajiv Gandhi in bringing this amendment was to give voice to those without voice in the governance of their own neighbourhoods. But the decentralisation sought has not thus far become a reality. The framework for this exists—allow every common Kashmiri the fullest use of this freedom.

But my plea was only a burned candle by the summer of 2016. An informed Kashmiri, Shujaat Bukhari, wrote in *Frontline*:

> On July 8 a party of the Special Operations Group (SOG) of the Jammu and Kashmir Police acted on a tip-off and reached Kokernag in south Kashmir to zero in on a house where Burhan Wani was spending time with two of his associates following Eid. The information was so correct that the party faced no difficulty in identifying the house and

> straightaway went to challenge the trio. According to the police, there was an encounter and by evening it was clear that Burhan, who had been giving the security establishment sleepless nights, was no more... The simmering discontent made it clear that Kashmir was heading for bad days after a peaceful Eid celebration. The government seems to have underestimated the spark that Burhan could ignite. Intelligence and administrative 'gurus' had dismissed him as another militant commander and denied the potential of the aura they had themselves built around him.

So I am beset with foreboding for the next phase of the relationship of Kashmiris with India, for we have lost Kashmir's youth, educated, talented and consumed with hatred, who will lead the state into its future.

Endnotes

1 Nandita Haksar, *The Many Faces of Kashmiri Nationalism,* (New Delhi: Speaking Tiger, 2015).

2 Josef Korbel, *Danger in Kashmir* (Toronto: Princeton University Press, 1954), pp. 146–47.

3 Nandita Haksar, *The Many Faces of Kashmiri Nationalism,* p. 219.

4 Village bully, often with political backing.

5 Omar Abdullah's speech to Parliament on the trust vote, 22 July 2008.

6 Wajahat Habibullah, *My Kashmir: The Dying of the Light* (Penguin Books, India 2014), pp. 91-94, 135.

7 *Crisis and Credibility: Report of the Press council of India January and July 1991,* Lancer Paper 4 (New Delhi: Lancer International), p. 127.

8 Ibid., p. 128.

9 See Jehangir Ali 'Indian 'nationalism': Why Kashmir won't move on', http://blogs.tribune.com.pk/story/11387/indian-nationalism-y-kashmir-wont-moveon/

10 Mahmud Ali Kasuri, *Neither a Hawk nor a Dove: an Insider's Account of Pakistan's Foreign Relations,* (Lahore: OUP Pakistan, 2015).

11 Emphasis mine.

What Ails the Northeast?

Rajeev Bhattacharyya

India's Northeast is a land distant from the national consciousness. It has a range of meanings to different people in different places, but is commonly viewed as a region on the fringe simmering with trouble. It is a frontier zone inhabited by people who look different, whose customs are different and who are fighting to break away from the country. News stories on the region are flashed in the media for all the wrong reasons—riots, killings by insurgents, natural disasters, and what not. Officials are never too happy to get posted in the Northeast and only committed missionaries and NGO activists have been coming to the region at regular intervals to carry on their work.

So is something wrong with the Northeast? Or is it a distorted image created years ago that simply refuses to wither away? Diverse opinions are found to be articulated from different quarters with equal enthusiasm. As a journalist who has covered the region for close to two decades, I find the situation complex and difficult to comprehend. The Northeast is extremely heterogeneous, with more than 160 tribal and non-tribal communities inhabiting the region and speaking over 200 languages and dialects. Different regions and groups have responded in different ways to the rapid changes in their socio-cultural milieu and the Centre's efforts to integrate them with the mainstream.

Very few zones in the world have given birth to as many rebel groups as the Northeast, where armed movements began soon after India attained Independence. In 2003, a think tank in New Delhi estimated that there were more than a hundred outfits active in the region with a range of ideologies and demands from secessionism to banditry. More than a decade later, the total number had come down to less than 60 with a majority demanding autonomy and a negotiated settlement within the constitution. The number of insurgency related incidents has also registered a downward trend in the past few years. In real terms, only a small region continues to be affected by insurgency in the Northeast, especially in Manipur, Nagaland, and Assam. The incident on 4 June 2015 in Manipur that resulted in the death of 18 soldiers of the Indian army is more an exception than the rule. Clearly, there is less support for insurgent groups now because people's aspirations have changed and there is a desperate yearning for peace. However, decreasing support for the rebels has not translated into increased support for the government, which still seems to be reeling under the impression that a military victory over the armed groups would mean an end to all violence in the region. Draconian laws like the Armed Forces (Special Powers) Act 1958 which gives extraordinary powers to the security forces during counter insurgency operations are in vogue in Assam, Nagaland, Manipur, and two districts of Arunachal Pradesh for tackling militancy. Is it not amazing that one of the largest and most professional armies in the world requires special powers to deal with a few thousand militants? The law has led to extra judicial killings and there has been a vociferous campaign for its repeal. However no government has ever dared to seriously question the army's contention that the law is needed to curb militancy in the Northeast.

There is a gamut of other dangers looming large over the horizon that could spell serious trouble for the Northeast if not dealt with soon. And they are quite apparent from a couple of examples from across the region. Guwahati the gateway to, and the biggest city in, the region, which was once described as a beautiful historical city on the banks of the Brahmaputra, is perhaps the dirtiest city in the country today. One cannot but be appalled by the heaps of garbage on the main roads for days on end. The citizens must consider themselves fortunate that an epidemic has not broken out so far. When there is wind and a downpour, the muck spills out of the huge containers producing an intolerably foul smell. Guwahati is also one of the very few cities in the country without a proper drainage system. Streets get flooded and there are traffic snarls whenever there is rain for a couple of hours. In September 2014, three persons died in the floods that ravaged the city for four days. The Congress government suddenly realised that the encroachments on the wetlands around the city were the reason for the crisis. The anti-encroachment drive began with tremendous fervour with bulldozers pulling down illegal structures. But as late as July 2015, there was no solution to the problem of floods in the city. Some garbage dumps are now cleaned but nobody knows for sure how the government plans to resolve the crisis.

The state of affairs would be apparent to anybody who stays in the city for a week. The city's list of woes is endless. The Congress has won the assembly polls for three consecutive terms since 2001. It is difficult to believe and accept that a solution to these problems could not be found in the last 15 years! The opposition parties had been equally ineffective and the performance and misdeeds of the Asom Gana Parishad (AGP) regime does not require elaboration. Deforestation continues at an alarming rate in the state; the one-horned rhino is poached almost every month and the Brahmaputra erodes a sizeable chunk of land every year. Corruption has reached an unprecedented level with the result that only a small percentage of development funds are actually utilised. Not surprisingly, the government has not been able to create employment avenues that could prevent the migration of young men and women to other cities of the country every year. Of course, there have been encouraging developments as well, in the state in these years. Insurgency related incidents have registered a sharp decrease and the corporate sector has shown a greater interest to invest in the state. There are now more roads and bridges in remote areas than ever before. But the list of achievements is not very long. Certain policies that have been pursued in the past two decades defy logic and explanation.

The figures in the last two censuses prove beyond doubt the danger to Assam and the Northeast from illegal Bangladeshi settlers. Repeated pleas from civil society organisations to the government for stringent measures have fallen on deaf ears. The vital clauses in the Assam Accord that sought to provide safeguards to the indigenous population remain unimplemented so far. As a result, more and more land is being encroached upon and the phenomenon has fuelled riots at regular intervals in the state. In 1998, the former governor of the state Lt Gen (Retd) S.K. Sinha had submitted an exhaustive report to the President detailing the measures that ought to be initiated to check the menace. The report is gathering dust and no government at the Centre has shown any interest to implement the recommendations. The BJP had always been vocal about infiltration from Bangladesh but banning the consumption of beef seems to be more important for the saffron party than checking illegal immigration. It was only after the Supreme Court responded in 2005 on some petitions filed by concerned individuals and local organisations that the controversial Illegal Migrants (Determination by Tribunals) Act 1983 has been scrapped and the National Register of Citizens (NRC) is being updated. Still, there is neither any long-term plan nor the necessary infrastructure to come to grips with the hazard that has already changed the social composition of the state and has the potential of triggering massive conflicts.

The muddle in Assam is visible across the region in varying degrees except Tripura and Sikkim. Tripura traversed a different path thanks to the relentless efforts of the Left government and its dynamic chief minister Manik Sarkar, who had been determined to wipe out insurgency and take governance to the grassroots. The rebel groups were also weakened by internal strife, lack of cadres and finance, and the aggressive posture adopted by the Awami League–led government in Bangladesh against rebel camps and hideouts. In Sikkim as well, the political leadership had been much more committed than the rest of the states in the region. Of course, it cannot be ignored that certain disadvantages suffered by the Northeastern states like remoteness and insurgency have never been the case with Sikkim. This border state is not free from the evil of corruption but it has not stood as a hurdle in the way of development. The same parties have won the assembly polls consecutively for many times in the twin states—the Left Front in Tripura and Sikkim Democratic Party in the case of Sikkim—but it has had the effect of improving governance unlike some other states like Assam, Manipur, and Nagaland where the same parties have also been winning elections.

Development has taken a backseat in every state crippled by insurgency. In disturbed areas there are hurdles in executing development projects and the governments have been focused on battling militancy. But what about peaceful states like Arunachal Pradesh and Mizoram? Or even Meghalaya where rebel outfits have not been able to make their presence felt as vigorously as in Assam, Manipur, and Nagaland? All the hill states are sparsely populated and endowed with resources for promotion of certain activities like tourism and horticulture. Startling results cannot be expected in a brief span but a beginning can always be made. Arunachal Pradesh, in particular, could have given competition to Himachal Pradesh and Uttarakhand had there been proper policies aimed at creating the necessary infrastructure for tourism and marketing. There are many spots in Mizoram and Meghalaya ideal for adventure trekking, camping, and allied activities. The inflow of tourists to the hill states has certainly registered an increase over the past few years but not to a significant extent.

The region should have witnessed more growth and development given the quantum of funds sanctioned by the Centre which has registered an upward trend every year. The Central sector fund for the year 2014–15, for instance, was Rs 4,84,532 crore. Therefore, about Rs 48,000 crore had been available to the region, in addition to the states' own plan allocations. However, the economic growth performance of the region is recorded at only 5.9 per cent during 2004–05 to 2013–14. If we look at the state-wise economic performance of the northeastern states during the same period, it suggests that Sikkim has recorded the highest economic growth of 13.5 per cent during 2004–05 to 2013–14, followed by that of Tripura and Mizoram with growth rates of 7.7 per cent each. Meghalaya and Nagaland have recorded a compound annual growth rate of 7.4 per cent and 6.9 per cent respectively. Arunachal Pradesh, Assam, and Manipur's economic growth rate is recorded as lower than the Northeast's average growth rate. Arunachal Pradesh has recorded a growth rate of 5.4 per cent, while Assam and Manipur have recorded a growth rate of 5.0 per cent each.

The government of India's Northeast Vision 2020 describes the economic situation in the Northeast as 'anarchic'. Partition in 1947, it says, has put the region in 'economic imprisonment'. A 'chicken's neck' corridor of 22 km links it to the rest of India, whereas its international boundary is 5,000 km long. A wealth of natural resources had given the region a sound economic foundation when the planning process started. Most northeastern states were above the national average in terms of State Domestic Product and per capita income. After 50 years of planning, the region laments that most of its states are almost at the bottom of the ladder, though there has been some positive movement in the past few years.

In reality, misgovernance and its attendant ills have taken a heavy toll on the Northeast. The anomalies are the outcome of a combination of factors that has only been reinforced over the years. While there has been a steady improvement in the delivery mechanism in most of the mainland states, exactly the opposite phenomenon is discernible in the Northeast. The status quo is sustained by vested interests cutting across political parties, bureaucracy, business houses, and even militant groups. Any attempt to dismantle the nexus and improve the system is met with opposition. There are protests through road blocks and agitations whenever scams and misdeeds are unravelled but they invariably fizzle out soon. At times, enquiries are ordered but hardly any action taken on the submitted report. Public memory is short and it is undoubtedly the shortest in the Northeast. The same politicians who have embezzled public funds are voted back to power by the people. There has been a sort of acceptance by the people of the misgovernance that has almost been legitimised in these states. In some states, there are fixed percentages to be given to ministers and bureaucrats on any contract that could be awarded to business houses. This phenomenon is also discernible in other states of the country, but perhaps it is not as blatant as in the Northeast.

It is difficult to accept that a country that has sent a space mission to Mars would have no answer to get rid of misgovernance and the anti-people character of the state administrations in the Northeast. Although development is a state subject, the Centre cannot and should not turn a blind eye to the misdeeds of the state governments even though the same party might be ruling at both places. In reality, the Centre doesn't seem too bothered about the Northeast beyond a certain point; it focuses attention on the region only when violence erupts and people are killed by militants. Officials without knowledge and ample experience of the region frame policies and advise the ministers. Most of them are careerists keen to ensure plum postings and post-retirement benefits. On the contrary, the Northeast should have been handled with utmost caution, since it is not only the most strategic region in the country—it borders Bhutan, China, Bangladesh, and Myanmar—but also hypersensitive geologically, ecologically, socially, and politically. It may not be known to many in the country that no two states are similar in the region. The eight states comprising the Northeast are populated by nearly 40 million inhabitants who vary in language, race, tribe, caste, religion, and regional heritage. Therefore, most often, the clubbing of all these states under the tag of 'Northeast' has tended to have a homogenising effect with its own set of implications for policy formulation and implementation, not to mention local aversion to such a construct. Every policy must take all stakeholders into account and must necessarily be fine-tuned to suit the local ambience. This would be possible only when policies and the implementation strategies are firmed up in Shillong by experts acquainted with the ground reality and not by generalists sitting in New Delhi.

As such, it is not at all surprising that ridiculous plans for the development of the region have been voiced from time to time, implemented and then sometimes stopped due to opposition. For instance, a special package called the North East Industrial Policy was unveiled in the late 1990s with a view to promote industrialisation of the region. The policy offered transport and capital subsidies besides other benefits to investors. However, investment from the corporate sector has been below expectations and only Assam has benefited with the few industries that have come up so far. It must be borne in mind that the same strategy of development cannot be applied everywhere. States like Jammu & Kashmir, Himachal Pradesh, Uttarakhand, and those in the Northeast are not meant for big industries. The Northeast is a biodiversity hotspot like the Western Ghats and establishing a manufacturing base in the region should not have been entertained at all.

The Northeast is largely dependent on agriculture and allied activities but the region lacks water for agriculture during the winter season, despite having abundant rainfall in summer. Therefore, lack of irrigation facilities and absence of water-retention practices severely limit the options of multiple cropping resulting in low land productivity. The states have not given priority to development of agricultural infrastructure and have so far recorded negligible investment in irrigation development. There are other issues in the agricultural practices that must be taken into account if the region were to witness a green revolution. Despite a large geographical area, the land available for cultivation in the Northeast is limited. Compared to an all-India average of 64 per cent, arable land under use in Assam, Meghalaya, and Nagaland is between 40–50 per cent. Only a small portion of this has irrigation facilities. In the hills, shifting (slash-and-burn) or *jhum* cultivation is the dominant agricultural practice which covers around 30 per cent of the total cultivable area in the region. The farming techniques have hardly undergone any change, although the population has increased over time. Soil erosion and destruction of forests are logical consequences as more and more areas have been covered under *jhum* cultivation. It is not known if there is a roadmap to wean farmers away and introduce them to better and sustainable techniques. The Shillong-based North Eastern Council, which was formed in 1971 for promoting development of the Northeast, should have focused its attention equally on these aspects and especially when the state governments have failed to fulfil their responsibilities.

There are endless instances to highlight the mockery in the Northeast in the name of development and integration. During the previous National Democratic Alliance regime, a scheme for converting Arunachal Pradesh into the 'powerhouse' of the country was designed, which entailed the construction of as many as 168 big and small dams across all the rivers in the hill state! Fiery debates on the viability of the projects began soon after it was announced by the government. The basic argument was over whether dams ought to be built in a zone that is highly earthquake prone. The Northeast, especially Assam, had been devastated by two earthquakes in 1950 and 1897, which measured and 8.3 and 7.1 on the Richter Scale. No matter how sturdily the dams are built to withstand earthquakes, it is extremely doubtful if the jumbo schemes would actually be able to survive catastrophes of such intensities. The 1897 earthquake raised the northern edge of the Shillong Plateau by more than 30 feet, resulting in the destruction of structures over much of the plateau and surrounding areas, and causing widespread liquefaction and flooding in the valley of the Brahmaputra River. In 1950, as many as 2,000 homes, temples, and mosques were destroyed and over 1,500 people were killed. Many rock falls and the destruction of forests were reported in the Mishmi Hills north of Assam. As a result, many of the tributaries of the Brahmaputra River were blocked. When some of these opened after a week they created a wall of water 30-feet high that destroyed several villages. On the mega dams, Assam was of the view that its districts on the north bank of the Brahmaputra would be obliterated in the event of a dam breach. Civil society organisations staged a protest for days on end to prevent the transportation of turbines to the site where the 2,000 MW Lower Subansiri project was executed in Arunachal Pradesh. Since 2012, work on the project has come to a grinding halt although the Centre has issued statements that it would be completed and taken to a logical conclusion. It may be too early to say whose opinion is true and whose is false. But the fact remains that parts of lower Assam have been regularly flooded whenever excess water is released from the dams in Bhutan. So why take the risk of constructing these projects in a region that is strategic but also sensitive, disturbed, and crying for a healing touch?

It is time for New Delhi to wake up from its slumber and take stock of the situation. It is not without reason that the US and some European nations have started taking active interest in the affairs of the Northeast. Top officials have been visiting the region regularly for information and acquaintance with the complexities across the eight states. They have clearly understood its strategic significance and the important role of the region in the future. The US has already opened a business centre in Guwahati and the British High Commission has employed a senior journalist as its adviser on the Northeast. The Northeast does not burn with the same intensity as it did two decades ago but it is far from normal. It is like an earthquake which shakes once in a while catching the nation's attention and triggering a flurry of activities and kneejerk reactions. A sensitive frontier zone like the Northeast would require a short- and long-term strategy for development and integration with the mainstream, based upon a realistic understanding of the region. This calls for reconceptualisation of the region at the soonest possible, a total restructuring of the North Eastern Council in both its planning and security dimensions and creating a new administrative ethos. A different planning model is the need of the hour that would be based on the peculiar circumstances and genius of the region. The effort must be to build on what is best in traditional community institutions that have been ignored in preference for norms that are universally applicable everywhere in the country. Exceptions tinged with pragmatism must be allowed to rule in exceptional circumstances.

Federalism Frenzy: India's Halting Centre–State Relations

Rajiv Jayaram

In the late 1980s, O.V. Vijayan, the renowned writer and cartoonist, drew a cartoon in a Malayalam daily in response to Sri Lanka's complaints about the implementation of the Indo-Sri Lanka Peace Accord inked by Prime Minister Rajiv Gandhi and President J.R. Jayewardene in 1987. In the cartoon, after a cursory glance at the Sri Lankan Prime Minister Ranasinghe Premadasa's grievances about the accord, Rajiv Gandhi deadpans: 'Oh, a minor quibble fit for the Sarkaria Commission'.

The cartoonist had a swipe at three things here. One, India's supercilious approach to ties with its smaller neighbours, even in a matter as grave as the one in Sri Lanka, where thousands of Indian troops were sent. Two, the derisive treatment given to federalism by the central government even after 40 years of Independence. Three, the cavalier fashion in which desultory commissions and committees are constituted to reform the country's federal structure, the reports of which the Centre had no intention of honouring.

If the cartoonish portrayal of Rajiv Gandhi's attitude to federalism was unexceptional, it was even more so during his mother Indira Gandhi's two stints as prime minister (1966–77 and 1980–84). State chief ministers of Congress-ruled states were, or were meant to be, nothing more than weak sycophants, to be used and thrown at her whims and fancies.

A classic example of the arrogant way in which state chief ministers were treated occurred in May 1982 when the then Congress general secretary and MP—at the time, but later, Mrs Gandhi's heir apparent—Rajiv Gandhi, on a private visit, publicly insulted Andhra Pradesh Chief Minister Tanguturi Anjaiah as a 'buffoon' for a minor crowd inconvenience in Hyderabad's

Begumpet airport. Indira Gandhi soon sacked Anjaiah. He didn't leave office screaming and kicking. Instead, he simply said: 'I came by the grace of Madam, I am going under her orders. I don't know why I came and why I am going.'

The impudence of the son and the petulance of the mother got an egregious response from the departing chief minister of a state as large and politically important as Andhra Pradesh. If there is a stronger word for buffoonery, it certainly applies here.

General secretary Rajiv Gandhi's affront was destined to go down in India's political history as among the costliest shows of arrogance of power. It upended forever the political calculus of Andhra Pradesh, where the Congress party long enjoyed a chokehold. In 1983, the newly-formed Telugu Desam Party (TDP), led by Telugu cinema's first megastar, N.T. Rama Rao or NTR as he was popularly known, won the state assembly elections with a huge majority. The victory could well have been the stuff meant just for the silver screen, had it not been an election in which the insult to Anjaiah was cleverly used by NTR as a test case of *Telugu atmagauravam* (Telugu self-respect).[1]

During Rajiv Gandhi's time as prime minister (1984–89), the Congress party was the dominant political entity, controlling a majority of states, and Centre-state relations hewed to the same mould. However, the political map of India suddenly changed in the twilight years of the 1980s. Rajiv Gandhi—a naive, diffident and feckless politician—presided over a Congress party that had begun its unprecedented decline. The decline gathered momentum due to the Mandir-Masjid agitations that rocked the country during 1989–90, and Congress was uprooted as the ruling party of most states in the country. The so-called Congress System[2] collapsed after the 1989 general elections, with regional parties increasingly filling the void. In every general election since the 1980s, the vote share of regional parties has gone up. From less than 20 per cent in 1984, they now garner votes nationally in the range of 48–53 per cent. Despite the Narendra Modi wave that swept the BJP into power in the 2014 general elections, national parties could manage only 52 per cent of the vote share.[3]

The Sarkaria Commission, after spending nearly five years to 'examine and review the working of the existing arrangements between the Union and States in regard to powers, functions and responsibilities in all spheres and recommend such changes or other measures as may be appropriate',[4] submitted a voluminous report running into 22 chapters, with 247 recommendations, in January 1988.[5]

Federal Distortions

The main sticking points in Centre–state relations related to fiscal, legislative, and administrative matters. The major administrative issues were the abuse of Article 356 (Centre's powers to dismiss state governments and dissolve state assemblies), the sending of Central forces to states without their concurrence (definition of the term 'internal disturbance' in Article 355) and the role of governors. Issues related to intrusions by the Centre into state-list subjects through the proliferation of centrally sponsored schemes and delays in obtaining assents for important bills passed by the state legislatures were some of the bones of contention in the legislative domain. Centralisation of powers in the Union government in matters of resource mobilisation and allocation and economic decision-making through central planning constituted the main areas of dispute in financial powers.

Judging from the evasive language used in the Sarkaria Commission report ('an expert Committee, with suitable representation from the States, may be appointed by the Union Government to recommend desirable directions of reforms….', for instance), it's clear that the committee did not recommend extensive changes in the last two areas. There were minor improvements in the financial sphere, such as giving powers to municipalities to issue tax-free bonds, endorsing chief ministers' decisions on consignment tax, extending slightly the timeframe for overdraft loans, etc. However, the Union government has implemented none of these recommendations.

In the first, the commission made some sensible recommendations, but the Centre had none of them. The misuse of Article 356 was one of the areas where the commission voiced its concern. It said:

> Article 356 should be used very sparingly, in extreme cases, as a measure of last resort, when all available alternatives fail to prevent or rectify a break-down of constitutional machinery in the state. All attempts should be made to resolve the crisis at the state level before taking recourse to the provisions of Article 356.[6]

On appointment of state governors, the commission stressed that the incumbent should be a 'detached figure and not too intimately connected with the local politics of the state and should be a person who has not taken too great a part in politics generally and particularly in the recent past'.[7] It recommended selection of the governor: '(i) from a panel to be prepared by the State Legislature; or (ii) from a panel to be prepared by the state government (in effect the state chief minister) or invariably with the concurrence of the state chief minister; or (iii) invariably in consultation with the state chief minister.'[8]

Governors are the most important lever the Centre uses when states enter a governance crisis, and so the commission's suggestion was a non-starter. For the Centre, governors are handmaidens who can be mobilised to manufacture constitutional crises where none existed, to give a pretext for the Centre to invoke Article 356 to impose President's rule.[9] Besides, Raj Bhawans are prestigious places where politicians or former government servants—who have to be removed from the state or central scene for long or a time being—can be parked.

Nearly two decades after the Sarkaria Commission's report, in February 2006, the Supreme Court observed, while indicting Bihar Governor Buta Singh's hasty recommendation of state assembly dissolution in the previous year:

> It is seen that one day a person is in active politics in as much as he holds the office of the chief minister or minister or a party post and almost on the following day, or, in any case, soon thereafter, the same person is appointed as the governor in another state with hardly any cooling period.
>
> Despite the supreme court's censure, governors continue to be appointed the way they were,[10] with little consultation with state chief ministers, especially of those ruled by Opposition parties.[11]

The Article 356 Gerrymandering Stops

But the supreme court had helped the country cross a milestone in federalism when it, in 1994, dramatically altered the Centre–state relations in a case called *S.R. Bommai vs Union of India.*[12] The case addressed the legality of the Centre's dismissals of six state governments in 1992. In a landmark judgement in March 1994, the apex court slammed the door shut on abuses of Article 356, sharply limiting the scope to impose President's rule in a state. This verdict is considered one of the critical turning points of Indian jurisprudence.

In fact, the judgement in the Bommai case had its basis in another turning point in India's judicial activism: the Supreme Court's own judgement in 1973 in the *Kesavananda Bharati vs State of Kerala* case.[13]

One notable contribution of the Sarkaria Commission was the establishment of the Inter-State Council in May 1990.[14] The council was designed as the platform that brings the union and the states into a partnership arrangement for identifying and investigating issues of common concern to arrive at agreed policy recommendations. The council is chaired by the prime minister and has all the chief ministers and selected union ministers as members.

However, the body proved to be an obtuse construct. Since it was formed, it had met only 10 times, and the last meeting it held was on 9 December 2006 (as of August 2015). In 25 years, apart from discussions on a few mealy-mouthed agenda issues and recommendations—almost all remained just that—marginal or even inconsequential to the constitutional provisions it was based upon, the Council could achieve hardly anything worthwhile.

In 2000, the NDA government (1998–2004) set up a commission headed by M. N. Venkatachaliah to review the working of the Constitution, but nothing changed.[15] The UPA government (2004–14) organised another commission, this time specifically to deal with Centre–state relations. The Madan Mohan Punchhi Committee, set up in April 2007, submitted its report in March 2010. In its six-volume report (with four more supplementary volumes),[16] the Punchhi panel made 273 recommendations. Again, there are no takers for them.

Some of the radical suggestions were 'localising emergency provisions' under Articles 355 and 356, contending that localised areas—either a district or parts of a district—be brought under Governor's rule instead of the whole state. Such an emergency provision should however not be of a duration of more than three months, it suggested. It recommended that a governor be given a fixed five-year tenure and selection of an apolitical person by a panel headed by the prime minister, home minister, speaker of the Lok Sabha and chief minister of the concerned state. It also laid down clear guidelines for the appointment of chief ministers. It called for a constitutional amendment to be brought about to limit the scope of discretionary powers of the governor under Article 163 (2). The committee urged strengthening of both the Inter-State Council and National Integration Council.

At another level, two path-breaking constitutional amendments that promised devolution to village and urban local bodies—the third tier in the federal system—were passed in 1992. Yet, progress on local governance as proposed through the 73rd and 74th Amendments for Panchayati Raj Institutions and urban local bodies, respectively, had been in fits and starts. One of the two key ingredients of strengthening local bodies is the devolution of functions, funds, and functionaries (3Fs) related to matters listed in the 11th Schedule of the Constitution. The other is the enablement of their function of preparing and implementing bottom-up participatory plans for economic development and social justice. The devolution of 3Fs had been unsatisfactory, increasing the immensity of capacity constraints faced by local bodies on the other front.

The report of the Second Administrative Reform Commission, which devoted an entire section to the subject of local governance, was a stark reminder to the slow and halting nature of decentralisation.[17] Although the government of India had constituted the commission to streamline the governance system, it is a sad reflection of the official apathy—a combination of resistance by states and lack of political will by the Centre—towards local democracy that a blind eye has been turned to the report's suggestions to strengthen and reinforce grassroots governance in India.

The lack of structural changes in the federal system has afflicted local democracy. The Centre lacks political will because if the local governance has to be effective, it has to first empower the states with greater financial, legislative, and regulatory powers. States, for their part, feel that there was no real downside to continue smothering local self-governance because, in the words of an analyst, though substantial expenditure powers have been given to the local bodies,

> there has been no decentralization of economic power from the Union government to the states. If anything, there has been an increase in the degree of centralisation essentially because of tax reforms, be it value-added tax or the proposed goods and services tax. The powers of the state governments have not only been constrained but actually curtailed.[18]

A New Beginning?

'If you know the *why*, you can live any *how*,' said the German philosopher Friedrich Nietzsche. In 2014, Narendra Modi, a man who purportedly knew the *why* and *how*, became the prime minister of the country. Modi made no bones about fixing the lopsided federal structure in the country, claiming that he understood better the problems states are beset with. He had been chief minister of a state ruled by the BJP for 14 years, a better part of it when the Congress party was running the government in the Centre at the head of a coalition.

After coming to power in May 2014, his refrain had been to apply cooperative, competitive federalism to obtain good governance—a healthy competition among states for socioeconomic development, investment and growth. His aim is to bring clarity in decision-making and make governance policy-driven. Red-tapism is being cut down, a speedy clearances system has been carefully constituted, key reforms—like labour and tax reforms—are either attempted or on the anvil, investment activity has picked up and the number of stalled projects has declined dramatically.

A major decision was the government's acceptance in February 2015 of the 14th Finance Commission suggestion to 'radically enhance'[19] the states' share in the net proceeds of union tax revenues from 32 per cent to 42 per cent, a significant jump. With more of its tax share going directly to states to spend at their discretion, the Union government had begun drastically pruning its allocations to the state plan and wound up some centrally sponsored schemes (CSS). In June 2015, the NITI Aayog, successor of the planning commission, decided to reduce the total number of CSS to 30 from 72. The panel has also recommended to increase the share of flexi funds to 25 per cent from the current 10 per cent.

The proliferation of CSS had soured relations between the Centre and states primarily because it substantially curbed fiscal federalism while denying states the flexibility in making or implementing schemes. On the other hand, many of their manifest faults have rendered them rip-offs, with nothing much to show for the heaps of dosh spent. No wonder that many of them, even those 'flagship' ones, faltered.[20] It was obvious from the very start, even when the Central government sunk its teeth into CSS in the late 1960s, that the Union government must desist from funding schemes in the social sector, which ought to have been the exclusive financial and administrative preserve of state governments.

All CSS run by the Central government were administered through the planning commission, which enjoyed decisive powers of discretion on resource allocation. By the time prime minister announced in his Independence Day speech on 15 August 2014 the government's decision to disband the commission (replaced by NITI Aayog on 1 January 2015), there were frequent complaints from states against the body. The criticism ranged from the commission making quixotic recommendations; the waste and lack of monitoring of plan goals; central governments' wanton disregard of plan expenditure targets; to state governments' frequent opposition to discretionary powers vested with the commission. It's often that piqued chief ministers would say they had come to Delhi just to be told by the commission how they should spend their own money.

The Finance Commission has no role to play in plan expenditure and grants for capital expenditure.[21] Yet, the increase in states' share does not change the significant tilt against the states in financial relations. Of course, the 10 per cent will certainly help correct the imbalance, and states will be on the hook for many social welfare schemes, as the number of CSS goes down, hopefully accelerating economic development in their jurisdictions.

But fiscal federalism has not been linked to resource federalism. India must now begin to establish a framework for natural resource revenue-sharing with the states. Natural resources—spectrum, minerals, oil, natural gas, and hydropower—offer lucrative avenues of resources mobilisation. They are a key instrument to alleviate the regional disparities in economic development, a cleavage the economic liberalisation post-1991 has worsened. It's untenable that even as their taxation powers are constricted, states continue to have little say in regulatory aspects of the economy and the market. Both these limitations destabilise federalism, and must be removed by Centre, giving greater elbow room to the states.

The establishment of NITI Aayog is a step in the right direction to strengthen federalism. An equally important move ought to be the conversion of the comatose National Development Council (NDC) and Inter-State Council into an approvals agency where contentious decisions are taken by majority vote, and not consensus. A revamped mandate for the NDC and Inter-State Council would result in better Centre–state coordination and iron out differences that hold back big-ticket initiatives like tax reforms to foreign direct investment in retail. That must be in tandem with decentralisation, in letter and spirit of the 73rd and 74th amendments.

A new exercise to restructure Centre–state ties should start with a review of the Concurrent List. And there was of course scope for expanding the states' powers in many fiscal, legislative, and administrative matters. Though the misuse of Article 356 is under check, the scandalous way in which governors are selected, appointed, and removed still blight Centre–state relations. This is a breach that makes the new-found cooperative federalism idea faulty.

Federalism has long been a prickly topic that generated just blather and reports. The renewed focus on reforming India's federal system is good, but how far-reaching it will turn out to be, remains to be seen. As Campbell's Law has it: 'Nature abhors a vacuous experimenter.'

Endnotes

1 Prime Minister Indira Gandhi could never reconcile to the fact that her party had lost Andhra Pradesh. Instinctively, she had scant regard for autonomy of the states granted by the Constitution, and her dictatorial mindset never deserted her. Acting on her instructions, her marionette Governor Ram Lal dismissed the 20-month-old NTR ministry of the state all of a sudden, on 15 August 1984 after engineering a comic split in the Telugu Desam Party. In a blatant violation of the Constitution of India (to begin with, Article 164(1), which was recited as the reason for the dismissal of the NTR ministry), Nadendla Bhaskara Rao, a Telugu Desam turncoat, was installed as Chief Minister. After a month of high drama of epic proportions, one of the acts was the parading of a majority of MLAs before the President at Rashtrapati Bhavan by a wheel-chaired NTR; his ministry was reinstated to power on 16 September and the governor was replaced. The patent abuse of power motivated the *The Economist*'s famous cover of Indira Gandhi, depicting her as Goddess Kali and holding in her hands a sword, a moneybag, and the Opposition. From its editorial: 'A ruler who regards opponents as demons is liable to start behaving like one... Mr Nixon, 10 years out of the American presidency, has yet to say sorry. Mrs Gandhi, four years back in power in India, is into her dirty tricks again.'

2 The phrase was coined by Rajni Kothari in *Politics in India* (New Delhi: Orient Longman, 1970).

3 Niranjan Sahoo, *Centre-State Relations in India: Time for a New Framework* (New Delhi: Observer Research Foundation, 2015).

4 Union Ministry of Home Affairs Notification No. IV/11017/1/83-CSR, dated June 9, 1983.

5 *Sarkaria Commission & its Recommendations*, (1988) http://interstatecouncil.nic.in/Sarkaria_Commission.html.

6 'Recommendation 6.8.01, Chapter VI: Emergency Provisions,' *Sarkaria Commission & its Recommendations,* (1988) http://interstatecouncil.nic.in/Sarkaria/CHAPTERVI.pdf.

7 'Recommendation 4.6.09, Chapter IV: Role of the Governor,' *Sarkaria Commission & its Recommendations,* (1988) http://interstatecouncil.nic.in/Sarkaria/CHAPTERIV.pdf.

8 'Recommendation 4.6.11, Chapter IV: Role of the Governor,' *Sarkaria Commission & its Recommendations,* (1988) http://interstatecouncil.nic.in/Sarkaria/CHAPTERIV.pdf.

9 The first instance of the Centre invoking Article 356 was to dismiss one of the first democratically elected communist government's in the world, the E.M.S. Namboodiripad ministry in Kerala on 31 July 1959. The Nehru government's action of sacking the two-year-old Namboodiripad government was a transparent misuse of Article 356. The Article has been used and abused many times thereafter.

10 In 2014, after the BJP-led NDA government headed by Prime Minister Narendra Modi came to power, the fortunes of many state governors appointed by the earlier Congress-led UPA government turned. In a notable instance, Kerala Governor Sheila Dixit, who was controversially appointed to the post in March 2014—just three months after she led the Congress party to a drubbing in Delhi where she was Chief Minister for 15 years until December 2013—was forced to resign from the post in August the same year. There are obviously no takers for the Sarkaria Commission's recommendation: 'Frequent removals and transfers of Governors before the end of their tenure have lowered the prestige of this office. Criticism has been levelled that the Union government utilises the Governors for its own political ends. Many Governors looking forward to further office under the Union or active role in politics after their tenure came to regard themselves as agents of the Union' ('Para 4.1.02, Chapter IV: Role of the Governor,' *Sarkaria Commission & its Recommendations,* (1988)).

11 In October 2004, the Tamil Nadu government placed before the Supreme Court the tape of a conversation between state Chief Minister J. Jayalalithaa and Union Home Minister Shivraj Patil. The state government was challenging the changing of the governor, P.S. Ramamohan Rao. In the tape, the Home Minister Patil, in reply to Chief Minister Jayalalithaa's query of whether he was consulting her or informing her about the change of governor, repeatedly said: 'I am informing you.'

12 SCR 644: AIR 1994 SC 1918: (1994) 3 SCC1.

13 AIR SC 1461 (1973), in which the court asserted its review power over the process and substance of Constitutional amendments, circumscribing the unlimited powers of Parliament to alter, amend, abrogate any part of the Constitution (Footnote: Fali S. Nariman, in *Judicial Independence in India* [Venkat Iyer, ed., *Human Rights and the Rule of Law* (New Delhi: Butterworths India, 2000)], had called this 'the greatest triumph of the Supreme Court as an institution..."[T]his

was the real turning point for the Indian judiciary—a glorious manifestation of its determination to retain custody and control of the Constitution, which, in the 1970s, was in grave danger of being usurped by Parliament."'

14 Though Article 263 of the Constitution of India stipulated for the establishment of an Inter-State Council, but it was not until the Sarkaria Commission report highlighted the need for it that the Centre explored the option. Incidentally, the decision to constitute the body was taken by the United Front ministry headed by V.P. Singh, the second non-Congress government at the Centre.

15 The National Commission to Review the Working of the Constitution, as it was called, submitted its report to the government in March 2002. The report related mainly to the areas relevant to the functioning of the Constitution, and endorsed the recommendations of the Sarkaria Commission in executive matters relating mainly to the role of governors and Article 356.

16 Report of the Commission on Centre–State Relations, March 2010, http://interstatecouncil.nic.in/ccsr_report.html.

17 *Second Administrative Reform Commission's Report on Local Governance*, New Delhi: Government of India, (2007), http://arc.gov.in/6-1.pdf. The Commission had excluded from its purview the detailed examination of Centre–state relations.

18 Haseeb A. Drabu, 'Modifying Federalism,' *Mint*, March 2, 2014. http://www.livemint.com/Opinion/x34c5ePS2iAsQpj4nIlmLI/Modifying-Federalism.html.

19 The Fourteenth Finance Commission (FFC),—'Implications for Fiscal Federalism in India?' Government of India, 2015http://www.indiabudget.nic.in/es2014-15/echapvol1-10.pdf.

20 In a newspaper article, Yamini Aiyar and T.R. Raghunandan of the Centre for Policy Research ('JNNURM: Cooperative federalism lessons,' *Mint*, July 08, 2014, http://www.livemint.com/Opinion/FhuL1nXRfERs6lb3zGvnSM/JNNURM-Cooperative-federalism-lessons.html) examined how the central governments' refusal to allow state governments take ownership over reform processes meant through CSS left many of them in shambles. They examined many of the manifest faults in the flagship scheme for urban renewal and rejuvenation, Jawaharlal Nehru National Urban Renewal Mission (JNNURM) and observed: 'Signing memoranda of agreements and bullying states with financial consequences do not create this sense of ownership. Rather, the Centre needs to loosen its controls and allow state governments the autonomy to take their own implementation decisions.'

21 Most revenues of the states come through transfers made by the Finance Commission, the erstwhile Planning Commission and transfers from central ministries. The Finance Commission manages over two-thirds of the total federal transfers. Significantly enough, The 14th Finance Commission (FFC) has also proposed a new horizontal formula for the distribution of the states' share in the divisible pool among the states. There are changes both in the

variables included/excluded as well as the weights assigned to them. Relative to the 13th Finance Commission, the FFC has incorporated two new variables: 2011 population and forest cover, and excluded the fiscal discipline variable. *The Fourteenth Finance Commission—Implications for Fiscal Federalism in India?*, New Delhi: Government of India (2015), http://www.indiabudget.nic.in/es2014-15/echapvol1-10.pdf.

What Happened to 'Land Reform'?

Robin Jeffrey[1]

'The single biggest reason for the kind of money visible in rural India is the skyrocketing price of land.'

—*India Today*, 15 February 2010, p. 37.

When I first lived in India in 1967, 'land reform' was a topic of conversation as prevalent as the weather or the state of Indian hockey. Today, the weather remains, but 'land reform' and Indian hockey have faded away like the Cheshire cat in *Alice in Wonderland*. If you googled 'land reform in India' in 2016, you would get about 55,000 hits; if you limited the search to the past year, you would get about 200. On the other hand, if you googled 'real estate in India', you would get 1,050,000 hits—within the past year alone.

This paper originates from my own puzzlement: 'Whatever happened to land reform?' At one level, the question is naive, as some friends have told me. 'Land reform' stopped being an issue with the beginning of 'economic liberalisation' in 1991, some will say. Others argue that it effectively went off the agenda once the CPI (M) government of West Bengal completed Operation Barga in the 1980s.

Yet India in 2012 still has a 'land question'. The 2011 census enumerated 69 per cent of the population as living in rural settings, even though only about 15 per cent of gross domestic product now comes from agriculture. Those numbers in themselves suggest a 'land problem': 69 per cent of the population generating, and in a sense depending on, only 15 per cent of the annual production of wealth. If we can formulate a convincing answer to the question of 'What happened to land reform?', we may learn something about the political and social dynamics of rural India and the degree to which changes that improve people's lives are possible and what those changes might be.

In 1969, a 'peasant war' raged in Vietnam, Eric Wolf published *Peasant Wars of the Twentieth Century*, and E.M.S. Namboodiripad's second stint as Chief Minister of a Communist government in Kerala came to an abrupt end, but left a significant land-reform bill for its successors to pass and implement. Naxalbari and Naxalite had become part of the national vocabulary since 1967, and scholars wrote books with titles that drew on Mao's strategy in China in the 1930s: *Kerala: Yenan of India.*[2]

Settling and taxing the land in an orderly, efficient and thorough way had been central to British rule. It was, after all, the foundation of the finances that paid for the Indian empire. 'Land' therefore was a challenge and an invitation to the early nationalists. 'The concept of land reforms was a part and parcel of our freedom struggle,' a key West Bengal land-reform official, D. Bandyopadhyay, wrote in 2008 as he wrestled with the question that I am trying to address now.[3] In the late 1960s, 'land reform' burned as hotly as an issue as it had at any time in the previous 100 years. In a recent important essay, R. Vijay suggests three periods that capture the post-independence experience of rural India: land reform, green revolution and industrialisation-urbanisation.[4]

It is fairly simple to divide the unfolding of land policy in India after independence into periods. The first might be called 'the long 1950s' from Independence to the China war in 1962 when so much of the *azadi* dream seemed to be going wrong. There was a lot of legislation and some notable changes, though none attempting to transfer 'land to the tiller'.

The second period marks a time when the food shortages of the mid-1960s led governments to turn their attention to agricultural production and to make the 'green revolution' happen. Simultaneously, peasant insurgency, driven by local conditions and inspired by the Chinese revolution, led to the oft-quoted remark of Y.B. Chavan that there was a danger that the Green Revolution could become Red. The third period represented a response to those conditions and a reflection of Mrs Indira Gandhi's 'Socialist' phase. A meeting of Chief Ministers in 1972, in the glow of the successful Bangladesh War, the 1971 election victory and Naxalite insurgencies, generated a wave of legislation addressing inequity in the countryside. The attempts to end bonded labour during the 'emergency' were part of such measures, though they were rarely implemented with persistence.

The fourth period begins in the early 1980s with Mrs. Gandhi's return to power, the rise of a post-freedom struggle middle class, embodied in Rajiv Gandhi, and a growing belief within that class that the 'socialist experiment' (or 'Nehruvian experiment') had failed. Tentative steps towards deregulating the economy began in the 1980s and accelerated with the financial crisis of 1991 and the new government of P.V. Narasimha Rao (1921–2004), which functioned from 21 June 1991 to 16 May 1996. 'Productivity', 'urbanisation' and 'land acquisition policy' supplanted 'land to the tiller' as discussion topics in policy-making conclaves.

Periodisation helps to organise facts and locate milestones, but seems to me less useful for getting to the root of my puzzlement: 'What happened to land reform?' How did its slippery meaning change? What did people at particular moments mean by 'land reform'? And why did those meanings—and the actions of politicians, policy-makers, and cultivators—change? To organise thoughts around a vast topic that has affected all of India across generations, I have tried to reply to the Big Question—'What happened to land reform?'—with Four Naive Little Answers. None of them, of course, is 'right', but working through them may provide a piñata to break open, help to tell a story and begin to isolate key events, policies, and social changes.[5]

Naive Little Answer No. 1: Land Reform Succeeded

This response is akin to one of the nostrums for wars in Vietnam, Iraq, and Afghanistan: 'Declare Victory and go home' regardless of what conditions might look like on the ground. Indian state governments from the 1960s produced materials and legislation that suggested 'land reform' was succeeding—had succeeded—in their jurisdictions. What was the record of 'land reform' after 1947? In north India, Uttar Pradesh (UP) and Bihar provided a striking contrast to Punjab. UP was a particularly noteworthy example since it produced not only a significant change in agrarian relations but also a body of literature analysing and sometimes celebrating 'success'.[6]

Big landlords—zamindars—characterised land holding in much of UP and Bihar under the British,[7] and some of the legendary struggles of the Gandhian Congress had occurred there. If we accept the conventional wisdom, the Congress mobilised substantial tenants, who had benefited from expanding cash crops and a monetised economy, against the British and their landlord allies.[8] G.B. Pant (1887-1961) and Rafi Ahmed Kidwai (1894-1954), two of the most influential leaders of the post-independence Congress Party, were named as authors of *Agrarian Distress in the United Provinces*, a report commissioned by the UP Provincial Congress Committee in 1931.[9] The report slammed British governments for accentuating rural distress and criticised zamindars for incidents where they had behaved badly, but it stopped short of discussion, much less advocacy, of land reform or redistribution.[10] The Mass Contacts Committee of the Congress generated the Agrarian Enquiry Committee Report, published in 1936. Again, it had to tread carefully to maintain a broad social coalitionopposed to the British government and capable of neutralising possible Indian adversaries.[11] Rajendra Prasad, member of the Mass Contacts Committee and later president of India, explained the requirements: 'The Congress is not a class organisation...the ideal of national independence is spacious enough for all...'[12]

After 1947, Congress governments had the delicate task of balancing the expectations of substantial tenants against the existing power and connections of the old landlord classes. The outcome in UP brought more fundamental change than in Bihar. The 'land reforms' in UP, for which Charan Singh (1902–87) took credit, broke up many of the old estates. Some of the landlord families lacked the skills and connections in law and administration to match the new rulers.[13] In UP, wealthy tenants became substantial landowners; but the actual tillers of the soil—landless labourers—found no change to their position. That position may have worsened in that the people they worked for were more secure now than ever before and more confident in their position than they had ever been; there was no possibility of appealing over them to the noblesse oblige of an old aristocracy.

The Uttar Pradesh Zamindari Abolition Act of 1952 and the Imposition of Ceiling on Land Holdings Act of 1960 pruned the old landlord class, though many families were able to preserve wealth and land through various stratagems. Large numbers of substantial tenant-farmer families became outright owners and employers of landless agricultural workers. In *Land Reforms in UP and the Kulaks*, Charan Singh presented himself as a key driver of the legislation enacted by the governments of Sampurnanand (1891–1969) (but always, one suspects, with G. B. Pant looking down from the Home Ministry in New Delhi).[14] 'Landlords,' Charan Singh wrote, 'performed no economic functions...and rendered no service in return for the rent they received and were...parasites...and thus contributed to lowering of the national character.' In the sense that such landlords were dispossessed to the satisfaction of Charan Singh—a lawyer from a Jat peasant family—and his followers, 'land reform' in Uttar Pradesh could be declared accomplished. However, if land reform meant a wider distribution of holdings, little had happened. National Sample Survey data showed the bottom 40 per cent of rural households in UP holding 2.5 per cent of land in 1954 and 2.9 per cent in 1982.[15]

In Bihar, similar public enthusiasm for land reform in the 1950s produced legislation that gave an appearance of commitment to agrarian change. The Bihar Land Reforms (Fixation of Ceiling Areas of Acquisition of Surplus Land) Act of 1961 was typical of the period, but its long parentheses suggested the legal tangles and political obstacles that stood in the way of wide and deep changes in land ownership. When the Communist Party of India held its 21st Congress in Patna in March 2012, it concluded that Bihar governments had 'scrapped the previous land reform legislations' and that 'landlords are committing atrocities on the rural poor'.[16] A Land Reforms Commission, which reported in 2008, found 75 per cent of the rural population was landless or 'near landless'.[17]

The states of Punjab and Haryana presented a contrast and perhaps the closest thing to comprehensive land reform that post-1947 India experienced. Indian Punjab had a land reform imposed on it by the Partition. The incoming refugees from Pakistan had left 6.7 million acres in West Punjab. The Muslim refugees driven from East Punjab abandoned only 4.7 million acres.

How to resettle so many people on substantially less land? A carefully calibrated solution imposed a class-based level. Great landlords of West Punjab might have had their holdings reduced by 95 per cent, but they were allowed to remain larger than anyone else; someone with four hectares in the West got three in the East; someone with 60 hectares in the old place might have got six hectares in the new. At the same time, the post-partition upheaval allowed plots to be consolidated; land was precious and thereby conserved; such consolidation laid the foundations for increased productivity. The Punjab 'land reform' was unintended, but it was as profound and as acceptable as any in India.[18] And of course it did not mean 'land to the tiller' nor did it give land to the previously landless.

Definition, of course, is crucial. If 'land reform' means adjustment in patterns of ownership, India of the 1950s nibbled round the edges. Enough legislation, bearing the right sorts of titles, was passed in most of the states to give an impression that change was in the wind. However, as the UP and Bihar examples suggest, the large majority of rural people living on the land did not acquire land or rights to land. Whatever happened to land reform was not that it succeeded and everyone, having got a prize, went home happy.

Naive Little Answer No. 2: Demands for Land Reform Were Extirpated

Could demands for land reform have simply been crushed by the forces of the state, their advocates jailed or killed and their supporters cowed into submission?

Independent India in its early years dealt sternly with two insurgencies founded on peasant grievance and resistance—the Tebhaga movement in West Bengal and the Telangana movement in the old princely state of Hyderabad. The Tebhaga movement grew out of share-cropper demands for two-thirds of the harvest from the land they cultivated. 'The movement failed,' wrote D. Bandyopadhyay, a Land Reforms Commissioner of West Bengal (and in 2012 a Trinamool member of the Rajya Sabha), 'after tremendous sacrifices by sharecroppers and their allies, the landless labourers and petty artisans.'[19] When the Naxalbari movement erupted in West Bengal in 1967, based in part on poor-peasant outrage at the inequity of land relationships, the Indian state crushed it in five years.

A similar timeline might be discerned in Telangana and Andhra Pradesh. The Communist Party of India (CPI) found a safe haven in Telangana during and after the Second World War and leading up to Independence. The government of the Nizam of Hyderabad, never particularly rigorous or effective, was losing both legitimacy and control, and the British, themselves about to decamp from India, were in no position to interfere in the domain of their longtime friend and ally, His Exalted Highness, the Nizam. By 1947, when the Nizam attempted to declare himself a sovereign ruler, areas of Telangana were being run as 'Soviets' or 'liberated areas' where the CPI called the shots and rough-and-ready local land reforms were undertaken. The Indian army was sent to Hyderabad in September 1948, within days of the death of Muhammad Ali Jinnah (1876–1948) in Pakistan. As well as overthrowing the Nizam, the army suppressed the Telangana revolt over the next two years. In 1951, the CPI dropped its ideological support for peasant insurgency when it abandoned the so-called Ranadive Line, which had called for Communist revolt because India was ripe for revolution.

As in West Bengal, agrarian discontent remained. A 'Naxalite movement' bobbed up in districts like Srikakulam in the late 1960s, and, as in West Bengal, police and paramilitary units suppressed these attempts to effect agrarian change through violence. Naxalite or 'Maoist' supporters retreated to the dry, underdeveloped Telangana districts and built bases that troubled landowners and distracted state governments until largely suppressed in the first years of the 21st century. Leaving Telangana, Maoist ideologues found refuge and followings, not in the agricultural plains of India, but in the hills and forests of the east among tribal people under pressure from mining, logging, and dam-building.

Peasant-based insurgencies, led by people deriving inspiration from Marx, Lenin, and Mao, never vanished. They emerged in eastern India—Bihar, West Bengal, Madhya Pradesh, Orissa, Andhra Pradesh, Jharkhand, and Chhattisgarh—through the 1980s and gathered support, under growing pressure from the extractive industries of a liberalised economy, in the 21st century. By 2006, the insurgency led by the Communist Party of India (Maoist) was often identified as the most serious threat faced by the Indian state. Control, ownership, and use of land were at the heart of the insurgency. State governments replied in some cases with brutal and clumsy suppression, but rarely with effective measures to change patterns of rural power. The central government attempted to put into operation legislation like the Panchayats (Extension to the Scheduled Areas) Act (PESA) of 1996. PESA was a well-intentioned attempt of the Union government to give local governments at the level of villages, rights to decide on land use and development. The act depended, however, on state governments for its implementation, and state governments were often cool to the point of refrigeration.

The Indian state and its components lurched between amelioration and suppression, and the Communist Party of India (Maoist) continued to lead a bloody resistance, ambushing armed police (more than 70 killed in a single trap in April 2010) and having their own leaders killed by the police or vigilantes (Azad in July 2010; Kishenji in 2011).[20] The grassroots support of the 'Maoist insurgency' was based on grievance and fear about the control and use of land.

Ideas about 'land reform' had not therefore been exterminated—driven underground and made unmentionable like religion in Soviet Russia. Ideas about what land reform would look like were canvassed in legislatures, proposed by inquiry commissions, published in newspapers and discussed by insurgents in jungle camps. Issues of 'land reform' flowed like hot lava just beneath the surface in many of India's states. They erupted occasionally like little volcanoes, and revolutionaries inspired by Mao pondered about how to produce a Krakatoa.

Naive Little Answer No. 3: Land Reform Was Defused and Dismantled

Could Congress governments, which had often confronted the British over questions of agrarian justice, totally abandon a cause that had been part of their rhetoric for more than 30 years? The Congress could not. But as the UP and Bihar examples showed, what constituted 'land reform' for the Congress after 1947 was a far cry from the slogan of 'land to the tiller'. The sorts of 'land reform' carried out in UP and Bihar installed a broad base of wealthier peasants across a swathe of north India, and in the 1950s, they were expected to support, and be part of, the Congress Party. If you were such a peasant, you might have endorsed Naive Little Answer No. 1: Land reform had succeeded.

However, it was in Kerala, and perhaps West Bengal, that land reform as an issue may be seen to have been 'defused' in a particularly obvious and distinctive way. Communist parties did it, and in some ways, blunted the class-consciousness that had been their strength from the 1940s.

The most ambitious attempt at comprehensive land reform in the 1950s was Kerala's abortive Agrarian Relations Bill of 1957, which (along with challenges to Christian and caste-Hindu educational institutions) led to the dismissal of the Communist government and the declaration of President's Rule in 1959. The agrarian legislation would have turned tenants, particularly in northern Kerala (the old Malabar District of the British-ruled Madras Presidency) into owners of the land they tenanted and all agricultural labourers into owners of the land on which their huts stood. After the dismissal of the Kerala government, the Congress-led coalition elected in 1960 followed an all-India pattern by enacting a weakened version of the Communist bill and then doing little to implement it. Landed supporters of the Congress smiled in 1963 when the Kerala High Court declared the Act unconstitutional.[21]

The legislative and legal contests of 1957–63 gave landowners warning of what might be coming. 'Hectic sales and transfers occurred,'[22] and by the time a Communist-led coalition government came to power in Kerala in 1967, many landholders had taken precautions to protect their assets and positions. Nevertheless, in the next two years, the CPI (M)-led coalition and then its successor, led by the CPI and the resourceful Chief Minister, C. Achutha Menon (1913–91), carried through the Kerala Land Reforms (Amendment) Act of 1969, which gave large numbers of people ownership of land. Tenants were transformed into landowners, but more importantly, landless labourers were given ownership of one-tenth of an acre of land on which their huts stood. This device—bestowing ownership rights on a tiny occupied house and small plot around it—became a favoured nostrum of other state governments thereafter. The West Bengal reforms that began in 1978 adopted it, and the Land Reform Commission in Bihar, which reported in 2008, recommended it.

In West Bengal, the Communist Party of India (Marxist) government elected in 1977, pursued Operation Barga to record share-croppers and to ensure that they received fair treatment. The programme followed the Kerala model and granted ownership of huts and 0.8 of an acre around a hut to agricultural labourers, who previously had been landless and without any entitlement. Left-wing critics asked why a Communist government should try to renovate what looked like a 'feudal' system of land control. Biplab Dasgupta, an intellectual leader of the CPI (M), replied that grinding poverty did not necessarily produce revolution and that the CPI (M) lived in a world of real politics in which *bargadars* were 'a significant proportion of the rural population'.[23] In the mid-1980s, Atul Kohli noted that 'concrete achievements have been made' and that 'programmes for sharecroppers are especially noteworthy'.[24] A large section of rural people in West Bengal were receiving tangible benefits.

Neither Kerala nor West Bengal became places of agrarian equality. In 1977, as a decade of agrarian legislation and dispute subsided in Kerala, 96 per cent of all landholders cultivated less than two hectares; they accounted for only two-thirds of cultivated land. The other one-third of cultivated land was controlled by four per cent of landholders.[25] Complete landlessness in Kerala, however, largely disappeared. In West Bengal, *bargardars* and small landholders appear to have stayed loyal in their support for the Communist Party of India (Marxist) party for more than 30 years until the state elections of 2011.

The political influence of rural landowners, even though they were far from being a majority of the rural population in any state, was too tough in most states to tangle with successfully. Legislation got challenged in the highest courts, which were often sympathetic to owners. Even when legislation was enacted and validated, governments could choose simply to ignore it and not implement it, as Dasgupta argued Congress governments had done in West Bengal in the 1970s. 'It is not easy to explain the dual character of the (Congress) regime of the period,' he mused. 'What motivated them to pass these progressive laws? And why, despite the passing of these laws, was their implementation blocked?'[26] It was perhaps, he concluded, to enable Congress to play a double game: to claim to be the friend of the poor while protecting the class interests that were the essence of the party. In short, to defuse demand for agrarian change.

One can interpret these 'land reforms' as examples of such defusing. In turning tens of thousands of landless households into tiny landowners, Kerala had, in the words of an old peasant leader, turned 'slaves into owners'. He called his autobiography *Atimakal Enngane Utamakal Aayi*—How slaves became owners.[27] By the 1980s, more than 90 per cent of rural labouring households owned the sites of their dwellings.[28] Scholars and politicians debated whether the acquisition of ownership rights had turned potential supporters of radical political change into very-petty bourgeois whose political loyalties were far less radical and predictable.[29]

There was another facet to arguments about defusing demands for land reform. It relates to the campaigns of Vinoba Bhave (1895–1982), a follower of Mahatma Gandhi who acquired a following in the 1950s and 1960s by walking the countryside appealing to landowners to surrender land to the landless. Bhave's claims to be carrying on a Gandhian tradition of appeals to the better instincts of humanity secured perhaps four million acres of not-very-good land and put him on the cover of *Time* magazine in 1953.[30] The Bhave phenomenon can be seen as a diversion which directed energy and attention into efforts that had little effect on patterns of landholding, security of the landless, or the productivity of land. But in absorbing the time of officials and the fascination of journalists, Bhave's campaigns suited those who had no wish to see repetition of the bitter class conflict generated by the Kerala Agrarian Relations Bill of 1957, in other states.

Naive Little Answer No. 4: Socio-Economic Forces Made Land Reform Obsolete

A fourth category of answers to the Big Question comes from what I might innocently call 'an economist's perspective'. A key measurement would be the declining share of agriculture in India's gross domestic product. Agriculture made up 50 per cent of GDP in 1960. The countryside was where the action was—where voters lived and where most wealth came from. No politician or official could ignore such facts. By 2010, agriculture's share had fallen to less than 15 per cent of GDP (See Table 1). Though 69 per cent of people still lived in the countryside, the major sources of wealth had shifted elsewhere.

Table 1: Share of GDP, 1950-2010

Year	Agriculture	Industry	Services
1950-1	55.8	15.2	29.0
1960-1	45.8	20.7	33.5
1970-1	45.2	21.9	32.9
1980-1	38.1	25.9	36.0
1990-1	31.0	29.3	39.7
2000-01	25.8	23.8	50.4
2008-09	20.0	26.3	53.7
2010-11	14.4	n.a.	n.a.

Sources: *Statistical Outline of India, 1999–2000* [hereafter SOI] (Mumbai: Tata Services, 1999), p. 15 and *SOI*, 2008–09, p. 14. CA Club India, 11 December 2011, http://www.caclubindia.com/forum/share-of-agriculture-sector-in-gdp-179511.asp, quoting Central Statistics Office (downloaded 25 March 2012).

Government investment in public infrastructure for agriculture shifted from the 1990s. A rough indicator lies in the record of land irrigated by public resources. It reached a modest 17 million hectares in 1991, but had fallen to 15.3 million hectares by 2006. In the same period, land irrigated by private tube wells doubled from 17.7 million hectares to 35.4 million hectares.[31]

Prosperous landowners deepened and diversified their links to town and cities and to relatives and connections in politics, the police and administration. The collapse of the Soviet Union and the discrediting of 'socialism' and socialist parties in the West contributed to a decline in class-based rhetoric in Indian politics. Caste and religion, always factors in Indian elections, assumed great influence in the late 1980s, illustrated in part by the intense emotions generated by the Mandal Commission and the implementation of some of its recommendations.

It had not always been this way. In Kerala in the 1950s and 1960s, and West Bengal from the 1970s, landless and land-poor people had to be taken note of because they consistently voted for Communist and Left parties that advocated land reform. Similarly, the Congress Party until the end of the 'emergency' in 1977 supported a 'left wing', including ex-Communists like Mohan Kumaramangalam (1916–73), who kept the rhetoric of land reform in the party's platform. Until the 1970s, too, there were 'socialist' parties drawing on the inspiration of people like the UP politician Narendra Dev (1889–1956), Ram Manohar Lohia (1910–67) and Jayaprakash Narayan (1902–79). The leaders of such parties were close to rural issues. They were reinforced in their beliefs about redistributive justice by the vitality of Western socialist parties and the existence of a Soviet bloc that in their eyes retained some virtue and achievements. Dev died in 1956, Lohia in 1967, and Jayaprakash in 1979, each death sounding a gong that signalled the progressive dilution of redistribution as an important component of Indian political argument.

'Agricultural' voices, never mind voices advocating land reform, had not been particularly strong among the elites of Jawaharlal Nehru's India. Under Nehru, the Rudolphs concluded in 1987, 'agricultural interests and values were poorly represented in New Delhi'. They argued that from Lal Bahadur Shastri's prime ministership (1964–66), 'agricultural producers have become increasingly visible and audible in national policy and politics'.[32] But these producers were, at the very least 'rich peasants', beneficiaries of Green Revolution incentives. Many were on the way to becoming 'farmers'—people who sold what they grew and were keenly aware of markets and the politics that affect markets. If conditions were right, such people would be interested in ways to acquire land, not redistribute it.

The growth of advocacy for rural capitalism from the 1960s, and the coming of the 'green revolution', led to the expansion of markets for land—to 'land reform' being replaced by 'real estate' as a discussion topic for Indian political elites. We get some sense of this shift from examination of the development of real-estate advertisements in Indian-language newspapers. It was only in 1992 that *Eenadu*, the king of Telugu dailies, launched a concerted programme to transform Telugu readers into 'real estate' advertisers. 'We had absolutely nothing,' an Eenadu executive said in 1993. 'Zero real estate ads. Then we... started off an ad campaign...and a real estate page.' Within a year, they had generated enough real-estate advertising to make it worthwhile to create 'an entire new segment'—a weekly supplement devoted to real estate.[33] By 2012, daily newspapers in all languages carried weekly real estate supplements that made hefty contributions to a newspaper's advertising revenue. Twenty years earlier, there had been almost nothing from this source.

Such evidence indicates that substantial change flowed from the 'liberalisation' of the economy that began in 1991. Comparisons of the Sixth Five-Year Plan (1980–05) and the Eleventh Five-Year Plan (2007–12) illustrate the change. The Sixth Plan, drafted after Indira Gandhi returned to power in 1980 and with Manmohan Singh as the Member-Secretary, aimed to implement land reform policies, including enforcement of ceilings, 'on a time-bound basis'. States that lacked appropriate legislation were to do so by 1982; acquisition of land that exceeded the ceilings was to be completed by 1983; land records were to be compiled and updated by 1985; consolidation of holdings was to be completed within 10 years; and house sites for the landless —Kerala-1970 style—were to be provided within five years.[34] By 1986, 'these tasks still remain unachieved', as Bandyopadhyay, tireless recorder of land-reform events, wrote.[35] The statements of the Sixth Plan did not accord with either the political pressures as understood by Indira Gandhi or her son and successor, Rajiv Gandhi.

The perceived popularity of 'land reform' as a rallying cry seems to have begun a long slow death about the same time as the deaths of two populists, Sanjay Gandhi in 1981 and Indira Gandhi in 1984. Indeed, Indira Gandhi herself had begun to move away from the 'socialism' espoused in the 1970s when 1982 was declared 'productivity year'. By the time the 11th Five-Year Plan (2007–12) was produced in 2007, little more than lip-service was paid to 'land reform':

'The poor are geographically concentrated in India...without effective (i) land reforms and (ii) agricultural services, none of these regions are likely to be able to reduce poverty.'[36]

Land reform, moreover, was portrayed as a way to increase productivity: 'Small-sized farms...have an advantage in using surplus family labour and saving monitoring costs, and this is the main argument for land reforms.'[37]

And jostling with 'land reform' for a place in the mind of the planners and the plan were the growing pressures of 'real estate':

> We have to evolve a National Land Policy which will allow both public and private developers to legally purchase land for conversion into urban habitats and townships through transparent rules and regulations. Inadequate availability of serviced land in the urban areas is a major constraining factor in taking up housing projects for the poor. [38]

From a focus in the early 1980s that still took as a starting point a vision of a 'Village India', the planners, representing an influential section of elite India, visualised a future India that by 2007 was proudly urban.

Yet the drift to the towns and cities was not dramatic in percentage terms. Absolute numbers were immense by world standards: An additional 90 million Indians moved from the country to the city between 2001 and 2011 (Table 2). But still only 31 per cent of India was urban, and the annual urban growth rate averaged about 2.5 per cent for 30 years, only slightly greater than the overall rate of population growth. India was not yet a country of deserted villages. One cannot, therefore, argue that widespread migration from the countryside accounts for the diminution of interest in land reform in politics or in social movements.

Table 2: Urban Growth, 1951–2011 Census

Year	Urban %	Number Urban (millions)	Number of urbanites added in the decade	Decadal % of urban growth
1951	17.3	62.4		
1961	18.0	78.9	16.5	21
1971	19.9	109.1	30.2	28
1981	23.3	156.2	47.1	30
1991	25.7	217.6	61.4	28
2001	27.8	286.1	68.5	24
2011	31.2	377.1	91.0	24

Sources: SOI and Census of India, http://censusindia.gov.in/2011-prov-results/paper2/data_files/india/paper2_at_a_glance.pdf (downloaded 25 March 2011).

R. Vijay presents data that suggests that 'non-cultivating peasant households... witnessed a phenomenal increase from 23.7 per cent (of rural households) in 1981 to 40.3 per cent by 2002'.[39] These figures masked various possibilities, but one of them was a growth of tenancy: landowners choosing not to cultivate land themselves but putting it out to others even though tenancy was, as a result of earlier land reform laws, illegal in many states. Vijay's findings, based on National Sample Survey data, also showed little change since 1981 in the proportion of landless labourer families which remained at about 11 per cent of rural households. Vijay's conclusions were sombre. The landless still needed access to land; they got it through (often illegal) leases from non-cultivating peasant households which had little interest in improving productivity once they had a guaranteed rent. If this analysis were correct, Vijay concluded, 'a different approach to dealing with the agrarian crisis' was needed—'either going back to land reform kind of measures' or finding ways to displace non-cultivating peasant households 'through market interventions like corporate farming'.[40]

Land Reform Becomes Real Estate: 'The Developer Ate My Homestead'?

The zeitgeist of the 1980s was marked by the despair of elites at the chaotic dissolution of the Janata Party government and the return to power of a shrewd, self-serving Mrs Gandhi. Rajiv Gandhi, an outward-looking airline pilot, aware of middle-class frustration, represented the first generation of adult Indians with no memory of the national struggle and British rule. Internationally, Margaret Thatcher rolled back 'Socialism' and Ronald Reagan reduced regulation of financial institutions, airlines, and telecommunications. India's 'Year of Productivity' and the arrival of colour television for the Asian Games in 1982, signalled that Mrs Gandhi too was leaving 'Socialism' behind. Rajiv Gandhi 'brought with him', according to the author of *Moguls of Real Estate*, 'an entirely new perspective for the economic development of the country' and was convinced by K.P. Singh of DLF, one of India's largest property developers, that 'archaic laws that came in the way of private sector townships needed to be scrapped'.[41]

'The real estate industry is at the core of India's growth story,' runs the first sentence of *Moguls of Real Estate*, published in 2007 to celebrate five leaders of the industry. 'The sector is booming with huge unmet demands, accelerating prices and increasing foreign investments. Growth, expansion, buy-outs and deals are the buzzwords.'[42] To be sure, the words are part of the Foreword, written by someone from the 'India Real Estate Practice' at Ernst and Young. And they were written just before the financial crisis of 2008 began. Nevertheless they portray a very different spirit from that embodied in titles like Daniel Thorner's *Agrarian Prospect in India* or P. C. Joshi's *Land Reforms in India* two generations earlier.[43]

A further marker of changing concepts about land and its uses was a conference in 2003 while the BJP-led government of A.B. Vajpayee was in power. Held in Seattle, Washington, 'Reforms in Land Policy for Accelerated Agricultural Growth and Rural Development' was a collaboration of two departments of the Government of India and the University of Washington.[44] The chief bureaucrat of the Department of Rural Development opened the conference with a statement that would have seemed glaringly inappropriate 30 years earlier. 'In the past,' he said, 'we have achieved very limited success in land reforms and poverty alleviation.' Emphasis ought therefore to shift to 'new reform approaches such as contract farming, land leasing and home-stead-cum-garden plots'. His opposite number from the Department of Agriculture 'highlighted the need for a paradigm shift from subsistence farming to market-oriented commercial agriculture'.[45]

Senior officials from a number of states echoed the need for change, including a new attitude to leasing and tenancy. Representatives from Andhra Pradesh told the conference that the ban on leasing out of agricultural land was probably relevant in the period immediately after independence when there was a demand and need for abolition of intermediaries/ zamindari. But in the present context, it was essential to liberalise land leasing in order to enable the large farmers to lease out land and take up non-farm activities, while allowing the marginal and small farmers to lease in land and improve their size of holding.[46]

From when do we date, and how do we explain, these changes in elite conceptions of what 'land' ought to be doing? As the halting discussion up to here may have indicated, I would suggest that change begins to become evident from the 1980s. In 1981, DLF, which by 2012 was India's largest real estate company, 'was given permission...to undertake a residential development... in Gurgaon' where DLF had 'managed to acquire 150 acres of land...from farmers'.[47] The Ansals started their development of gated communities at

Gurgaon a few years later.[48] Another of the 'Moguls', Niranjan Hiranandani of Mumbai, also got out of the textile business and into real estate in Mumbai in 1980–81, and Irfan Razack, 'Bangalore's leading developer, sold his first piece of property in 1980'.[49]

At the 2003 conference in Seattle, the highest ranking official in the Department of Agriculture argued that 'very limited success in land reforms' in close to 60 years of independence dictated that 'new reform approaches...should be properly examined and exploited'.[50] 'New reform approaches' included:

- contract farming
- land leasing
- land share company in agriculture
- allotment of homestead-cum-garden plots.

Vijay's 2012 essay echoed one of these possibilities: 'market interventions like corporate farming' seemed one way out of rural distress. (This essay has not attempted to analyse the extent of such distress or one of its markers, rural suicide).[51]

Contract farming would involve cultivators agreeing to plant particular crops, achieve a satisfactory crop quality, and sell crops at a pre-agreed price to the company with whom they had made the deal. The advantages to the cultivator were said to be improved seeds and technology and guaranteed sale; the country would benefit from reduced spoilage and efficient movement of crops to markets. Land leasing proposed a retreat from one of the tenets of 'land reform' as understood in the past. Laws would be changed to allow agriculturalists to lease out land or lease it in. The idea, of course, was that knowledgeable cultivators would make the most sensible deal for themselves and their land, depending on market prices and their personal needs.

The land-share company had echoes of the old cooperative: farmers would become shareholders in a company run on modern business lines, which would pay dividends based on harvests and prices, in proportion to the land farmers had committed. The homestead-cum-garden plots proposal was the old Kerala programme, repeated in West Bengal, of granting every hut dweller ownership rights to their hut and a tiny plot around it.[52] This measure seemed to bring increased independence and confidence to the poorest people in the countryside;

but even it was not easy. The Bihar government of Nitish Kumar received a report of its Land Reforms Commission in April 2008 which recommended the homestead initiative. Four years later the report appears to have been buried.[53]

'Reverse tenancy' has also become a common practice. Capital-rich interests, either individual farmers or agricultural businesses, rent land from marginal holders and put the owners back to work to grow a particular crop on their own land.[54] Montek Singh Ahluwalia alluded to this shift nearly 20 years ago when he pointed out that 'the rights of the tenant may need redesigning in a situation where the landlord is actually the weaker party'.[55]

Transition from agricultural societies to urban, industrial, life has been painful in every country for the past 300 years. In 1770, Oliver Goldsmith lamented the destruction of the English peasantry and the drive to the cities, which then was only beginning, in 'The Deserted Village':

If to the city sped—what waits him there?
To see profusion that he must not share;
To see ten thousand baneful arts combined
To pamper luxury and thin mankind;
To see each joy the sons of pleasure know
Extorted from his fellow-creature's woe.

One of the 'Moguls of Indian real estate' could count himself fortunate to have come from a family that anticipated rural agony. The grandfather of Sushil Ansal of the property developers Ansal API, noted for its 'ability to "see and seize" opportunities in the real estate field', had been 'a sugarcane farmer' of Jalandhar.[56]

In the past 30 years, land in India has steadily become as important for what you put on it as what you grow on it. Legislative energies have gone into drafting bills to facilitate the acquisition of land for 'development' and to mitigate the disadvantage and distress of rural people whose land is acquired.[57] Confrontation between agriculturalists and developers, with governments taking sides, erupted in West Bengal over the car factory planned by Tata at Singur (and moved to Gujarat in 2008) and at New Okhla Industrial Development Authority (NOIDA) on the eastern borders of New Delhi in the state of Uttar Pradesh in 2011.[58] The NOIDA dispute highlighted the difficulties, pressures and temptations. It appeared that the land in question was originally acquired by the state government for 'industrial purposes' but later reclassified for residential use and sold at great profit to developers. The original owners received a fraction of what the 'open market' now deemed the land to be worth.[59] Such collisions were not unique to India, but they were made even more difficult by widespread lack of trust. Harrowing stories of tribal people displaced by the Sardar Sarovar and other dam projects were well known. Promises of 'rehabilitation and resettlement' were often scoffed at. Moreover, India's transition from a system in which well-defined 'markets' for land were rare to one in which 'market value' was made a key feature of mechanisms for protecting land-losers was, most scholars agreed, unprecedented.[60] Understanding and influencing such change pose urgent challenges to activists, scholars, politicians and policy-makers.

Appendix—The Beginnings of a List of Legislation related to Land

- Bengal Tenancy Act, 1885
- Land Acquisition Act of 1894
- U.P. Zamindari Abolition Act of 1952
- West Bengal Estate Acquisition Act, 1953
- West Bengal Land Reforms Act, 1955
- Kerala Agrarian Relations Bill, 1957
- U. P. Imposition of Ceiling on Land Holdings Act, 1960
- Bihar Land Reforms (Fixation of Ceiling Areas of Acquisition of Surplus Land) Act, 1961
- Kerala Land Reforms Act, 1963.
- Kerala Land Reforms (Amendment) Act, 1969
- Gujarat Agriculture Lands Ceiling Act, 1972
- Haryana Ceiling on Land Holding Act, 1972
- Himachal Pradesh Ceiling of Land Holding Act, 1972
- Jammu and Kashmir Agrarian Reforms Act, 1972
- Punjab Land Reforms Act, 1972
- Rajasthan Imposition of Ceiling on Holding Act, 1973
- Forest Conservation Act, 1980
- Panchayats (Extension to the Scheduled Areas) Act (PESA), 1996
- Scheduled Tribes and Other Traditional Forest Dwellers (Recognition of Forest Rights) Act, 2006
- Land Acquisition, Rehabilitation and Resettlement Bill, 2011

Endnotes

1. The views expressed are those of the author alone and not of any institution with which he is associated.
2. Victor M. Fic, *Kerala: Yenan of India. Rise of Communist Power*, 1937–69 (Bombay: Nachiketa, 1970).
3. D. Bandyopadhyay, 'Does Land Still Matter?', *Economic and Political Weekly* [hereafter *EPW*], vol. 43/10 (8 March 2008): 37.
4. R. Vijay, 'Structural Retrogression and Rise of "New Landlords" in Indian Agriculture: an Empirical Exercise,' *EPW*, Vol. 47/05 (4 February 2012): 37.
5. P. C. Joshi, *Land Reforms in India* (Bombay: Allied, 1975): p. 87, suggests another way to think about 'changes in agrarian structure': those that happen in response to 'socio-economic forces' and those that happen through the intervention of governments.
6. Charan Singh, *Land Reforms in UP and the Kulaks* (New Delhi: Vikas, 1986). Paul Brass, *An Indian Political Life: Charan Singh and Congress Politics*, 1937–61 (New Delhi: Sage, 2011).
7. Peter Reeves, *Landlords and Governments in Uttar Pradesh: a Study of their Relations until Zamindari Abolition* (New Delhi: Oxford University Press, 1991). Stephen Henningham, *Peasant Movements in Colonial India: North Bihar 1917–1942* (Canberra: Australian National University, 1982).
8. Peter Reeves, *Landlords and Governments in Uttar Pradesh: A Study of their Relations until Zamindari Abolition* (New Delhi: Oxford University Press, 1991). Gyanendra Pandey, *The Ascendancy of the Congress in Uttar Pradesh, 1926–34: A Study in Imperfect Mobilization* (New Delhi: Oxford University Press, 1978).
9. *Agrarian Distress in the United Provinces, Being the Report of the Committee appointed by the Council of the U.P. Provincial Congress Committee to enquire into the Agrarian Situation in the Province* (New Delhi: Prabhu Publications, 1982; First published 1931). I am indebted to Maxine Loynd of the Australian National University for help with the discussion of UP.
10. Ibid. p. 61.
11. D.A. Low, 'Congress and Mass Contacts 1936-1937', in Low, *Rearguard Action: Selected Essays on Late Colonial History* (Cambridge: Cambridge University Press, 1996), p. 141.
12. Quoted in ibid. p. 150.
13. Brass on Charan Singh.
14. Charan Singh, *Land Reforms in UP and the Kulaks* (New Delhi: Vikas, 1986), p.v. I am grateful to Maxine Loynd for this and other UP references.
15. H.R. Sharma, 'Distribution of Landholdings in Rural India, 1953–54 to 1981–82: Implications for Land Reforms,' *EPW*, vol. 29/13 (24 September 1994), Table 3, p. A-120.

16. http://cpixxicongress.blogspot.com/#!/2012/03/resolution-on-land-reform-in-bihar.html (accessed April, 6 2012).
17. *Mainstream*, 1 August 2009, http://www.mainstreamweekly.net/article1547.html (accessed April, 6 2012). The account published by *Mainstream* was extracted from '*ML Update*, a CPI-ML (Liberation) weekly news magazine.'
18. M. S. Randhawa, *Out of the Ashes* (Chandigarh: Public Relations Department, Punjab, 1954), p. 97.
19. D. Bandyopadhyay, 'Tebhaga Movement in Bengal: a Retrospect,' *EPW*, Vol. 36/41(13 October 2001): 3901.
20. See the 'Introduction' to *More than Maoism*, eds. Robin Jeffrey, Ronojoy Sen, and Pratima Singh (New Delhi: Manohar for the Institute of South Asian Studies, Singapore, 2012).
21. Robin Jeffrey, *Politics, Women and Well-Being* [hereafter *PWWB*] (London: Macmillan, 1992), pp. 173–74.
22. *Land Reforms Survey in Kerala, 1966-67: Report* (Trivandrum: Bureau of Economics and Statistics, 1968), p. 95.
23. Biplab Dasgupta, 'Sharecropping in West Bengal. From Independence to Operation Barga,' *EPW*, Review of Agriculture, Vol. 19/26 (30 June 1984): p. A-90.
24. Atul Kohli, *The State and Politics in India* (New York: Cambridge University Press, 1987), p. 143.
25. Jeffrey, *PWWB*, p. 175.
26. Ibid., p. A-86.
27. V.M. Vishnu Bharatheeyan, *Atimakal Enngane Utamakal Aayi* (Trivandrum: Prabath Book House, 1980).
28. *Report of the Survey on Socio-Economic Conditions of Agricultural and Other Rural Labourers in Kerala, 1983–4* (Trivandrum: Bureau of Economics and Statistics, 1985), p. 13.
29. Jeffrey, *PWWB*, p. pp. 183–4.
30. *Time*, 11 May 1953, http://www.google.com/imgres?imgurl=http://img.timeinc.net/time/magazine/archive/covers/1953/1101530511_400.jpg&imgrefurl=http://www.tim.com/time/covers/0,16641,19530511,00.html&h=527&w=400&sz=45&tbnid=KiwkSssgAl_GGM:&tbnh=90&tbnw=68&zoom=1&docid=0XG4PP0TbHf5KM&sa=X&ei=OpptT5rKOM2HrAeGr7igDg&ved=0CFQQ9QEwBg&dur=94 (accessed March24, 2012). http://www.mkgandhi.org/vinoba/bio.htm (accessed Apri l6, 2012).
31. *SOI*, 2008-09, p. 49.

32. Lloyd I. and Susanne H. Rudolph, *In Pursuit of Lakshmi: The Political Economy of the Indian State* (Chicago: University of Chicago Press, 1987), p. 312.
33. Interview, Piush Bahl, Assistant Manager (Advertising), *Eenadu*, Hyderabad, 1 March 1993.
34. *Sixth Five Year Plan (1980-5),* para 9.100, http://planningcommission.nic.in/plans/planrel/fiveyr /6th/6planch9.html (accessed March 25, 2012).
35. D. Bandyopadhyay, 'Land Reforms in India: An Analysis,' *EPW*, Review of Agriculture, Vol. 21/25-26, (21 June 1986): p. A-50.
36. *Eleventh Five Year Plan (2007–2012),* Vol. 3, *Agriculture, Rural Development, Industry, Services and Physical Infrastructure* (New Delhi: Oxford University Press for the Planning Commission, 2008), p. 85.
37. Ibid., p. 33.
38. Ibid.
39. Vijay, 'Structural Retrogression', p. 40.
40. Ibid., p.45
41. Ibid., p. 26.
42. Manoj Namburu, *Moguls of Real Estate* (New Delhi: Roli Books, 2007), p. ix.
43. Daniel Thorner, *Agrarian Prospect in India* (Bombay: Allied Publishers, 1976) and P.C. Joshi, *Land Reforms in India: Trends and Perspectives* (Bombay: Allied Publishers, 1975).
44. The Government of India's Department of Agriculture and Cooperation and Department of Rural Development, and the Rural Development Institute at the University of Washington.
45. T. Haque, 'Reforms for Agricultural Growth and Rural Development,' *EPW*, Vol. 38/48 (29 November 2003): 5031.
46. Ibid., p. 5032.
47. Ibid., pp. 24, 26.
48. Ibid., p. 151.
49. Ibid., pp. 69–70, 213.
50. Haque, 'Reforms', p. 5031.
51. See, for example, P. Sainath in the *Hindu*, October29, 2011, http://www.thehindu.com/opinion/columns/sainath/article2577635.ece (accessed April 9, 2012) and the accompanying table of rural suicide 1995–2010.
52. Haque, 'Reforms', pp. 5032–33.
53. *Mainstream*, 1 August 2009.
54. For discussion of 'reverse tenancy' in the Approach Paper to the 12th Five Year Plan see, N. C. Saxena, 'Land for landed,' *Frontline*, (21 October 2011): p. 21.

55. Paraphrased in G. Parthasarathy, 'The New Economic Policy, Rural Development and Land Reform', in *Land Reforms in India*, Vol. 5, *An Unfinished Agenda,* ed. B.K. Sinha and Pushpendra (New Delhi: Sage, 2000), p. 66.

56. Namburu, *Moguls*, pp. 127–28, 133.

57. For example, Panchayats (Extension to the Scheduled Areas) Act (PESA), 1996, Scheduled Tribes and Other Traditional Forest Dwellers (Recognition of Forest Rights) Act, 2006 and Land Acquisition, Rehabilitation and Resettlement (LARR) Bill, 2011. Sanjoy Chakravorty, 'A Lot of Scepticism and Some Hope', *EPW,* Vol 46/41(8 October 2011): 29–31, for a discussion of the LARR bill.

58. *India Today*, May 11, 2011, http://indiatoday.intoday.in/story/land-acquisition-stir-rahul-gandhi-meets-farmers-in-greater-noida/1/137749.html (accessed April 11, 2012).

59. *Frontline*, June 17, 2011, pp. 4–11.

60. Ashwin Mahalingam and Aditi Vyas, 'Comparative Evaluation of Land Acquisition and Compensation Processes across the World', *EPW*, Vol. 46/32 (6 August 2011): 94–102.

Can India Afford not to Eliminate Corruption?

T.S.R. Subramanian

Corruption can be categorised in different ways, petty vs. grand; transactional vs. policy related, political vs. administrative, centralised (mafia type) vs. decentralised etc. A form of low-level corruption, the equivalent of a 'tip' has existed in India and elsewhere from times immemorial. Indeed 'baksheesh' as a word is still used in Germany and many other countries, as in India, to connote low-level corruption, the word probably originating from Persian. The concept of a bribe relates to when 'rent' is demanded as a right, for a legitimate service supposed to be rendered free of charge. Such corruption at the thana and tehsil levels have been known in India for centuries. With massive development funds flowing to rural areas in the post-independence era, large leakages ingeniously devised, blending with ascendancy of local politics, poor supervision, and weak punitive action have encouraged rapid growth of this phenomenon. Thus the policeman's job is coveted—If a new police recruit at the lowest level has to pay Rs 2 or Rs 3 lakhs for being selected (the prevailing rates about 10 years back—the numbers probably these days closer to Rs 10 lakhs), one can imagine that he would have to borrow the money from relatives and money lenders at usurious rates—no wonder his compulsion to repay the loans force him into corrupt practices from the very day he enters the service; in course of time his bloodthirst increases by the day as it advances to rapacious levels.

The 2-G, coalgate and other recent scams have abundantly illustrated how corruption is now a normal way of life in our political sector—politics is now big business; heavy investments are made with a view to get major returns. Just to illustrate how open the issue is, a Union Minister (belonging to Congress Party) in a TV programme a couple of years back categorised the Congress chief of a major state as 'a mafia don – he is a don in mining, liquor and land'. Rajiv Gandhi as Prime Minister had once commented that only 17% of development funds reach the intended beneficiary—indicating the enormity of leakage and the extent of corruption with which the common citizen has to contend.

That the large-family-owned business houses, relatively few in number, were able to influence policy making in a significant manner, was well established by the mid-1960s. The advent of Dhirubhai Ambani into the industrial scene of India raised this to a new dimension. Nearly from scratch, within a few years, the Ambani group was able to build a large empire, mainly enabled by ensuring that an extremely friendly and beneficial policy atmosphere was continually created and improved at the occasion of each budget or import/export policy announcement, and in-between. The fine art of building a business empire not so much by work in the field but through a liaison network based in Delhi became established. In due course this included influencing Members of Parliament to lobby effectively in and out of parliament, and ensuring that key ministries in Delhi at the secretariat and political levels were populated by the nominees of a business house became normal practice. In the 1990s it was not uncommon to hear of this or that Chief Minister amassing a fortune of 500 crores—by today's opulent standards, these may be seen as small change! But the seeds were planted into the politico-administrative scene at the centre and the states during those days. It was also the era when Indira Gandhi wanted 'committed' civil servants—initially the commitment referred to was to policy, then to the party, then to the minister concerned, with whom eventually the civil servant who would cooperate, moved on to become a collaborator, and anon a co-conspirator, sharing a part of the spoils. Politics rapidly became a new lucrative field for making money—much like when a new petroleum field or gold mine opens up, people entered politics exclusively with the idea of making a large fortune.

It needs to be understood that the active assistance and collaboration of the civil servant is imperative in this process of determined and reckless money-making that the political executive has reduced itself to. Officers are assessed with great care to see who will collaborate and eventually conspire; who will be squeamish and needs to be sidelined ruthlessly. Thus the civil service was broken into three categories—the majority who would quietly implement orders without looking left and right, the relatively few who were totally upright and dared to express their views (and were consequently sidelined), and the chosen few who became partners yielding power and collaborating closely with the rulers.

There are other many equally important reasons. These include state control of major investigative agencies like CBI, Enforcement Directorate, State vigilance directorates; ineptitude of Constitutional and Statutory watchdog agencies like the CVC, etc. Not long ago we have witnessed what one person heading the CAG could do if he took his job seriously, realises that he is serving the people of India and not the government or political masters, and is bold and courageous in his investigations and his conclusions. It is a pity we have not seen too many examples of erstwhile civil servants, experienced and competent, who when given elevated responsibilities could not shed their lapdog attitude, and transcend and assume the full powers given to them by the Constitution or the statutes. T.N. Seshan showed the way in removing muscle power from the election scene during the 1990s. We now need a new Seshan to rid our elections of money power.

Corruption is endemic in India

The Santanam Committee, as early as in the 1960s, had identified the main strands in the Indian corruption scene and had prescribed remedial measures—it is not a coincidence that nearly every major corrective proposed by Santanam has not been implemented till now. Indeed the Lok Pal or its equivalent, which was prescribed by Santanam in early 60s is still not a reality 50 years later. Even after Anna Hazare's movement and other similar outpourings of recent anger, there is no clarity when this will happen—left to our politicians, we may have to wait another 50 years or more.

Wherever you go, whichever agency you look into at the Centre or at the State which deals with people's issues (as all do), you will find corruption to an extent ranging from very large to extremely large. An amateur some time back found out that 36 beat-policemen, in different parts of the same town in Maharashtra, on the same day, were photographed on camera taking bribes, on an average ranging from Rs 200 to Rs 500; in one instance Rs 4000, from passing motorists, motorcyclists and others. Repeat this scenario in every small town, every village, every metro; repeat the search in every office everywhere in India—passport office, ration card office, driving licence office; the block, the thana, the tehsil, the collectorate, the list can go on and on—the conclusion is inescapable that petty corruption at field level is universal. Every District Magistrate, every Superintendent of Police, every field Head of Department knows exactly how much and where the corruption is. If they are made responsible, accountable, with the fear of God put in them with their career at stake, and interference eliminated, it is a safe bet that corruption levels will come down by 75% (my loose estimate—don't ask me to prove it mathematically) in short order. Clearly everyone concerned is happy—nothing needs to be done—the citizen should learn to pay bribes, cheerfully and happily!

A significant ethical question is involved—is the bribe-giver and the bribe-taker equally culpable? The conventional wisdom is that it takes two hands to clap—there will be no bribe taken, if none is given. All of this is true; but in practice can one treat the bribe-giver on the same footing as the bribe-taker. There can be no moral, ethical, or legal way to condone the actions of the bribe-giver—but does the world consist entirely of bribe-givers and bribe-takers—is there no role for governance, administration, a sanitised atmosphere for pre-empting bribes or to provide an effective, swift, punitive retribution to bribe-takers and givers alike. Imagine the plight of a truck-driver who has obtained a job in the Middle-East, wanting an International driving licence in a hurry, or a passport as the case may be, without which his major career opportunity will go away; imagine a student desperately wanting to stay in a particular town for higher education, which he cannot do unless he pays a 'capitation' fee for college entry, without which his whole career can be pre-emptively blighted; imagine a philanthropist wanting to establish a high quality charity-oriented school or college or hospital, who has to obtain one of several 'NOCs' required for the same, which can be done only through a hefty bribe—are these people committing crimes by paying bribes to get their legitimate objectives achieved—can they be equated, on the same footing, as the persons who demanded and received the illegal gratification. What they have done clearly is unethical, surely illegal—are there credible extenuating circumstances? In Indian prevailing conditions, can an outsider, who does not stand in the shoes of these people take the 'holier-than-thou' position that the bribe-giver is as much to blame, that circumstances are not relevant. In Western countries, transactional corruption is largely eliminated, through a combination of swift, efficient, incorruptible investigating agencies, and a judiciary to mete out swift exemplary punishment—the cost of being caught is very heavy.

Corruption at the operational levels

There is no question that there is widespread corruption at the "cutting edge" level. This has been endemic in India and has thrived through the Mughal times, also survived the British times. This deep-rooted practice is a definite menace to society. It is the failure of the civil services class, the IAS and the other central services, that we have not been able stamp out or at least keep in-check, the 'transactional' corruption. The classical excuses relate to political patronage, lack of political backing, etc. This 'routine' type of corruption needs to be distinguished from the kind of new post-independence corruption phenomenon where the business classes have abstracted licenses, approvals, changes in law and the like, and encouraged a wide variety of tampering with the regulatory structure, for mutual reward between the businessmen on one side and the politician (supported by the bureaucrat) on the other, at the expense of the public. The tragedy is that with 'opening of the economy' in the past two decades, the menace has grown to monstrous proportions.

A significant part of India's domestic transactions is funded by black money; various estimates have placed the numbers at a very high level. Indeed, the 'parallel economy' is surmised to be at least as large as the official economy. In the period following the international financial crisis of October 2008, one wag had mentioned that its impact on India will be quite limited because the Indian economy does not function merely on banking finance; it has other fuel through black money, to keep it going! A Swiss Banking Association report estimates bank deposits in the territory of Switzerland by Indian nationals, at a staggering US$ 1,500 billion. This is three times as large as the deposits from the next country, Russia; the Indian deposits are many multiples of those from other countries including USA, Germany, Japan, Brazil, etc. There is no doubt that this represents the stashing of ill-gotten wealth of corrupt businessmen, politicians, bureaucrats and other Indian crooks. Naturally these numbers don't represent Indian money hiding in other 'safe-havens', elsewhere in the world.

Much of the citizens' contact with the Government is at the district and sub-district level—the thana, the tehsil, the block, etc. The existing systems have no credibility left with the public in these cutting-edge areas. The nexus between lower officials and local politicians is ever-present and a reality of life. No citizen can expect any assistance from these agencies except with significant doses of speed money. In Tamil Nadu, avowedly a well-run state, I was recently speaking to a field joint director of rural development—her estimate of the amount that reaches the beneficiary was about 30%. It is the same story nearly wherever you turn. Surely, the massive levels of unauthorised construction in our metropolitan cities could not have happened without the knowledge of local authorities and the local politicians and without the transfer of thousands of crores cumulatively of 'blinker money'. One's own experience and all anecdotal assessments indicate a progressive increase in corruption levels in the past decades.

Does anyone want corruption eliminated from India?

Who indeed is interested in stemming the growth of corruption, not to speak of reining it in, indeed reversing it? What are the forces working to not only keep corruption on a leash, but to diminish its range and scope? Can the technology steps and policy moves alone reduce or mitigate corruption levels? Is anyone actually doing anything about it seriously, apart from lip-service? If one were to think about these dispassionately, the picture is bleak indeed. Let us take a reality check.

Indeed the country, nominally a 'democracy' is ruled by five classes of people—the politicians, the bureaucrats, the judiciary, the business class and increasingly the media of late. Let us examine the position of each one of these.

The politician surely can live with corruption—indeed he cannot live without it! Reference to this politician or the other having amassed 1,500 crores or 2,000 crores is now accepted without a blink of the eye. It is well known that most transactions of politicians are in cash and that too in large amounts, and totally unaccounted for. The reality is that politics is now the biggest business in the country, with no accounts, or accountability; nor with any checks and balances or overlooking ombudsman. In fact, the fountain for all corruption starts in the foundations of our democratic process—the election process is riddled with corruption. In recent years, the 'investment' to get initially a nomination and thereafter the cost of fighting the election has shot up astronomically, nearly for every elected post—an unerring indication that these are no more public service opportunities, indeed they are major openings to make fortunes, through an untrammelled, unregulated system deliberately created to foster high level corruption; no wonder the politician as a class is unwilling to take any concrete step to reverse the situation. One recently heard that in municipal boards/corporations of major cities, a corporator needs to spend upto 30 crores to get elected—one may only surmise that he will amass wealth over 200 crores in one tenure. Alas, there was once only one T.N. Seshan, who single-handedly eliminated physical force as the key element in deciding electoral outcomes; despite new technological aids, successive Commissions have not showed the spunk to take serious measures to eliminate this menace—it can be surmised that if real will is there, this is one of the easiest problems that can be addressed.

The bureaucrats are at best disinterested. Whereas the field-level functionary is steeped in corruption (though mostly on a petty case-to-case basis), the senior bureaucrat does not want to know about this. Most or many of them are probably financially honest, (though it is increasingly difficult to make this statement of late); but most of them definitely are intellectually dishonest. They will not get their hands soiled by grappling with corruption—this could ruin their career. They prefer to look the other way.

The business community actively welcomes opportunities for corrupting others. With greed they look for politicians and bureaucrats who are 'amenable', and there is no shortage of targets to stalk. So long as giving a 'bribe' is not seen as a crime in India, the businessman will look for short cuts at every turn. Indeed he has no choice; he will be left stranded in the current situation, if he doesn't play an active part as a bribe-giver.

The media has shown sporadic interest in the matter, particularly when large raids take place and the target is newsworthy. Their interest flags the moment the news-value wears off. There is no follow-up on work done by intrepid journalists. Indeed a noteworthy performance by one television channel in unearthing a major scandal is frequently totally ignored by the rest of the media. The media lives for viewership /readership percentages alone. If any fight ever raged against corruption, we had better make it newsworthy, or the media would not be involved.

One would not say much about the judiciary, for obvious reasons; all that could be said is that one has seen no marked sustained enthusiasm exhibited to combat corruption. After all, chief ministers and union ministers have had cases against them for over a decade and are happily in the public eye, controlling public affairs—we do not know if they are major benefactors to the public or just plain crooks. Perhaps the theory is that the quality of evidence will improve with age! Surely, whatever may be the reality, the public has the right to expect a verdict in short order. More complicated cases abroad are settled much quicker, particularly where personalities with impact on public issues are involved. Procedure is king—substance may wait—and the beneficiary is the legal profession and the guilty; the loser is the citizen. While one has much admiration for the major contribution by the judiciary to standing up on occasion to the shenanigans of the executive and callousness of the legislature, they have shown an astonishing level of reluctance to make changes in the system—in short, there is no justice available to the ordinary citizen—justice delayed is justice denied. Would Rajat Gupta have gone anywhere near jail in 50 years if he had been in India? The system cries for reform.

The truth is that nobody is fighting the battle against corruption; the structures have been created in such a manner that it is not in the interest of any group in joining the issue. Are we still naive enough to think that a couple of administrative measures will trigger enough significant impact on corruption. No wonder people are apathetic; civil society apparently has no role.

Corruption—linkage with backwardness

The direct linkage between backwardness and poverty on one hand, with corruption on the other has not found general recognition in India. It is no coincidence that countries high in the corruption index are generally the same as those which fall very low in the human development index—the correlation is too marked to be accidental. Surely, a country with 40% of the population living in abject poverty and another 40% quite poor, living with bare minimum standards can hardly be called a true democracy. A key reason for this is corruption. Economists and planners are generally preoccupied exclusively with economic growth; indeed many economists privately dismiss corruption as an issue, as it is merely a 'domestic transfer payment', with no impact on GDP. However, corruption has a huge impact on income transfer, and contributes to income disparity, backwardness and poverty. Its impact on equity and income distribution are most marked. While policy makers and politicians in power frequently refer to 'programmes for the poor' in a patronising manner, addressing the corruption issue effectively will be key to reducing income disparities. In fact, the 'rights' of the majority of the people have been trampled due to corruption.

Steps taken so far

In the past decade or so many significant beginnings have been made in addressing the corruption issue—the Right to Information Act and bringing technology into administration are significant steps in the right direction. Industrial and financial sector reforms have also led to near-elimination of the quota-permit raj, which are welcome. Providing competition to the public sector agencies in the services field, like banks, civil aviation etc., and introduction of technology, like in Railway bookings has reduced the impact of corruption in many sectors. Significant new initiatives on e-governance have recently been undertaken which are also in the right direction. It should, however, be added that most of these initiatives have impacted only the affluent and middle classes in India, and have not meant much for rural India and the urban poor.

The best role that can be played by a Lok Pal is to be entrusted with the role of swift, non-dilatory, impartial examination of prima facie information/ evidence. He needs to have wide-ranging powers to do this, and be enabled to act suo motu. Clearly the Lok Pal should not be allowed to become a large bureaucracy, an administrative dinosaur, whose head may not know what the tail is thinking or doing. Clearly this institution should be slim, have a specific role to play, and should have the authority to call, as the occasion demands, on the services of any other government or quasi-government agency for information, advice, or investigation. This should preclude the Lok Pal from being a 'corruption Czar', with the role to examine all actions by everybody in the country—such a move would be counter-productive—it may indeed create a parallel system which would impede the work of the legitimate government.

As has been mentioned, in the case of the civil service, there is a well-established procedure, requiring the person to stand down from office temporarily, pending investigation—this 'suspension' procedure is not deemed to be punishment or admission/declaration of 'guilt'. The official awaits the progress of the investigation, and is quickly 'reinstated' if he is exonerated at the investigation stage, or he is acquitted honorably after due process by the competent 'judicial body'. It is well established in the case of civil servants that 'suspension' is no punishment. A similar dispensation is currently not being applied in the case of the political executive, who are equally public servants. None has the 'fundamental right' to hold public office. The really effective role that the Lok Pal can play is to ask a public servant to step down from his office till he is cleared through due process in a court of law; this would be based on the assessment of the Lok Pal, taking into account the first-cut evidence, preponderance of probability and other circumstances in respect of a politician or senior bureaucrat against whom allegations have been leveled. After all there will be more harm to society in allowing a delinquent public official to hold office till he is finally convicted after exhausting all appeals, than the occasional 'miscarriage' of denying public office to an innocent person. Besides one cannot think of any politician or minister or official in the past four decades that the country would have seriously missed, if he had been denied public office!

The way forward

If there is political will at the top, the levels of corruption will definitely sharply diminish. The evidence of the last two years of governance in the Central Government since 2014 can be cited in this regard. By all accounts, corruption at policy-making levels has sharply diminished. The key has been a watchful eye from the top that decisions are taken on merit swiftly and that interested parties are not allowed to meddle in the policy-making process. If the present momentum is sustained, this is a good augury. Resort to technology, using such devices as Aadhaar card, Digital India and delegated powers to implement at the field-level with adequate supervision can go a long way to address operational corruption.

Alas, the same cannot be said now of the state governments in general. The general perception is that in nearly every state government, corruption is not only rampant, but it is gathering pace every year. Nothing can be done in all operational matters without a bribe. Surely there are honourable exceptions; alas, no chief minister has given the clear call that corruption will not tolerated and that he will take swift action against offenders. Apparently no chief minister considers this necessary—clearly his political calculation is that the voters don't care. The country will only get the 'democracy' it deserves.

A major thrust on e-governance, meaningful administrative reforms, carefully focussed judicial interventions with much greater use of 'commissioners', perceptive assistance by the media can all go to mitigate the problem to a large extent.

If there is the will, corruption is one of the easiest areas to address and tackle in a relatively short period. Hong Kong, which was known as one of the most corrupt countries in the world was able to transform itself in short order—many other examples can be cited. All insiders know of the major areas where transactional and policy corruption flourish in the country at the central and state levels. If there is determined effort, if only the ruling classes resolve to root out corruption, the levels can be drastically reduced, if not totally eliminated. Sadly the ruling classes are the main beneficiaries—it may be utopian to ask them to create a Damocles' sword to hang over their own heads.

Exemplary swift punishment of prominent cases will change the scene in short order. If people are brought to book, and in three-to-six months are given effective prison sentences, which if highly publicised, will have a powerful deterrent effect indeed. Swift, strong and exemplary highly visible punishment under the law is an important deterrent.

The Hand and the Fist: Human Rights and State Power in India

Manu Bhagavan

Introduction

As a democracy, India is perpetually guided, and restrained, by the principles laid out in the Constitution. All major disagreements are subject to judicial review, to ensure fidelity to our fundamental charter. The Constitution is a living document, and our understanding of it is informed by generations of interpretations and application, what is known in legal circles as precedent.

Of course, each clause of the Constitution was originally drafted and debated in the Constituent Assembly, which functioned from 1946 to 1950. Looking back to this time, and understanding the framers' intent, provides us with an additional, and perhaps alternate, lens through which to see the core values that have defined the idea of India, that do so now, and will continue to as the country transitions to the future. Original intent is especially important in India because of the basic structure doctrine, the idea that certain facets of the Constitution, like Fundamental Rights and Directive Principles, are so key that they cannot be altered by any act of Parliament or even by amendment.

Debates over human rights in India today often fall into one of two broad camps. The first, primarily concerned with the welfare of individual citizens and groups, demands certain kinds of interventions to help to redress current but historically informed inequities and deep-rooted discrimination. Inversely, the second begins from the premise that any authority can potentially become dangerous, and so individuals and groups must be protected from ill-informed actions as well as mal-intent. These varying perspectives mirror concerns raised at the dawn of the human rights era in discussions taking place in the United Nations: the necessity for the state to right wrongs and to actively provide for the needs of people under its care versus the necessity to check the power of the state to ensure that it did not encroach upon liberty by interfering in the private lives of individuals. With Indian leadership that saw this as the tension between duties and rights, the United Nations recognised the two different trajectories of rights, the need for them both, and the benefit accrued by harmonising the two principles, ultimately manifesting in the twin covenants on human rights, one on economic, social, and cultural rights, and one on civil and political rights. Indians were successful in pushing their point of view at the UN on the need for both types of rights, in part because they themselves had adopted a similar framework in their new Constitution, distinguishing between Fundamental Rights and Directive Principles.

Kanaiyalal Maneklal Munshi, a famed lawyer who had been involved in innovative Indian constitutional initiatives in the princely states from the 1920's, had driven much of this conversation in the Constituent Assembly. Munshi saw himself as a staunch democrat as well as close friend and ally of Mahatma Gandhi. When the two disagreed in the 1930s over the creation of *akhadas* (gymnasia), Munshi was taken aback but held firm to his views, leading to his departure from the Indian National Congress shortly thereafter. But by the late 1940s, with the ending of World War II and new challenges looming on the horizon, Gandhi invited Munshi to rejoin the Congress. In the intervening years, Munshi had grown more concerned with identity politics, and he often focused his attention on ways democratic representation could be made to shore up the will of majorities. Still, Munshi leapt at the opportunity Gandhi offered and proudly recast himself above mere ideology. As a proclaimed nonpartisan, interested only in thinking through each issue fully and to its logical conclusion, he offered powerful counterpoints to many of his colleagues' opinions. As a result, Munshi was at the center of many of the Assembly's biggest debates, especially those that dealt with human rights.

This essay attempts to grapple with the central tension at the heart of rights discourse: where to draw the line when empowering the state so that it might provide a hand to the underprivileged and dispossessed while simultaneously shielding individuals from an overreaching state's fist. Through an analysis of constitutional debates that hinged on the placement of this line, notably in conversations featuring Munshi over a due process clause, this chapter will hopefully illuminate the kinds of challenges that society faces today as it seeks to best implement international human rights norms.

What Rights Fundamental?

In 1946, the British Prime Minister Clement Attlee announced that there would be a Cabinet Mission to lay the groundwork for constitutional creation and a transfer of power to a new government in India. Over the next several months, the Mission came up with several ideas, and eventually settled on a constituent assembly comprised of members indirectly elected from existing legislative assemblies.

The plan did not meet the demands of the Muslim League, and of Muhammad Ali Jinnah, whose primary concern was the category of the minority. He wanted parity between Hindus and Muslims so that both would be seen and treated equally by the other. After considerable back and forth, the League eventually opted to stay out of the new assembly.

The League's ultimate decision, really only finalised towards the end of 1946 and just before the Constituent Assembly met for the first time, made moot the plan's rejection of a proposed 'proportional representation' scheme put forward earlier by K.M. Munshi. In 1934, Mahatma Gandhi had asked Munshi to draft a note on what a constituent assembly for India might look like. Munshi produced a document that explored the historical nature and purpose of constituent assemblies around the world, touching on Montesquieu and Rousseau and the Congress of Philadelphia before lingering on steps taken within the British Commonwealth.

Gandhi edited the piece before Munshi published it in July in the *Hindustan Times*.[1] The takeaway was that constituent assemblies might be formed in one of only two ways. The first, which Munshi claimed was used in countries 'where Anglo-Saxon influences predominate' allowed assembly members to be elected from 'provincial bodies' which themselves may or may not have been comprised of members put there by unrepresentative elections. The second option, which Munshi claimed was 'the only one which [would] suit India,' was 'achieved by adopting adult suffrage and proportional representation, which is more or less a scientific form of providing separate electorates.' Munshi's 'science' was really a reactionary response to Ramsay MacDonald's Communal Award of 1932, which provided for separate electorates to provincial legislatures. The Cabinet Mission Plan meant that

Munshi would not get what he wished, which he saw as essential from a majoritarian perspective, but the ever-shifting terrain on which the game was being played meant that it perhaps did not matter as much as he feared.

The Mission's Plan took up some of the aspirational elements of the Nehru Report[2] and agreed that questions of fundamental rights had to be discussed and spelled out, and that the Constituent Assembly had subsequently to grapple with whether and in what manner to include such rights. One of the reasons for the Cabinet Mission's support for listing rights, a departure from British tradition, was that support was building globally at precisely the same moment for something called 'human rights'. The new United Nations, created in 1945 in the aftermath of World War II, was preliminarily grappling with these matters, and the ongoing Nuremberg Trials were revealing how far-reaching human injustice could truly go without proper checks. The Interim Government of India, formed as a result of the plan with Jawaharlal Nehru at the helm in September of 1946, spearheaded the proto-conceptualisation of human rights when Nehru's sister, Vijaya Lakshmi Pandit, led India's delegation to the UN to a rousing victory over South Africa over the question of its treatment of people of Indian origin within its borders.

By this point, Nehru had already begun to formulate the broad contours of an integrated international and domestic grand strategy meant to bring about a radical vision for the world that he and Gandhi jointly shared. Internationalist in nature, Nehru's vision was one in which the new India was but the prototype for a new transnational order, one where people would move freely within and between states while protected by a universal constitution centered around 'human rights'.[3]

So the work of the Fundamental Rights Subcommittee (which began its task in February 1947, shortly after the Objectives Resolution passed and gave breath and purpose to the Constituent Assembly) was truly 'fundamental', not only because it was going to be a true break from the colonially imbricated legal past, and not only because it was going to wield tremendous influence over the course of any new state to emerge, but also because its decisions would also have an impact internationally. The fact that Hansa Mehta sat on both this committee and the UN's Commission on Human Rights reinforced this conclusion.

Munshi was influential from the start, always drafting the preliminary documents on which subsequent discussion or debate followed in whole or in part. Munshi loosely categorised the committee into three groups: the drastic leftists, the idealists, and the pragmatists. K.T. Shah was the only member of the first group, while Hansa Mehta, Rajkumari Amrit Kaur, and M.R. Masani comprised the second. Munshi, along with the rest, including Ambedkar, were in the last group.

One of the first issues to come up was what nature of rights were to be included in the Constitution. Munshi, along with Sir Alladi Krishnaswami Aiyar, argued that rights had to be enforceable by law, and urged that the American and Irish models be used as templates. K.T. Shah and Sardar Harnam Singh both argued that there was another type of rights, 'precepts', that should also be considered, and Singh referenced the Soviet model as an example of a constitutional framework built on these.[4]

Munshi was opposed to placing non-justiciable rights into the Constitution, claiming that such directive principles would overly restrict the parliament, which he felt had to be unfettered in making its policy, provided they were in line with Fundamental Rights.[5] Most of the committee disagreed, and Hansa Mehta and Rajkumari Amrit Kaur were particularly adamant, so ultimately both categories of rights were included in the sub-committee's recommendations, justiciable composing Fundamental Rights, and those considered non-justiciable making up Directive Principles. Mehta and Kaur emphasised that they believed that both types of rights were 'fundamental' and that the state had a duty to carry out the principles, even if no entity could actually go to court over them. Their wording was placed virtually verbatim into Article 37 of the final Constitution.[6]

Munshi never accepted the argument that both types of rights were equal, instead arguing that the types of rights were tiered, and that justiciable civil and political liberties had to be considered superior and more important. So if legislation were to be passed promoting the Directive Principles, signposts for moving society in a particular progressive direction in the economic, social, and cultural sphere, it had to 'conform to and run as subsidiary to the Chapter on Fundamental Rights'.[7]

Years later, Munshi railed against what he saw as the breakdown of Fundamental Rights facilitated by mechanisms to promote the Directive Principles. The villain? The very legislature that Munshi had originally argued had to be free from undue constraints on its freedom to enact policy as it saw fit, only encumbered by a commitment to Fundamental Rights.[8]

The Hand and the Fist

There was not necessarily any inconsistency in Munshi's positions, since he saw civil and political liberties as fundamental in both his original comments and his later ones, and argued that anything that impinged on them was problematic. But an alternate reading is that Munshi was disturbed that the parliament was moving in a direction that he disliked, one that bound the state to deliver on obligations to its citizens. The idea of rights and obligations had expressly been laid out by K.T. Shah in the first subcommittee meeting, and Mehta and Kaur had embedded the word 'duty' into the article defining the nature of the principles.[9] That Munshi's was more of a politically enabled concern than an authentic defense of Fundamental Rights qua Fundamental Rights is underscored by the fact that he defended his point of view, claiming:

> None of us who were connected intimately with the drafting of the Fundamental Rights and Directive Principles ever envisaged that the firm foundation of guaranteed Fundamental Rights could be dislodged by currently accredited theories sponsored by the Legislature and read into the Directive Principles. It is true that where there are competing demands of social control allegedly exercised for the welfare of the people and of liberty, there should be reasonable accommodation between them; but it is the function of the Courts to see that such accommodation does not imply the surrender of Fundamental Rights.[10]

Here Munshi simply denies that others on the committee saw the directive principles as equally fundamental. His acknowledgement that the boundary between justiciable and non-justiciable rights was negotiable only serves to highlight that he felt that the line was drawn in the wrong place. But why? The answer I believe lies in Munshi's majoritarian proclivities, his preference for 'proportional representation', and his observation regarding social control. This can be better seen in the debate that ensued over a due process clause.

Munshi described the due process clause as one of 'the most controversial topics in framing the Constitution'.[11] He felt that the clause was a necessity to protect democracy from 'extreme positions'. On 3 April 1947, the Sub-Committee submitted its report to the Advisory Committee detailing its overall recommendations, which, for the most part, moved forward and were adopted as formal constitutional clauses. One exception was item number 11, listed under the 'Rights to Freedom', that read: 'No person shall be deprived of his life, liberty or property without due process of the law'.[12] The passage was almost verbatim taken from the Vth and XIVth Amendments of the United States' Constitution.[13] Some members of the Advisory Committee objected to the use of the word property, so it was stricken from the sentence adopted, and now known as Clause 9, by the full Constituent Assembly on 30 April 1947.[14]

Munshi believed that property had to be protected, but he was satisfied with giving ground here, since he thought he would win the property fight elsewhere—a fascinating debate worthy of analysis in its own right, but unfortunately outside the scope of this chapter. The new due process clause had near unanimous support in the Constituent Assembly. Yet the article that ultimately made it into the Indian Constitution reads: 'No person shall be deprived of his life or personal liberty except according to procedure established by law'. What happened?

The new language, which avoided the phrase 'due process' altogether, came from the new Constitution of Japan, created in 1946. And liberty was personal to precisely exclude property (and contract).

The shift began when US Supreme Court Justice Felix Frankfurter reviewed a draft version of the Indian Constitution. Frankfurter warned against the due process clause, arguing that it had caused 'many complications' in the US. The Justice was an ally of former President Franklin Roosevelt, who had named him to the court in 1939. Frankfurter stood for judicial restraint, which meant that he generally wanted the Legislature to make decisions and that he believed in upholding judicial precedent.

The key issue had to do with the difference between *procedural* due process and its much more muscular cousin, *substantive* due process. Essentially, the former mandates that the government has to follow a set of clear rules and steps in enacting laws that affect individuals and that theoretically might contravene their fundamental rights. The latter grants to individuals the power to 'do or possess certain things' even if the government desires otherwise.[15] While in the abstract substantive due process appears an important mechanism to protect against a runaway state, in practice in the United States substantive due process was seen by many as a possible tool to block the freight train that was the New Deal.[16]

Frankfurter's concerns swayed several members of the Drafting Committee, most notably Ambedkar, who switched his previous position in support of the due process clause to the modified Japanese-based procedural language. The issue exploded into a fierce debate in the main Assembly on 6 December 1948, where an amendment was offered to reinsert the due process phrase, and Pandit Thakur Dass Bhargava explicitly claimed that 'due process' empowered courts to investigate both procedural and substantive matters.[17] Munshi agreed and chimed in:

> Now, the question we have to consider, I submit, is only this. What are the implications of this 'due process'? 'Due process' is now confined to personal liberty. This clause would enable the courts to examine not only the procedural part, the jurisdiction of the court, the jurisdiction of the legislature, but also the substantive law. When a law has been passed which entitles Government to take away the personal liberty of an individual, the court will consider whether the law which has been passed is such as is required by the exigencies of the case, and, therefore, as I said, the balance will be struck between individual liberty and the social control.[18]

Ambedkar too agreed for the most part, and largely saw a need for a due process clause to protect against state overreach, buttressing an example Munshi provided of an unchecked police force, but he also saw danger in relying on a small number of justices to know better than elected representatives. As a result, Ambedkar decided not to advocate for one position over the other, and the due process amendment as a whole went down to defeat, leaving only the procedural language in the final Constitution.

For Munshi, the central question in the due process debate, as with justiciability, involved the tension between 'individual liberty' and social control. And this, I believe, stemmed from, and was determined by, a majoritarian viewpoint. This is a connection that cannot be made using Munshi's public comments from the time, though context provided by other writings and actions from the 1940s lends credence to the claim.[19]But in commentary he later provides for a retrospective collection of documents related to his work on the Constitution, Munshi at last reveals the real concerns animating his actions. Talking about religious freedom, part of the Fundamental Rights package he had appeared to so consistently and ardently defend, he lamented that in the name of secularism, politicians in power adopt a strange attitude which, while it condones the susceptibilities, religious and social, of the minority communities, is too ready to brand similar susceptibilities in the majority community as communalistic and reactionary.

> These unfortunate postures have been creating a sense of frustration in the majority community. If, however...every time there is an inter-communal conflict, the majority is blamed regardless of the merits of the question; if our holy places...continue to be converted into industrial slums by establishing huge industries, the springs of traditional tolerance will dry up. While the majority exercises patience and tolerance, the minorities should learn to adjust themselves to the majority; otherwise the future is uncertain, and an explosion cannot be avoided.[20]

In his initial 1934 note on constituent assemblies, Munshi had argued that proportional representation was necessary for a constituent assembly to be viable and legitimate in India. When his plan was not adopted, Munshi then argued that the constitution should guarantee only civil and political liberties, justiciable rights, because positive, non-justiciable rights might otherwise hamper the parliament, which had to be free to pass laws as it saw fit, provided they did not interfere with Fundamental Rights. His position not adopted, Munshi then pushed fiercely for a due process clause which would empower the judiciary to pass judgment on substantive law, thereby placing a check on parliament that might otherwise unduly infringe upon people's rights. And that tactic too failed in favor of procedural protections. Munshi's sour position on religious freedom then undermined his stated commitment to Fundamental Rights. Without the focus on Fundamental Rights, Munshi's designs appear much more about majoritarian power. The parliament had to reign supreme, until it was mandated to progressively provide for the needs of all its citizens to the best of its ability. Then Munshi feared the parliament, a potentially aggressive body no longer restricted to the will of the majority that conceivably could use its power to force even the majority to abide by rules, possibly even in the name of protecting the minority. Substantive due process was conceived of as a means to then shield the majority from an overactive parliament, in a way that popular perception suggested had been attempted in the United States to halt the New Deal.

All of these efforts to insert majoritarianism into the constitution-making process, and in the resultant constitution as well, were rejected. Munshi remained proud of the democratic state that emerged, but his resentment at perceived leftist ascendance, and his overall bitterness with India's direction grew ever more palpable. During the 1950s, as Kulapati of the Bharatiya Vidhya Bhavan, Munshi turned from the world of policy-making and the law to that of culture to make his mark.[21] His efforts culminated in the effort to rebuild the Somnath Temple. Despite success in these areas, Munshi remained concerned with battles he had lost and recast himself as a forlorn Cassandra, wise but unheeded and frustrated by his own marginality.

Conclusion

K.M. Munshi's majoritarian vision for India's Constituent Assembly and resultant constitution was, for the most part, rejected, as exemplified by the triple loss he suffered, illustrated in this chapter. But the concerns that came up during the due process debate, and the positions that various assembly members took, make clear the complexity of nearly every question that came before the body. While Munshi may have been tactically manoeuvring for his larger majoritarian strategic objective, his warnings of a police run amok ring eerily true in today's India. Ambedkar too saw the great danger in a state that did not fear to trample on Fundamental Rights, though his conception included both the justiciable and non-justiciable kinds.

We must be wary, though, of drawing too straight a line from the constitutional creation of the late 1940s to any particular crises currently consuming India. The Constitution, as the founders foresaw and intended, is a flexible, living, and breathing document. Current predicaments stem not from the document itself, but in its political implementation over the last sixty odd years. There are no easy answers. But the cacophonous voices of the Constituent Assembly nonetheless remind us that engaging in debate is key to ever more effectively negotiating the boundary between a strong state necessary to break the chains of inequality, and a state that is a threat to the civil liberties and fundamental freedoms of its citizens.

Endnotes

1 K.M. Munshi, *Indian Constitutional Documents,* [hereafter *IDC*] *Volume II* (Bombay: Bharatiya Vidya Bhavan, 1967), pp. 1-5. See also *Volume I*, pp. 33-41.

2 In 1927, an all-white commission was created at the behest of Viceroy Lord Irwin and Secretary of State for India Lord Birkenhead to explore constitutional reforms in the Indian subcontinent. The British were late to the game, as a number of constitutional initiatives had already been launched in princely states over the course of the 1920s, largely at the behest of Sir Manubhai Mehta, with supporting counsel from Munshi and a number of others. So it particularly stuck in many an anti-colonialist craw when Birkenhead proclaimed that he could find no 'Indians' qualified to serve on such a body. Facing controversy, the Secretary of State stepped back and offered to consider any indigenous alternative put forward. People from many different organisations and backgrounds collaborated to create what became known as the Nehru Report, after the chair of the drafting committee, Motilal Nehru, and its secretary, his son Jawaharlal. The report, only meant to set signposts for a constitution, not to serve as one, departed from British constitutional tradition to an extent by including a specific section on Fundamental Rights. While rights were not enumerated in any detail, the report declared in favour of religious freedom and the equality of all citizens. See *Ibid.*, *Vol. I*, pp. 19-28.

3 See Manu Bhagavan, *The Peacemakers: India and the Quest for One World* (New Delhi: Harper Collins, 2012).

4 B. Shiva Rao, *The Framing of India's Constitution: Select Documents,* [hereafter *TFICSD*] *Volume* 2 (Delhi: Universal Law Publishing, 2006, 1st published 1967), Minutes of the Meetings of the Subcommittee on Fundamental Rights, February 1947, pp. 114-116.

5 Munshi, *IDC, Vol. I,* p. 296.

6 This in turn became the basis for Indian efforts to split the International Covenant of Human Rights into two, one on Civil and Political Rights, and the other on Economic, Social, and Cultural Rights.

7 Munshi, writing in 1967, quoting a 1951 court case, *Madras v Champakam.*

8 See Munshi, *IDC, Vol. I,* pp. 291–321.

9 Minutes of the Sub-Committee, *TFICSD, Vol.* 2, pp. 115, 147.

10 Munshi, *IDC, Vol. I,* p. 297.

11 Ibid.

12 Draft Report of the Sub-Committee, 3 April 1947, *TFICSD, Vol.* 2, p. 139. Cf. Munshi, *IDC, Vol. I,* p. 298.

13 B.N. Rau,'Notes on the Draft Report,' *TFICSD, Vol.* 2, p. 148.

14 http://parliamentofindia.nic.in/ls/debates/vol3p3.htm; Munshi, *IDC, Vol. I,* p. 298.

15 http://www.stanford.edu/group/psylawseminar/Substantive%20Due%20 Process.htm

16 There is some debate as to whether or not the New Deal led to the 'abandonment' of substantive due process. See G. Edward White, *The Constitution and the New*

Deal (Cambridge: Harvard University Press, 2001, 1st published 2000), p. 309. One opinion held that critics of the New Deal were particularly vocal in defending substantive due process, and this in turn would have been on Frankfurter's mind. More investigation of these issues is required.

17 http://parliamentofindia.nic.in/ls/debates/vol7p20b.htm

18 Ibid.

19 See my observations on some of Munshi's actions as Agent-General of Hyderabad during the police action. 'The Hindutva Underground: Hindu Nationalism and the Indian National Congress in Late Colonial and Early Postcolonial India,' *The Economic and Political Weekly*, XLIII (37), 13 September 2008: pp. 39-48.

20 Munshi, *IDC, Vol. 1*, p. 312.

21 'The Hindutva Underground,' pp. 43-45.

Debating Judicial Reforms in India

Sukanya Natarajan

Typically, countries are interested in restructuring institutions to increase their economic performance. Scholars such as Douglas North allude that the rate of economic growth is reliant upon the operation of a country's social, economic, legal and political institutions.[1] There is abundant literature on the role played by structural reforms in facilitating economic development in particular instances of individual countries such as India. Policymakers and academics have keenly sought to comprehend the affiliation linking legal institutions and judicial reforms with economic growth. This quest has been motivated by a dedicated interest in understanding how the legal apparatus aids in poverty reduction. Enormous literature exists in perceiving the connection between legal apparatus, judicial reforms, and economic development, particularly in developing countries.[2]

In the past, many scholars have devoted themselves to understanding myriad factors including that of a country's legal apparatus that ascertains and establishes the link between economic growth and development and thereby have sought to comprehend the link connecting law with economic growth.[3] Some of these studies reveal the following outcomes: predictability and transparency, minimal judicial corruption, legal proceedings without delays, and augmentation in investment atmosphere for overseas investors to trigger economic development.[4] Existing literature suggests that in order to sustain and promote economic growth, efficient legal apparatus, and enforcement of laws are compulsory. Kenneth Dam argues that there exists a strong connection between legal apparatus and economic development. He claims:

> No degree of substantive law improvement—even world 'best practice' substantive law—will bring the Rule of Law to a country without effective enforcement. Rule of law, in the primary economic sense of protecting property and enforcing contracts, requires a judiciary to resolve disputes between private parties. And protection against the state itself is made easier where the judiciary can resolve a controversy raised by a private party against the state based on constitutional provisions or parliamentary legislation. One conclusion widely agreed upon, not just in the economic literature but also among lawyers and legal scholars, is therefore that the judiciary is a vital factor in the Rule of law and more broadly in economic development.[5]

To understand the role of law in influencing economic development in the Indian context, research commissioned by the Asian Development Bank which was later published as a book by scholars including T.C.A. Anant and M.L. Mitra, put forth the following inquiry: 'Did law matter for economic development in India between 1960 and 1995?'[6] Also published as a Development Discussion Paper for the Harvard Institute for Economic Development, the findings are as follows:

> In the early periods, the changes enhanced the procedural discretion of the bureaucracy, which began to decline in the last period. Also in the early periods, the legal changes gave the State increasing power over the allocation of resources, which also declined during the last period. In an interesting finding, compared to many of the other countries in the study, the judiciary emerged as a major challenger of executive power during the early periods and a major defender of certain economic rights in the later period. So while law and legal institutions tended to follow economic strategy, at least one institution, the Supreme Court played an important independent role.[7]

Legal scholars such as Fali Nariman, Soli Sorabjee, and Upendra Baxi argue that the supreme court holds a crucial position in determining the political, social, and economic progress in the country. On the contrary, there is an argument that confirms that India's courts in the process of protecting civil rights as well as political rights might not contribute to economic growth.[8]

Investors who come to India and citizens who live within are bothered by judicial corruption, lack of resources, long delays, pendency of cases and largely view the system as inefficient.[9] Many legal luminaries have appreciated the essential features of the Indian legal apparatus before analysing the challenges that judicial reforms pose and its impact on the current situation as well future scenario of the Indian economy. In India, there exists an indispensable interplay with respect to judicial independence and judicial accountability. Judicial institutions act as an important check on the executive and legislative branches of the Indian government. The chapter critically assesses the diverse challenges pertaining to judicial reforms.

Scholars such as Stephenson claim that three main issues crop up when judicial reforms are being discussed.[10] He claims: in order to improve the efficiency of a judicial apparatus, one requires financial as well as human resources that fall in diminutive supply in developing countries, consequently, the possibility of the judiciary to bear a helpful role in promoting development depends on the compliance of concerned parties to make use of the courts for settling disputes.[11]

'Justice delayed is justice denied' is a familiar phrase one comes across, whenever the Indian legal system is discussed and debated.[12] Before we proceed to discuss the same, it is important to understand the history, configuration, and pathologies of judicial pendency of cases. The Indian judicial system is a three-tiered system with roughly 16,000 courts[13] under the helm of the supreme court of India[14] headed by the chief justice of India (CJI). The supreme court has a total approved strength of 31 judges, out of which there are 6 vacancies at present.[15] High courts have a total sanctioned strength of 1,056 judges, out of which there are 465 vacancies.[16] Smaller district level courts have an approximate vacancy number of 4,432 judges yet to be appointed out of the sanctioned strength of 20,502 judges. There is shortage of courtrooms for the sanctioned strength of 21,589 judges. Therefore, judicial infrastructure has to be improved and given priority.

In a globalised economy, especially when the present government is keen to win over investors from all over the world, specialised commercial courts are being set up recently to deal with investors' issues and problems.[17] A recent Law Commission report noted that the US and UK courts are increasingly admitting cases which technically should have been filed before the Indian courts on the ground that in India almost all cases consume 25 years for disposal.[18] Commenting on the setting up of commercial courts, the CJI[19] claimed that 'simply putting old wine in a new bottle will not serve the purpose'. As a solution, the CJI proposed that retired judges be hired for 2–3 years to dispose cases that are delayed for more than 10 years.[20]

Judicial reforms need to be systemically implemented not in a haphazard piecemeal manner with appropriate importance given to solving the problem of judicial delays and judicial appointments. In this context, it is important that India streamline its judicial system to be effective and make judicial reforms an integral part of the economic reform agenda. Permanent Member of the NITI Aayog,[21] Bibek Debroy claims that there are three layers to judicial reform in the case of India. He states:

> First, there is an element of statutory law reform weeding out old and dysfunctional elements in legislation, unification and harmonization. Second, legal reform has to have an administrative law reform component, meaning the subordinate legislation in the form of rules, orders, regulations and instructions from ministries and government departments. Third, the element of legal reform is what may be called judicial reforms, though faster dispute resolution and contract enforcement are not exclusively judicial issues.[22]

Debroy discusses how to further efficiency within the judiciary in India.

> Court cases will not disappear even if demand is brought down. Therefore, the efficiency of disposal also needs to be improved. Other than lengthy legal procedures, a need for more judges and filling up vacancies in time invariably figures in any cataloguing of the efficiency problem. There is a mandatory and Constitutional obligation on the part of the President to periodically assess needs of various High Courts and appoint additional judges wherever necessary. But in practice, even sanctioned positions of judges are left vacant. It may be argued that Chief Justices must play a more active role in determining the judge strength and this must be enshrined in law. The President also has the power to appoint additional judges for a period of two years at a time. The appointment of additional judges was for the express reason of reducing the load of over-burdened High Courts. However,

> this provision has been misused. With the same number of judges, it is possible to increase court productivity.[23]

Debroy and Hazra's work on judicial reforms in India examines how economic understanding of judicial reforms is not necessarily the correct approach as they measure efficiency of the system largely pertaining to property rights, enforcement of contracts and maintenance of order. Their contribution reviews property and contract laws in addressing legal and judicial problems listing few of them such as judicial strength, judicial productivity, judicial infrastructure and management of judicial administration.[24] Arun Mohan in *Courts, Justice and Delays* argues that delayed justice slows down economic development and growth. He claims:

> A proper set of laws that are fine-tuned and an efficient judicial system that acts as an accelerant while an improper set of law, tardy justice, poor governance and inefficient administration act as a retardant. An inefficient law and justice system could become a dead weight to development efforts. An agreement or a business transaction must be enforceable at law and so in a reasonable time. The ability of the law to settle matters quickly and make itself more agile is imperative. The greater the justice system's support the faster is the growth of the economy and therefore development.[25]

Several scholars have attempted to understand the link between the judiciary and the India story on economic development by assessing the quality of the legal systems according to various parameters. In addition to work carried out by Bibek Debroy and Hazra, Wolfgang Koehling worries about the significance of speedy legal proceedings as opposed to pendency, backlog of cases, and predictability of the outcome of the cases.[26] Mathhieu Chemin advanced a game theoretical model to appreciate the manner in which efficiency of the Indian legal system would disturb the contracting behavior of firms. Chemin's asserts that negative implications of having an inefficient judiciary are enormous.[27]

Nick Robinson's work throws light on the manner in which the supreme court micromanages and undermines the judicial system rather than focusing on the pendency and backlog of the cases.[28] Robinson analysed the Indian

Supreme Court docket from 1993 to 2011 and concludes that court data is imperfect in a certain way.[29] He further claims that the number and the type of cases the court accepts rather than having far fewer judges who handle the cases cause the backlog. He argues that 'the low barriers to petitioning to the supreme court, combined with the high percentage of cases the court ultimately accepts, lie at the root of the high backlog'. He presents the international system of admission policy in other countries to give a broader context to his argument.[30] He argues:[31]

> The Supreme Court has centralized judicial authority in Delhi, micromanaging the decisions of the rest of the judicial system, with seemingly counterproductive results. By taking on so many cases, the Supreme Court instead of clarifying precedent has confused it. Instead of making the system more accessible, it has normalised an expensive layer of appeal that the wealthy and those closer to Delhi are best positioned to navigate. The current arrangement has enriched Supreme Court lawyers but arguably weakened the health of the rest of the judicial system.

Robinson argues that despite this situation, the 'Supreme Court by and large remains popular. Yet, if one digs a bit, beneath the surface is an institution that has strayed from its mission and may even be undermining the rest of the judicial system.'[32] He demonstrates how the supreme court centralises and creates uncertainty deliberately. He claims: 'Such an extremely active Supreme Court demoralises High Court and lower court judges, who now have difficulty determining what the law actually is, and exasperates litigants, who can now expect that any given case will be appealed to the Supreme Court, which means squandering years and money in the process'.[33] He argues that public interest litigation and important constitutional cases have a high entry barrier as opposed to the other cases. He claims that increasing the number of judges alone will not solve the backlog problem.

The traditional understanding of the literature available on the supreme court portrayed how the main advantage lay in understanding how the importance of judiciary lay in checking abuses of state power, enforcing property rights, enabling exchanges between private entities, as well as ensuring public order. Presently, there is a proposal in the public domain on creating a

National Court of Appeal to reduce the burden on the Supreme Court so that it may only consider matters pertaining to constitutional law and public law.[34]

The Chief Justice of India, T.S. Thakur in April 2016 during a public address in the presence of Prime Minister Narendra Modi put forth an emotional appeal to escalate the number of judges from the present number of 21,000 to 40,000 judges. He cited the 1987 Law Commission report, which recommended increasing judges per 10 lakh of the population from 10 to 50.[35] Barry Walsh's work on judicial productivity in India depicts a stark comparison that the disposal ratio in Australian courts was twice that of India in the year 2005.[36] In April 2015, Law Minister Sadananda Gowda claimed that about 18.9 million cases were pending in subordinate courts as of 2014, whereas in higher courts the cases stood at 89,164 cases. In April 2016, the Chief Justice of India, Thakur showcased the historical perspective on pendency of cases during his address. He claims:

> The apex court came into being in 1950; it had strength of 8 judges, including the CJI with 1,215 cases pending. Then, he said, the pendency was 100 cases per judge. In 1960, the strength of the SC rose to 14 judges and the cases increased to 3,247. In 1977, the strength was 18 and the cases were 14,501. By 2009, as is the case today, the strength of SC judges rose to 31 and the pending cases spiralled by 77,181. In 2014, the cases were 81,582 which were reduced to 60,260. On December 2 when I took over as CJI and now, 17,482 cases were filed out of which 16,474 cases were disposed. The high courts have over 38 lakh cases to dispose and the number is increasing.[37]

The 20th Law Commission submitted its recommendations for judicial reforms to foster economic growth in January 2015. The report shows 32,656 civil suits are pending in 5 high courts, an increase of 6.27 per cent in pendency every year as noted, overload of cases on few judges, for e.g., the Madras High Court contains only 4 judges who were disproportionately allocated 41,702 cases pending on the original jurisdiction.[38] The report discusses the 'Commercial and Commercial Appellate Division of High Courts and Commercial Courts Bill, 2015' that includes promised increase in the judicial strength of high courts which was passed in December 2015 and became an act in January 2016.[39] Commercial Divisions are being set up in high courts with ordinary original civil jurisdiction relating to commercial disputes. Commercial courts (comparable to district level courts) are being set up in states and Union territories where the high courts do not have ordinary original civil jurisdiction. The Chief Justice of India in April 2016 criticised and appealed to the government that merely creating new commercial courts without improving infrastructure[40] and the judge pool would not serve the purpose.[41] For a historical perspective of pendency and disposal, see Figure 1, for an overview of pendency in commercial disputes see Figures 2, 3, and 4.

Figure 1: Historical Perspective: Supreme Court Case Status—Admission, Disposal and Pendency

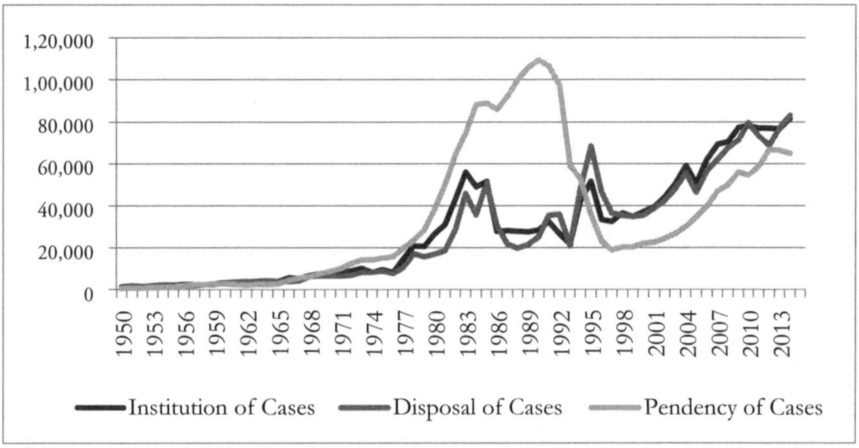

Source: Annual Report 2014-15, Supreme Court of India.[42]

Figure 2: Percentage of Commercial Disputes in High Courts with Original Jurisdiction

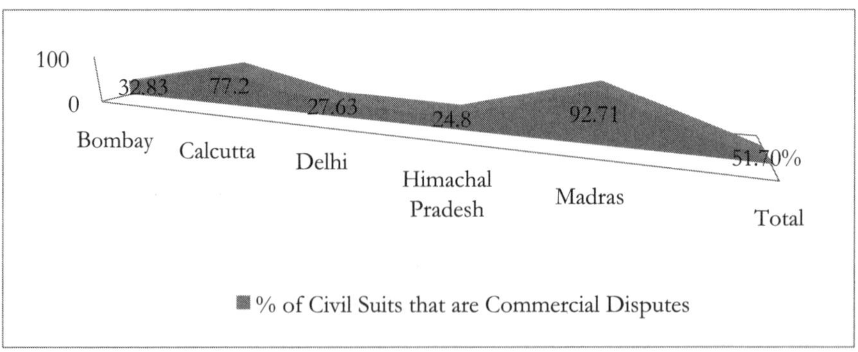

Source: The Law Commission of India Report no 253, 2015, Ministry of Law and Justice, India.[43]

Figure 3: Pendency of Commercial Disputes in High Courts with Original Jurisdiction

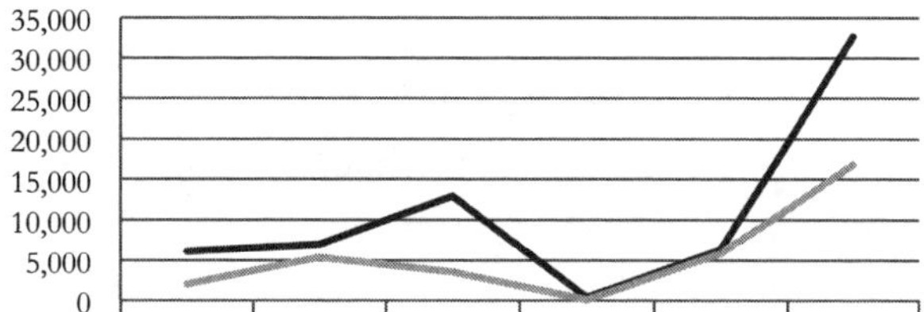

	Bombay	Calcutta	Delhi	Himachal Pradesh	Madras	Total
Total Number of Civil Suits Pending	6,081	6,932	12,963	354	6,326	32,656
Total Number of Commercial Disputes Pending	1,997	5,352	3,582	88	5,865	16,884

Source: The Law Commission of India Report no 253, 2015, Ministry of Law and Justice, India.

Figure 4: Breakdown of Delays in Disposal of Civil Suits in Each High Court with Original Civil Jurisdiction

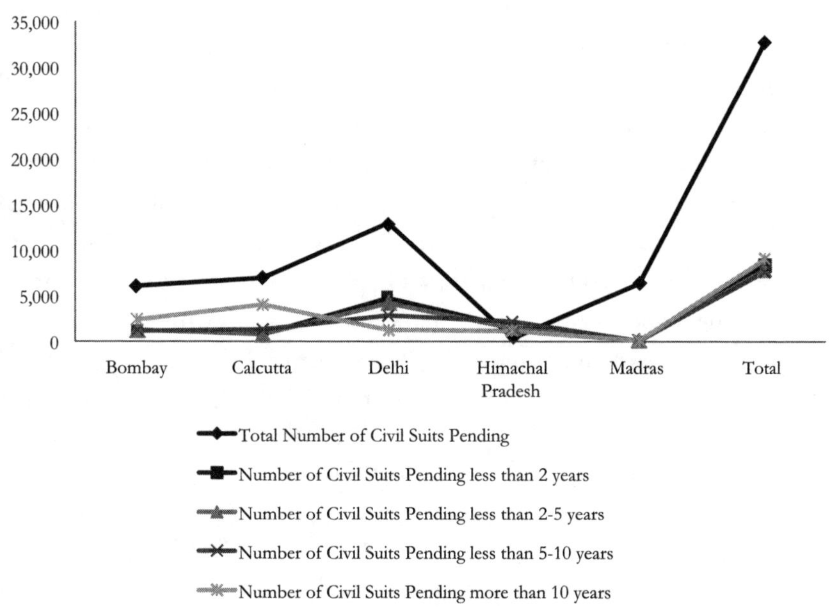

Source: The Law Commission of India Report no 253, 2015, Ministry of Law and Justice, India.

As per the bill, the power to constitute commercial vision within high courts or commercial courts will now lie with the central government.[44] To establish these commercial courts, new norms of practice will be set up for commercial litigation, which can be expanded to civil litigation in India. Some measures to be introduced include e-courts, online operations to maintain voluminous accounting, and efficacy of functioning.[45]

In addition, judges of commercial courts will be made to undergo training at the National judicial academy that will improve the level of exposure. In terms of court infrastructure, better maintenance of court records, digitisation of proceedings of commercial courts and e-filing as well as facilities for audio visual recording will be instituted.[46] From the increase in commercial dispute definition to speedy disposal of cases and effective training of the judiciary, the law commission has suggested the enhancement of professionalism of the Indian legal system.

In the context of broader judicial reforms being discussed about, the judicial accountability bill has been long dormant due to some of the clauses proposed to lay down prescribed codes of conduct for the supreme court judges as well as the judges of the high courts. The judicial standards and accountability bill which was passed by the previous government in the Lok Sabha in 2012, essentially tries to lay down enforceable standards of conduct for judges, in addition requiring judges to declare details of their assets as well as liabilities.[47] This bill lapsed soon after, once the dissolution of the 15th Lok Sabha took place.

In May 2015, the present government delayed introduction of the Judicial Standards and Accountability Bill until the announcement of the National Judicial Appointments Commission (NJAC) was made. The passage was intended to swap the collegium system of appointing judges to the Supreme Court and the higher courts to usher in transparency in the judiciary. The Bill was passed by the parliament in August 2014.[48] Later, 16 Indian states ratified the bill ultimately assented by the President of India in December 2014.The NJAC Act came into being in April 2015. In October 2015, both the NJAC Act as well as the 99th amendment to the Indian Constitution made by the Parliament were obliterated by the Supreme Court in the SCAORA Vs Union of India (Fourth Judges Case).[49]

Public intellectuals like Pratap Bhanu Mehta point out that the method of appointing judges through a system of collegiums of judges, had excluded the other branches of government. He says:

> The current method of appointment was a usurpation of sorts. Some input from outside is important. Judging is too important to be left only to judges. In this light, the proposed NJAC is worth trying. The formal arguments against it are weak. It is not a violation of the basic structure, another fuzzy judicial invention that served an institutional purpose but has no principled basis if used indiscriminately. The mere presence of non-judicial members on a committee to appoint judges does not compromise independence. Is there a potential conflict in that the government is a major litigator and this puts the chief justice directly in a 'negotiating' position with it? Possibly. But our apprehensions on this come more from our lack of faith in our chief justices.[50]

The main responsibility of the commission was to recommend and oversee the appointment of chief justice of India, supreme court judges, chief justices of high courts and high court judges. The purpose of the commission was intended to make sure that the persons suggested are of capability, excellence, and other criteria to be satisfied by the office of the high court/ supreme court judge.[51] Indira Jaising argues that an assessment of the new law introduced to appoint judges will make the independent judiciary subservient to the executive and that it poses a fundamental challenge to the Constitution and Indian democracy. According to her, the long pending calls for transparency and accountability for judges and for instituting the judiciary as a more inclusive institution have been long-forgotten in these aforementioned new bills.[52]

After the supreme court quashed the NJAC and declared the constitutional amendment as unconstitutional. It maintained that the previous collegium system will continue and that it is open to bring changes in the collegium system. Due to this logjam on the judicial appointments, no appointments were made for almost a year. The 22-year-old collegium system set up in 1993 has no explicit mention in the Indian Constitution, although it has been deemed constitutional so far. Furthermore, in several countries across the world, the executive is a part of the appointment process of judges, unlike India. The tussles between the executive and the judiciary on the issues of separation of powers and independence of the judiciary are being handed down as reasons for thwarting judicial reform and in particular, judicial accountability.

According to the majority opinion of the judgement, 'judicial primacy is lost by veto accorded to 2 eminent members'.[53] The court claims that the conferment of a veto to any member of the NJAC, eminent person or otherwise, undoubtedly constitutes an unconstitutional check on the authority of the president and the chief justice of India wherein one eminent member will be either woman/minority/Other Backward Class/Scheduled Caste/Scheduled Tribe.

In addition to the aforementioned reforms, the National Litigation Policy (NLP) is being reviewed.[54] The NLP[55] was drafted to solve the pendency problem for several courts in India under the National Legal Mission to reduce average pendency time duration from 15 to 3 years. This policy intends to regulate the manner in which the state should behave as an efficient litigant in handling disputes.[56] The states and the center together amount for 70 per cent of the 30 million cases left pending, thereby making government the largest litigant in India.[57] The aim of NLP is to reduce this percentage to roughly about 50 per cent. Even this percentage is not enough. The report states:

> The National Litigation Policy is based on the recognition that Government and its various agencies are the pre-dominant litigants in courts and Tribunals in the country. Its aim is to transform Government into an Efficient and Responsible litigant. It is the responsibility of the Government to protect the rights of citizens; to respect fundamental rights and those in charge of the conduct of Government litigation should never forget this basic principle.[58]

A recent commentary claims 'If the judiciary fails to deliver meaningful justice in a reasonable time, we try and find reasons everywhere except within the judiciary. The total number of sanctioned judge strength is 21,542 as of September 2015. Although 462 judge vacancies are to be filled for high courts, only 170 names have been recommended by the collegium. Despite the fact that the government is justly targeted for not accommodating the names immediately, one has to ask why suggested names for the outstanding positions have not been selected by the collegium.[59]

In this context, judicial reforms, promised and assessed so far, need to be implemented in a non-piecemeal manner to foster an impact on economic growth. Obvious tussles and tensions between the judiciary and the legislature on the various judicial reforms including judicial accountability and appointments represent fundamental differences rooted between political constitutionalism and judicial constitutionalism.

Endnotes

1 Douglas C. North, 'Institutions and economic growth: An historical introduction, *World Development*, September, 17/9 (1989): 1319–32; Douglas C. North, 'The New Institutional Economics and Development,' Economic History 9309002, EconWPA, 1993; and Douglas C. North,' The Role of Institutions in Economic Development,' ECE Discussion Papers Series, UNECE, 2003.

2 Alvaro Santos, 'The World Bank's Uses of the "Rule of Law" Promise in Economic Development,' in *The New Law and Economic Development: A Critical Appraisal*, ed. David Trubek and Alvaro Santos (New York: Cambridge University Press, 2006), pp. 253–300; Amanda Perry. 'An Ideal Legal System for Attracting Foreign Direct Investment? Some Theory and Reality,' *American University International Law Review* 15/6 (2000): 1627–57.

3 Kenneth Dam, *The Law-Growth Nexus: Rule of Law and Economic Development* (Washington D.C.: Brookings Institution, 2006a) and Kenneth Dam, *Judiciary and Economic Development* (Washington D.C.: Brookings Institution, 2006b); Amartya Sen, 'What is the Role of Legal and Judicial Reform in the Development Process?' (paper presented at the World Bank Legal Conference, Washington D.C., 2000); Richard A. Posner, 'Creating a Legal Framework for Economic Development,' *The World Bank Research Observer* 13/1 (1998): 1–11; Richard E. Messick, 'Judicial Reform and Economic Growth: What a Decade of Experience Teaches' (paper presented at the conference on 'A Liberal Agenda for the New Century: A Global Perspective,' Moscow, Russian Federation, 2004); Stefan Voigt, 'The Economic Effects of Judicial Accountability—Some Preliminary Insights,' Discussion Papers in Economics 72/05, (Kessel, Germany: University of Kassel, Institute of Economics, 2005).

4 Katharina Pistor and Philip A. Wellons, *The Role of Law and Legal Institutions in Asian Economic Development, 1960–95* (New York: Oxford University Press, 1999), p. 294; Robert S. Brown and Alan Gutterman, *Asian Economic and Legal Development: Uncertainty, Risk and Legal Efficiency* (Boston: Kluwer Law International, 1998), p.477; Kanishka Jayasuriya, ed. *Law, Capitalism and Power in Asia: The Rule of Law and Legal Institutions* (New York: Routledge, 1999), p. 345.

5 Kenneth Dam, *Judiciary and Economic Development* (Washington D.C.: Brookings Institution, 2006b).

6 T.C.A. Anant and N.L. Mitra, 'The Role of Law and Legal Institutions in Asian Economic Development: The Case of India,' in *The Role of Law and Legal Institutions in Asian Economic Development, 1960-1995*, ed. Katharina Pistor, Philip

A. Wellons, Jeffrey Sachs (Oxford University Press, 1999) and T.C.A. Anant and N.L. Mitra, 'The Role of Law and Legal Institutions in Asian Economic Development: The Case Of India', Patterns Of Change In The Legal System And Socio-Economy, Harvard Institute for Economic Development, HIID Development Discussion Paper no. 662, 1998.

7 T.C.A. Anant and M.L. Mitra, 'The Role of Law and Legal Institutions in Asian Economic Development: The Case Of India, Patterns Of Change In The Legal System And Socio-Economy,' Harvard Institute for Economic Development, Discussion Paper no. 662, http://www.cid.harvard.edu/hiid/662.pdf.

8 Peerenboom, R. (2008). 'Law and Development in China and India: The Advantages and Disadvantages of Front-Loading the Costs of Political Reform,' La Trobe Law School Legal Studies Research Paper No. 2008/15.

9 Law Commission of India, 'Proposal for constitution of Hi-tech Fast Track Commercial Divisions in High Courts, *188th Law Commission Report*, (New Delhi: Government of India, December 2003).

10 Matthew Stephenson, 'Judicial Reform in Developing Countries: Constraints and Opportunities,' in *Beyond Transition*, ed. Francois Bourguignon and Boris Pleskovic (New York: Oxford University Press, 2007).

11 Stephenson (2007) argues that 'when the judiciary is in a suboptimal stage improving the courts along one dimension might not improve overall institutional performance.'

12 The famous phrase 'Justice delayed is justice denied' is attributed to William E. Gladstone although some claim that it is attributed to the Magna Carta (1215).

13 Maneesh Chhibber, 'Do we need more judges? CJI Thakur's plea to the govt raises key questions,' *Indian Express*, May 1, 2016, http://indianexpress.com/article/india/india-news-india/india-judiciary-cji-t-s-thakur-supreme-court-judges-pending-cases-2778419.

14 '30 Million Cases & Counting; The Law Fights Back,' October 23, 2012, India Spend, http://www.indiaspend.com/snapshots/30-million-cases-the-law-fights-back.

15 http://doj.gov.in/sites/default/files/Vacancy-statement-1.3.2016_1.pdf

16 Ibid.

17 Ibid.

18 Law Commission of India, *Law Commission Report no 245, Arrears and Backlog*, (New Delhi: Government of India, July 2014), http://lawcommissionofindia.nic.in/reports/Report245.pdf.

19 Comment made at the annual conference of chief justices and chief ministers by CJI Thakur in the presence of the prime minister and the law minister, April 2016.

20 'Hon'ble Prime Minister, the commercial courts project is one of your prime agenda but what's happening? These commercial courts are being designated out

of the existing courts. Will that serve the purpose when the concept was to provide a different environment for commercial disputes? Simply putting old wine in a new bottle will not serve the purpose,' Justice Thakur said, http://timesofindia.indiatimes.com/india/How-can-18000-judges-tackle-3-crore-cases-CJI-TS-Thakur-asks-PM-Modi/articleshow/51971782.cms.

21 NITI Aayog is the new institution that has replaced the Planning Commission which was under the helm of Montek Singh Ahluwalia during the United Progressive Alliance government. Presently, Bibek Debroy is a permanent member of the NITI Aayog.

22 Bibek Debroy, 'Judicial Reforms: Law and Contract Enforcement' in *Documenting Reforms: Case Studies From India*, ed. S. Narayan (New Delhi: Macmillan and Observer Research Foundation, 2006), pp. 89–104.

23 Ibid.

24 Arnab Kumar Hazra and Bibek Debroy, *Judicial Reforms in India: Issues and Aspects* (New Delhi: Academic Foundation and Rajiv Gandhi Institute for Contemporary Studies, 2007).

25 Arun Mohan, *Justice, Courts and Delays*, Volume I and II, (New Delhi: Universal Law Publishing, 2009).

26 Wolfgang Koehling, 'The Economic Consequences of a Weak Judiciary: Insights From India,' Law and Economics, EconWPA, 2002.

27 Matthieu Chemin, 'Does Judicial Quality Shape Economic Activity? Evidence from Judicial Reform in India,' CIRPEE Working Paper 07-25, (Montreal: Department of Economics, University of Quebec, 2007).

28 N. Robinson, 'A Quantitative Analysis of the Indian Supreme Court's Workload,' *Journal of Empirical Legal Studies*, 10 (2013): 570–601.

29 N. Robinson, 'A Quantitative Analysis of the Indian Supreme Court's Workload, '*Journal of Empirical Legal Studies*, 10/3, September (2013): 570–601. In this work, Robinson concludes that court data is imperfect in a certain way and analyses court data and pendency to show that 'the Supreme court is disproportionately accessed by those close to Delhi and with more resources and that the Supreme Court's multiplicity of benches and cases may be undercutting precedent following in the Indian judicial system.'

30 The importance of the court's admission policy becomes clearer when placed within an international context. In the United States, for instance, an appeal to the supreme court is fairly easy, but its court only accepts about 1 per cent of these appeals and so generally hears less than 100 cases each year. Several European constitutional courts have very high acceptance rates but the legislature or a lower court judge can often only generate appeals upon request. Because of this, the Italian constitutional court decides about 500 cases a year, while the French constitutional council, which has, even stricter grounds for appeal may decide only 50 cases in

a year. For a detailed report by Robinson titled 'Too many cases', see Frontline, http://www.frontline.in/static/html/fl2601/stories/20090116260108100.htm

31 Ibid.

32 For a detailed report by Robinson titled 'A Court Adrift,' see *Frontline* http://www.frontline.in/static/html/fl3008/stories/20130503300800400.htm.

33 Ibid.

34 All you need to know about National Court of Appeal, http://www.thehindu.com/news/national/national-court-of-appeal-the-hindu-explains/article8532094.ece

35 'Teary Chief Justice Tells Modi He Must Help Reduce Burden on Judiciary,' The Wire, April 25, 2016, http://thewire.in/2016/04/25/teary-chief-justice-tells-modi-he-must-help-reduce-burden-on-judiciary-31318/

36 Barry Walsh, 'Judicial Productivity in India,' *International Journal for Court Administration*, 1/1, (2008): 23–30.

37 'Teary Chief Justice Tells Modi He Must Help Reduce Burden on Judiciary,' The Wire, April 25, 2016, http://thewire.in/2016/04/25/teary-chief-justice-tells-modi-he-must-help-reduce-burden-on-judiciary-31318/

38 Maneesh Chhibber, 'Do we need more judges? CJI Thakur's plea to the govt raises key questions,' *Indian Express*, May 1, 2016, http://indianexpress.com/article/india/india-news-india/india-judiciary-cji-t-s-thakur-supreme-court-judges-pending-cases-2778419/

39 Commercial Courts Bill Accessed at http://www.prsindia.org/uploads/media/Commercial%20courts/Commercial%20courts%20Act,%202015.pdf

40 http://doj.gov.in/national-mission-justice-delivery-and-legal-reform

41 http://www.livelaw.in/commercial-courts-cannot-work-way-propose-cji-pm/

42 *Annual Report 2014–15*, Supreme Court of India,http://supremecourtofindia.nic.in/annualreport/annualreport2014-15.pdf

43 The Law Commission of India, *Report No 253*, 2015, (Ministry of Law and Justice, India).

44 Ibid.

45 Ibid.

46 Ibid.

47 The bill was later amended in the Rajya Sabha following protests by several members of the judiciary.

48 http://rajyasabha.nic.in/rsnew/bill/bill_main.asp;

49 *SCAORA vs Union of India*, http://supremecourtofindia.nic.in/FileServer/2015-10-16_1444997560.pdf.

50 http://supremecourtofindia.nic.in/FileServer/2015-10-16_1444997560.pdf.

51 For a detailed report on the same, please see PRS Legislative Research, http://www.prsindia.org/billtrack/the-national-judicial-appointments-commission-bill-2014-3359/.

52 Indira Jaising, 'National Judicial Appointment Commission, A Critique,' *Economic and Political Weekly* 49/35 (August 30, 2014).

53 *SCAORA vs Union of India* (NJAC) case, Supreme Court of India.(Para 156, Order of Merits)

54 National Litigation Policy, Ministry of Law and Justice, http://pib.nic.in/newsite/erelease.aspx?relid=62745.

55 http://lawmin.nic.in/la/status%20note%20on%20nlp.pdf.

56 National Litigation Policy, Ministry of Law and Justice, http://pib.nic.in/newsite/erelease.aspx?relid=62745.

57 Ibid.

58 Ministry of Law and Justice, http://www.electroniccourts.in/blog/wp-content/uploads/2014/10/National-Litigation-Policy-Of-India-NLPI-2010.pdf.

59 Shailesh Gandhi, 'Buck stops at Bench,' April 29, 2016, *Indian Express*, http://indianexpress.com/article/opinion/columns/india-judiciary-supreme-court-judges-t-s-thakur-cji-buck-stops-at-bench-2771750/.

Governing the Ungoverned: Challenges from Below

Abinash Chaudhary

In the spring of 2014 when Chief Minister Narendra Modi successfully spearheaded the political campaign to be prime minister of India, he primarily focused on two themes: (a) good governance (b) Cooperative federalism. In the history of Independent India, there have been only five chief ministers prior to Modi, who have gone on to become prime minister of India—Morarji Desai, Charan Singh, V.P. Singh, P.V. Narasimha Rao and H.D. Deve Gowda. Except for Narasimha Rao none of them could complete a full term as prime minister.

Thus, Modi's transition from being the chief minister of Gujarat for 12 years to becoming prime minister of India was quite significant from the perspective that he supposedly understood governance at the grass-roots level. When the rubber hits the road i.e. the districts, Prime Minister Modi has to focus on a few simple things to deliver his two primary poll promises.

In India the principal challenge is scale. Any policy measure has to navigate through the bureaucratic channels of bloated central/state ministries to the district and then the block-panchayat level. This size of the bureaucracy is larger than any country except China. When we add to this the 5-tier electoral system in India, it is huge. The fundamental unit of governance in India is inherited from the Mughal and British Empire in the form of the district system. Today India has 640 districts functioning as administrative units. The district as administrative unit is large enough to be relevant to policy and immediate enough to be responsible for implementation. All the policies at the centre or state have to navigate through the district administrative system. The Tax to GDP (Gross Domestic Product) ratio (Centre and states combined) is estimated at 17.24 per cent for 2012–13.[1] The IMF estimate for India GDP (nominal) is a US$ 2.04 trillion economy. Therefore, from tax revenue, US$ 320 billion (20 lakh crores) accrues every year to run the affairs of the State.

Aruna Sharma's UN study in 2008 has indicated that on an average a district receives US$75 million (approximately 400 crore) for development schemes. This is in addition to non-plan expenditure. Further to this, take a small sample of the Rural Development Ministry. Under the nine schemes it sponsors to the state, in the financial year 2012–13 it transferred 5,175.89 lakh in East Godavari district of Andhra Pradesh alone.[2] Add to this the budget a district zila parishad has annually and the number is staggeringly high.

In our zeal for good governance, the state is increasingly compared with the private sector for efficiency, transparency, and customer service. Increasingly, with the state playing the role of facilitator, this requirement has become great. Also, given the fact that due to a revolution in information and communications technology (ICT), and consumption, people's expectations are rising and determining political-electoral outcomes. Therefore the question of capacity and relevance of taluk/tehsil, village/ward-level increases multifold.

Let us for a moment assume a private/public sector unit has a turnover of US$75 million per year. The deployment of human resources will be massive—strategic planning/deployment of human resources/change management, communications strategy would be adopted and continuously improved. Substantial investment would be made in PR/media relations and linkage with global markets.

In fact 640 such firms would be a formidable pressure group for the policymakers. In contrast, the district administration is subordinate jurisdiction for state governments and thus its affiliated agencies cut a sorry figure. The capacity to plan a budget, implementation and accountability for US$75 million is missing.

A typical district planning officer is in his/her late 50s, has a few years left to retire, possesses little training, and his/her capacity to operate in changing circumstances has been disempowered by a system so cumbersome that the ability to think strategically is largely missingdespite the unique advantage of years of experience of working at grass-roots level.

With regard to budgeting, the districts have little leverage in the use of untied funds, which are meant to be used by Panchayati Raj institutions. Even as the district treasuries have been successfully computerised across India, they don't have any competent chief finance officer and finance professionals working in district administration. Instead of being a competently managed agency they are merely treated as a fund disbursement agency, often with little understanding of accounts, audit and risk management.

At the implementation level, large district machinery and its block level officials are constrained by lack of capacity, training, and conducive work environment. Given the fact that district level planning is weak and constrained, any results that the implementer delivers is despite the system, not because of it. Moreover, there are a large number of districts with a continued history of vacancy and non-recruitment. The absenteeism of teachers and doctors has to be viewed in this context and their ratio has to be understood.

Now contrast this with Central Government ministries, which are bloated with staff. Each ministry is a private empire with their own scheme, under which they have funds, staff and all other required services. The so-called mission of health, education, urban renewal, and smart cities are certainly not finishing in a mission mode. It is either renamed/relaunched or kept on lingering government after government. This trend has nothing to do with political parties in power either at the centre or the state. Requiring district governance to be in tune with its scale and salience, fund and relevance, delivering the result is very much an unfinished agenda.

For cooperative federalism to work, public institution reform needs to be undertaken at the outset. In the past a lot of work has been undertaken reflecting insights from 'new institutional' economics,[3] and historical institutionalism[4] emphasising the critical role of institutions and how they play a pivotal role in the functioning of the state.

> Institutions perform a variety of functions: they structure incentive for actors within society and provide mechanisms for coordination, sometimes enabling and some time impeding it. As anthropologists have long argued, institutions have considerable impact on the process of recognition and classification that go on in any society (Douglas 1986). In short, most aspects of our collective existence are unintelligible without taking the role institutions play seriously.[5]

The role of institutions is increasingly becoming critical in the light of the liberalisation process started in 1991 and the increasing globalisation of the market. Neither good governance nor cooperative federalism can function without robust institutions which can manage public demand of delivering timely and affordable justice. Successful delivery of the promise of good governance through the mechanism of cooperative federalism can be delivered only through institutions: legislature, executives, judiciary, police and through rule of law.

Let us take stock of the aforementioned institutions and the reforms required to achieve good governance as promised by Prime Minister Modi. The founding fathers of our constitution clearly earmarked the role of the three branches of the government, i.e. Legislative, Executive, and Judiciary with clear checks and balances. In recent times there is clear impingement and overreach of one branch over the others' role and functioning.

First, under the larger rubric of legislative reform, electoral reform constitutes the cornerstone. There is an old saying: 'A fish rots from the head down'. Legislatures are custodians of lawmaking and running the government as per the rule of law. The entire idea of institutional reform hinges on electoral reform. Unless, we reform from the top, it will be difficult to reform at the middle and lower levels and other arms of the government.

Legislative reform has to start with reform in specific of the Representation of the People Act, 1951. It is needless to say that the high cost of elections and corruption go hand-in-hand, because electoral expenses over and above the sanctioned limit are met by means of unaccounted funds, which entail a quid pro quo. To quote Mark Twain, the situation is one where 'every election is an advance auction of stolen public goods'. It also vitiates the condition of 'free and fair elections' which require a level playing field. When all candidates or parties do not have equal access to such funds, the asymmetry in funds leads to asymmetry in reaching out to voters and helping them to make an informed choice. 'Big Money' is used in a non-transparent manner and undermines the rule of law. The elected representatives become captive in the hands of those who provide such funds. Besides, vote buying is another manifestation of such non-transparent use of money in elections. The excessive use of money power in elections has been reported by some parties, candidates, media and civil society organisations. Many parliamentarians have also raised concerns in the House about the use of excessive money in election campaigns and have asked the Election Commission to take urgent steps to curb such a malaise.

Reforming the Representation of the People Act, 1951, is absolutely essential. Debaring criminals from contesting elections is absolutely essential in a system of good governance.

In a 97-page judgement, the supreme court bench of justices Dipak Misra and P.C. Pant highlighted the criminalisation of politics, calling it an 'anathema' to the 'sanctity of democracy'. The court defined the essentials of a democracy. The electoral process is sacrosanct to a nation's democratic fabric and the voter's 'right to know' is paramount, as 'a free and fair election stabilises the democratic process which leads to good governance'.

Though the Election Commission has taken several steps in this regard in the recent elections, it faces challenges in enforcement, including the absence of express legal provisions. The Law Ministry in association with the Election Commission had initiated a national consultation on electoral reform, including the reform in political, finance, and transparency norms. The matter was referred to the Law Commission, which has submitted its 255th report in March 2015.[6]

It will be critical for the government to implement this report if they want their promise for good governance be delivered.

Second, under the Executive reform, the government needs to urgently take up the Administrative Reform Commission (ARC)-II report for implementation. The Second ARC was set up with a resolution no. K-11022/9/2004-RC of the Government of India as a committee of inquiry to prepare a detailed blueprint for revamping the public administration system.[7]

The Commission was given the mandate to suggest measures to achieve a proactive, responsive, accountable, sustainable, and efficient administration for the country at all levels of the government. The Commission was asked to, inter alia, consider the following:

(i) Organisational structure of the Government of India (ii) Ethics in governance (iii) Refurbishing of personnel administration (iv) Strengthening of financial management systems (v) Steps to ensure effective administration at the state level (vi) Steps to ensure effective district administration (vii) Local self-government/Panchayati Raj institutions (viii) Social capital, trust and participative public service delivery (ix) Citizen-centric administration (x) Promoting e-governance (xi) Issues of federal polity (xii) Crisis management (xiii) Public order.

The report was submitted to the Government of India and it is yet to be implemented by it. The report will be pivotal to bring structured institutional reform in India. To meet the twin promises of good governance and cooperative federalism Prime Minister Modi will have to undertake this exercise immediately.

Third, Judicial reform—Article 50 of the Indian Constitution says: 'The State shall take steps to separate the judiciary from the executive in the public services of the State.' An independent and impartial judiciary, with efficient and speedy systems should be the cornerstone of any democratic republic. The overreach of the judiciary has become quite evident in recent times. However, our judiciary, by its very nature, has become ponderous, excruciatingly slow and inefficient. Imposition of an alien system, with archaic and dilatory procedures, proved to be extremely damaging to our governance and society. As Nani Palkhiwala observed once, the progress of a civil suit in our courts of law is the closest thing to eternity we can experience!

Fourth, police reform—it may be the last but not least. The police doesn't come under direct purview of the Central Government. But it is the most important cog in the wheel of good governance and institutional reform. The need for police reforms in India is a long-pending demand. There has been almost three decades of discussion by government-created committees and commissions. Way back in 1979 the National Police Commission (NPC) was set up to report on policing and give recommendations for reform. The Commission produced eight reports, dozens of topic-specific recommendations and also a Model Police Act. In *Prakash Singh & Ors vs Union Of India And Ors*, on 22 September 2006, the supreme court of India delivered a landmark judgement on police reforms. It identified seven key areas for police reforms in India and its states. The seven points are as follows:

1. Constitute a State Security Commission (SSC) to: (i) Ensure that the state government does not exercise unwarranted influence or pressure on the police (ii) Lay down broad policy guidelines and (iii) Evaluate the performance of the state police.
2. Ensure that the Director General of Police (DGP) is appointed through a merit-based transparent process and secures a minimum tenure of two years.

3. Ensure that other police officers on operational duties (including Superintendents of Police in charge of a district and Station House Officers in charge of a police station) are also provided a minimum tenure of two years.
4. Separate the investigation and law and order functions of the police.
5. Set up a Police Establishment Board (PEB) to decide transfers, postings, promotions and other service-related matters of police officers of and below the rank of Deputy Superintendent of Police and make recommendations on postings and transfers above the rank of Deputy Superintendent of Police.
6. Set up a Police Complaints Authority (PCA) at state level to inquire into public complaints against police officers of and above the rank of Deputy Superintendent of Police in cases of serious misconduct, including custodial death, grievous hurt, or rape in police custody and at district levels to inquire into public complaints against the police personnel below the rank of Deputy Superintendent of Police in cases of serious misconduct.
7. Set up a National Security Commission (NSC) at the union level to prepare a panel for selection and placement of Chiefs of the Central Police Organisations (CPO) with a minimum tenure of two years.

Without police reforms any institutional reform in India will be a window dressing and half-hearted approach. True, the Central Government cannot intervene directly in the states to implement police reforms, however it has enough leverage to force states to start police reforms as per the directive of the court. Before that the Central Government itself can lead by example, by enforcing police reforms in union territories where the Centre is in charge of the police, particularly, the capital, Delhi, where the police comes under direct purview of the Union Home Ministry.

Institutional reform of the Legislative, Executive, Judiciary and Police level should be taken up immediately. Otherwise, results will be achieved in the files of the ministries, located in Delhi and state capitals and not on the ground, where it is critically required. Prime Minister Modi has to remember the bandwagon is there, but the wheels are rickety.

The views expressed are those of the author alone and not of any institution with which he is associated.

Endnotes

1 http://finmin.nic.in/reports/IPFStat201213.pdf.

2 http://rural.nic.in/sites/dist-scheme-wise.asp.

3 Douglass North, *Institutions, Institutional Change and Economic Performance* (Cambridge: Cambridge University Press, 1990); James March and Johan Olsen, 'The New Institutionalism: Organizational Factors in Political Life,' *American Political Science Review*, 78 (1984): 734–49.

4 Peter Hall, *Governing the Economy: The Politics of State Intervention in Britain and France*, Cambridge: Polity Press, 1986; Theda Skocpol, *Protecting Solders and Mothers: The Political Origins of Social Policy in the United States*, (Cambridge, MA: Harvard University Press, 1992).

5 Devesh Kapur and Pratap Bhanu Mehta, eds. *Public Institutions in India: Performance and Design* (New Delhi: Oxford University Press, 2005).

6 http://lawcommissionofindia.nic.in/reports/Report255.pdf.

7 http://arc.gov.in/.

ECONOMICS AND DEVELOPMENT

The Indian Economy: Looking Back to go Forward Differently

Jayati Ghosh

Obviously, the future of an economy cannot be delinked from its past. And so if we are to imagine what the Indian economy will be like around three decades from now, we must necessarily view it from the vantage point of the economic structures that are in place now and the processes that are currently underway. I will consider this issue first in terms of the current status of the development project and industrialisation, then examine the likely implications of the demographic transition that will occur over these decades. I will address the political economy of change in India, and dream of alternative, more positive, and desirable trajectories of economic expansion that are also possible for India to achieve with a different set of political economy forces.

The Development Project and Industrialisation

Until recently, India was regarded (along with China) as one of the 'success stories' of globalisation, likely to emerge into a giant economy and global economic power in the 21st century. The perception of a vibrant democracy on the move, especially in economic terms, was reinforced by an economic boom that has been relatively prolonged, with a confident capitalist class increasingly taking on the world not only in exports but also through investment abroad, euphoria in the financial markets, and growing self-confidence among the elite, professional, and middle classes.

Of course, that happy picture has since been blurred, and global investors have suddenly come to recognise the features that were evident even during the boom phase to those with the willingness to look: the fragility of the

Indian balance of payments, the internal imbalances, and lack of employment generation and infrastructure development. Yet there is still a somewhat perverse and misleading rendering of the economic trajectory of the past two decades, one in which it is assumed that growth in the period until the end of the first decade of the current century was driven by the inherent strengths of the Indian economy that were unleashed by forces of globalisation and liberalisation, while the slowdown has been ascribed to 'policy paralysis' and lack of continuing market-oriented and privatising reforms.

This is a substantial misinterpretation of both the past boom and the current slowdown. Recent high economic growth in India was related to financial deregulation that sparked a retail credit boom and combined with fiscal concessions to spur consumption among the richest sections of the population. This led to rapid increases in aggregate Gross Domestic Product (GDP) growth, even as deflationary fiscal policies, poor employment generation, and persistent agrarian crisis reduced wage shares in national income and kept mass consumption demand low. There was a substantial rise in profit shares in the economy and the proliferation of financial activities. As a result, finance and real estate accounted for more than 15 per cent of GDP in 2009–10. This combined with rising asset values to enable a credit-financed consumption splurge among the rich and the middle classes, especially in urban areas. And this in turn generated higher rates of investment and output over the upswing. The earlier emphasis on public spending as the principal stimulus for growth in the Indian economy was thus substituted in the past two decades with debt-financed housing investment and private consumption of the elite and burgeoning middle classes.[1]

The recent Indian growth story in its essentials was therefore not unlike the story of speculative bubble-led expansion that marked the experience of several other developed and developing countries, and was therefore subject to similar problems of lack of sustainability. It is well-known now that debt-driven bubbles usually end in tears, whether in rich developed countries or in 'emerging markets' or even in resource-rich least developed countries. In the Indian case, the lack of sustainability is accentuated by the social and political problems that are increasingly emerging, driven by the unequal pattern of growth. Extremist movements are powerful and dominate in 150 backward and relatively undeveloped districts that are the location of extractive industries; lack of productive employment generation has given rise to powerful demands for regional autonomy and exclusion of 'non-natives' within the different states; other forms of criminality are increasing; and there is widespread public anger not only at the evident corruption that has been characteristic of this phase but also at the explicit ways in which state policy has favoured the rich. These create potent sources of instability that may rebound on the growth process in unpredictable ways.

Further, to paraphrase Charles Dickens, while these were the best of times for some, particularly the elite and some sections of professional middle classes, they were also the worst of times for others. And the 'others' in this case may well include the majority of Indians, given the growing divisions in conditions of living. Despite more than six decades of independence, the development project is nowhere near completion in India. It is also clear that over time, some elements of that project seem even less likely to be achieved than in the past, despite relatively rapid economic growth.

Taking a long view, there are some clear achievements of the Indian economy since Independence—most crucially the emergence of a reasonably diversified economy with an industrial base. The past 25 years have also witnessed rates of aggregate GDP growth that are high compared to the past and also compared with several other parts of the developing world. Significantly, this higher aggregate growth has thus far been accompanied by macroeconomic stability, with the absence of extreme volatility in the form of financial crises such as have been evident in several other emerging markets. There has also been some reduction (although not very rapid) in income poverty.

However, there are also some clear failures of this growth process even from a long-run perspective. An important failure is the worrying absence of structural change. The experience of the Indian economy is startling in the extent of its deviation from almost all of the expected features of the 'classic pattern' of industrialisation and development that was experienced in today's developed countries, of the movement of labour from agriculture to industry and then services (reflected also in changing shares of national incomes) as well as growing formalisation of all work. The Indian economy has shown hardly any of this, and remarkably, these peculiar features have persisted through different growth models and policy regimes in the post-Independence period, whether Nehruvian mixed economy or open economy market-based strategies, and through varying periods of slow growth, stagnation, and rapid growth. This has been particularly surprising in the most recent period, when the accelerated expansion of economic activity over the past two decades was widely expected to generate significant structural changes. Some of the central paradoxes of the recent pattern of growth and employment in India can be briefly stated as follows.

First, growth has not been associated with much employment generation, even with the rather loose and flexible definition of work that is adopted by our National Sample Surveys. Indeed, total employment (in terms of usual status of work, principal and subsidiary activities) actually grew faster when the economy was growing more slowly, and has tapered off significantly in the period since 2004–05, with rural employment showing a decline in absolute numbers and urban employment growing by only 2.5 per cent annual compound rate between 2004–05 and 2011–12. Employment elasticities of output growth have declined as the economy has become more exposed to global competition that was supposed to have favoured more labour-intensive activities.

The share of manufacturing in both output and employment has been stubbornly constant at relatively low levels. Low productivity work continues to dominate in total employment, so in the aggregate there is little evidence of labour moving to higher productivity activities. This is true both across and within sectors, such that low productivity employment coexists with some high-value-added activities in all of the major sectors, and there are extremely wide variations in productivity across enterprises even within the same sub-sector. The persistence of low productivity employment has been evident in the continuing significance of primary activities in total employment and the domination of low productivity service activities accounting for the bulk of non-agricultural jobs. While the share of agriculture and allied activities in GDP fell from around 55 per cent in 1960–61 to less than 18 per cent in 2011–12, the share of employment it accounted for declined much more slowly over the entire period, from 72 per cent in 1960-61 to 48 per cent in 2011-12. The most rapidly expanding activities in terms of GDP share, such as finance, insurance, and real estate (FIRE), IT-related services and telecommunications, which together now account for nearly 20 per cent of the GDP, still employ less than 2 per cent of the work force. More than 60 per cent of the workforce is employed in sectors with very low labour productivity, such as agriculture and unregistered manufacturing.

Meanwhile the share of manufacturing has stagnated at low levels of both output and employment—in 2011–12 it accounted for only 14.4 per cent of GDP and 12.6 per cent of the work force. This has led some to argue that India can successfully become a post-industrial 'service-driven' economy on the basis of modern services that are associated with rapid productivity increases that generate positive spillovers to the rest of the economy. But it would be foolhardy to presume that the difficult but necessary stage of industrialisation can simply be bypassed in this manner, especially as the newer services also generate very little additional employment. Although this has been increasingly recognised in official circles (as in the National Manufacturing Policy of 2012 and the 'Make in India' exhortation of 2014–15)current trends still point to industrial underperformance.

Even within sectors that are perceived as more dynamic, the majority of workers persist in low productivity activities, with only a small minority in each sector involved in highly remunerated and high productivity work. For example, there are extremely large variations in productivity within the manufacturing sector, with the registered (organised) manufacturing industry showing nearly seven times the labour productivity levels of unregistered (unorganised) manufacturing in 2009–10, and also employing less than one-third the numbers of workers. This is in marked contrast to the experience of China, for example, where the period of rapid growth has been associated not only with industrialisation but more particularly the emergence and preponderance of medium and large-scale units that provide formal employment to workers.

The expected formalisation of work and the concentration of workers into large-scale production units has not occurred—rather, there has been widespread persistence of informal employment and increase in self-employment in non-agricultural activities.[2] Informal work overwhelmingly dominates total employment. In 2004–05, informal workers were estimated to account for 96 per cent of all workers, and there is little to suggest that the share of formal work would have increased greatly since then. It is important to bear in mind that many informal workers are actually employed in the formal sector, in registered manufacturing and service companies, as contractual workers or even daily wage workers. In 2004–05, the number of informal jobs in the formal sector (at 3 per cent of the total estimated work force) was nearly as large as the number of formal jobs in the formal sector!

The incidence of self-employment (most of it highly fragile and vulnerable) has actually increased as a proportion of non-agricultural work, and the only reason for its overall stagnation is the decline in agricultural employment, particularly in the number of women workers self-employed in agriculture. Meanwhile, the share of the informal sector in GDP has fallen quite sharply during this period of high growth. Indeed, the recent period of most rapid acceleration of national income was also the period of sharpest fall in the share of unorganised incomes. Thus, while the formal organised sector has substantially increased its share of national income, it has done so without drawing in more workers.

Chart 1: Structure of employment in 2004–05.

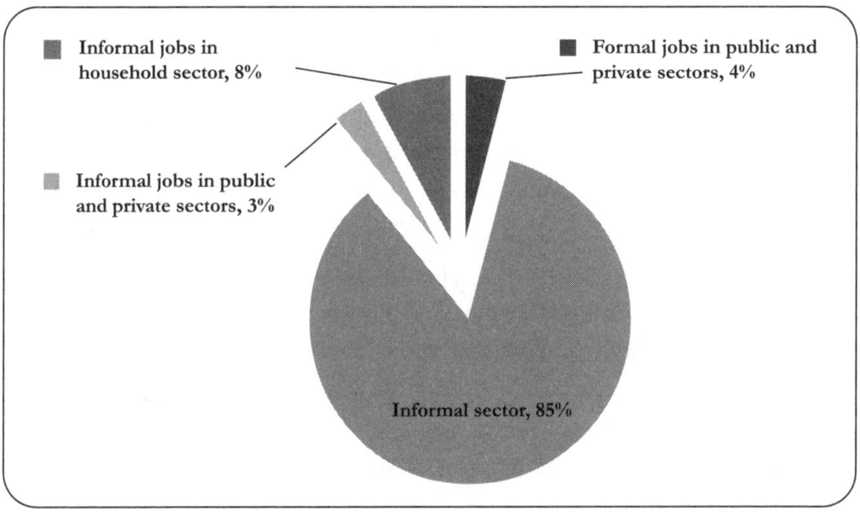

Perhaps most striking of all is the fact that the period of rapid GDP growth has been marked by low and declining work force participation rates of women, in a pattern that is unlike almost any other rapidly growing economy in any phase of history over the past two centuries. This is significant for several reasons. It is now generally accepted that most women work, even when they are not recorded as 'workers' by official and other data gatherers. The tasks associated with social reproduction and the care economy are largely (though not solely) borne by women, but in many societies these are not counted among economic or productive activities. Similarly many women are engaged in what is recognised otherwise as productive work, but as unpaid household helpers who are therefore only marginally seen as workers in their own right. The general invisibility of women's work is itself a mostly accurate reflection of their status in society: where women's official work participation is low, this is typically a sign of less freedom and mobility of women, lower status and lower empowerment. Indeed, where more women are active in the labour market and are employed (especially in formal activities), the share of unpaid work tends to come down and even the unpaid labour performed by women is more likely to be recognised and valued. This is why looking at the extent, coverage, conditions and remuneration of women's work is often a useful way of judging the extent to which their broader status in society has improved.

Thus in India, the low and declining rates of recognised work participation by women can be traced to several features:[3] lack of recognition of women's work; a backward bending supply curve of household labour as increased wage rates actually cause more women to shift back to unpaid domestic labour; the associated continued and even increased unpaid labour of women in household activities, care economy, and reproductive services; social restrictions on women's autonomy, mobility and agency, even with educated women. Whatever be the specific causes in particular regional contexts and class categories of women, it is clear that this tendency is both reflective of the continued inferior position of women in Indian society, as well as a huge waste of resources and human potential for the economy.

Social perceptions about women and their capacities are also important factors. It is ironic but true that mechanisation has tended to displace women workers, particularly in agriculture and construction. Just as some activities becomes less arduous and physically taxing, women who were previously engaged in such work are replaced by male workers. But there is really no physical reason why women should be less able than men to drive tractors and harvester-threshers or to operate construction machines. Rather, it reflects the persistence of what should be archaic attitudes towards women and the work that they are fit to perform.

However, it is also likely that women themselves may wish to quit the labour force when there is no pressing need, simply because the paid work that is available for most of them is so arduous, taxing, and poorly paid. Indeed, this is why it has been noted that much of women's work participation in India is of the 'distress' variety, engaged in when the household is very poor or when there is a natural calamity, economic shock, or other decline in household income.[4] Since paid work is not so readily available, and what is tends to be both difficult and low remuneration, as well as associated with the double burden of paid and unpaid work, it is not implausible that some improvement in household income levels could result in reduced pressure for women to seek outside employment.

In many ways, these features also indicate why 'the development project' is still incomplete. Other major failures, which are directly reflective of the still poor status of human development in most parts of the country, are in many ways related to this fundamental failure. These include: the persistence of widespread poverty; the sluggishness of employment, especially in the formal sector; the absence of basic food security (and growing food insecurity) for a significant proportion of the population; the inability to ensure basic needs of housing, sanitation, and adequate health care to the population as a whole; the continuing inability to ensure universal education and the poor quality of much school education; the sluggish enlargement of access to education and employment across different social groups and for women in particular. In addition there are problems caused by the very pattern of economic growth: aggravated regional imbalances; greater inequalities in the control over assets and in access to incomes; dispossession and displacement of people from land and livelihood without adequate compensation and rehabilitation.

The Demographic Transition

For many years population was seen as a problem rather than a source of growth potential. However, the recent discussion on the 'demographic dividend' turned the argument around. It is based on the idea that economic growth is critically dependent upon the dependency ratio (the proportion of non-workers to total population) which in turn is determined by the age structure, and specifically by the proportion of the population in what can be called 'the working age group' (say 15 to 60 years or 19 to 64 years). It has been observed that both the size and the age structure of the population (and the dependency ratio) change over time and with economic development. Death rates tend to decline (because of better public health, etc.) before birth rates do, as these depend on age of marriage and fertility rate. The initial fall in infant mortality and improvement in child survival results in a boom generation, with a larger number of people in the younger ages. After some time, the lagged fall in fertility rates reverses the baby boom, resulting in a 'bulge' in the younger ages. At some point the population in the working age peaks relative to children and older people, creating the lowest dependency ratio, and thereby high potential for rapid economic expansion. Finally, the bulge enters the old age bracket, as in Japan and several other mature capitalist countries now).

India is and will remain one of the youngest countries in the world. In 2020, the average Indian will be only 29 years old, compared with 37 in China and the US, 45 in West Europe and 48 in Japan. The arguments for the demographic dividend assume that this will deliver a large and growing labour force, falling dependency ratio, no labour shortages and a growing youth workforce that can be trained to acquire the skills needed by newer and technologically more dynamic industries. These potential advantages clearly do exist, but the dependency ratio must be defined not as the ratio of the non-working age to working age population but the ratio of actual non-workers to workers. This is determined by absorption into work of the available labour force, taking account of underemployment besides unemployment. This depends on job creation in the economy and matching available skills to economic requirements. So the ability to benefit from a demographic transition will depend upon some critical features that are not mentioned in this more positive perspective: the ability of the country to ensure that this work force is healthy, well-fed and well-educated; and the ability of the economy to generate suitable jobs to meet the needs and aspirations of this expanding labour force. Without these, what could be a demographic dividend could very easily become a ticking time bomb. And yet in these critical areas, the society and economy are currently lacking. *(See chart 2 on the next page).*

Education is very significant. The East Asian miracle, for example, was driven by increased productive investment along with sharply increased public expenditure on education. Recently India has witnessed a substantial increase in the proportions and numbers of young people engaged in education, as shown in Charts 3 and 4. This is clearly positive. However, the numbers are still well below those of other countries at the point of their 'take-off' into a sustained higher growth trajectory. And there are concerns even within this. More than two-thirds of tertiary education enrolment is now in private institutions that are often expensive and are of uneven quality. Young people and their families are willing to sell family assets and take on debts in the hope that these investments in higher education will lead to more lucrative income opportunities in future. Tens of millions of young people with relatively expensive tertiary education will enter the labour force in the next decade, and will not find jobs that meet their expectations or aspirations. All this is of particular concern because, as already noted, formal employment is not growing fast enough.

Meanwhile, the market is generating socially undesirable incentives for education and employment choices. Major skill mismatches are already evident, and there is growing evidence of significantly increased social

Chart 2: Age-wise population break-up of India in 2000, 2025, and 2050.

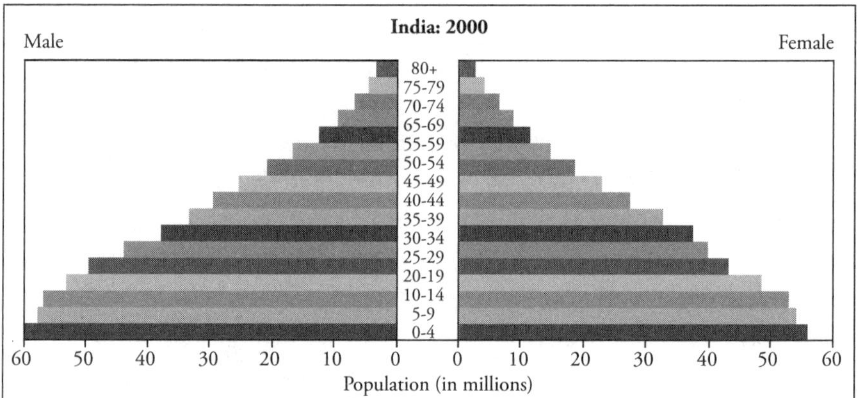

Source: U.S. Census Bureau, International Data Base.

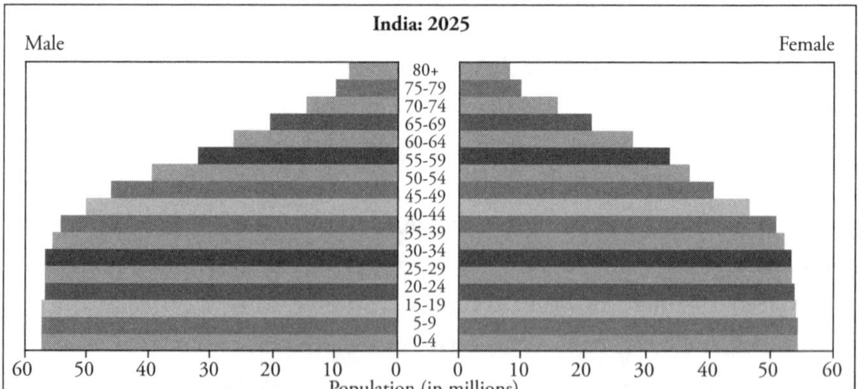

Source: U.S. Census Bureau, International Data Base.

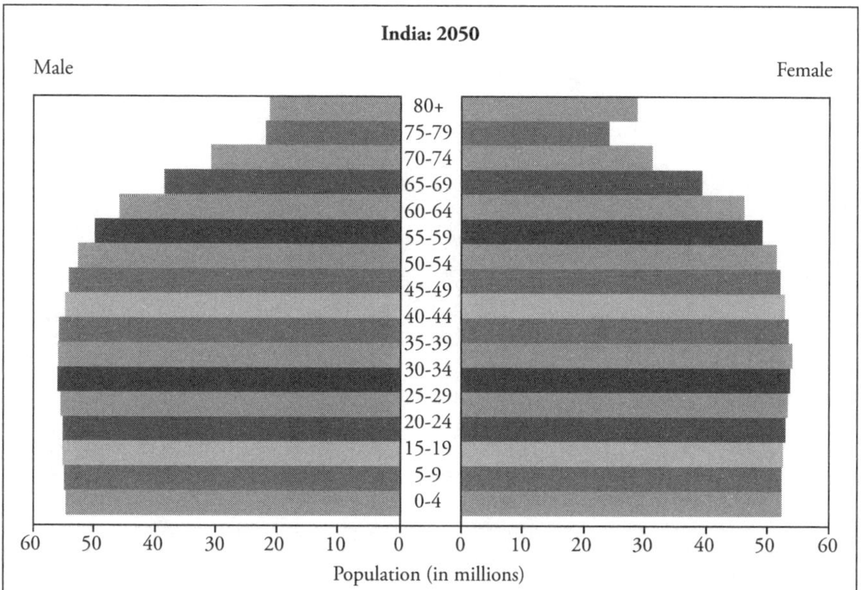

Source: U.S. Census Bureau, International Data Base.

tensions related to inadequate employment generation and the gaps between aspirations and reality. This in turn suggests a likely increase in political instability, violence of different kinds and other unpleasant social phenomena, unless the economy is geared to generating a much greater number of more varied and more remunerative jobs.

The other aspect of the demographic transition is the growing number of elderly people. As is evident from Chart 2, by 2047 and even well before then, there will be significantly larger numbers of people above 65 years, especially more older women. But India has hardly any provision for the elderly and there is little planning for it, whether in the form of infrastructure requirements, social pensions, health facilities, etc. Elderly women in India face particularly challenging circumstances. The need to consider the elderly is often viewed only as a strain on fiscal resources, but in fact it can be an opportunity for generating different kinds of economic activity and more equitable outcomes.

Political Economy Forces

It has become apparent that a basic feature of the process of economic development thus far has been exclusion: exclusion from control over assets;

Chart 3: Per cent of youth aged 15-19 years in education

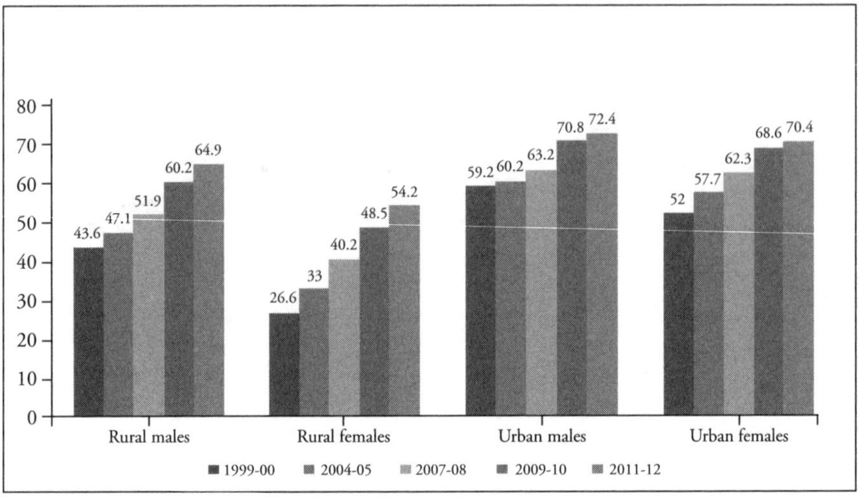

Chart 4: Per cent of youth aged 20-24 years in education

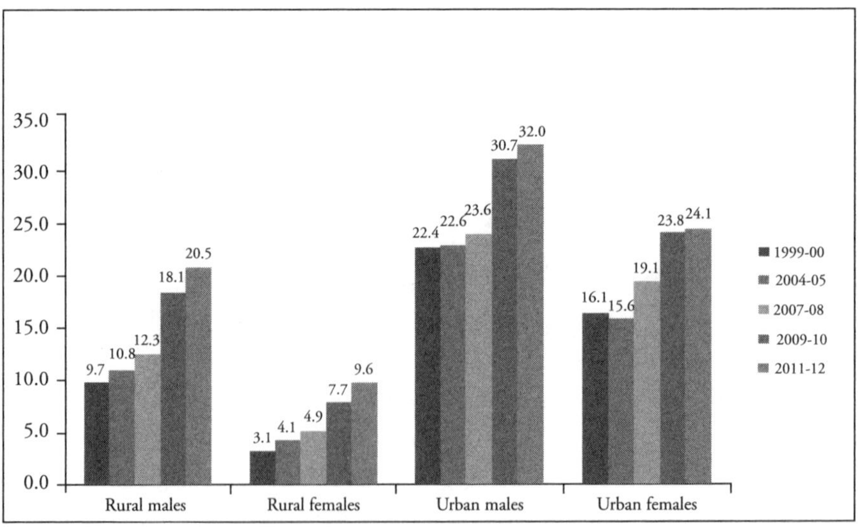

exclusion from the benefits of economic growth; exclusion from the impact of physical and social infrastructure expansion; exclusion from education and from income-generating opportunities. This exclusion has been along class or income lines, by geographical location, by caste and community, and by gender. However, exclusion from these benefits has not meant exclusion from the system as such—rather, those who are supposedly marginalised or excluded have been affected precisely because they have been incorporated into market systems. We therefore have a process of exclusion through incorporation, a process that has actually been typical of capitalist accumulation across the world, especially in its more dynamic phases. Thus, peasants facing a crisis of viability of cultivation have been integrated into a market system that has made them more reliant on purchased inputs in deregulated markets while becoming more dependent upon volatile output markets in which state protection is completely inadequate. The growing army of 'self-employed' workers, who now account for more than half of our work force, have been excluded from paid employment because of the sheer difficulty of finding jobs, but are nevertheless heavily involved in commercial activity and exposed to market uncertainties in the search for livelihood. Those who have been displaced by developmental projects or other processes, and subsequently have not found adequate livelihood in other activities, are victims of the process of economic integration, though excluded from the benefits.

The reasons for this can be traced to the very strategy of accumulation and its location in certain social structures. An important element of this is the reliance on growth strategies that did not seek to develop the home market for mass consumption goods through asset redistribution and dismantling of traditional monopolies. Indeed, the absence in post-Independence India of comprehensive land reforms (which were so instrumental in dismantling traditional structures of economic control in Japan, South Korea, and Taiwan, China) has been a major underlying feature of the continuing structural inequality that has prevented broad-based economic growth. This was related to the (possibly resulting) persistent hold of gender, caste and other forms of social discrimination, which in turn allowed segmented labour markets to persist and even intensify.

So workers in the informal economy have not simply been excluded from formal employment—they are deeply integrated into it both directly and indirectly. The perception that the informal economy exists because low wages allow it to compete with the formal sector in a host of non-agricultural activities is essentially misplaced in much of the Indian economy. Rather, in many instances the informal economy is not in competition with the formal sector, but actually services its requirements, and low wages in the informal economy help sustain profits in the formal sector. Consider for example the software industry, which is generally seen as a shining example of hyper-modernity, an outlier of high productivity that is somehow separate from the vast sea of low-productivity work that surrounds it. In actual fact, the ability of this industry to be competitive globally relies crucially on the very cheap supporting services in the form of logistics, security, transportation, cleaning, and catering that are provided by companies or individuals that use workers on informal contracts that are well beyond the pale of labour protection. Similarly, the ability to hire highly skilled professionals in this industry at what are clearly salaries below global averages is dependent upon such workers' ability to access goods and services provided cheaply by India's informal workers.

This is equally true of other formal sectors. There is strong evidence of substantial increases in subcontracting by the formal manufacturing industry to more informal production arrangements since 2001.[5] The value chains evident in a number of important exporting industries in sectors as varied as readymade garments, gems and jewellery, automotive components, leather and leather products and sports goods, which are often co-ordinated by large and possibly multinational corporate entities, provide evidence of the significant and increased contribution of informal activities to what are seen as formal sector production.[6] These are only some examples of a wide and pervasive process of extremely close intertwining of formal and informal sectors, and the effective subsidisation of the formal sector by low-paid informal activities.

These tendencies have been reinforced by the nature of the growth strategy adopted in India over the past two decades. The focus of the Indian state (and of most state forces at the regional level) has been on generating growth through various incentives designed to encourage the expansion of private capital. It is now obvious that this can very quickly become prey to corruption, crony capitalism, and the like. But it is possibly less obvious that this strategy in itself generates incentives for such private players that effectively militate against a more broad-based and egalitarian economic expansion. So new forms of capital certainly do emerge and proliferate as a result of this strategy, but they do so in a wider context in which capitalist accumulation is based essentially on extraction: of land and other natural resources, of the labour of differentiated workers, of the products of peasant cultivators and small producers of goods and services. This has reduced the incentives to focus on productivity, growth, and innovation as routes to more rapid growth, since state-aided primitive accumulation and socially determined extra-economic relationships provide easier and more reliable means of generating private surpluses. All this has actually been reinforced under globalisation, rather than being diminished by external competition.

The point is that these transactions in land, labour, and product markets are not simply voluntary exchanges between equivalent parties. Instead, the game is played with dice that are heavily loaded in favour of capital, especially large capital, through various means: social institutions that allow for discriminatory labour market practices; legal and regulatory institutions that can be and are mobilised to enhance the bargaining power of capital; and political forces that actively engage in supporting all of these. The process of capitalist accumulation in India has utilised the agency of the state to further the project of primitive accumulation through diverse means (including land use change as well as substantial fiscal transfers) and has also exploited specific socio-cultural features, such as caste, community, and gender differences, to enable greater labour exploitation and therefore higher surplus generation. These are in turn associated with various other more 'purely economic' patterns that pile on the imbalances: financial institutions, input and product markets that do not provide reasonable credit access, and so on.

It can be argued that the greater part of the modern Indian economy is implicitly regulated or determined by social institutions derived from 'primordial identity' such as gender, caste, and community.[7] These interact with political forces, generating forms of patronage, control and clientelism that vary across regions. This makes the outcomes of government strategies, including those connected with liberalisation, privatisation, and deregulation, different from those generally expected. Take the large bourgeoisie, for example, which is dominated by diversified joint family enterprises extending across different economic sectors. Even in the phase of globalisation, caste, region and linguistic community have been crucial in shaping these groups, determining their behaviour and influencing their interaction with each other as well as with global capital.[8] The very emergence of such capital has often reflected social forces: for example, there are no major business groups in the North and East that are not from 'traditional' business communities, and nationally no Dalit business group of significance. Existing practices, such as gender discrimination in property ownership and control, have often been reinforced by corporate behaviour, such as the ability to utilise the existence of legal forms (such as the Hindu Undivided Family form of ownership) that deny any role to women.[9] These obviously added to the weight of socially discriminatory practices—and they affected how business houses at large and medium levels dealt with more purely economic forces, and their attitudes to investment, employment, and output.

Yet it could also be argued that these features of the Indian economic landscape are precisely what have been crucial in generating the recent phase of rapid growth, even as they have allowed the persistence of backwardness and accentuated inequalities in the course of that expansion. The complex nexus between politics and different levels of local, regional, and national businesses has allowed for the appropriation of land and other natural resources that has been an integral part of the accumulation story and fed into the way that central and state governments have aided the process of private surplus extraction. More overt economic policies such as patterns of public spending and taxation are only one part of this—a substantial part relates to laws, regulations, and their implementation (or lack of it) that provide the contours for the expansion of private capital.

These processes of direct and indirect underwriting of the costs of the corporate sector have been greatly assisted by the ability of employers in India to utilise social characteristics to ensure lower wages to certain categories of workers. Caste and other forms of social discrimination have a long tradition in India, and they have interacted with capitalist accumulation to generate peculiar forms of labour market segmentation that are unique to Indian society. Studies have found that social categories are strongly correlated with the incidence of poverty and that both occupation and wages differ dramatically across social categories.[10] The National Sample Surveys reveal that the probability of being in a low-wage occupation is significantly higher for STs, SCs, Muslims, and OBCs (in that order) compared to the general 'caste Hindu' population. This is only partly because of differences in education and level of skill, which are also important and which in turn reflect the differential provision of education across social categories.

While in many cases class and caste do overlap, the latter always supersedes the former at least in socioeconomic factors. Caste is an extra-economic factor that acts in two forms, inequality of opportunity and inequality of outcome. Economic wellbeing cannot always overturn the inequalities of caste distinction, and that is reflected in the education levels, job opportunities, wage levels, access to social benefits, and basic facilities, etc. Caste clearly affects family income, consumption, and other parameters like education, health, etc.

Such caste-based discrimination has operated in both urban and rural labour markets. One study of Delhi[11] found that significant discrimination against Dalit workers operating dominantly through the mechanisms of recruitment and assignment to jobs led to Dalits largely entering poorly-paid 'dead-end' jobs that are essential but significantly lower paid. Similarly, empirical studies of caste behaviour in rural India have found that there are many ways in which caste practices operate to reduce the access of the lower castes to local resources as well as to income-earning opportunities, thereby forcing them to provide their labour at the cheapest possible rates to employers.[12] In addition to the well-known lack of assets, a large number of social practices effectively restrict the economic activity of lower caste and Dalit groups and force them to supply very low wage labour in harsh and usually precarious conditions. These practices in turn can be used to keep wages of Dalit workers (who are extremely constrained in their choice of occupation) low, even in a period of otherwise rising wages. The persistence of such practices and their economic impact even during the period of the Indian economy's much-vaunted dynamic growth has been noted.[13]

Gender-based differences in labour markets and the social attitudes to women's paid and unpaid work are also reflections of this broader tendency. The widespread perception that women's work forms an 'addition' to household income, and therefore commands a much lower reservation wage, is common to both private and public employers. So for private employers, women workers within Dalit or other discriminated groups typically receive even lower wages for similar work. In public employment, the use of underpaid women workers receiving well below minimum wages as Anganwadi workers or Accredited Social Health Activists (ASHAs) has become institutionalised in running several major flagship programmes that are designed to deliver essential public services of health, nutrition, support for early child development, and even education. Further, the role played by the unpaid labour of women in contributing not only to social reproduction but also to what would be recognised as productive economic activities in most other societies has been absolutely crucial in enabling this particular accumulation process.

So it may not be surprising that private agents find little value in accumulation strategies that are designed to enable structural transformation. Indeed, such transformation may even be to the detriment of their short-term interests, if it reduces their bargaining power. The low tolerance levels of capitalists in India to anything that can even slightly improve the bargaining power of workers is evident in the growing impossibility of even forming workers unions in most activities controlled by the private sector. It is clearly indicated by the ferocious and orchestrated backlash against something as limited as the Mahatma Gandhi National Rural Employment Guarantee Act (MGNREGA), only because it has provided some relief to rural workers who could at last begin to demand wages closer to the legal minimum from employers.

The point to note here is not simply that such practices continue to exist, but that they have become the base on which the economic accumulation process rests. In other words, capitalism in India, especially in its most recent globally integrated variant, has used past and current modes of social discrimination and exclusion to its own benefit, to facilitate the extraction of surplus and ensure greater flexibility and bargaining to employers when dealing with workers. So social categories are not 'independent' of the accumulation process— rather, they allow for more surplus extraction, because they reinforce low employment generating (and therefore persistently low wage) tendencies of growth. The ability to benefit from socially segmented labour markets in turn has created incentives for absolute surplus value extraction on the basis of suppressing wages of some workers, rather than requiring a focus on relative surplus value extraction resulting from productivity increases. High productivity enclaves have not generated sufficient demand for additional workers to force an extension of productivity improvement to other activities; instead the accumulation process has relied indirectly on persistent low wages in supporting activities or on unpaid labour to underwrite the expansion of value added. So the particular (possibly unique) pattern of Indian inequality has led to a long-run growth process that generates further and continued inequality and does not deliver the expected structural change.

Potential for Transformation

The future of the Indian economy depends largely on the extent to which it will be able to overcome these various failures and reduce the associated disparities. These problems are not unsurmountable: indeed, they essentially require a different vision of how the economy should be organised, in whose interests institutions should function and how society and economy must change towards greater justice and dignity for all citizens.

So let us allow ourselves to dream for a moment, and imagine some sort of ideal society: one in which some things that you cannot control (where you are born, what you are born as, the family into which you are born) do not affect your basic conditions of life (having a secure home; peace and security; access to nutritious food and other basic health; access to education; opportunities for work, leisure, self-expression, and social participation). This would not mean putting an end to all social and cultural differences, because after all, that is what makes life interesting. But it would mean that one's life chances are not fundamentally different because of the accident of birth. So if a person is born as a girl of a minority ethnic group in a rural area of a poor region, she would still have access to minimum conditions of life and opportunities for developing her capabilities that are not too different from a boy born in a well-off household of a dominant social group in an affluent society.

What would this require in terms of how Indian society and economy are organised? First, economic arrangements would not be oriented around the simple expansion of aggregate incomes and profits as the most significant goals. It is actually irrational to be obsessed with GDP growth. Consider just one example: a chaotic, polluting, congested, and exhausting system of privatised urban transport generates much more GDP than a clean, efficient, affordable and 'green' system of public transport. Second, other goals would matter: reasonable living conditions for all, development of people's capabilities and space for their creativity, decent employment opportunities, safe and clean environments. Access to the essentials of life—food, water, basic housing, and so on—would not be determined by the ability to pay but treated as human rights, made available to all in an affordable way. Third, market forces that help in achieving these goals would be encouraged, while those that operate to reduce standards of living and quality of life of ordinary people would be regulated, restricted or even abolished. Fourth, extreme inequalities would not be tolerated. Systems of taxation and distribution, as well as methods of monitoring and regulating pay and other returns, would ensure that material differences between people do not grow too large. Social discrimination and exclusion of all kinds would be actively discouraged and sought to be done away with. Fifth, there would be much greater social respect for nature. Economic activities would be monitored and assessed for the damage they do to nature, with a focus on reducing this as much as possible. Sixth, since the role of governments would obviously be much more important, they would have to be more genuinely democratic, transparent, and accountable, and adjust policies to changing conditions. There would be more people's voice and participation in the decisions that affect their lives. Governments would respect both the collective rights and concerns of groups and communities as well as the individual rights of all citizens.

Consider, for example, how demography is both threat and opportunity: to ensure that the opportunity is what dominates, forward-looking strategies need to be developed and implemented immediately. So public economic strategies must be oriented to the generation of decent work, especially for young people, rather than only focussed on GDP. This requires changes in economic policies, social policies, and educational policies. For the latter, the expansion of public secondary and higher education to generate skills relevant to the needs of Indian society is important. This in turn means less obsession with 'world class' and more focus on 'socially relevant and necessary'. Along with this there should be incentives to those who choose employment that is socially required and serves less privileged constituencies.

This may appear to be utopian, but in fact at least some of these are not so hard to achieve or at least to strive for, with the right political and social conditions and greater recognition of their importance. So ultimately, the future of the Indian economy is inextricably linked with the future of politics and social relations.

Endnotes

1 C. P. Chandrasekhar and Jayati Ghosh, 'The costs of coupling: The global crisis and the Indian economy,' in *Cambridge Journal of Economics* Symposium on the Financial Crisis (July 2009) 33: 725–739, doi:10.1093/cje/bep034.

2 K.P. Kannan and G. Raveendran, 'Growth sans employment: A quarter century of jobless growth in Indian organised manufacturing,' *Economic and Political*

Weekly, 44/10, 7 March (2009); Anshika Arora, 'Economic dualism, openness and employment in manufacturing industry in India,' (M. Phil thesis, Jawaharlal Nehru University, 2010).

3 Himanshu, 'Employment trends in India: A re-examination,' *Economic and Political Weekly*, 46/37, September 10 (2011); Nisha Srivastava and Ravi Srivastava, 'Women, Work and Employment Outcomes in Rural India,' *Economic and Political Weekly*, 45/28, 10 July (2010); Jayati Ghosh, *Never Done and Poorly Paid: Women's Work in Globalising India* (New Delhi: Women Unlimited, 2009); Jayati Ghosh, 'The curious case of the jobs that did not appear: Structural change, employment and social patterns in India,' *Indian Journal of Labour Economics*, 57/1 (2014).

4 Nisha Srivastava and Ravi Srivastava, 'Women, Work and Employment Outcomes in Rural India,' *Economic and Political Weekly*, 45/28, 10 July (2010); Himanshu, 'Employment trends in India: A re-examination,' *Economic and Political Weekly*, 46/37, September 10 (2011).

5 Indrajit Bairagya, 'Liberalization, Informal Sector and Formal-Informal Sectors' Relationship: A Study of India' (paper presented at 31st General Conference of The International Association for Research in Income and Wealth, St. Gallen, Switzerland, August 22–28, 2010).

6 Sumangala Damodaran, 'Global Production, Employment Conditions and Decent Work: Evidence from India's Informal sector,' ILO Working Paper (2010), http://www.ilo.org/legacy/english/protection/travail/pdf/rdwppt27b.pdf.

7 Barbara Harriss-White, *India's Market Society: Three Essays in Political Economy* (Delhi: Three Essays Collective, 2005).

8 Harish Damodaran, *India's New Capitalists: Caste, Business and Industry in a Modern Nation,* (London: Palgrave Macmillan 2008).

9 Chirashree Das Gupta 'Gender, property and the institutional basis of taxpolicy concessions: Investigating the Hindu Undivided Family,' 2012, http://www.macroscan.net/index.php?view=search&kwds=Chirashree%20Das%20Gupta.

10 Amit Thorat, 'Ethnicity, caste and religion: Implications for poverty outcomes,' *Economic and Political Weekly*, 45/51, December 18 (2010).

11 Biswajit Banerjee and John B. Knight, 'Caste discrimination in the Indian urban labour market,' *Journal of Development Economics*, 17/3, April (1985): 277–307.

12 Ghanshyam Shah, Harsh Mander, Sukhdeo Thorat, Satish Deshpande, and Amita Baviskar, *Untouchability in Rural India* (New Delhi: Sage Publications, 2006); Sukhdeo Thorat, Prashant Negi, Motilal Mahamallik, Chittaranjan Senapati, *Dalits in India: Search for a Common Destiny*, (New Delhi: Sage Publications 2009).

13 Human Rights Watch. 'India: Hidden Apartheid: Caste discrimination against India's "Untouchables",' Shadow Report to the UN Committee on the Elimination of Racial Discrimination, (2007), http://www.chrgj.org/docs/IndiaCERDShadowReport.pdf.

Human Development: Conceptual Foundations and Practice in India

Sandeep Dikshit

The post-World War-II era saw decolonisation accompanied by democratisation and the pre-eminence of welfare state philosophy and planned economic development. National leaders and policymakers displayed a greater understanding of the processes of economic growth, more concern for pro-poor growth that reduces drudgery and destitution, enables people to prosper and break from the shackles of birth, background, social and economic standing, and so on. Many scholars and 'social scientists' concerned themselves both theoretically and with evidence of what has been happening. Especially with the advent of the World Bank's World Development Reports, IMF's Article IV Reports, and UN Global Reports, the period since 1980 has seen more nuanced thinking of how growth and development must be taken forward, or managed, or controlled. As democracy deepens, and people and their misery and difficulties and aspirations for prosperity and progress become more and more important for governments, rulers, thinking people, and academics, recent periods have produced many ways of looking at how to push, manage, and direct growth and changes in our society, economy, and governments.

This contestation of ideas and ways of running and managing life, the extreme 'isms' have been the outposts between which we think and take our decisions on which side our nations and our society must go. They give us knowledge and tools to understand and then decide policy and programmes. Just as these are the broad and over-arching guides, and help create platforms and frameworks, there has also been critical thinking on how and what to invest in, how and what to enable, and how and what to ensure, even within the broad ideology inspired thrusts or frameworks of governments.

The entire discourse and outlook of 'human development' is precisely this—showing what growth, progress, investments by government and society, programmes for welfare, and initiatives aimed at providing better lives for people, should really ensure, and how. It draws very much on writings of economists such as Prof. Amartya Sen, and then thought through and designed into the form of 'human development' and written as human development reports by Prof. Sen and the Pakistani economist Dr Mahbub-ul-Haq. Not repeating its theoretical arguments, it states that we must bring people into the centre of development. To governments (in India for the state and central governments), it emphasises the importance of building peoples capabilities, by being adequately educated, and leading a long and healthy life. Added to this, is the need for accessing basic minimum services and a quality of life that ensures food, clothing, and shelter, security and dignity, respect and opportunities to fulfil ones reasonable dreams and desires. Governments must invest their resources, both financial and human, and policy and programmes into ensuring better education, better health, basic enabling infrastructure, basic services such as drinking water, sanitation, electricity, etc., and an environment that makes possible a life of dignity and security—good law and order, human rights, lack of discrimination, freedom of thought, expression, practise and beliefs, and respect and security for what one is.

Human development also emphasises the means for achievement of goals—otherwise a dictator or jailor can also deliver food and housing with a library and claim success. Or a genocidal or homicidal ruler can just eliminate the worse-off through massacres, mass starvation, or ethnic cleansing. Human development is humane development—its interrelated precepts being Equity, Efficiency, Sustainability, andParticipation (henceforth EESP).

All these together would make for better living conditions for people in a region/nation, than just economic growth. Evidence from the world over shows that nations that invested in their citizens and provided an enabling environment, recognising provision of services and civic amenities and infrastructure as entitlements, have done better than other nations. This was brought out convincingly in the first global *Human Development Report* (HDR) authored by Mahbub-ul-Haq and produced by the United Nations Development Programme (UNDP) in 1990.

The global HDR (published annually since 1990 and focussed on a different theme in every edition[1]) did two very important things, or had a significant impact. It succinctly put down in black and white, with evidence and solid data, that if you invest in people, in their education, health, basic infrastructure, and ensure better participation and democratic governance, then quality of people's lives improves much more than what just growth and other investments can bring about. Second, the reports also showed, that however rich a nation might be, and however impressive its growth rates and its per capita incomes, it does not always translate into 'human development'. Nations with better track records of people-centred investments and institutional development were measured better in human development. Many such instances surprised people, and in India's case, people suddenly woke up to find that neighhbours such a Sri Lanka had better human development indicators than us, and Bangladesh was doing better in indicators of gender and health than we were.

The human development reports also attempted to put together a simple composite index measuring human development and ranked nations on it. This measurement and ranking became much discussed and the ranking a matter of much concern to lower-ranked countries. In a way it brought a sense of competition amongst nations, a competition to increase the Human Development Index (HDI) and the rankings, as successive years of HDRs brought annual HDIs.

Both these points led to changes in the way nations and organisations talked of development, their discourse both within and outside their nations and in shaping development policy. India, was particularly impressed with this, and the decade of the 1990s saw a spurt, in what we outline below.

Human Development Reporting and India

Strong steps were being taken in the early 1990s to revive and speed up the Indian economy by substantial policy changes to spurt growth, through 'liberalisation, privatisation and globalisation'. These three words are often used to describe the changes of the time led by the then Finance Minister Dr Manmohan Singh.[2] The international HDRs had meanwhile brought international attention to 'human development', especially the human development indices, which ranked nations. The attention was both a sense of competition, as well as a more serious look at how and why did the country stand where it did, and since India was being ranked amongst the worst performing nations, the HDI became a number we could not hide from.

So while the Central Government focussed on putting the economy on track and going for accelerating it, there was a sense that we may forget elements of real development, looking at concerns of the poor, provisioning for them, spending on social sectors and social security, and inviting in backward regions and on backward communities. This discomfort with economic reforms found a support in the growing focus on and vocabulary of human development, and helped to maintain focus on social sectors, on direct anti-poverty measures, on social security, and on insisting that the state remains the major provider of services in education, health, basic infrastructure, and essential amenities like drinking water.

India had had for a long time a strong tradition of academicians, experts, and practitioners cautioning against just growth-led development, and in many ways articulating just what 'human development' was saying. This tradition gave human development its thinkers and experts.

In 1993, the international report was released in India in New Delhi, bringing human development and its writing to a much larger audience. In 1995, the state government of Madhya Pradesh published its own state-level human development report,[3] sponsored by the government but written independently. A brave report, it talked openly of the gaps in development, a habit that Indian governments did not have, and this reported kick started a few things.

One was opening up of writings and discussions on complimentary and/or alternate paths to development, alongside national-level economic reforms. These writings underlined the experience of some states like Kerala, Himachal Pradesh, and even Tamil Nadu, Maharashtra, Uttarakhand etc., as states that had invested in education, health, in peoples' organisations, in local self-government, and had achieved remarkable progress in human development indicators, much ahead of their performance on the economy front.

While today we hear about the 'Gujarat model', in India each state is a model in different aspects of human development, and clearly may have done so without sacrificing at the altar of economic growth. Kerala, perhaps a mid-level economic performer, rivalled the world's best in educational and health achievements. Clearly one did not have to wait for high growth to deliver a better quality of life in terms of health and education. Tamil Nadu, showed impressive gains in health, fertility, nutrition, women's development, etc. Himachal Pradesh had impressive education and health outcomes and last mile infrastructure, and Uttarakhand had much better human development indicators than Uttar Pradesh, inspite of a common 50-year government, only because of better investments and public participation in social sectors. That such a line of policy action and investing of public funds will bring in greater and more equitable impact could not be denied by these reported and analysed state-level experiences. Human Development had come to stay in India.

Following the example of Madhya Pradesh, many other states started similar assessments and put them in the public domain. Karnataka came out with a report in 1998, Rajasthan in 2002, etc. The United Nations partnered with the Planning Commission to support state governments to write their reports,[4] leading both to nearly all states bringing out HDRs and also spurning action on HD. Within states, the reports brought attention to regional imbalances, social imbalances, to critical gaps, say in Infant Mortality Rates (IMRs), or immunisation, or child sex ratio, or discrimination, or disparity, etc. Inter-district comparisons on the basis of district-level HDIs became the deciding tool for allocations and focussed action. Good examples of achievements within a state and from other states caught the attention of policymakers.

A clique of public policy thinkers and experts concerning themselves with tackling the new economic policy, found this an attractive line to pursue. There were two reasons for this, one that it was a powerful set of ideas in which they believed sincerely, complementing the economic changes would cover questions of equity, justice, and impact on the poor and disadvantaged. Second was that for many of these public policy experts, it was a good sugar-coating to usher in reforms that were not finding great resonance amongst a large section of Indians, especially since these reforms were coming without popular political support.

There was an equally vocal and powerful group of policy influencers, who were cautioning against this line, since they actually believe that growth trickles down to eventually affecting lives of all people positively. They were worried that the emphasis of human development should not dilute financial and policy priorities to anything apart from reforms, opening up the economy, industrialisation, and apportioning resources to easing industrial and financial growth.

HDRs brought much action on the human development front. In Madhya Pradesh, allocations to these sectors increased from 19 per cent in the Eighth Plan period to 42 per cent in the Ninth Plan period, with missions on human development, more effective decentralisation to panchayat, and conceptualisation of the idea of district governments. Karnataka prepared its first report in 1998, and followed it up with sustained action. The report had bipartisan support and was used in elections to forefront development issues. Using the report, the government set up task forces on education and health, and even the World Bank used these reports to set development conditionalities in their structural adjustment loan. Sikkim made its report the basis for the Tenth Plan, created a legislator's forum to debate on HD issues, so that there was political support, and many research projects were initiated to promote livelihoods.

Maharashtra undertook wide consultations for the report, undertook regional strategy discussions, and initiated action research on determinants of human development such as quality of education, access of tribal community to health, diversification of rural economy, and a District Human Development Programme for low HDI districts.

As the momentum of HD writing caught speed, there were efforts at the national level also to not just write a national human development report but also to mainstream this into government policy, and significantly the Eighth Five-Year Plan stated that 'Human development will be the ultimate goal of the Eighth Plan. It is towards this that employment generation, population control, literacy, education, health, drinking water and provision of adequate food and basic infrastructure are listed as the priorities'.[5] Subsequent five-year plans focus on human development targets as national development goals. The *Economic Survey* published by the Union Finance Ministry also began to have a separate chapter on Human Development.

It would not be an exaggeration to say that these reports, international and local media and public attention drawn by them, led to further mainstreaming of education, health, social security, gender equality, and greater detail paid to outcome indicators. Indicators such as the infant mortality rate, maternal mortality rate, human development indices, gender-related development index (showing male-female disparity in human development), retention rate in schools, mean schooling years, gender ratio and so on, gained policy and public attention as never before. These also graduated into more details covering other aspects of measuring development.

Phases of Human Development Writing

In a period when economic growth was centre stage and when nearly all political formations and governments, state and central, moved to believing and acting for growth and promoting economic diversification, industrial and service sector growth, albeit in modern sectors, the continued stress on human development balanced the set of priorities. Starting in 1995 with Madhya Pradesh writing its first state-level HDR,[6] many states followed. The thematic focus of these reports initially in every state focussed on problems and issues in human development, the gaps and financial, institutional, and other issues, as well as how and what could be done to take the state forward. In time, as some states went beyond just one edition, they entered into different relevant themes, and these themes can be related with the state governments own commitments and balance between action, its output and their propaganda.

Some of the reports acted as part of the overall conviction of state leadership to invest in and better the human development conditions of their people. In such cases, the reports usually were honestly written, did an in-depth assessment of where the state stood and then the states complemented it with action. The bureaucracy played a proactive role in ensuring honesty in writing and then in turning the document into a push for work. The other side were states that really did it to just tick off that they too had written it. In such cases, action did not really correspond to these reports, and in fact in such states, human development did not become a priority for state policy.

The purpose and independence of state reports has changed in time. As politics became more bitterly contested, some states went back from producing an honest appraisal to coded reports with propaganda as its principal purpose. In some cases, state governments did not even own their reports or take them seriously, rejecting them as vehemently as they ignored the prevalent human development faultiness in their states. This break from the tradition of independent writing is a serious concern. Just as honest appraisal and identifying gaps in development and in programmes led to positive action, hiding these and propagating manufactured data and half truths in recent years is leading to a near irrelevance of human development reports for many states. Earlier, work on human development acted as companion documents to state action on human development, unfortunately now they appear as companions to less serious handouts by publicity departments.

As we stand today, twenty years from the first Indian human development report, the changes or lack of them since the 1990s agitate for taking a fresh look at the strategy of writing on human development, and seeking areas for action. There has been progress on the human development front, evidenced by nearly universal school enrolment, accessible and better equipped schools, drop in infant and child mortality, decrease in malnutrition (although very slow), focussed policy and programme attention on improving sex ratios, especially child sex ratio, closing of the gender gap in many development indicators, provision of basic infrastructure such as approach roads, electricity connections, and even in safe drinking water, and decline in income poverty. But now, we seem to be in a period of dullness in the urgency that the last two to three decades saw. Initiatives in human development appear to become appendages to economic growth, liberalising the economy, putting financial, natural, and national resources for productive purposes rather than for social purposes and social justice.

While the way to becoming even a moderately developed HD nation is a long way away for India, Its national and state governments seem to be moving into other spheres of focus. India has not been able to improve its relative ranking in HDI to any substantial level, moving in the range from the 130s to 120s and then back again to the 130s. Investments in human development are not including the serious issue of growing inequality that leads to social unrest, and inefficiencies. The focus on equity in distribution of national resources is not a priority, as natural resources, taxation benefits, subsidy regimes, and governments promotional expenses are looking to industrial, and service industries, foreign investments, and skills described as those serving modern industrial and domestic demands, as against improving the existing skill base of our own industrial, artisanal, small-scale to tiny-scale manufacturing strengths. Sustainability, an inalienable concern of human development, the latest commitments to Climate Change agreements post-Paris notwithstanding, is not being prioritised in most instances in government's action. Priority clearance for projects with environment concerns, attempt to give clearances to and ease norms for diverting forests lands for the purposes, and open invitations for capital to partner in natural resource–based manufacturing, with the promise of eased environment protection is one side of the issue. Working against sustainable goals is also the growing dependence on fossil fuels both in transport and power, unplanned urban growth, a missing policy for urban growth, and how to manage and dispose solid waste, water management, and urban green cover. Participation, which makes the fourth of the EESP structure of human development, is also in a state of withdrawal from the high days of the 1980s and 1990s. While, the power and governance division between the states and Central Government has now stabilised, the third tier of local self-government has become nothing more than an executing branch of the government, with no legislative powers, hardly any financial powers, except for in an urban setting, no personnel, and poor institutional strengthening to turn them into powerful units of self-government. Not only has people's participation in government reduced due to this, there is also a change in the implementation practices of government. People's or community-based organisations, except for in thrift and credit are now no longer a preferred medium to implement programmes. Cooperatives have failed to take off except in isolated cases as in dairy, and in some states like Maharashtra, Gujarat, and Tamil Nadu. Voluntary organisations or what is also termed as civil society has been facing a backlash from governments, and revenue, and law and order administrations to squeeze them from the space of questioning and articulating people's concerns, and as keepers of public consciousness.

These changes have slowed considerably the momentum to impact of human development as far as government action is concerned. While some challenges have been adequately met, and some in smaller measure, real turnovers haven't taken place. What Kerala and Mizoram have been able to achieve, and what Maharashtra, Himachal Pradesh, Uttarakhand, Tamil Nadu, Karnataka, etc., have achieved to some extent, is even within these states highly uneven, with some districts and communities lagging far behind their state averages. States like Uttar Pradesh, Bihar, Jharkhand, Madhya Pradesh, Odisha, Assam, and to a lesser extent West Bengal, Gujarat, Haryana, and Punjab, are all still struggling to ensure honourable declines in IMR, in Maternal Mortality Rate (MMR), in ensuring seven years of quality schooling, in stopping declining child sex ratios, in eliminating malnourishment, leave alone the more serious prevelance of 'stunting'and 'wasting'amongst children, etc. The disparity is not only geographic, it is, of course, also rural-urban, but within a region, there are marginalised communities, women suffer much worse conditions, scheduled castes and scheduled tribes remain backward, and amongst them there are groups who are even worse off.

While the human development status improves, but remains unacceptably low, policy and programme concerns are becoming more and more economic. There have also been some large shifts. From these arise new concerns that the umbrella of human development must take into consideration and link with its existing concerns and prescriptions. A major issue is the one of increasing disparities/inequalities in incomes, of course, and also in a substantial manner in wealth. Estimates show that the top 10 percentile of wealthy people own 74 per cent of the total wealth of India, while the bottom 50 per cent own just 9 per cent, and bottom 30 per cent just 4.7 per cent.[7] Another estimate says that the wealth owned by the top one per cent, the wealthiest, is 49 per cent of the total wealth, that is to say that one per cent of Indians own more than what the other 99 per cent own, and the same study also shows that the total wealth of 100 of India's richest individuals is more than the wealth of two-third of all Indians.

Such severe wealth inequality, and on the increase since the liberalisation era of the 1990s impacts social balance, and has its own connotations of law and order. Apart from that it also tells of an unjust taxation system, and the dangers, already evident in our society, of highly concentrated wealth and what it does to destabilise true democracy, subvert institutions necessary for democracy such as the elected executive, policy making, media and messaging through the world of entertainment and visual and verbal mediums, including control of the internet. This kind of wealth concentration also perpetrates these conglomerates favouring further accumulation, and also in turn makes the policy, taxation, and investment climate such that returns of their wealth become higher than returns on smaller capital, on owners of capital, knowledge, and other assets. It seems today as if the question of inequality has disappeared from being a concern, and is being lauded and celebrated as a national good.

The other emerging red zone is the entire issue of natural resources, their ownership, management, sustainable exploitation, share of profit, profiting or profiteering, and to how much extent can private enterprise make profits out of a public good/public asset. Let us for our convenience divide natural resources into three groups—the minor minerals, using the official definition of all basic construction material derived from mining like stones, sand, etc.; major minerals, the expensive minerals that, once treated, provide critical elements for production like steel, zinc, aluminium, copper etc.; and the natural resources of daily usufruct usage like water, timber, minor forest produce, etc. In case of minor minerals, right from the auction or allotment of mining rights mines, to illegal mining, to over-exploitation, to unsustainable exploitation, to unacceptable labour practices, it is a quagmire. The exploitation of other natural resources once again is loaded in favour of powerful persons or groups with ownership of political, financial, and social capital, and access to power. While fisherfolk are pushed away from traditional rights to fishing in flowing waters, companies are being apportioned water fronts for withdrawal of water for their factories. While people who live in forest areas are allowed the bare minimum of usufruct and minor forest produce to keep their livelihoods, large-scale timber felling goes on, and forest lands are being diverted to industries and tourism facilities. In the case of major minerals, the solid financial resources of a nation, ever since mines are being handed over for mining to private parties, genuine questions of pricing, of duties of auction/sale/ allocation rates/cess are being raised. And questions are not just on how much does a private party pay? The question to be asked is who does eventually pay? If you raise coal allocation rates by auction, do mining companies pay from their own costs or are they passed onto coal users?

The regime of natural resources should be analysed with different lenses. The ability to exploit natural resources, both that require capital and technology and even those that require managing local administration, put them out of reach of communities and common people. The cross between sustainable mining, maximising profits, environmental protection, state actors and private collusion, and illegal mining, leads to the simple question of whether public assets or resources can be turned into cornered profit for some?

Another sphere is the role, and impact of non-state actors. Non-state actors have always been influencing both society and the economy, and state polity and policy. It is not very easy to define non-state actors. In our context they would straddle quite a few typologies. Non-state actors range from those running quasi-governments in Naxalite belts to highly wealthy and publicly influential religious gurus; from large voluntary organisations registered, formalised, and doing on-field-level effective work, to those that influence policy and public thinking through advocacy, whether of rights or governments' actions or of cultural and political ideas, but remain funded, and are able to take morally superior grounds, without the trudge of agencies actually working on the field.

Non-state actors would also include civil society organisations, but there must be a careful read of them, as many are only disguised outreaches of the state, led, nurtured, funded, promoted and supported by governments, by those running and supporting governments, and many are elite initiatives. They also include the large number of persons and organisations that are using distant communication mechanisms to spur and excite small-scale to large-scale movement, through propaganda, both progressive and which is made from half-truths, to downright lies. These have in recent years affected good changes on a large-scale affecting governments, unleashing violence, distorting systems and destabilising regimes, countries, governments, political parties, and cultural and social patterns.

The gender question, along with the same for other marginalised communities remains one of unequal rights, development, capability attainments and access to entitlements. These specially include the girl child, girls in the adolescent stage, women of reproductive age, scheduled castes, scheduled tribes, tribal people living in or at the margins of forests, displaced people, people living in mining zones, etc.

To summarise, it seems clear that both work on human development by governments, as well as action on it, is now no longer in the exciting period ofthe 1990s. The new concerns that were not addressed earlier and neither seem to be on anyone's scanner must be now looked at by governments, public policy mandarins and development practitioners. We have listed just some that appear to look crucial. An important way of expanding the scope is to expand the constituency or audience of the HDRs, focusing more on directly influencing political will. However, for this to happen effectively, the focus could move away from increasing technical sophistication and formulas. It could be more on popular discourse that political leaders and influencers of opinion in the political space. This audience may not have the elegance and erudition of international agencies and forums, but it would have an immediacy of impact and action that would improve the credibility of the HDR.

India has the largest portfolio globally of HDRs, experts, and projects—it is time it showed the way to the world of how HDR messaging can be simplified to be effective in the political domain and how data can be used as a trigger for action. After all, HDRs are important but Human Development is more important!

Endnotes

1 Details of the HDRs can be found at http://hdr.undp.org/en.

2 In 1991, when DrManmohan Singh became India's Finance Minister, the Indian economy was in shambles. The fiscal deficit was at unsustainable levels of almost 8.5 per cent of gross domestic product (GDP). The current account deficit was close to 3.5 per cent of GDP, and India's international ratings were so low that no one was willing to finance this deficit. There was barely a forex reserve of a billion US dollars that could just about sustain two weeks of imports.

3 The Madhya Pradesh report can be found at http://www.dif.mp.gov.in/downloadhdro.htm.

4 To get an idea of this collaboration and impact on public policy in India, please see http://planningcommission.nic.in/sectors/hdbi/rep_analysis.pdf.

5 Planning Commission, *8th Five Year Plan*, Vol. I., Section 1.4.4, (New Delhi: Government of India, 1992–1997).

6 The Madhya Pradesh HDR in 1995 was the world's first sub-national HDR. I have had the privilege of being associated with the writing of this report, and have seen with interest and excitement the change in human development reporting and focus on it over the last 20 years.

7 Credit Suisse. *Global Wealth Databook 2014,* (Zurich: Credit Suisse Research Institute, 2014), https://publications.credit-suisse.com/tasks/render/file/?fileID=5521F296-D460-2B88-081889DB12817E02.

Whither India's Economic Reforms?

Jaithirth Rao

Way back in the balmy 1950s, in a little town in Tamil Nadu (then Madras State) called Avadi, at a session of the Indian National Congress, an important resolution was passed. It committed the party and presumably the country (since that party had undisputed political control of the country) to something known as a 'socialistic' pattern of society. One always wonders what difference there is between 'socialist' and 'socialistic'. Be that as it may. Several fateful decisions followed. It was decided by the powers that be that all major industries (the Stalinist vocabulary referred to it as the 'core sector') would be made by the state through so-called Public Sector Undertakings (PSUs). The private sector would be tolerated, but was required to be 'subservient' to the public sector, which would always get preferences and special accommodation.

The private sector would be gingerly and hesitantly 'allowed' to start industries, but only after spending three years chasing paperwork through 17 government departments/agencies/commissions (in those days one new department was being created in socialistic Delhi every month). Naturally, only persons/families/companies that were already entrenched in business would get these licenses and those who got these licenses worked hard at preventing others from getting them. And within the private sector, foreign investors were treated particularly harshly. They had to pay high taxes, their funds were blocked in India for long periods of time due to a bewildering set of exchange control regulations and of course, they were given very few licenses.

With regard to agriculture, we decided that the only service to be rendered by the state to farmers was 'lip service'. We mercilessly taxed industrial imports and made industrial products expensive to the detriment of farmers. We even taxed the export of agricultural products (remember our famous export duties on tea which encouraged Kenya to go in for tea planting and ensured that we conceded market share to other countries?). Agricultural growth was sluggish and we had to frequently fall back on 'crisis imports', for which we could not afford to pay. The countries who 'aided' us attempted to extract their political pound of flesh.

Finally, we woke up. But instead of taking the obvious step of eliminating the distortions in relative prices, we decided to go in for guaranteed procurement prices for select crops and high subsidies for fertilisers and pesticides. The inevitable happened. The production of those crops where we had high procurement prices, shot up; even areas of the country unsuitable for growing water-intensive crops like rice, started using precious aquifer water to grow rice. We soon started having mountains of wheat and rice. A lot of these grains rotted as our 'public sector' storage facilities were inadequate. In some years, we actually exported some of these food grains at a loss, thus becoming generous benefactors of countries much richer than us. The inevitable happened again. The consumption of subsidised fertilisers and pesticides shot up.

Here there was a sub-plot. We subsidised some kinds of fertilisers more than others. So these fertilisers got consumed in excess of what might be technically desirable. These fertilisers and excessive pesticides poisoned our fields and our crops. Indian fertiliser plants which were technically less efficient than foreign plants (in some measure due to licensing restrictions keeping them smaller in size than economies of scale would warrant) stayed remarkably profitable. The industrialists favoured by our socialistic government did quite well. In fact, the favoured friends of our government did extremely well in terms of having protected profit margins, but they remained midgets in size under their licensing constraints, compared to their counterparts in other countries.

In the meantime, socialistic state governments decided that it made sense to supply free power to farmers. This encouraged the farmers to pump out 'free' water and started a process of long-term desertification. Because the socialistic state governments were sometimes unable or unwilling to supply regular good quality power, the socialistic central government decided to heavily subsidise diesel so that farmers could continue to over-mine precious deep aquifer water and continue with accelerated desertification. Between the socialistic central government and the socialistic state governments, sector after sector got nationalised—electricity generation, electricity distribution, passenger road transport, banking, insurance, coal mining, airlines, telephones, radio, television, and so on.

All these sectors which had worked reasonably efficiently in a competitive private sector, now slowly and steadily deteriorated. The governments also entered new areas: hotels, bakeries, pharmaceuticals, photo films, film finance, fisheries—you name it—socialistic thoughts occupied the commanding heights and commanded lows of our economy! The socialistic governments also decided that it was their duty to take over private companies that were heading for bankruptcy. So quite a few loss-making mills, factories and other establishments became 'public sector undertakings'.

There were plenty of jobs for IAS officers and railway engineers to have and to hold in the ever-growing tropical jungle of PSUs. There were nice contracts for those who were friendly with the political powers that be. There was immense featherbedding and large unionised labour forces were created, provided of course the unions were affiliated to the great Congress Party! As time went by, things got worse (or better if you were of the socialistic persuasion). The sacred Constitution of India was amended with a lie. The preamble now states that on 26 January 1950, we decided to call ourselves a Socialist Republic—something that is at variance with history. In all these years, many countries, especially to the east of India, became rich and prosperous and improved the lives of their citizens. India trundled along. Our persistent poverty created plenty of job opportunities for economists, sociologists, political pundits, bureaucrats, and members of various honorable committees and commissions, empowered committees and so on. Our socialistic government grew like Topsy. Where we had seven secretaries in imperial Delhi in 1947, running a larger country (which included present day Pakistan, Bangladesh, and possibly Aden) we now had three hundred secretaries and thousands of joint secretaries or jet-secs as they liked to be called. We had ministries galore—all successfully claiming to help citizens, while oppressing them no end. India really had proved that it was a sui generis country!

And then came Narasimha Rao—another name for a whirlwind. Narasimha Rao abolished industrial licensing, denied the public sector its automatic right to commanding heights and commanded lows, abolished the quaint British wartime office of the Controller of Capital Issues and substituted it with a modern Securities and Exchange Board of India (SEBI), got rid of the draconian Foreign Exchange Regulation Act (FERA) and substituted it with a benign, mildly irritating Foreign Exchange Management Act (FEMA), encouraged exporters as distinct from penalising them and so on. The somnolent economic energies of the Indian people were dragged into a waking state. After an aberrant interregnum, Narasimha Rao was followed by Vajpayee, who though a tad more hesitant, did by and large build on the foundations laid by his eminent predecessor.

The cardinal mistake that both Rao and Vajpayee succumbed to was that all their reforming good works were acts of stealth. The country simply did not have the courage to drop the silly socialist word from the new false preamble to its constitution. Businesses still operated under hostile sufferance, not in a neutral world, let alone an encouraging ecosystem. The numerous ministries in Delhi and their counterparts in the states worked at cross purposes erecting barriers and hurdles to entrepreneurship. The tax czars were unrelenting with any sector that did well. They forgot the tenets of Kautilya and Raja Todar Mal.

They continued with inexorable energy to try and kill each and every golden goose that was just beginning to emerge. Again, India trundled along as other countries continued to move ahead at a faster pace. 'Operation Stealth' was good enough to double the growth rate of the economy. It just was not good enough to make that all-important breakthrough from poverty to prosperity. The country at large, did not embrace the view that business and entrepreneurship could be a force for good, could create jobs, make goods and services available, and make the citizens prosperous.

The residual legacy of the Permit-License Raj (possibly more tyrannical than the predecessor British Raj apropos of the economic activities of its citizens) ensured that several 'favoured' businesses got good deals thus sapping the moral basis of Rao's reforms. The inability of both Rao and Vajpayee to openly embrace economic reform and to blatantly give up silly socialistic mantras, meant that the country lurched forward—it did not move forward and certainly not fast enough. Vajpayee's coy nomenclature 'Ministry of Disinvestment' instead of a *khullam-khulla* 'Ministry of Privatisation' comes to mind. Tragically, even this feeble ministry was shut down in the next dispensation.

Then came the backlash. Manmohan Singh, who as Rao's lieutenant had been an intrepid reformer, seems to have interpreted his unexpected mandate as a sign from the electorate to go back to the salad days of the Avadi Congress session. Because so much had been done by stealth, because there had been no open love of markets as shown by Ronald Reagan and Margaret Thatcher, not even the partial love shown by Tony Blair, the intellectual and political foundations of economic reform gave way. More ministries in Delhi were empowered. More secretaries and jet-secs were appointed and they all got together to make sure that gears were reversed.

The fashionable expression in the revived socialistic atmosphere of unfazed Kremlinesque Delhi was that of 'economic rights'. Suddenly the hapless citizens of India were showered with a new set of rights (despite the fact that their original Fundamental Rights, were not necessarily very well guarded)—the rights to information, education, employment, land, food, and so on. Clever, clever socialistic embrace through the backdoor! One cannot forget that the much-maligned 'right to property', which had been by a sleight of hand made non-fundamental (assuming that is a passable word) was not given any central position.

The right to property had been attacked by the mandarins of Avadi as supportive of maharajas, zamindars, industrialists, and businessmen. No one was willing to name and shame the unclothed emperor. If property had been a Fundamental Right, the farmers of India would have been protected against unfair acquisitions undertaken to help large businesses set up car manufacturing plants. Again, be that as it may. Meanwhile sundry despots (Telecom Regulatory Authority of India, Department of Telecommunications, Central Board of Direct Taxes) and others continued their attacks. The poster boy, the IT Industry, started getting tax notices about on-site earnings despite pledges to the contrary made on the floor of parliament by several ministers with the taxman typically using a subclause in a circular to justify rapacious demands.

The one foreign investor who actually set up a plant to manufacture telephones and who gave jobs to tens of thousands of young women was frontally assaulted by the taxmen of the state and the center and driven out. Another foreign investor, who discovered oil and gas in the desert and who should have been a poster boy of the creative success of foreign investment, was repeatedly hounded on one technicality after the other. And when the shenanigans of the government's favoured businesses were exposed by courts and by government auditors—what did we do?

We decided that all businesses were crooked and brought the pace of all economic activity virtually down to a trickle. Because of the persistence of the strategy of 'stealth', no one was or is willing to say that businesses become crooked when laws give them incentives to be crooked. If someone can arm-twist a government bank and obtain an easy loan, if someone can get cheap land under the guise of setting up a special economic zone (one wonders why the whole country cannot be special—why are only some zones special? Is that inherent to crony socialistic behavior?), then as night follows day, these atrocious events will come to pass. The solution is to embrace wider reform and genuinely competitive markets, not to stop all businesses.

The nadir of the Manmohan Singh government's regime was reached when it finally decided to destroy India's reputation as a country ruled by laws, not by whimsical tyrants. Having lost a case in the supreme court, the government retrospectively amended a tax law laughably and untruthfully arguing that the new attempt at fiscal plunder was actually the intent of the parliamentarians of 1961! The argument we had in our armoury that we differed from our more efficient and more prosperous neighbour to our north, in that we had fair laws and fair courts was lost—probably irretrievably for decades to come.

This was not sufficient. The government came up with an infantile Companies Act imitating the worst provisions of the hysterical and ill-conceived Sarbanes-Oxley Legislation of the US. The new version of the Companies Act, plus hasty moves of an otherwise well-run SEBI, plus unwarranted intrusions by the Reserve Bank of India, plus silly tax provisions (no options for directors/advisors/consultants; taxation when companies raise subsequent rounds of funding at higher levels, no contingent sale to foreigners, etc.) all proceeded to make the environment hostile for new enterprises, which promptly started locating themselves in Singapore, to their benefit and our detriment. Not to be far behind in the act of comical imitation, our imperious income tax czars came up with a multi-page form copied almost word for word from the US Internal Revenue Service—forms which are universally derided around the world as stupid and counterproductive. Our uncanny ability to copy the weaknesses of other countries (mind you, not their strengths) never ceases to amaze us hapless Indian citizens. As for agriculture, the underlying

Gordian knot progressively gets more knotted and paralyses the country. We kept raising prices of wheat and rice creating mountains of grains; we kept mispricing fertilisers, distorting their usage, and—except in one state—we kept giving away free power unintelligently. We must be the only country in the world using ground water to grow water-hungry sugarcane. We kept promising high prices to cane farmers and we kept confusing and hobbling sugar mills, always lending a helping hand to friends, of course.

In the meantime, no one seems to care that we are not making any progress with pulses and oilseeds. No one seems to care that we have the lowest crop yields in the world, not just marginally behind, but orders of magnitude behind other countries. No wonder our farmers keep encroaching on forests. If yields were high, we could possibly give up farm-land for forests. But such intelligent and optimistic developments are unlikely to be part of our national destiny. The worst tragedy to hit our agriculture was the Luddite move to ban/postpone/effectively smother genetically modified (GM) crops. We can take joy from that fact that not only were we among the last countries to introduce televisions, we will be the last country to benefit from the Genetic Revolution.

And now, we have a new government that needs to grapple with the issue of reform by stealth. It is a tough one. As an obdurate Opposition, they had opposed foreign investment in insurance (with an elaborate and sanctimonious committee report), they had blocked the Goods and Services Tax Bill, they had vociferously defended retrospective taxation, they had for patriotic and other reasons opposed GM crops, and they had actually supported a Land Acquisition Law which is impossible to implement. Now what does one do?

The biggest source of optimism is the change in vocabulary—which is the first step to abandoning the stealth' strategy. It is good to acknowledge that the Indian state has been indulging in 'Tax Terrorism' and that this needs curbing. It is good to acknowledge that the government cannot (despite the promises of Avadi) do everything. It is good to acknowledge that we must actually make an attempt to climb the rankings of business-friendly countries. But that is not enough. The ghosts of Avadi are still present everywhere and these are powerful ghosts. The supporters of crony capitalism both inside and outside the state apparatus are still around in large numbers. Numerous government departments, commissions, ministries and committees exist which are fundamentally and almost implacably hostile to businesses, entrepreneurship, and wealth creation.

And of course, the socialists of India remain strong, loud, and hysterical, almost as if they do not know that the Berlin Wall has fallen and the Gosplan in the Kremlin has been dismantled. The 2008 financial crisis, the Great Recession (December 2007 to June 2009), and the recent setbacks in China have now become powerful arguments to stymie and perhaps even to roll back economic reform in India.

Unless our leadership is able to openly and convincingly communicate with the entire country and build a constituency for a state that supports businesses—small and big—the roadside hawker (who is needlessly harassed by the minions of the state—what would they rather have the hawker do to make a living? Commit crimes?), the young entrepreneur who gets blatantly unfair service tax notices, the foreign investor who is always unclear about ever-changing rules, the Indian company which never knows how much money to raise from which investor as the domestic/foreign nature of the company and the investor can remain forever in doubt, the company Chief Executive Officer (CEO) who is now required to spend more time on the new Companies Act compliance matters than on meeting customers or making products—all of these need protection, support, help and nurturing, not hostility and harassment.

Franklin Roosevelt, Margaret Thatcher, Ronald Reagan and Deng Xiaoping were all great communicators. They knew that in the final analysis, progress requires large sections of the population to be carried along. The required changes cannot be implemented by stealth. If and only if India embraces market-friendly (note, not friendly businessman-friendly!) policies openly, loudly, unabashedly, and unapologetically, will the country finally move to higher levels of prosperity and speedier elimination of poverty.

Otherwise, we risk trundling along—mostly moving sideways as other countries cruise ahead.

Black Money: We Won't Get it Back

Vivek Kaul

In the campaign of the 2014 Lok Sabha elections, Narendra Modi had been very vocal about getting the black money that had escaped Indian shores, back to India. This focus has continued even after he took over as the prime minister of the country on 26 May 2014. Though, two years later, there is little to show for all the effort that may have been put in to get this black money back, despite a lot of noise being made.

The question is, does it make any sense to go chasing all the black money that has left Indian shores? Before we get into answering this question, it makes sense to define what 'black money' is. At the most simple level, black money is essentially income that has been earned and on which taxes have not been paid.

The 'White Paper on Black Money' released by the Ministry of Finance in May 2012, defines black money as: 'any income on which the taxes imposed by government or public authorities have not been paid.' The wealth that has been accumulated in this way 'may consist of income generated from legitimate activities or activities which are illegitimate per se, like smuggling, illicit trade in banned substances, counterfeit currency, arms trafficking, terrorism, and corruption,' the White Paper goes on to suggest.

Of course, this wealth that has been accumulated through tax evasion has 'neither been reported to the public authorities at the time of their generation nor disclosed at any point of time during their possession.'

This money does not lie idle. Some of it escapes the shores of this country. An estimate made by Washington-based research and advocacy group Global Financial Integrity in a report titled *Illicit Financial Flows from Developing Countries: 2003-2012,* suggests that around $439.6 billion (henceforth in US$) of black money left Indian shores, between 2003 and 2012.[1]

Also, this estimate does not take into account hawala transactions and the misinvoicing of trade. As the report points out: 'Many illicit transactions occur in cash to prevent an incriminating paper trail. For these many reasons our estimates are likely very conservative.'[2] Even with these weaknesses, there is no denying that a substantial amount of money seems to have escaped Indian shores between 2003 and 2012. And there is no reason to suggest that this process wouldn't have continued in the years to come.

India is ranked number four (behind China, Russia, and Mexico) when it comes to the total amount of black money leaving a developing country. The interesting thing nonetheless is that the quantum of money leaving India has increased dramatically during the Congress-led United Progressive Alliance (UPA) years. In 2003, around US$10.18 billion left the country. By 2012, this had jumped by more than 9 times to US$94.8 billion. Interestingly, the number in 2009 was at US$29 billion. This clearly tells us that the second term of the Congress-led UPA which started in May 2009 was fairly corrupt, leading to a lot of black money leaving Indian shores

Also, the amount of money leaving China grew by 3.9 times between 2003 and 2012. In the case of Russia the increase was 3 times, whereas in the case of Mexico the increase was 1.6 times. Hence, the jump in the Indian case was clearly the most. The US$439.6 billion that has left the country works out to around 23 per cent of the Indian GDP of US$1.88 trillion in 2013. Given this, it is a large amount of money and hence, the Modi government's interest in getting this money back, seems justified. While things may always be possible, what we need to look at is whether they are probable. And the answer in this case is no. Conventional wisdom has it that all this money is lying in Swiss banks. But that is an incorrect assumption to make.

As Cambridge University economist Ha-Joon Chang writes in *Bad Samaritans—The Guilty Secrets of Rich Nations and the Threat to Global Prosperity*: 'Switzerland is *not* a country living off black money deposited in its secretive banks...It is, in fact, literally the most industrialized country in the world.'[3]

Data released by the Swiss central bank, the Swiss National Bank, suggests that Indian money in Swiss banks was at around Rs 14,000 crore in 2013. In 2006, the total amount had stood at Rs 41,000 crore. The reason for this fall is simple. Over the last few years as black money and Switzerland have come into focus, it would be stupid for individuals or companies sending black money out of India, to keep sending it to Switzerland.

What further needs to be realised is that there are around 70 tax havens all around the world. An estimate made by the International Monetary Fund suggests that around US$18 trillion of wealth lies in international tax havens other than Switzerland, beyond the reach of any tax authorities. An estimate made by *The Economist* in 2013 suggested that: 'Nobody really knows how much money is stashed away: estimates vary from way below to way above $20 trillion.' Another estimate made by the Tax Justice Network, an international coalition of researchers, suggests that around US$21 million was hidden across various tax havens, as of the end of 2012.

Also, it needs to be pointed out here that even though Switzerland may not seem to be at the centre of the global black money business anymore, that is really not the case. As Gabriel Zucman writes in *The Hidden Wealth of Nations—The Scourge of Tax Havens*:

> There has, in fact, never been as much wealth in tax havens as today. On a global scale, 8 per cent of the financial wealth of households is held in tax havens. According to the latest available information, in the spring of 2015 foreign wealth held in Switzerland reached $2.3 trillion.[4]

Since the 1980s, the black money has moved into newer tax havens. Nevertheless, as Zucman writes:

> To view Swiss banks in opposition to the new banking centers [i.e. tax havens] in Asia and the Caribbean doesn't make much sense. A large number of the banks domiciled in Singapore or in the Cayman Islands are nothing but branches of Swiss establishments that have opened there to attract new customers.[5]

Some of this black money that has found its way into Switzerland and other tax havens, has originated in India. Given that there are so many tax havens, the money that has left Indian shores could be anywhere. Tax havens maintain secrecy in order to ensure that they remain attractive options for those who are looking to hide their black money. As Pooja Rangaprasad of the Centre for Budget and Governance Accountability (CBGA) writes in an article titled '*Issues Related to Black Money*': 'Individuals and corporations...set up a layer of *benami* trusts...using this network of tax havens and loopholes in domestic laws.'[6]

This makes it very difficult for the government authorities to figure out who the ultimate beneficiary is. And figuring this out will require massive international coordination and cooperation. Nevertheless, as mentioned earlier, Switzerland is still at the heart of it all. As Zucman writes:

> In the past, Swiss bankers provided all services: carrying out the investment strategy, keeping securities under custody, hiding the true identity of owners by the way of famous numbered accounts. Today only securities custody really remains in their purview. The rest has been moved offsite to other tax havens—Luxembourg, the Virgin Islands, or Panama—all of which function in symbiosis. This is the great organization of international wealth management.

Given this, India alone cannot deal with the issue. Combined international pressure needs to be applied on Switzerland in order to get anywhere with the idea of bringing black money that has left the shores of the country, back. And given that the chances of getting back the black money that has left the shores of the country, remain low.

What makes the situation even more difficult is the fact that a lot of money that goes abroad comes back to India through a process known as round-tripping. In fact, the Finance Ministry's White Paper on black money makes this point in the context of foreign direct investment:

> The two topmost sources of the cumulative inflows from April 2000 to March 2011 are Mauritius (41.80 per cent) and Singapore (9.17 per cent). Mauritius and Singapore with their small economies cannot be the sources of such huge investments and it is apparent that the investments are routed through these jurisdictions for avoidance of taxes and/or for concealing the identities from the revenue authorities of the ultimate investors, many of whom could actually be Indian residents, who have invested in their own companies, though a process known as round-tripping.[7]

A similar sort of round-tripping also happens in the stock market through an instrument known as participatory notes (PNs). As the White Paper points out:

> Investment in the Indian Stock Market through PNs is another way in which the black money generated by Indians is re-invested in India. PNs or overseas derivative instruments (ODIs) are issued by FIIs [foreign institutional investors] against underlying Indian securities, which can be equity, debt, derivatives, or even indices. The investor in PNs does not hold the Indian securities in her/his own name. These are legally held by the FIIs, but s/he derives economic benefits from fluctuation in prices of the Indian securities, as also dividends and capital gains, through specifically designed contracts.[8]

This makes the issue of trying to recover the black money that has left the Indian shores, even more complicated. Nevertheless, this hasn't stopped the government from coming up with the Undisclosed Foreign Income and Assets (Imposition of New Tax) Bill, 2015, which was passed by the parliament in May 2015.

The Black Money Act

The Act states that undisclosed foreign income as well as assets will be taxed at the rate of 30 per cent, without allowing for any exemptions or deductions, which are allowed under the Income-Tax Act, 1961. This will be accompanied by a penalty equal to three times the amount of tax. Hence, the tax and penalty on undisclosed overseas income as well as assets can amount to as much as 120 per cent (30 per cent + 90 per cent). Further, the amount of tax to be paid on foreign assets will be computed on the basis of its current market price and not the price at which it was bought.

Nevertheless, there was a way out of this. The government offered a short compliance window, which would allow those with undisclosed foreign assets and income to declare them, pay a tax of 30 per cent and a penalty of 30 per cent. The Act also has a provision which allows the government to charge a penalty of Rs 10 lakh for the inaccurate disclosure of foreign assets, along with a rigorous imprisonment of six months to seven years, the first time around. Second and subsequent offences are punishable with fines of Rs 25 lakh to Rs 1 crore and a rigorous imprisonment three to 10 years.

On the face of it, the Act seems like an honest attempt to crack down on black money that has already left the country and that might leave the country in the days to come. But there are several questions that crop up here. Why is a short compliance window being offered? It makes the taxpayers who have been honestly declaring their income (foreign and domestic) as well as assets till date, look a tad stupid. Just because someone is willing to pay a fine of 30 per cent and declare his foreign assets, does that make him less guilty? Or is this another tax amnesty scheme in disguise being offered by the government?

Taking advantage of the compliance window 638 declarants declared assets and income of Rs 41,470 million in total. This meant that the government will be able to collect around Rs 2.48 crore (60 per cent of Rs 4.14 crore) as tax revenues. This means around Rs 3.9 crore of tax and penalty will be collected on an average from every declarant.

For all the hype and hoopla that has happened around black money since Narendra Modi came to power, this is barely peanuts. And given this, a collection of Rs 2.48 crore is basically a bad joke, especially once you take into account the tremendous amount of political capital that the Narendra Modi government has spent on the black money issue.

Further, why is a distinction being made between domestic and foreign black money? The definition of black money in the Ministry of Finance White Paper does not make any distinction between black money in the country and black money that has left the shores. Ultimately, almost all black money originates in the country, when people earn an income and do not pay a tax on it. So why is this artificial distinction being made?

Further, in the budget speech finance minister Arun Jaitley made on February 29, 2016, he proposed:

> a limited period Compliance Window for domestic taxpayers to declare undisclosed income or income represented in the form of any asset and clear up their past tax transgressions by paying tax at 30 per cent, and surcharge at 7.5 per cent and penalty at 7.5 per cent, which is a total of 45 per cent of the undisclosed income.

So, if you have black money, and are willing to pay 15 per cent extra to the government, over and above the top tax rate, the laws of the land won't apply to you. As Jaitley further said in his speech: 'There will be no scrutiny or enquiry regarding income declared in these declarations under the Income Tax Act or the Wealth Tax Act and the declarants will have immunity from prosecution. Immunity from Benami Transaction (Prohibition) Act, 1988 is also proposed subject to certain conditions.'

In an interview to the national broadcaster Doordarshan, Jaitley later said: 'It's not a VDIS (Voluntary Disclosure of Income Scheme) and it is not an amnesty.' Like a good lawyer, he did not specify what the scheme really is.

The answer for the distinction being made between domestic and foreign black money, perhaps lies in the way political funding works in this country. An analysis carried out by the National Election Watch and Association of Democratic Reforms reveals that during the period 2004–05 and 2011–12, the total income of the national political parties was Rs. 4,899.46 crores. The Congress party declared the highest income of Rs 2,365.02 crores. It was followed by the Bhartiya Janata Party which declared an income of Rs 1,304.22 crores. Between 2004–05 and 2011–12, there were two Lok Sabha elections (in 2004 and 2009) and multiple state assembly elections. It doesn't take rocket science to come to the conclusion that the amount of donations declared by the political parties were clearly not enough to fight so many elections.

Within 90 days of completion of the General Elections, political parties are required to submit their election expenditure to the Election Commission of India. The National Election Watch and Association of Democratic Reforms have analysed this expenditure for the last Lok Sabha election and it makes for a very interesting reading. This expenditure statement contains the 'details of the total amount received as funds in the form of cash, cheques and demand drafts and the total amount spent under various heads.'

The total amount of funds collected by national political parties for the 2014 Lok Sabha election was at Rs 1158.59 crores. This was 35.5 per cent higher than the funds collected for the 2009 Lok Sabha elections. The total declared expenditure of the national political parties was Rs 1308.75 crore, up by 49.4 per cent from 2009. Now compare this to an estimate made by the Centre for Media Studies in March 2014. It estimated that around Rs 30,000 crore would be spent during the 16th Lok Sabha elections which happened in April and May 2014. Of this amount, the government would spend around Rs 7,000–8,000 crore to conduct the elections. The remaining amount of around Rs 22,000–23,000 crore would be spent by the candidates fighting the elections.

Of course, national political parties are not the only parties fighting elections. Nevertheless, the difference between the officially declared expenditure and the 'real' expenditure to fight elections, is huge. Where does this money come from? The domestic black money essentially finances political parties and in the process elections in India. And given this, no government (and political party) can really go after it. Meanwhile, they will keep talking about foreign black money.

Foreign Account Tax Compliance Act

One school of thought is that if the United States can work towards getting its black money back, why can't India? The Black Money (Undisclosed Foreign Income and Assets) and Imposition of Tax Act, 2015 (popularly Black Money Act) is inspired by the Foreign Account Tax Compliance Act (FATCA) of the United States. This Act was passed in 2010 and was brought in after it was revealed that Swiss banks were helping American citizens hide their earnings.

As per the Act, American taxpayers are required to file a new form (Form 8938) declaring their foreign financial assets with a value greater than US$50,000. This form needs to be filled up along with the annual tax return. If the taxpayer does not file the Form 8938, he can face a fine of US$10,000, which can go up to US$50,000 for subsequent offences. Any tax payer who pays lower tax because he does not disclose foreign financial assets could be subject to a penalty of 40 per cent.

The provisions of the foreign black money Act, which we have already seen earlier, are along similar lines. As per FATCA, every financial institution outside the United States needs to figure out whether it has American citizens as clients. Having done that, it needs to report the information to the Internal Revenue Service of the United States.

Due to this, the conventional view now seems to be coming around to the idea that tax havens are now cooperating with the United States and handing over information regarding their clients. Hence, the question is, if the United States can do it, why can't India? And the answer lies in the fact that the United States is a global superpower. In 2013, the military expenditure of the United States amounted to US$640 billion. This was nearly 36.5 per cent of the global military expenditure of US$1.75 trillion. In comparison, the total budget for the Indian defence services in 2015–16 was around US$2.5 billion.

With so much money being spent by the United States, the military apparatus of the United States can drop bombs anywhere in the world at a few hours' notice. As David Graeber writes in *Debt: The First 5000 Years*: 'The U.S. Military ... maintains a doctrine of global power projection: that it should have the ability, through roughly 800 overseas military bases, to intervene with deadly force absolutely anywhere on the planet.'[9] It is this military might of the United States that has led to the tax havens cooperating with it.

Nevertheless, as the Americans like saying: 'show me the money'. Or to put it simply, how much revenue has the Internal Revenue Service of the United States managed to collect because of FATCA? Jane G. Gravelle writing in a research paper titled Tax Havens: *International Tax Avoidance and Evasion* for the Congressional Research Service estimates that FATCA is expected to 'have a relatively small effect, $8.7 billion over 10 years, when compared with estimated costs of international evasion of around $40 billion a year.'[10] So on an average the United States expects to recover $870 million per year, when the international tax evasion by Americans is around US$ 40 billion per year. Hence, the recovery rate for FATCA is 2.2 per cent on an average.

What this clearly tells us is that even the United States does not expect much out of FATCA, initially. This, despite being the only global superpower. In this scenario, how much chance does India have of recovering the black money that has left its shores?

Domestic Black Money

In 2011, the Congress-led UPA government had asked three institutes, National Institute of Public Finance and Policy (NIPFP), National Institute of Financial Management (NIFM) and National Council of Applied Economic Research (NCAER), to estimate the total amount of black money in India. The reports from these institutes still have not been put up in the public domain. 'Reports received from these institutes are under examination of the government,' the Finance Minister Arun Jaitley told the Rajya Sabha, in May 2015.

The Hindu newspaper had accessed the NIPFP report in August 2014. The NIPFP puts the size of the black money economy at around 75 per cent of the gross domestic product (GDP). This estimate is much bigger than the previous estimates. The last official study for estimating black money had been carried out by NIPFP way back in 1985 on the request of the Finance Ministry. The study put the size of the black money anywhere between 15–21 per cent of the GDP.

If we compare the 1985 study numbers to the latest NIPFP black money number there has been a huge jump in black money generation, with the black money economy now accounting for nearly 75 per cent of the GDP. The question is where is this black money being generated from? The first is property transactions. A FICCI report on black money published in February

2015 points out: 'The Real Estate sector in India constitutes for about 11 per cent of the GDP of Indian Economy, as these transactions involve high transaction value. In the year 2012–13, Real Estate sector has been considered as the highest parking space for black money.' [11]

The Hindu report referred to earlier states that the black money from real estate is estimated to be bigger than the plan expenditure of the government. The plan expenditure of the government for the financial year ending March 31, 2013, had stood at Rs 4,53,327 crore. Now that is a huge amount of money. The other major sectors generating black money are private education and mining. Politicians running this country have significant interests in real estate, mining, and the education businesses. In fact, as is well known, many real estate companies and education businesses are fronts for politicians.

The other major black money spinners are the subsidies given by the government. *The Hindu* reported: 'Diversion of subsidised kerosene to the open market is estimated to have generated as much as Rs 11,910 crore.' This was half the total amount of kerosene subsidy provided in 2013–14. It wouldn't be surprising to know that black money is being generated from other subsidies offered by the government as well. Conclusion: The *Annual Report of the Ministry of Finance* points out that in a country with a population of more than 120 crore, the number of income tax assesses in the 2013–14 stood at a mere 4.7 crore. By laying out the red carpet for the tax cheats who have managed to move their black money abroad or have it in India, what message is the government sending out to the individuals who have been paying their taxes?

This is not the best way to go about trying to increase the number of people who pay income tax. In fact, the annual report of the Ministry of Finance points out that between April and December 2014, just 24.35 lakh fresh assesses were added. The point being that the rate of growth of tax compliance is anyway very slow and on top of that if the government keeps welcoming those who have black money, what future does tax compliance really have in this country?

There is other data that suggests that enough people are not paying income tax in this country. In fact, former finance minister P Chidambaram in his February 2013 budget speech had said that India had only 42,800 people with a taxable income of Rs 1 crore or more. In April 2016, top finance bureaucrat Hasmukh Adhia said: 'There are only 1.5 lakh individuals whose total income would be above Rs 50 lakh,'

Now compare this with the fact that around 30,000 luxury cars are sold in India every year. Both Audi and Mercedes sold more than 10,000 cars in India in 2014. A February 2015 report brought by business lobby FICCI makes a similar point. The report estimates that the number of dollar millionaires (i.e. with assets of Rs 6 crore or more) in India in 2014 stood at around 2.27 lakhs, up from 2.14 lakhs in 2013. But the number of taxpayers with a taxable income of more than a crore is less than 50,000.

What this tells us clearly is that there is widespread tax evasion in the country. This tax evasion continues to generate a lot of black money, a major part of which continues to remain in the country. This is the black money that the government should be going after.

Information technology can play a huge part in this. In fact, it already is. As the *FICCI* report cited earlier points out: 'The Integrated Taxpayer Data Management System is a data mining tool implemented by the I-T department that is used for detection of potential cases of tax evasion. The tool assists in generating a 360-degree profile of the high net-worth assessees.' The government should work towards making this tool even more robust by building in more data into it, in the days to come.

Further, it has to get cracking on the real estate sector where the maximum amount of black money is invested. This black money generates more black money. Going after the biggest property dealers of the National Capital Region (NCR), where most black money changes hands, might be a good starting point.

One view point is that black money that remains in the country has some benefits. As Cambridge University economist Ha-Joon Chang writes in the context of a minister taking a bribe (which is also black money, given that the minister is not going to declare the bribe as an income). 'A bribe is a transfer of wealth from one person to another. It does not *necessarily* have negative effects on economic efficiency and growth.'[12] If the minister taking the bribe decides to spend/invest that money in the country, it has a positive impact on economic growth, as the spending creates economic demand and the investment creates jobs. At least in theory, the idea seems to make sense. In comparison, the black money leaving the country is a total waste. As Chang writes: 'A critical issue… is whether the dirty money stays in the country. If the bribe is deposited in a Swiss bank, it cannot contribute to creating further income and jobs through investment—which is one way odious money can partially "redeem" itself.'[13]

Hence, as per Chang, black money if invested properly can create jobs as well as economic growth. In the Indian case a lot of this money gets invested into gold and real estate. Money going into gold does not create any jobs. And money that goes into real estate has driven up home prices in particular, all over the country, to extremely high levels. Most middle-class Indians cannot afford to buy a home now. Anshuman Magazine, chairman and managing director of CBRE South Asia Pvt. Ltd., wrote in an article that 'around 1.2 crore completed houses' are 'lying vacant across urban India'. That is where the Indian black money is.

Given this, it makes tremendous sense for the government to crack down on domestic black money, instead of making noises about recovering black money that has already left the shores of this country. Further, focus should be on ensuring that the number of people paying income tax goes up in the years to come. Finance Minister Arun Jaitley told the officials of the Income Tax department in May 2015:

> You have the responsibility to recover every rupee which is due to the government...A tax is either payable or not payable, if it is not payable, then no attempt has to be made to recover it, but if it is payable, then there is no scope for any collateral consideration why it must not be recovered for the government.[14]

All this boils down to the Income Tax department and how it goes about recovering black money. The past evidence isn't very encouraging. As the annual report of the ministry of finance for the year 2013–14 points out: 'During the financial year 2013–14 (upto December, 2013), 3069 (provisional) search warrants were executed leading to the seizure of assets worth Rs 559.04 Crore (provisional). During the financial year (upto December, 2013), 3263 surveys (provisional) were conducted which yielded a disclosure of undisclosed income of Rs 6,968.82 Crore (provisional).'

So, the Income Tax department performed better when it came to seizing assets and identifying undisclosed income in 2013–2014 than it did in 2014–2015. In 2013–2014 it seized assets worth Rs 559.04 crore. In comparison it managed to seize assets worth only Rs 538.23 crore in 2014–2015. It identified a total undisclosed income of Rs 6,989.82 crore in 2013–2014. This number fell to Rs 4,673.11 crore in 2013–2014. How was the performance of the

Income Tax department in the years prior to these two financial years? The accompanying table shows that clearly:

Financial year	Seized assets (in Rs crore)	Undisclosed income (in Rs crore)
2014–2015	538.23	4,673.11
2013–2014	559.04	6,989.82
2012–2013	450.18	8,254.41
2011–2012	Data not available	Data not available
2010–2011	716.66	2,700.59
2009–2010	602.34	1,832.00

Source: Annual reports, Ministry of Finance.

The table on seized assets and undisclosed income makes for a very interesting read. The value of seized assets was significantly higher in 2009–10 and 2010–11. The undisclosed income identified peaked in 2012–13 and then fell dramatically. What this clearly tells us is that the record of the Income Tax department in going after black money over the last few years has been very weak.

One possible explanation for this is the fact that corruption in the second term of the UPA peaked, the Income Tax department stopped going after people with a serious amount of black money and has still not managed to change its course. While we may keep thinking of reasons, what this data clearly tells us is that Arun Jaitley was being overtly optimistic regarding the black money recovery skills of the Income Tax department. And that clearly is not good news for all the black money recovery plans that the government has.

Postscript: On 8 November 2016, in a late-evening broadcast to the nation, Prime Minister Narendra Modi, announced that the Rs 500 and Rs 1,000 notes had been demonetised. Come midnight, they would be useless pieces of paper. These notes can be deposited in banks and post offices up to 30 December 2016, and will be credited into user's accounts.

By demonetising these notes the government hopes to take on the twin ills of fake currency as well as black money. The hope is that the black money held in the form of cash will be destroyed. The hope is that a portion of black money held in the form of cash will not make it to the banks because that would generate an audit trail for the income tax department. On the flip side, if it is deposited into banks, the government can tax and fine it, and earn a quick buck in the process.

But the government has messed up the implementation part. While 86 per cent of the currency by value has been demonetised, less than 10 per cent of it had been replaced through new notes of Rs 500 and Rs 2,000, until 18 November 2016.

Without enough currency going around, transactions across markets have come to a standstill. Estimates suggest that it will take the government at least five months to replace the currency it has demonetised with new currency, given the limitations of the printing capacity of the note printing presses. This will have a negative impact on economic growth. Further, it remains to be seen how much black money is destroyed in the process. That will become clear only in January 2017.

Endnotes

1 Global Financial Integrity, *Illicit Financial Flows from Developing Countries: 2003-2012* (Washington D.C.: Global Financial Integrity, 2014).

2 Ibid.

3 Ha-Joon Chang, *Bad Samaritans—The Guilty Secrets of Rich Nations and the Threat to Global Prosperity* (New York: Random House Business Books, 2008).

4 Gabriel Zucman, *The Hidden Wealth of Nations—The Scourge of Tax Havens* (Berkeley: University of Chicago Press, 2015).

5 Ibid.

6 Pooja Rangaprasad, 'Issues Related to Black Money,' *Employment News,* February 8, 2014.

7 Ministry of Finance, 'White paper on Black Money' (New Delhi: Government of India, 2012).

8 Ibid.

9 David Graeber, *Debt: The First 5000 Years* (New York: Melville House, 2011).

10 Jane G. Gravelle, *Tax Havens: International Tax Avoidance and Evasion* (Washington D.C.: Congressional Research Service, 2013).

11 FICCI, *Widening of Tax Base and Tackling Black Money* (New Delhi: FICCI, 2015).

12 Chang, *Bad Samaritans,* pp. 163–64.

13 Ibid., p. 164.

14 Arun Jaitley, 'Address at the 31st Annual Conference of Principal Chief Commissioners of Income Tax,' 25 May 2015.

India's Employment Guarantee Act: In a Nutshell

Reetika Khera

The National Rural Employment Guarantee Act (NREGA), later renamed Mahatma Gandhi NREGA (MGNREGA) was enacted in September 2005. It promises up to 100 days of employment per rural household to all adults at the minimum wage. Any adult residing in rural areas can demand work and is entitled to get it within 15 days of asking. If the government failed to provide employment, applicants were entitled to an unemployment allowance.

While the demand-driven aspect and the unemployment allowance aspect have not been activated due to poor levels of awareness—people still do not know that they can ask for work, employment has been provided to millions of households (see Figure 3: State-wise Level of NREGA Employment) since the law came into force in February 2006. Starting with 200 districts in 2006, over a period of three years, the Act was extended to all 650-odd districts in the country by 2008.

Why NREGA is Supported by People with Diverse Views

The NREGA received wide-ranging support from entrepreneurs (e.g., Jaithirth Rao, MphasiS), to corporate economists (Ajit Ranade, Aditya Birla group), even *The Economist* supported the idea of an NREGA-type intervention.

The economic rationale for a programme such as NREGA comes from the recognition of the need for social security in poor countries, but a perception that not enough resources are available to implement a full-fledged 'welfare' programme in India (e.g., unemployment benefits are widely provided in Europe). With 'workfare' programmes such as NREGA, it has been observed that the non-poor automatically select out of the programme. The requirement of performing physical labour and being paid the minimum wage for it keeps the non-poor with better opportunities out of the programme. The NREGA is a universal programme, yet it automatically selects-out the non-poor. This is no mean achievement in policy design—correct identification of beneficiaries has been the undoing of many other welfare initiatives. This 'self-targeting' design has earned NREGA the support of many economists.

Why Richer People do not Benefit: Self-targeting Works?

The self-targeting works over the agricultural cycle (e.g., during sowing and harvest season when agricultural work is available, many withdraw from NREGA), it works across geographical areas (e.g., employment levels tend to be higher in poorer districts within states) and it also works within population groups (attracting more people from vulnerable population groups such as Dalits, Adivasis, and women). Liu and Barrett find that "the self-targeting design of MGNREGS leads to greater rates of self-selection into the programme by poorer and scheduled tribe or scheduled caste households.'[1] Zimmerman finds that 'private-sector wages increase substantially for women, but not for men, and that these effects are concentrated during the main agricultural season'.[2] Figure 1 of a paper by Engler and Ravi shows how NREGA employment picks up in the lean season.[3] Government data presented here also shows high rates of participation in NREGA from disadvantaged groups.

What Works: A Quick Check on NREGA's Facts

Expenditure: The cost of the programme has always been a cause of worry. NREGA expenditure peaked in 2010–11 at Rs 39, 400 crore and has since come down in to Rs 33,000 crores in the financial year 2013–14 (see Figure 1). (The decline began in the previous government's term.) In relative terms, e.g., as a percentage of GDP, today the expenditure on NREGA is at 0.3 per cent of Gross Domestic Product (GDP). At its peak, it was 0.5 per cent of GDP.

This is a substantial amount of money. But it is also important to put NREGA expenditure in perspective. One possible comparison is with the 'tax revenues foregone' reported in the budget documents. Tax revenues foregone are tax breaks given in order to encourage industry.

Expenditure on NREGA is less than the tax revenue foregone (in 2013–14) on the 'gold and diamond' industry which was over Rs 65,000 crore in

Figure 1: Average Daily Labour Cost and Consumer Price Index for Agricultural Labourers

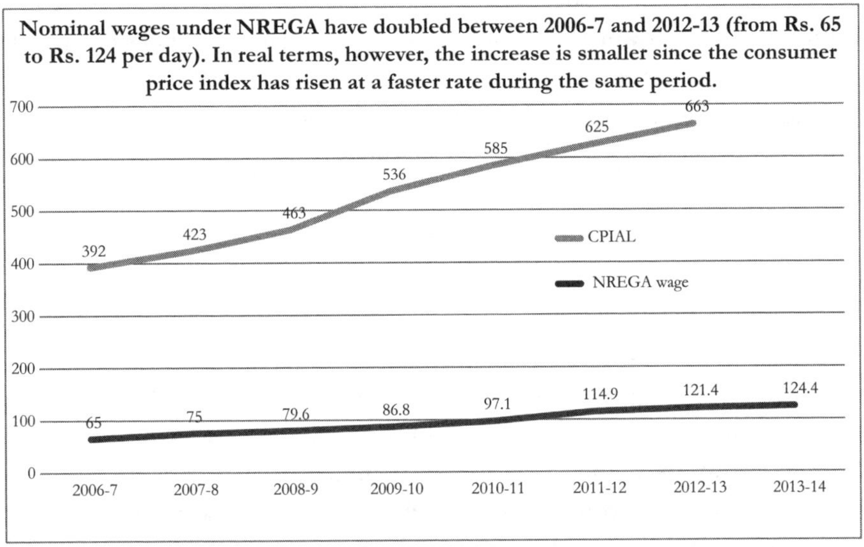

Figure 2: Trends in NREGA: Expenditure and Employment

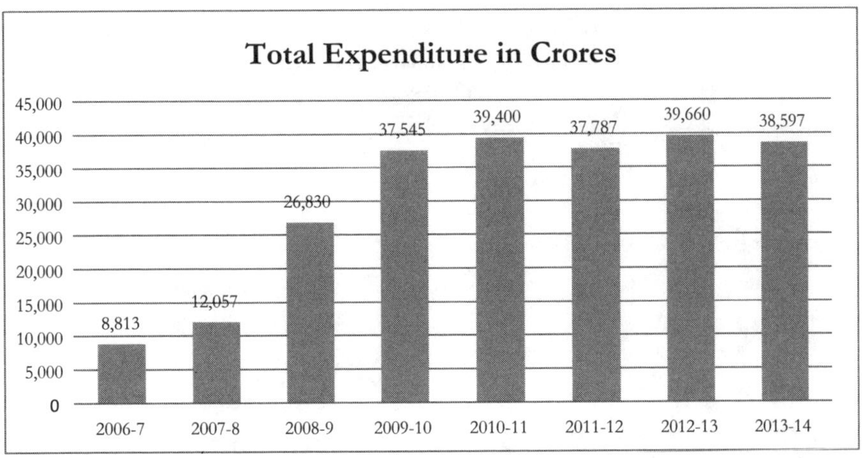

2012–13. As noted elsewhere, such tax breaks are justified on the grounds of the employment potential of the gems and jewellery industry.

According to Invest India, a website of the Ministry of Commerce and Industry, 'The sector provides employment to around 1.8 million people. In the next five years, the sector is expected to create additional employment for around 1.1 million people.' The target employment represents 0.7 per cent of the workforce. On the other hand, an expenditure of Rs 33,000 crores on NREGA has provided employment to around about 25 per cent of the rural households, or about 50 million people.

Corruption: Jean Drèze has written on the uphill but relatively successful battle against corruption in NREGA. Three different estimates of wage corruption are available: matching days of work recorded in the India Human Development Survey (IHDS) 2011–12 with official data in the same year, we find that only 4 per cent is not confirmed by respondents. Using National Sample Survey data, there is a mismatch of 20–30 per cent in 2011–12 compared with approximately 50 per cent in 2007–8. In our smaller survey in May–June 2013, we found that on average sample households reported getting 22 days of work while official records indicated 24 days of work in their name.

Figure 3: State-wise Level of NREGA Employment

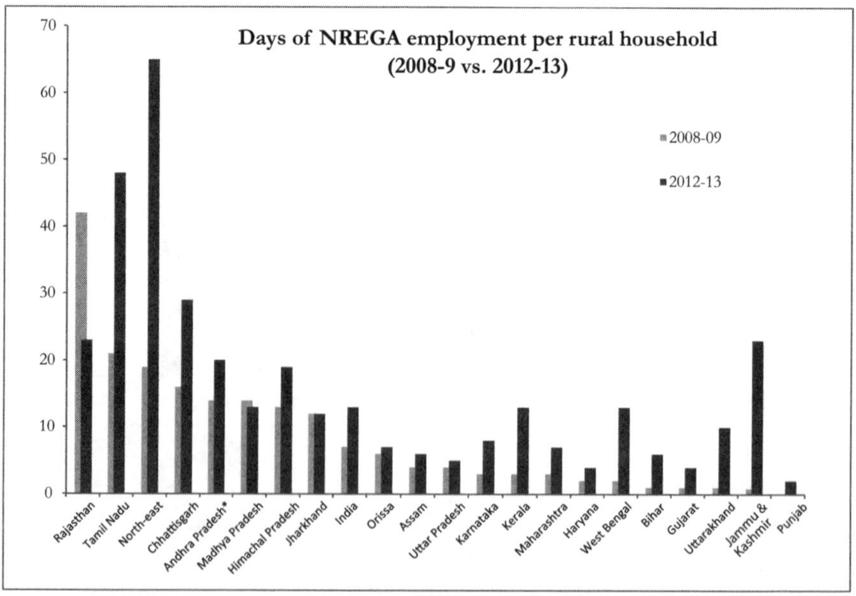

Work culture: In a speech made by Vasundhara Raje at the India Today conclave in March 2014, she said that NREGA had taught people to become lazy. She is not the only one to hold such a belief. On a recent BBC radio show, two callers from Rajasthan made the same accusation. Not many are aware that in most states NREGA workers are not paid on a daily basis (i.e., wages are not based on being marked present). They are paid on a piece-rate basis—if a prescribed 'task' is completed, they get the minimum wage. If their output is less than the prescribed norm, they get less than the minimum wage. Yet the impression from mainstream media is that NREGA workers are only sitting around at worksites. (Yes, workers do 'sit around' to take a break. But who, among us, doesn't check the cricket score, the latest tweet or most recent 'like' for a facebook post, while at work?).

What are the Government's new Proposals to cut back NREGA?

Restricting NREGA: The recent proposal to restrict it to selected districts or blocks is an unwise move. Firstly, it amounts to revoking people's rights. Rights-based programmes are meant to provide security, and if rights can be removed arbitrarily, it defeats their purpose. (In some ways, it is like saying, women's autonomy is particularly low in 200 districts, so the government will ensure women can choose who to marry in those districts, but not the rest.)

Secondly, there is bound to be some arbitrariness in the selection of these districts and blocks. Just as no foolproof mechanism or yardstick is available to identify 'needy' people (even NREGA is not foolproof—e.g., the elderly and disabled persons are likely to be most in need of social support, but are least likely to be able to participate in NREGA), no mechanism exists to identify such districts, *even* if it were desirable.

There is confusion about the need for the proposed restriction: some say there is 'no demand' for NREGA employment in the better-off areas (a line often taken by the previous government also), whereas others say that better-off areas get too much of NREGA expenditure.

For the former, even the reduction in NREGA expenditure is a reflection of a reduction in 'demand' for employment. The argument that there are no poor in better-off districts has been debunked already. Other surveys have consistently shown that there is a large unmet demand for NREGA work.[4] We have also found that there is a huge unmet demand for NREGA work: in a survey in 10 states, while 83 per cent reported wanting 100 days of work, only 8 per cent had actually done 100 days of NREGA work in the same period.

Others say that it needs to be restricted because the bulk of the employment has gone to non-poor areas; that currently, the highest spending states (e.g., Andhra Pradesh, Tamil Nadu) are not the poorest (e.g., Uttar Pradesh).[5]

It is true that the employment generation has been higher in, say, Tamil Nadu than in Bihar. However, this is also a reflection of greater administrative capacity in the former. Perhaps a better parameter would be whether within a state, employment has been higher in the poorer districts. Further, there is evidence from previous studies that administrative rationing (e.g., restricting NREGA for a few blocks or districts) dilutes the 'self-targeting' feature of NREGA (see figures on pp. 4–6 of Liu and Barrett). Work by Martin Ravallion has also shown similar results.

Finally, the minister's office responded to a letter by economists by stating that NREGA had been politically 'exploited for pure partisan purpose'. (They overlooked the fact that the potential for political opportunism will be greater if districts or blocks are to be selected.)

The top three states in terms of NREGA employment since the Act was implemented have tended to be non-Congress states. For instance, it was under Vasundhara Raje's chief ministership (2003–2008) that NREGA saw its 'golden period' in Rajasthan, averaging more than 60 days of employment per rural household between 2006 and 2008. During the following Congress government (led by Ashok Gehlot) it crashed from 42 in 2008–09 to 19 in 2013–14.

Chhattisgarh ruled throughout the nine-year period by BJP has steadily improved its performance, with the average days rising from 16 days in 2008–09 to 31 in 2013–14. Andhra Pradesh is often cited as a big success though employment levels in the state have been quite modest (lowest of 14 in 2008–09 and highest of 18 days in 2013–14). Remarkable improvement in NREGA employment is observed in Tamil Nadu (from 25 to 43 days between 2009–10 and 2013–14). It has been ruled by DMK and AIADMK since 2006.

Increasing material share: The second proposal is to increase the labour–material ratio in favour of material. It is justified on the grounds that it is necessary for asset creation. Implicit in this argument is another 'fact'—that NREGA has been uniformly unsuccessful as far as asset creation is concerned, a popular perception that is not entirely supported by existing studies.

No doubt, the record on asset creation is weak, however, there are now a clutch of studies which suggest that the potential exists—*within the existing labour–material ratio*—and also that in some pockets this potential has been realised. Sudha Narayanan finds that

> Already, well over 60 per cent of the works have been supportive of agriculture. For example, a study of over 4,100 MGNREGA assets across 100 villages in 20 districts in Maharashtra indicate that 87 per cent of the works exist and function and over 75 per cent of them are directly or indirectly related to agriculture.[6]

A cost-benefit analysis of 117 'best-performing MNREGA water assets' in four states, including Bihar, Gujarat, Kerala, and Rajasthan, finds that they 'recovered the investment within a single year of use'.[7] Similarly positive findings have been reported in a study of 11 NREGA wells in Jharkhand. The bottom line here is that within the current policy design assets can be (and in some cases, are being) created.

The proposed increase in material component can end up harming the NREGA. As noted above, as far as wage corruption in NREGA is concerned, there has been some improvement. Corruption in the material expenditure is likely to be the main opportunity for corruption in NREGA. Increasing the share of material will also bring in contractors and suppliers, who have been the main cause of corruption in earlier public employment programmes. (Currently, contractors are banned under NREGA). Combined with the fact that increasing material will not guarantee better quality assets, the case of increasing material expenditure is also very weak.

What Should the Verdict be?

The World Bank which had called NREGA a 'barrier to development' in the 2009 *World Development Report* (WDR)[8] had revised its opinion by 2014 when the WDR called it a 'stellar example of rural development'.[9] However, public debate in India has tended to be very resilient to the mounting evidence of its successes along with its failures.

We need to move away from the lazy resort to statements such as 'out of every rupee spent only 15 paise reaches the poor' and 'digging holes and filling them up' to something that matches current ground realities more closely.

Once that happens, a more productive debate—on how to fix all that is wrong with NREGA (delays in wage payments, lack of awareness, corruption, asset quality)—can be initiated.

This article has been previously published at: http://www.indiaspend.com/cover-story/the-whys-and-whats-of-indias-rural-jobs-scheme-99284, *and is reproduced here with the permission of the author.*

Endnotes

1 Yanyan Liu and Christopher B. Barrett, 'Heterogeneous Pro-Poor Targeting in the National Rural Employment Guarantee Scheme,' *Economic and Political Weekly*, 48/10 (9 March 2013).

2 Laura Zimmerman, 'Labor Market Impacts of a Large-Scale Public Works Program: Evidence from the Indian Employment Guarantee Scheme,' IZA Discussion Paper No. 6858, September 2012, http://ftp.iza.org/dp6858.pdf.

3 Monika Engler and Shamika Ravi, 'Workfare as an Effective Way to Fight Poverty: The Case of India's NREGS,' Social Science Research Network, February 13, 2013,http://papers.ssrn.com/sol3/papers.cfm?abstract_id=1336837.

4 Martin Ravallion, 'MGNREGA is unwell,' *The Indian Express*, October 24, 2014, http://indianexpress.com/article/opinion/editorials/mgnrega-is-unwell/.

5 Jagdish Bhagwati and Arvind Panagariya, 'Rural inefficiency act: Despite protests about diluting NREGA, the PM is right to confine it to 200 poorest districts,' *The Times of India*, October 23, 2014, http://blogs.timesofindia.indiatimes.com/toi-edit-page/rural-inefficiency-act-despite-protests-about-diluting-nrega-the-pm-is-right-to-confine-it-to-200-poorest-districts/.

6 Sudha Narayanan, 'Saving people's livelihoods,' *Livemint*, April 20, 2016, http://www.livemint.com/Opinion/hz2CLtVBL7q45SrIfg1BfL/Saving-peoples-livelihoods.html.

7 Shilp Verma and Tushaar Shah, 'Beyond Digging and Filling Holes,' Water Policy Research Highlight no 42, International Water Management Institute, 2012, http://www.iwmi.cgiar.org/.

8 'World Bank sees NREGA as a barrier to economic development,' *The Economic Times*, March 15, 2009, http://articles.economictimes.indiatimes.com/2009-03-15/news/28464057_1_migration-mobility-nrega.

9 'World Bank calls NREGA a stellar example of rural development,' *The Economic Times*, October 10, 2013,http://articles.economictimes.indiatimes.com/2013-10-10/news/42902947_1_world-bank-world-development-report-safety-net.

Audit, Good Governance, and Sustainable Development

Vinod Rai

Democracy is a system in which the rule of law is allowed to take its course and the ultimate goal of the government is the pursuit of the collective good. The auditor, keeping vigil on the functioning of all the institutions of the executive, is a key player in this process. Such an atmosphere will ensure that economic growth is inclusive. Audit, good governance, and sustainable development are the concerns uppermost in the minds of all citizens in India today. Economic development, however rapid it may be, cannot be sustained in the long run unless it is driven by good governance. This has been the experience of nations around the world. Hence, its relevance in the Indian context.

I propose to approach the issues involved in three parts: First, we will address the historical perspective of these factors and the background leading to why and how good governance has become so critical to India today. In the second part, we shall see how good governance helps in making development efforts more sustainable in the long run. We shall draw on lessons in history wherein the lack of a responsive and accountable administration led to a frittering away of the benefits of economic development. We shall then proceed to examine how audit can contribute to good governance and how it can help sensitise awareness and public opinion which, in turn, helps the citizenry to maintain vigil on the actions of government.

To view the entire issue in the appropriate perspective, let us begin with events at the turn of the millennium. At the turn of the century, the Indian economy was displaying excellent signs of growth and buoyancy. A matter of great elation was the uplifting thought that the vibrant Indian democracy was capable of delivering near-double-digit economic growth. India had successfully overcome the stressful situation that preceded the 1991 reforms, consolidated the initiatives taken after the reform agenda was unfolded, and indeed withstood the shock which had hit the Asian Tigers in 1997.

In fact, the 'India shining' story was being projected during the 2004 general election with great gusto. Private investment indeed was encouraging. Manufacturing was being freed of licensing; banking and insurance had been liberalised. Road and telecom sectors were clocking good growth. Value Added Tax (VAT) had been introduced, and it was believed that Goods and Services Tax (GST) would follow soon. The country even managed to survive the initial setbacks of the financial meltdown which was traceable to the toxic assets originating from the United States of America. India had grown out of the shadow of an albatross around its neck for 40 years since Independence—the tag of its economy growing at the 'Hindu rate of growth' namely, 2.5 per cent to 3.5 per cent per annum.

However, as almost all major developed and emerging economies are now globally networked through trade and financial institutions, the gathering economic consequences of the meltdown did create difficulties for India. The adverse turn in India's external economic environment proved to be the real test, wherein exports began to decline and, as a consequence, the manufacturing sector began to suffer upon the emergence of supply side problems. Trade imbalances began to arise, leading to serious deficits on the current account.

It was around that time when some recent decisions of the government came up for adverse notice in the public space as well as in parliament. The decline in investments on infrastructure, and the poor quality of public spending, sparked allegations of 'cronyism', opacity in the decision-making process and a feeling of so-called 'policy paralysis'. There appeared to be a decline in the trust between the government and its people. The government did attempt the usual macroeconomic solutions to overcome the slide in the economy. These did not yield the desired results. Something had very seriously gone wrong. Was it only about economic issues? Was it only because of the Indian economy being plugged into the global economy, which in itself was stalling? Or, was it that India had not unleashed its 'national spirit'?

Something had gone wrong, horribly wrong. This was the time when the citizens' dissatisfaction peaked, and the civil society movements took centre-stage to demonstrate that the common man was no longer willing to accept the ineptitude that seemed to afflict the management of the economy and the government itself. The citizen began seeking accountability for some very obvious misdoings, instances of which had become public knowledge. The bungling in the preparations for the Commonwealth Games of 2010, the perceived opacity in the distribution of finite national resources such as coal and radio waves, became the subject matter of discussions at bus stops, tea shops, on television channels, in living rooms, and, indeed, the parliament, too.

There was an all-pervasive feeling among the citizens that the government had faltered, and governance had become a casualty. In public perception 2012 became the defining year, as the discerning Indian citizenry, awakened to the perceived misdeeds of government, demanded a responsive administration, and set out to debunk another myth: the myth of a 'silent majority'. The majority decided it could no longer afford to be silent and that it should hold its government to account. This heralded a maturing of India's democratic forces. It became clear that the citizens were seeking a dialogue—a dialogue in which they could participate in governance. This was indeed the old order changing, yielding place to the new.

The era of a new discerning and very-demanding class of citizen had now come to stay. The citizen was now seeking to develop a new moral and ethical framework to guide the elected representatives and the populace as well. With the citizenry seeking transparency, responsiveness, and accountability in the operations of government, the requirements of good governance had clearly come centrestage. By now, there were very distinct signs of the urban Indian middle class mobilising itself politically. This mobilisation was again debunking the conventional wisdom of the white-collared urban citizenry being unwilling to take to the streets to pursue the public cause.

This class of people had earlier confined itself to living-room discussions, TV debates, and maybe, college-level politics. They even took pride in not caring to cast their vote. They had looked askance at caste- and regional-politics, and were never sought out by the political parties. But this disparate group began aggregating and uniting for a cause. It seemed to feel its strength. What stirred them? Maybe, corruption at every government office; in the issuance of a birth certificate, a driver's licence, a hospital bed, a gas connection. Maybe, it was a series of episodes that related to a Jessica Lal, a Director General of Police Rathore or a Manu Sharma, a series of events that outraged the public' sense of justice and propriety.

Maybe, it was the realisation that the citizens should no longer tolerate being denied basic amenities such as drinking water, power, and security. Maybe it was a TV clip of a state minister telling officials that it was okay to steal a bit but one should not loot. The proverbial last straw on the camel's back certainly was the unfolding of human barbarity at its worst, on the night of 16 December 2012, in New Delhi, against a young lady. A churning of public conscience among the civil society had commenced. A new paradigm was now emerging.

In a parliamentary democracy, the three main pillars such as the legislature, the executive and the judiciary have an equal role to perform. They have their own checks and balances too. The supremacy of the elected political executive in a parliamentary democracy cannot be denied. The administrative bureaucracy is meant to facilitate the implementation of the policy parameters enunciated by the political executive. The conventional wisdom of good governance is premised on the basic tenet that democratically elected governments will conduct public affairs with probity and accountability.

Governments are entrusted with the responsibility of exercising power and taking decisions on behalf of the people. The well-being and development of all people depend on the choices made by their representatives. It is easier to misuse or not use this authority. A government is administered well or practices good governance when its authority and institutions are accountable, effective and efficient, transparent, responsive, equitable and inclusive, under the rule of law. Good governance is not the responsibility of the government alone. It is an equally important requirement in the corporate sector too.

It also extends to the civil society, the non-governmental organisations, and citizens' groups. However, as the governments collect money from the public and spends it on behalf of the public, such spending does place an element of higher accountability on governments. Such accountability requires that the actions and decisions taken by public officials are transparent and capable of withstanding public scrutiny: such accountability in respect of government decisions and actions ensures that the government initiatives meet their stated objectives and are indeed responsive to the needs of the people. History speaks of such accountability being a cornerstone of virtually all definitions of democracy and good governance, since time immemorial.

The idea of governance and accountability is as old as organised government. The preservation of the resources of the king in ancient times was accorded topmost priority. As early as in the 3rd Century BC, Kautilya in his magnum opus, *Arthashashtra*, had observed that it was the disposition of human nature to acquire public money for private gain. He wrote: 'Just as it is impossible not to taste honey or poison that one may find at the tip of one's tongue, so it is impossible for one dealing with government funds not to taste, at least a little bit, of the king's wealth'. He added: 'Just as it is impossible to know when a fish moving in water is drinking it, so it is impossible to find out when government servants, in charge of undertakings, misappropriate money'.

Therefore, Kautilya went on to formulate a series of checks and balances in the administrative system. He wrote that 'in all cases (where) an official has caused loss of revenue to the state....his property shall be confiscated'. The Greek philosopher Aristotle wrote: 'Some officials handle large sums of money: it is therefore necessary to have other officials to receive and examine the accounts. These inspectors must administer no funds themselves. Different cities call them examiners, auditors, scrutinees, and public advocates'.

In medieval England, we find that the concern for fiscal accountability was paramount. As early as the 13th century, parliament had sought to scrutinise accounts, even from the royal household, and the attempts in the succeeding centuries met with an objection from Henry IV that 'kings do not render accounts'. After the Glorious Revolution of 1688, the Commons felt that they 'might claim a more extensive function, that of investigating the wisdom, faithfulness and economy with which grants had been expended'.

This led to the setting up of 'commissioners of accounts'. Later in 1780, the creation of statutory commissions by Lord North was a significant step in the process of accountability, as these commissions were independent agencies as distinct from the earlier political institutions. We need to ponder why there is so much of emphasis on good governance and more so for sustainable development. History speaks of so many instances in the development of nations, where despite good steps being initiated by governments and emperors alike, the lack of transparency and accountability had rendered the entire effort fruitless. A remarkable example is from the administration of the East India Company.

The company is often believed to be the forerunner of the modern multinational firm. Starting as a humble trader in Asian spices, the company soon emerged as the face of the British Raj. Today, there is no sign, not even a plaque in any building or location, as a reminder of the existence of the world's most powerful corporation of yesteryear. What did bring about the decline of this powerful company in an era which was otherwise promoting an earlier phase of globalisation? Private trading by its managers became one of the cancers that gnawed at the company's ethical fibre.

Accepting 'presents' in order to secure business for the East India Company had become commonplace at one stage. Those 'presents' influenced the quality and cost of the commodities traded. The cancer spread as intrigue, corruption, and speculation, leading to that company's decline and its demise. The company's legacy provides compelling lessons on how to ensure accountability and probity in today's global business. The most fundamental challenge that all institutions face is to ensure that their employees promote the collective rather than the individual self-interest.

History has repeated itself with Barings Bank, Bears Stearns, and Satyam—personal greed versus corporate interest. The community of nations seeks development which is sustainable over the long run. Such sustainability is possible only when it is premised on the delivery of public services based on core values such as integrity, transparency, and accountability. It is imperative that the rule of law is allowed to prevail and the system delivers on its own. To further strengthen the delivery process, it is essential that public sector agencies possess or develop the capability and expertise to perform in that sector.

Domain capability is very critical to sustainable performance. Such capability will have to be dovetailed with the objectives of the public sector institutions to ensure that prioritisation of the service-delivery is based on the felt-Audit, as one of the instruments of accountability, is a powerful tool of good governance. Accountability and transparency, the two cardinal principles of good governance in a democratic set-up, depend to a large extent on how well the public-audit function is discharged. Effective audit strengthens governance by providing for accountability and protecting the core values of government.

It helps in enhancing transparency in operations of the government and bringing to light improprieties committed by persons holding high positions. It plays a significant role in safeguarding the interests of various stakeholders, thereby facilitating good governance. For any vibrant parliamentary democracy, an effective system of accountability of the executive to parliament is fundamental. It is in this background that the framers of the Constitution of India decided to provide an independent authority in the form of the Comptroller & Auditor General.

The Comptroller & Auditor General's external audit provides confidence by which parliament, on behalf of the tax payer, scrutinises how the government uses the authorised appropriations of money. The CAG helps to hold the government financially accountable to the legislature. It is a critical link in the chain of public accountability in a democratic system of government. In democracies across the world the provision of such an institution is premised on the universal belief that public oversight of government policies and actions is essential for inclusive and sustainable economic growth.

Worldwide, governments have empowered supreme audit institutions in response to the changing models of governance and the rising demands of citizens for greater transparency and accountability. Mandates of several national auditing offices have been broadened to secure not only the legality and probity of government's spending but also its efficiency and effectiveness. A symbolic demonstration of how public-audit has evolved to bring into focus its accountability-role is the repositioning of the Supreme Audit Institution of the United States. In July 2004, recognising the critical role that the GAO, the equivalent of the Indian Audit and Accounts Department, would be called upon to play, the 110th Congress, introduced several proposals to augment the mandate of the external auditor.

The US Congress decided that, the erstwhile 'General Accounting Office' be re-designated as the 'Government Accountability Office' and its mandate be accordingly modified. This sent a very clear signal about the repositioned role of the national auditor. In Canada, the parliament passed the Federal Accountability Act in December 2006 to amend the Auditor General Act to give the Auditor General authority to conduct performance audits. The Australian National Audit Office, in its centenary celebration, published a book, *From Accounting to Accountability* to record the change, over the last century, from an emphasis largely on the practice of compliance-audit to a norm based on value-for-money and accountability-for-performance.

As models of governance evolve and newer systems to purvey government schemes are conceptualised, auditors have also to keep upgrading their skillsets. This is the way in which audit can add value and not detract from the process. Working together, auditors and the executive can improve the efficiency of administration and the effectiveness of government's spending. Whilst the executive has been given the freedom to frame and architecture schemes and projects to fulfil the requirement of growth, it is essential to ensure that subjective elements do not enter the implementation process.

Hence, the need to have an independent agency—the auditor to ensure objectivity. I also wish to emphasise that between 'audit' and the 'administration' there is no 'WE' and 'THEY' relationship. Both are on the same side of the table. Their goals are common. While the administration is the spending agency of governmental resources, the auditor is merely the validation agency to provide comfort not only to the legislature but the man on the street that the monies extracted from him have been most efficiently expended. In the newly emerging scenario, the public, besides seeking a more participative governance, is getting more vocal in its observations on the performance of the government agencies.

There is thus a perceptible paradigm shift in the approach towards public spending. Should there not be a paradigm shift in the approach of auditors too? The oft-raised query is that, in an era where the government has itself introduced the concept of social audit and transparency through the Right To Information Act, should not the public-auditors seek to sensitise public opinion about audit-observations, especially so in respect of the audits of the social sector departments such as those dealing with public health, primary education, rural employment, air pollution, environment, and drinking water.

It is incumbent on auditors to sensitise public opinion towards the way government expenditure is undertaken and how the nation's resources are being tapped for its economic development. It is towards this role that auditors-general, worldwide, have been mandated to conduct performance-audits to assess the efficiency and economy of public spending. In a reference made before the supreme court of India in 2013, the court had passed a judgment stating as follows:

> The CAG is not a Munim (accountant) to go into the balance sheets. The CAG is a constitutional authority entitled to review and conduct performance audit on revenue allocations relating to the centre, the states and the union territories and examine matters relating to the economy and how the government uses its resources. Don't undermine the office of the CAG.

The Indian political system faces many critical challenges today. Bottlenecks impinging on accountability have to be removed. Good governance cannot be relegated to a secondary position in pursuit of power and money. Typically people with vested interests in the system attempt to subvert the rules of government's accountability, on the one hand, and free-market competition, on the other. Several transformational developments taking place in India present opportunities for this section of players to try to divert decision making in government and public institutions for their personal agenda. These people then become the most insidious threats to a healthy democracy. It is, therefore, crucial that the accountability-institutions must reposition themselves to the changing scenario and must assist to serve the interests of the public.

It must be recognised that good governance is not an end in itself. It is merely the means to create an enabling environment in which every individual gets to benefit from the fruits of economic development on a continuing basis, and in which each institution of the country performs its role with impartiality and transparency. It is a system in which the rule of law is allowed to take its course and the ultimate pursuit is that of the collective good and not any partisan interests. In such a pursuit, the auditor is a key player, keeping vigil on the functioning of all the institutions of the executive. Such an atmosphere would nurture and perpetuate economic growth, thereby ensuring that it is inclusive and leads to the benefit of the welfare of society at large.

Economic prosperity is not an option—it is a necessity. Economic empowerment of the people in India, and its emergence as a superpower, can be possible if growth is founded on good governance. Such growth is sustainable only if it is premised on an ethical code of governance. When the story of India is written, it should be written that governance has been the solution and not the problem, wherein the state has been the facilitator and not the predator. These edicts in India's governance structure have to be an essential ingredient, as a lot is at stake, and that too for a huge population, whose democratic aspirations deserve the best efforts of the government.

This article is based on a speech delivered at the Indian Institute of Public Administration, Karnataka Branch, Bengaluru, on 30 May 2015. The views expressed are those of the author alone and not of any institution with which he is associated.

Falling For the Village Romantics

Manu Joseph

Idealists and Pragmatists Battle for the Future of Indian Agriculture

Gurgaon in plain sight is a dismal city near New Delhi, India's self-absorbed capital. Flanking a national highway and hedged on one side by a forest of hardy shrubs, Gurgaon lies in a suburban sprawl that has no center even though there are several buildings that proclaim 'City Center'. Builders claim it is 'modern,' but what they mean is new. Its inhabitants do not know the names of most of its roads. They too are new, chiefly seniors who have fled Delhi and young couples from all over the nation who work in the corporations that have set up offices in Gurgaon. Just a few years ago, a different kind of people used to live in Gurgaon, leading a very different life. They were farmers who used to grow grain, millets, and mustard. Then the builders made them offers they could not refuse. Hectares of land were sold to the builders transforming villagers into sudden millionaires. They went with bags filled with cash to buy cars. They started businesses and many became land brokers. Their diet changed, their habits changed. As one of them told me, about seven years ago when the transformation was still fresh, they were introduced to 'heart attack'. They bought fancy villas. A resident of one of Gurgaon's villas, the wife of a retired railway officer, told me that one day she saw a woman at her gates. 'I thought she wanted a job as a maid but then I realised she wanted to buy a house.'

Farmers have not entirely vanished from Gurgaon, but they have retreated into the ever-receding margins where they live on small farms with ever-masticating camels and cows. They await the builders. That is what agriculture in India is today—land awaiting the builders, farms waiting to become real estate.

The productivity of Indian agricultural land has improved vastly over the decades but it lags far behind not just developed economies but also other middle-income countries. India's rice productivity per hectare is half of that of China's, and its wheat productivity is less than 60 per cent. About half of India's population is employed in agriculture or associated industries, but contributes less than 20 per cent of the nation's gross domestic product. But India is vast, and more than 60 per cent of its land is used for agriculture. Only the United States has more arable land than India. As a result India is a statistical giant in farm produce. According to the United States Department of Agriculture, Indian agricultural exports in the decade between 2003 and 2013 grew faster than those of any other nation. India is among the largest producers of several crops. India can feed all its people and more. In fact, one of its major problems is that huge quantities of grains that are meant for the poor rot in warehouses.

So, the question that Indians with socialistic leanings—nationalists, traditionalists, and others who are suspicious of science and foreign corporations—ask, is why India should bother at all with seemingly risky genetically modified crops. Isn't all well as things are?

Genetically modified crops have better yields, are more resistant to conventional pests than organic crops, and use less fertiliser. India permits the use of genetically modified seeds only in cotton cultivation. Since 2002, when the technology was allowed, India's otherwise doomed cotton production increased manifold and the nation is today one of the major cotton producers in the world. But the technology has also been mired in controversy with activists alleging that seed companies, chiefly Monsanto, which produces Bt Cotton, have exaggerated the benefits and played down the reverses. They have accused Monsanto of being responsible for farmers falling into debt traps, and for their suicides. Several independent studies have disproved this hypothesis but the issue has become a matter of belief. Years of campaigning against the technology by both honest and spurious activists, and the tendency of Indian journalists who cover rural affairs to be suspicious of multi-national corporations, have instilled the fear in the minds of farmers that the products of biotechnology would make them beholden to seed companies like Monsanto.

The fact is that India has an exemplary law in place that protects the Indian farmer from becoming a slave to the monopoly of private corporations. Also, India has consistently demonstrated its will to stand up to the whole world to protect the commercial interests of the farmer, who is politically crucial. Yet, Indian politicians, who are usually practical men of the world, and as a result short-term players, see no immediate gain in risking the wrath of farmers, activists, and nationalists.

»»»»»»

In May 2014, after the new government was sworn in, India's agriculture minister, Radha Mohan Singh, said on his first day in office, 'I have spoken to government officials and feel GM technology is important'. But he added, 'If it is very essential then we will implement it.'

The Bharatiya Janata Party, which was triumphant in the general elections held this year, had maintained throughout its campaign that it would permit genetically modified crops only after serious scientific evaluation in Indian conditions. It was an admirable stand but the new government, like its predecessors, has succumbed to the pressures of activists and put on hold its valiant plans to understand the technology better from a purely scientific point of view. There is a case for India to be circumspect, but it has done nothing to comprehend its own circumspection and to make an informed decision. Instead, the Indian government has yielded to the threats and campaigns of activists.

There are several reasons why there is an urgent need for India to overhaul its agriculture through modern technology, bio-technology being just one of the many sciences it must prospect.

Farming is venerated in India, chiefly by those who are not farmers. An overwhelming majority of India's farmers are unable to share this quaint adoration because they are impoverished. Working on an Indian farm is among the least paying jobs in India. Not surprisingly, the aspiration of young rural Indians is to find liberation from farming. In fact, it is the lack of good opportunities in agriculture that is driving millions of young Indians to seek their future in the cities, where they live in inhuman conditions. Skilled farm workers are arriving in cities to become unskilled security guards in paramilitary uniforms, who are so malnourished even stray dogs taunt them. They also become drivers, gardeners, and maids. The educated are luckier but they struggle against the more sophisticated urban graduates. Many of India's social problems and urban nightmares emerge from the crushing poverty meted out by India's agricultural sector to its own.

States like Punjab and Maharashtra have shown that increasing the productivity of agricultural land and the associated industries such a growth would create, can transform societies within the lifespan of a government. Biotechnology is not the answer, but it is a part of it. For instance, Indian agriculture is a perennial victim of the extreme forces of nature. India is constantly hit by droughts and floods, and by pests. The Indian government has an unambiguous humanitarian reason to investigate whether biotechnology can solve some of the nation's unique problems. If India can create crops that can withstand droughts and floods, it would be an achievement that is far greater than sending a colour camera to orbit Mars.

In February 2014, Manmohan Singh, in his final months as prime minister said, 'Use of biotechnology has great potential to improve yields. While safety must be ensured, we should not succumb to unscientific prejudices against' genetically modified crops.

But it appears that he could not convince his own government to adopt the technology. The Genetic Engineering Approval Committee (GEAC), which has the mandate to regulate the development and cultivation of genetically modified organisms in India, had cleared several GM crops for field trials in 2013, but the Minister of Environment and Forests, Jayanthi Natarajan put them on hold. She was replaced by a man who claimed that she had misread a court directive. He approved the trials. But in May, after the general elections, the government headed by Manmohan Singh ceased to exist, and a new government headed by Prime Minister Narendra Modi was sworn in. In July, the Approval Committee, cleared 13 crops for field trials, but a few days later the government put the trials on hold. The turnabout was influenced by objections raised by two outfits, one of whose philosophy is to reject, 'materialistic and imperialistic homogenisation and aimless transnationalism of the Western assumption'; and the goal of the other outfit is, 'to collect, experiment, innovate, improve and publicise the centuries old practices and usages in the agriculture field …'

It is not hard to comprehend the nature of the opposition to biotechnology in India. The current Indian government is not opposed to genetically modified organisms. Nor was the government that it replaced. Their reluctance cannot be attributed to scientific scrutiny or concern for the commercial well-being of its farmers or the health of its citizens.

In almost every sphere of life, India shows no regard for the welfare of its citizens. Indian cities are among the most polluted in the world. Vehicles that are long past their usability are allowed to ply on the road. Children travel to school in open rickshaws, a dozen crammed into one that can fit only four. Several die in accidents on the way to school or on their way back. Chemical factories have very poor safety precautions. Buildings collapse because they have been built on loose soil or with poor material. Almost every restaurant is a serious fire hazard. Poorly designed roads, as much as wild driving, cause hundreds of fatalities every day. In Mumbai's suburban trains, men dangle from the doorways because those trains do not have automatic doors—hundreds die every year by falling. Yet, it is possible that such a nation would be concerned about the health implications of a technology, even if developed economies have deemed it safe for their citizens. Such a concern would have been honourable, even touching. But then the fact is that India's biotech policy has been disproportionately influenced by a mob of urban and provincial elites who hold on to traditions to sustain their own relevance in a changing world.

The two outfits that coerced the government to put the trials of genetically modified crops on hold—Swadeshi Jagran Manch and Bharatiya Kisan Sangh—are affiliated to the Hindu nationalistic Rashtriya Swayamsevak Sangh (RSS), the ideological mothership of the party that governs India today. The RSS, in Indian public conscience, is a fellowship of adult males in billowing khaki shorts and shirts, who perform morning drills as rudimentary physical exercise. Membership is not open to women. The stated purpose of the organisation is to preserve and promote India's Hindu ideology. It is a society of fierce intellectuals, academics, writers, and thugs, which is despised by the nation's westernised liberals. But the requirements of activism have brought together the fellowship of male ideologues and urban liberals, among them 'eco-feminists,' whatever that might be, on the same side in the battle against GMOs.

The aristocracy of these liberals are the village romantics. They are usually affluent, western educated, city-dwellers who are the beneficiaries of hailing from the top layers of India's social hierarchy. They inherited not just wealth, but also class, privileged education, social contacts, and other forms of exceptional advantages that ensured that they would remain the aristocracy even if the world changed fast. Like Gandhi. He too, unsurprisingly, was a village romantic.

They like the idea of the unchanging Indian village inhabited by colourful unchanging rustics who work on their small organic farms. Yet, what they love is the illusion of the Indian village, a village that does not now exist or ever actually existed. Deep within, the Indian village was a perpetually miserable place. The primary author of the Indian Constitution, B.R. Ambedkar, said six decades ago, 'The love of the intellectual Indian for the village community is of course infinite, if not pathetic...What is a village but a sink of localism, a den of ignorance, narrow mindedness and communalism?'[1]

Its oppressed have prayed for the village to be transformed. But the village romantics, who live far away in their bungalows, do not like the evolution of the village. They find economic progress, which transforms farms into real estate, visually ugly. They wish everything remains the same, because when everything remains unchanged they have something beautiful to marvel at from the outside—small, lush fields that are not very productive, good natured rustics who are stranded in their lives, and zero-emission bullock carts.

To the western world, the most famous of the contemporary Indian village romantics is Vandana Shiva, who is also among the world's most prominent activists against genetically modified organisms.

»»»»»

An article by Michael Specter in *The New Yorker* has cast serious doubts on her campaign.[2] It is inevitable that a story of this nature would provide Shiva's perception of India's Green Revolution that began in the 1960s and transformed Indian agriculture through innovations and the use of fertilisers and pesticides. 'Shiva believes that it destroyed India's traditional way of life,' Specter writes,

> She told me that, by shifting the focus of farming from variety to productivity, the Green Revolution actually was responsible for killing Indian farmers. Few people accept that analysis, though, and more than one study has concluded that if India had stuck to its traditional farming methods millions would have starved.[3]

Vandana Shiva is among the Indian intellectuals whom the West looks up to for an interpretation of Indian maladies. There are times when what 'intellectuals', such as Vandana Shiva, say is so ridiculous to an Indian ear that one wonders if they realise that Indians, too, would be reading their analyses.

Shiva's imagination of a pastoral paradisiacal India before the Green Revolution is so outrageous it borders on hilarious. Almost all of Indian literature and cinema of an age are essentially about the crushing, numbing poverty on the Indian farm before the Green Revolution began to transform the society. In fact, India was so food deficient before the Green Revolution that there would be police raids on wedding feasts to check if the guests were being fed too much food.

India paid a price for the advancement, of course, through ecological damage. But generations of Indians would agree with Specter's analysis that the incontrovertible fact is that the Green Revolution saved millions of Indians from starvation. In a way, the Revolution created India's vast educated middle class, the progeny of farmers who did not essentially get rich but prospered enough to send their children to schools and colleges, who in turn formed a formidable mass of first generation literates that straddled across metros and small towns, and became the very backbone of modern India.

The New Yorker story seriously challenges the credibility of many of Shiva's claims, and of Shiva herself. Specter writes,

> Shiva said last year that Bt-cotton-seed costs had risen by eight thousand per cent in India since 2002. In fact, the prices of modified seeds, which are regulated by the government, have fallen steadily… Shiva also says that Monsanto's patents prevent poor people from saving seeds. That is not the case in India. The Farmers' Rights Act of 2001 guarantees every person the right to 'save, use, sow, resow, exchange, share, or sell' his seeds. Most farmers, though, even those with tiny fields, choose to buy newly bred seeds each year, whether genetically engineered or not, because they insure better yields and bigger profits.[4]

These are vital facts, and Shiva is unable to contest them in her written response to the article. All through her response, which she posted on her website, she adopts the classic activist strategy of appearing to rebut the specific points raised in an article but discussing a range of issues that the story never stated or implied in the first place. Shiva denies that she ever said that the Bt-cotton seed costs had risen by 8,000 per cent in India. Then she goes on to show the difference in prices between natural cotton seeds before Monsanto entered the market and Bt, which was not the comparison the article was claiming to make.

Also, the story raises the serious question whether activists like Shiva are, in fact, responsible for the starvation or malnutrition of millions in the world's poorest nations. By protesting against genetically modified crops that are enriched by vitamins, crops that are developed by non-profits and have been proven to be safe, are they not denying the poor their right to better foods? Shiva's response does not address this crucial question.

On the plates of India's poor, when they do find food, there is always a huge portion of grain. Their meals are chiefly mere starch. The free or cheap food that they receive is almost entirely in the form of grains. India has a responsibility to scientifically investigate the genetically modified crops that add nutrition to grains, and clear them for consumption if they are indeed safe. Even if Shiva would raise hell.

More than *The New Yorker* story it was Shiva's insubstantial response that indicted her as a person who employs hyperbole to stir the emotions of her western audience. It is an outdated mode of activism. In the age of information, the smartest activists stick to facts.

Her most powerful claim—that Monsanto was responsible for the suicides of indebted farmers in India, and that the company was responsible for 'a genocide'—is largely discredited in India's mainstream news media, which was once instrumental in the wide dissemination of the hysteria when it began. Several independent studies by highly regarded academics have attempted to explain the so-called 'farmer suicides' and they have found Shiva's favorite hypothesis outlandish.

India can yet ban genetically modified life in India, but it should have an honourable reason for doing so.

This piece was first published in The Common Reader, *a publication of Washington University, St. Louis. It is reproduced here with the permission of the author and* The Common Reader.

Endnotes

1 Ambedkar's speech in The Constituent Assembly, 1948.

2 Michael Specter, 'Seeds of Doubt,' *The New Yorker*, (August 25, 2014), http://www.newyorker.com/magazine/2014/08/25/seeds-of-doubt.

3 Ibid.

4 Ibid.

The 'Real Other' of the World's Largest Democracy

Atul K. Thakur

Although it is almost 70 years now since we gained Independence, the leaders of independent India are not yet open enough to be sensitive to the needs of the poor. While making efforts to maintain sustained economic growth, they primarily undermine the merits of an equitable society. It is universally true that 'economic growth' is a prerequisite for running 'welfare programmes', but it alone should not be expected to cure all the socio-economic ills, which more often solicit active policy interventions to check the 'wild desires' of market capitalism.

In recent years, the misplaced notion of 'superpowerdom' has gripped the psyche of a section of Indian leaders, to an alarming degree. The Lok Sabha elections of 2014 decisively established a new political culture that for functional normalcy juggles between the 'medieval parochialism' and 'marketisation of critical resources'. A complete failure to admit and check various scams made the country's oldest political party, the Indian National Congress, shockingly redundant with its organisational morale fallen to an unprecedented low. This made a thumping majority possible for the Bharatiya Janata Party (BJP), a radically polarised political party under the leadership of Narendra Modi.

Modi's phenomenal rise within his own party and in national politics could be attributed to many factors, but the most prominent among them would be 'unrest among India's top 1 per cent wealthy businessmen' with the state's sustained capability to control business and resources. Thus, the Nehruvian socialistic vision was suddenly found to be at odds with the new political aspirations of the ruling party that helms the Centre, without counting its responsibilities for India's diverse demography and history.

The claims on governance and economic remodelling are grossly exaggerated and misleading—and the chauvinistic fog is too thick at the decision-making level. The rhetoric, overall, is helping to set a sort of totalitarianism—and fast changing the values in social, political, and economic realms. As the country's core fabric is under attack, the public policies are naturally moving in tandem—and necessitates for priorities to be reordered. The nature of the state today, having taken a decisive turn, is one where large corporate and business interests are the biggest influence. The glaring shift of a 'welfare state' in this fashion, intimidates, and raises genuine angst among the masses.

Left-Wing Extremism (LWE), more commonly represented and known in India as Maoists and Naxalites, have been gaining in strength and influence over the years. They maintain a high intensity in their operations while cracking down on the security forces or the 'comprador elites', who for them are the 'class enemies'. As reported widely, there are more than 30 LWE groups active in the country. A majority of them pursue 'armed-struggle', maintain armed cadres, and do not recognise parliamentary politics. Although some of them have been participating in democratic processes, with a mixture of success and failure.

They do not recognise the legitimacy of government—and the government on its part, attempts to crush these movements. Both sides instinctively perceive each other as a deadly threat to the other's existence. On a misplaced existential turf, the 'threat factors' work so much that India's former Prime Minister Manmohan Singh termed LWE, as 'the biggest internal security threat the country has ever faced'. Here, he boosted it out of proportion—so much that even the grave security issues of Kashmir appeared to him, less dangerous than this. He wrongly took it as only a side-game of a 'distracted economic view' that incorrigibly stands against the popular but deviated notion of globalisation.

Since 1991, when India opened its economy in lieu of reforms—market capitalism was given unprecedented prominence. Ushering in economic reforms was not completely an impulsive step, taken by the Narasimha Rao government—an impoverished economy and deteriorating governance had made it inevitable to change the course of the economy and the nature of government. Though much hyped, the actual gain of economic reforms didn't reach the vast segment of the humongous Indian population. Even worse, it created a ground of extreme inequality and 'relative deprivation'—where the difference in fortunes between two humans could be at an unimaginable level.

At the macro level, the economic reforms have helped services and businesses to attain a new scale—and certainly have enhanced the materialistic fundamentals of a higher socio-economic echelon. A compressed 'trickle down' has also touched some other sections but never with a uniform pace and magnitude, resulted in fuelling frustration among those who had hitherto been discriminated against—and were now on the verge of pauperisation under the new economic buoyancy around. Amidst the fancy of figures, the Indian economy has a fissure within that is threatening the very core 'idea of India', which promised equitable growth and an egalitarian social system. Both are missing completely—and India today as a nation, fulfills all the criteria that make it an abnormal unit of 1.2 billion vulnerable human masses and super-creatures.

The condition forces the desperate groups to go from pillar to post, to seek their rights, which are enshrined in India's well-written Constitution. But the 'fundamental rights' of the land are privy to those from a privileged background—otherwise, these don't go too far. The archaic judicial system, with its heavy 'elitist bias' is the biggest enforcer of structured procedures and verdicts, which gravely harms the 'idea of justice'. It would be grossly wrong to say that the third pillar of Indian democracy has really justified its prominence, placed stoutly on the pages of the Constitution. The 'separation of power' is a real must for a representative democracy like India—but when it is essentially laid out for action, not only for technicalities. The ethical decline of Indian courts should be a matter of grave concern, as the syndicates of Westernised and wealthy lawyers are hell-bent to secure 'selective verdicts' for people with easy and abundant riches. Justice has a high cost attachment in resurgent India.

Migrating to the governance side, it is imperative here to recall how unlike the present government at the Centre that so far has abstained from dealing with complex public policy matters, the previous United Progressive Alliance government at least had some genuine policy stands on crucial issues. Almost eight years back, the Ministry of Home Affairs had set up a high-level committee to come out with ways to check the growing LWE resurgence. The finding of the committee's report, noted:

> While the mechanism constituted for countering naxalism envisaged a multi-pronged approach, over the years the State response has tended to remain largely police-centric, with the main effort being to counter the movement with superior force. The approach has often swung from one extreme—that of using overwhelming force—to the other, structured around 'ceasefires' and 'peace talks'. While it is recognized that the naxal problem goes well beyond mere law and order dimensions, the broader socio-economic issues have not attracted serious attention.

Earlier in 2006, a Naxal Management Division was created in the Ministry of Home Affairs to effectively address the LWE insurgency in a holistic manner. But it proved a damp squib and didn't bring any noble ideas, or ways to contain the growing influence of LWE.

In December 2008, P. Chidambaram took charge of the Home Ministry, and that was the phase when the Maoist insurgency was gaining in the states of Chhattisgarh, Madhya Pradesh, Jharkhand, Bihar, Uttar Pradesh, Odisha, West Bengal, Maharashtra and Andhra Pradesh. The same parts together comprised the 'red corridor'—the prime base of LWE. As per the Ministry of Home Affairs statistics the violence in the red corridor peaked in 2009, with 2,258 incidents (a bureaucratic term) that resulted in the killing of 317 security forces personnel, 220 Naxals, and 591 civilians.

The numbers of incidents and scale of losses spiked again in 2010. That year, a total of 2,213 incidents caused the death of 720 civilians and the total security personnel and Naxals killed were 285 and 172, respectively. From 2011 onwards, there was a marginal fall in the death toll, nevertheless, there was no sharp fall in violent incidents. The further statistics show not a very different picture, as the carnage continued: in 2011, 469 civilians, 142 security forces, and 99 Naxals were killed in 1,760 incidents. In 2012, 301 civilians, 114 security men, and 74 Naxals were killed in 1,415 incidents. The number of incidents touched a low of 1,129 in 2013, yet 279 civilians, 115 police personnel, and 99 Naxals were killed that year.

As per the Home Ministry data, and as widely reported, there is a conformity that Chhattisgarh and Jharkhand are the hardest-hit by LWE violence. Next comes Bihar and Odisha. West Bengal had witnessed a high in 2010 but it has fallen down thereafter. The cases of Maharashtra, Andhra Pradesh, and Uttar Pradesh are akin to that and follow a similar trend. In the last one-and-half decades, LWE activities have shifted toward the north and east and it is a little surprising that Andhra Pradesh, where the People's War Group (PWG), Maoist Communist Centre (MCC), and other groups were hyperactive in the 1980s and 1990s, in fighting a 'class war', suddenly appear to have been tamed.

In 2009, the Ministry of Home Affairs adopted a two-pronged strategy to combat LWE, which laid emphasis on security and development-related interventions by the state. That clearly didn't work as the approaches were not addressing the 'real cause of dissent'—hence the ministry went further to strengthen central paramilitary forces, with a major infusion of funds. Keeping aside the conventional practice of not using air support for anti-LWE operations, the ministry made its mind clear. Next in line, the government brought about an overhaul in the training of security forces for specialised jungle/guerilla warfare.

Commando Battalions for Resolute Action (COBRA), a specialised force trained for counter-insurgency and jungle warfare, came into force to annihilate the LWE from its core base. Another strategic move made from a counter-insurgency point of view during Chidamabaram's tenure was to shape a two-year Integrated Action Plan (IAP) for the 60 most-affected Naxal-hit districts. IAP was presented as an economic development package for the 'red corridor', spread over nine Indian states. It primarily aimed to build critical physical infrastructure in those tribal and backward districts, which disconnected in the course of time from the usual developmental loop.

The plan was forwarded in order to implement the Provisions of the Panchayats (Extension to the Scheduled Areas) Act, 1996 and the Scheduled Tribes and Other Traditional Forest Dwellers (Recognition of Forest Rights) Act, 2006. The Ministry of Panchayati Raj and the Planning Commission were given institutional charges to deal on the district and state level, respectively. In 2010–11, each of the 60 districts was given a grant of Rs 25 crore. The next year, the grant was increased to Rs 30 crore and 12 more districts, to extend the plan.

The funds worth Rs 4,177.65 crore were spent covering 82 districts in nine states during 2010–13. Intent-wise and in effect, IAP was a soft plan that made some impact—but it would be a misnomer to believe that it made any transformation in LWE. Yet, the government had valid reason to extend it for four more years in 2013—but the one-sided action plan didn't last long and on 25 May, a massive attack by the Naxalite insurgents of the Communist Party of India (Maoist) on a convoy of Congress leaders in the Darba Valley in the Sukma district of Chhattisgarh caused at least 27 deaths, including that of Mahendra Karma, former State Minister and founder of Salwa Judum (a local armed militia group deployed against LWE groups), state Congress chief Nand Kumar Patel, and Vidya Charan Shukla, a senior Congress leader and former Union Minister who succumbed to his injuries on 11 June 2013). This halted the momentum to bring the tussle back on top.

The tribes of central India—Gond, Vaiga, Korwa, Muria, among others—have been the biggest sufferers of the state's insensitive handling of natural resources by allowing corporate plundering. Noticeably, the tribes depended on these natural resources for their survival. They grew up in ways where their existence couldn't be separated from the inhospitable jungles and rough mountains. The 'modernism' which otherwise impacted the world as a progressive set of ideas, made them reduced to subhuman conditions, where they couldn't converge with the outside world—and also lost their zone of survival in their native jungles.

Their perennial victimhood was primarily caused by three factors—the government's selective interest in natural resources, large corporates' greed for natural resources and prevalence of many LWE outfits, which are simply reactionary groups, using violence without any sense of purpose among the local communities. There is no uniformity in either sides' stories—but it is undeniable that the tribal people were not given basic human treatment by corporates operating in these regions. In the blind moves of commercialisation, they have been reduced to 'showpieces', who often appear during Corporate Social Responsibility (CSR) Conferences, hosted by the plunderers of their lives.

Through primary, secondary, and tertiary sources, I found that a large number of people who are hiding in the jungles around their villages or periodically fleeing to the jungles are the fearful local people, who frequently get attacked by the security forces and cadres of Salwa Judum (which was ordered disbanded by the supreme court in July 2011).They are forced to live precariously on the margins and often they too get labelled as 'the biggest threat to the nation', while the other stakeholder too choses to see them with suspicion, assuming they are potential informers to the security agencies.

They are the true wretched on earth, without any meaningful affiliation with the institutions of modernity or those who want to overthrow it all. They are the victims, as they are not really into the system—they are being unwaveringly exploited, cheated, and killed—in the name of insurgency and anti-insurgency. For them, no system represents their causes—the ideologies are just too naive for them. They live from day-to-day as the days ahead do not hold any promise of a better prospect. They are not fit to be in the schemes of the government, which owes a lot to payback to its corporate friends or of the armed insurgents, as they don't find them capable enough to wage the same war they have been carrying forward—without zeroing in on the justifiable goal.

There is another category, who are forced to live in Salwa Judum camps. Nandini Sundar has been working at the grassroots, and she makes a good point when she thinks it is fallacious to contend that 'inequality, poverty, or lack of development per se' lead to people joining the armed insurgency. She proposed a rehabilitation plan to the supreme court of India, which included: individual compensation for injury, death, and sexual violence; household compensation for property loss and damage; rebuilding of village infrastructure; restoration of tribal society, which has suffered damage due to the breakdown of trust and fratricidal violence; and restoration of district administrative, police, and judicial machinery.

The plan also included contributions from the National Commission for the Protection of Child Rights (NCPCR) for restoring village schools and rehabilitating minors who were employed as combatants and addressing the psychological trauma of children who are caught in the conflict. The National Commission of Women (NCW) would be enlisted to counsel female victims of rape and sexual violence and help them file cases. What the plan intended was to ensure a fair representation of victims' voices. Bibek Debroy, now a member of NITI Aayog, had argued in 2010 about the limits of expenditure-based counter-insurgency. The BJP-ruled governments at the Centre and state should give some heed to his views on this.

Sudeep Chakravarti, who chronicled his extensive travels to the nooks and corners of India's insurgency lands in his book *Red Sun: Travels in Naxalite Country* came out with a detailed finding that Maoists have moved away from their earliest priorities of the 1960s, when the movement was about class tension between sharecroppers and landless peasantry. Chakravarti says:

> In states like Chhattisgarh and West Bengal, uprisings are concerned with tribal rights; in Orissa and Jharkhand it's over the rich mineral deposits there; in Bihar, Uttar Pradesh, and parts of Haryana it's about caste and land. Now the movement is even spreading to Punjab where the area is over-farmed and undergoing a serious water crisis. The movement is growing as injustices proliferate. All the inequities of India are beginning to add up.[1]

He adds:

> The government can't wish away resentment and rebellion. Repeatedly, since the 1960s the Maoist movement has been 'annihilated.' But from the time it started with three villages, it has come back stronger, and now it's in 223 districts. These are not your frothing individuals. There's a method to what they do. You have to accept that these are angry, yet thinking people.[2]

While delving further on the ultra Left, it is imperative to look back on the role played by the democratic Left in India. Although there is a paucity of analytical literature on the mainstream Left at the national level, journalist Praful Bidwai's posthumously published book *The Phoenix Moment: Challenges Confronting the Indian Left* is a significant work.[3] This book remarkably covers the ground of a communist movement—unique within the world's capitalist democracies—that flourished for so long in India, and examines what accounts for its initially gradual and then rapid decline.

Bidwai attains a distinction here in his investigation on the mainstream Left's core agenda of progressive or socialist transformation, which can yet be reinvented and restored to relevance—either with its own agency or through other forces, formations, and initiatives. Despite operational flaws and lack of organisational Left unity, undoubtedly India still has a significant and relatively powerful communist movement. This is noteworthy, since communist parties have suffered massive setbacks in electoral politics, where they didn't become able to secure the safer bastions of West Bengal and Kerala. The setback became the strongest during the 2014 national elections, but the overall decline took place during the last decade.

Despite touching a new low, the Indian Left remains a significant component of the wider political spectrum. It has a glorious past and respectable present in representing almost every state with trade unions, peasant associations, and student unions—and in state legislatures, municipal bodies, and village councils. However, in counting the failures of mainstream communism in India, the first recognisable factor was their unwillingness to end factionalism—and stay under a single centralised canopy. With the India-China war of 1962, an operational weakness took root in the democratic Left—and that fragile collaboration in the name of 'Left unity' remains elusive, keeping at bay any chance of unification.

The same is true with the trade union movement, another area where actual chances existed for progressive unity. Today, Left parties by themselves are not in a position to contest all the Lok Sabha seats. That is why they must get extra active to forge a Left and democratic unity, which will take along with the Left all other secular democratic parties, forces, and individuals. Moreover, what the Left parties need most is electoral reforms, which will save the electoral process from the grip of money/muscle-power. The Left parties have been talking of the proportional representation system, which will do away with the first-past-the-post system prevailing presently in which moneyed individuals use all tricks to get elected, even with minority votes.

I interviewed Comrade A.B. Bardhan, then the Communist Party of India (CPI) General Secretary and he replied to my query 'Why is communism still being determined by the texts rather than contemporary contexts?'

> The world has changed but imperialism and capitalism continue to exist; what we see today is a big crisis that has overtaken capitalism. It can't solve the problems of unemployment, poverty, and even illiteracy and disease. India has also changed in the course of the last six-and-a-half decades since Independence but facts reveal that the capitalist path of the government that's being pursued and the so-called neo-liberal policies of privatisation, liberalisation, and globalisation have only aggravated all our problems. Disparities between the super rich and affluent sections, which are only 10 per cent of our population, and the overwhelming mass of the poor and vulnerable sections has deepened and widened as never before.[4]

In a nutshell, he exemplified his party's genuine binding with the 'contemporary contexts'—and also shared the limiting factors, which are keeping the democratic Left movement at a low pace.

In an interview with me, Senior CPI leader and former Union agriculture minister comrade Chaturanan Mishra spoke on the existential aspects of Left unity:

> Despite hard efforts during my stint as the President, All India Trade Union Congress (AITUC, 1983–89)…'I couldn't succeed in ensuring its merger with the Hind Mazdoor Sabha [HMS]; due to internal hindrances, the overall merger of the Left-led trade union movement remained a pipe-dream. I attribute this division to our failure in emerging as a truly national party; today civil rights activists like Medha Patekar, Arundhati Roy etc. are raising their voice on issues that should be our concern.[5]

Both the leaders admitted not joining the United Front Government was a blunder for the Communist Party of India-Marxist (CPI-M), which adversely impacted the possibilities for Left forces in the country. Jyoti Basu, as a prime minister would have scripted a new chapter in Indian politics—and for the Left forces. The failure to understand the call of time transcended negatively on mainstream Left parties—and also alienated radical groups, which otherwise would have come closer to the state to negotiate their demands. The end of the 1990s and the early years of the next decade witnessed a new beginning of intensified violent activism, where the radical forces were seen increasingly at loggerheads with the security agencies and institutions of the state.

The divergence has been glaring among the Indian communists; their being so has harmed the prospects of the masses, and lately their own existence—despite having an impressive past to reckon with and a current possibility to emerge as an alternative. Every stakeholder has to acknowledge that in the long run, the solution to the LWE lies in understanding and addressing key ailing factors in governance, not in merely cracking down on them and flexing muscles the wrong way by allocating a large amount of resources for ostensible developmental projects. The lack of proper focus on bringing major changes in existing paradoxical governance frameworks will not let security and development actions go very far. Those who are on the other side of the fence, with little belief in the state's intentions are surely seeking a better package of solutions.

If one takes a closer look one can see the instances, which show the lack of political commitment to improve governance in the Fifth Schedule Areas, by honouring the Panchayats Extension to Scheduled Areas (PESA) Act, 1996. This Act was enacted to address the issues of 'self-governance', meeting the demand of local ethnic communities. The PESA meant to give the tribal population a free voice in democratic forums—and allow them to make decisions locally on their surroundings, culture, natural resources, and development programmes. The Act offered a fair amount of reservation to the tribes in local self-government—but alas, not all provisions were followed at ground level, finally leaving the PESA too failing on the ground.

Negating the imminence of a holistic framework on counter-insurgency, many crucial dimensions have been overlooked—which broadened the chasm further between the blocks. The present government at the Centre, which is under the shadow of its predecessors,—a phenomenon that was termed by the senior BJP leader and former minister Arun Shourie as 'Congress + Cow'. The NDA government at the centre is strongly controlled by Narendra Modi, the Prime Minister of India, with a mission to overhaul the existing system. This ardous task appears like a move to depart from the past.

This same man has a customised taste for polices—at home or beyond borders ... The unkept promises are piling up rapidly and managing them would be challenging for him or the faithful people in his company. On security matters, he has his man in Ajit Doval, the National Security Advisor, who had once summed up LWE in these words:

> Majority of the people in Maoist affected areas and even their supporters and cadres have little to do with Maoism at ideological level. They are only alienated and angered people with real or perceived sense of injustice, oppression and indignity. Maoists are cleverly exploiting this sentiment to their advantage—caste conflicts in Bihar, resentment against landlords in Andhra, discontent against forest laws in tribal areas, unemployment amongst youth, and radicalism among Muslims, are all given prescription of capture of power through gun as the ultimate solution of all their problems. While the local grievances need to be effectively addressed through improved governance and ruthless

> accountability, there is also a need for creating mass awareness of the ultimate designs and consequences of what the extremists stand for.[6]

Doval, the man with a heavy burden to understand the complex security scenarios and prepare measures to handle them appears through this piece, a big admirer of the modern day ideologue of Fourth-generation warfare, William Lind. His understanding of LWE doesn't prove him someone with a 'distinct approach'—he is on the same page, where the new brigade of the ruling BJP is positioned. Rajnath Singh, Union Minister of Home Affairs, is not regularly engaged with these issues—and his statements usually come in the wake of incidents or for clarifications.

India now is being ruled under a new system, which is not in a mood to let democracy go on the same track that it has travelled on for the last almost seven decades. Yet the 'real others' should be given the attention they deserve. The mode could be wrong for a few but the angst and alienation of the majority, as their livelihood and identity are in danger, are justified. This government or any other should not keep matters in hibernation. The problems always merit a solution.

Endnotes

1 Sudeep Chakravarti, *Red Sun: Travels in Naxalite Country* (New Delhi: Penguin India, 2008).

2 Ibid.

3 Praful Bidwai, *The Phoenix Moment: Challenges Confronting the Indian Left* (New Delhi: Harper Collins India, 2015).

4 Atul K Thakur, 'Comrade in Introspection!', *Mainstream*, Vol. XLIX, No. 50, 3 December (2011).

5 Atul K Thakur, 'Comrade in Introspection!', *Mainstream*, Vol. XLIX, No. 29, Reproduced 9 July (2011).

6 Ajit Doval, *Left Wing Extremism – The Threat and Response* (New Delhi: Vivekanand International Foundation, 2010).

SECURITY AND FOREIGN POLICY

Indian Strategy in a Non-Strategic Age

Dhruva Jaishankar

As India emerges in the 21st century, evolving gradually into a middle-income country with increasingly global interests, it will find itself adapting to a rapidly evolving international system. India's resources today are greater than at any time in its history, and it no longer confronts existential threats. But while the country may now be less vulnerable, it will have to confront different—and sometimes unprecedented—challenges.

Are India and its leaders up to the task? Sceptics often point to an absence of strategy. Indeed, a widely-held view, both domestically and abroad, is that India—its leaders, its polity, and its culture—is not strategic.[1] This is simply untrue. India would not have remained unified, grown stronger, slowly prospered, achieved military victories, or emerged as a de facto nuclear weapons power without some kind of strategy; these developments were not merely the product of accident or good fortune. In fact, a slew of histories and accounts document detailed deliberations and strategic decisions behind each of these outcomes.[2]

But the image of India as non-strategic is so widespread and so deeply ingrained that it is worth considering how and why it became so popular. One reason is that India has no single defining national strategic document. In fact, there rarely is one. Indian leaders—like their counterparts elsewhere—have often found value in ambiguity. Another view is that India's strategic culture has often been guided by the spoken—rather than the written—word, or that elements of strategy are intuitively understood rather than explicitly stated.[3] Furthermore, analysts and commentators, particularly outside India, are often unable to discern a strategy amid the noise of the Indian public sphere, mistaking public debate for strategic incoherence. At a very superficial level, democracy muddies the strategic waters. Finally, an absence of strategy is often inferred from India's poor or *ad hoc* implementation. India's record as an executor of strategy is at best uneven, although critics often overlook India's resource constraints. Yet while implementation has perhaps been India's greatest weakness, it is not for want of strategic acumen.

Strategy is a much misunderstood, misused, and maligned concept. In general, it refers to how individuals and organisations set goals and attempt to achieve them under uncertain conditions and with limited resources. In the context of national policymaking, the term 'strategy' is often used as shorthand for 'grand strategy'. Grand strategy is how a national leadership controls and utilises resources to effectively promote a country's vital national interests and secure those interests against adversaries. Strategy is, perhaps, illusory.[4] It may also be overrated. The mere presence of a strategy is not, in itself, a good thing. Major historical debacles—from Napoleon's Waterloo campaign, Hitler's invasion of the Soviet Union, or the US involvement in Vietnam—were all motivated by clear-eyed strategies, even if they were flawed in hindsight.[5]Nor is a good strategy a pure reflection of public opinion, as can be attested to by numerous cases of extreme nationalism and populism gone awry. A successful strategy depends in large part on its feasibility and sustainability.

The Elements of India's Grand Strategy

I. Resources

Grand strategy requires drawing a connection between three elements. The first is national resources, which a leadership must identify, enhance, and control. This might include a country's ability to apply force, including through the use of its military or a covert action capability; its economic resources such as raw materials, industrial output, capital, and market access; its diplomatic abilities; and the information at its disposal, such as technological expertise, intellectual property, intelligence, and ideas.

India's resources are still modest, but are growing. Its military is large, professional, and battle-experienced, but has limited offensive capabilities and is not always adequately equipped. Its covert action capability is restricted. And although an existential nuclear deterrent has been established, many steps are still required before India has a credible minimum deterrent.[6] While warfare is becoming increasingly rare, especially between states, there are many conceivable scenarios that might require India to use force. Security challenges within the country remain a concern, although violence of all kinds—including terrorism—has been steadily declining since the early 2000s.[7]

Economically, India has seen meaningful progress from a very low base. In a quarter century since the economic liberalisation of 1991, India's economy has grown seven-fold and per capita incomes have multiplied by five. It retains several structural advantages, including a large and youthful workforce and internationally competitive wages. But India remains resource-poor relative to the size of its population, and is heavily reliant on raw material imports. Its industrial output is still marginal, although its manufacturing base is gradually increasing. India's research and development capabilities in many sectors are still wanting, although it has been able to compete globally in such areas as software and space. The Indian government has a growing ability to provide international assistance and loans, including through joint initiatives with the private sector. India also remains a lucrative export destination and it is developing into one of the largest untapped consumer markets. This is in fact a source of influence, giving India greater leverage when imposing sanctions or threatening other discriminatory economic measures.

Although diplomatically overstretched, India wields considerable diplomatic power in its immediate neighbourhood, particularly with its smaller neighbours. It also has effective veto power over many decisions of global significance.[8]India is also a rich fount of ideas—from Buddhism and democracy in the developing world to yoga and Bollywood—all of which can be used to increase India's attraction or soft power. These military, economic, diplomatic, and information resources constitute but a sampling of the national resources at India's disposal. Along almost every dimension, including in areas where there is considerable room for improvement, India's capabilities are increasing, even if gradually.

II. Interests

The second element of a grand strategy involves interests, which a national leadership must define. In any polity, the national interest reflects a general consensus among ruling elites. In democratic societies such as India's, this consensus about the national interest is influenced by a broad spectrum of public opinion, through the ballot box, the media, and formal and informal lobbying. In most countries, the national interest involves the preservation of national unity and sovereignty, improved welfare through increased prosperity and security, and the defence of national values.

It is important to note that national interests can evolve over time. The United States' national interests as a newly-independent country in the late 18th century were very different from its objectives two hundred years later. Similarly, Germany's grand strategy in 1990 bore no resemblance to that of 1938. These changes were the result of changes to the national character and the structure of the international system. The end of the Cold War in 1991 altered the global context in many ways. For India, advancing the same national interests required establishing a relationship with the Soviet Union in the early 1970s but necessitated deeper relations with the United States in the 2000s. Yet there was not a fundamental change in India's national character that completely overturn edits interests, even if the *means* of advancing those interests may have changed in significant ways.

India's national interests, like those of many other countries, stem from its foundational document: the Constitution. The national interest therefore involves the preservation and strengthening of the Indian republic and its system of governance; the preservation of India's territorial unity and sovereignty; and improvements to public welfare, through increases in prosperity, security, and the rule of law. If much of this seems obvious, it is precisely because it has become hardwired into India's democracy. It is natural —even healthy—that there are robust debates about how to achieve these ends, and to what degree certain interests should be prioritised over others. But, by and large, these broad objectives of national security and public prosperity have guided India's leadership since Independence.

III. Adversaries

The third element of a grand strategy involves adversaries, against whom a state must secure its national interests. Adversaries can sometimes be other states, occasionally on specific issues, but they can extend to non-state or sub-state actors. In India's case, certain adversaries are easily identifiable: those non-state actors who explicitly seek to undermine India's existence, unity, and well-being. They include those groups based in other countries, often with those countries' tacit support (e.g. Lashkar-e-Taiba) as well as those entities within India that do not recognise or abide by India's Constitution, such as various violent separatist groups and revolutionaries (e.g. Naxalites). Non-state adversaries may also encompass those actors that directly threaten Indian citizens and interests farther afield, such as pirates in the Gulf of Aden or the so-called Islamic State of Iraq and Syria (ISIS).

Identifying other states as adversaries is, in today's world, more problematic. However, there are two—China and Pakistan—that explicitly contest India's territorial integrity. This does not make them enemies in the classical sense. Both China and Pakistan officially recognise India's right to exist, enjoy diplomatic relations with it, and cooperate with India in a variety of ways. India is not in a declared state of war with either of these neighbours. But an adversarial relationship will exist at least as long as they claim Indian-controlled territory and use, or threaten to use, force in a bid to seize it. Although territorial disputes may be the most direct manifestation of an adversarial relationship, competition can extend beyond the territory in question, to third countries, multilateral bodies, economic competition, and the ideological realm. The view of the national interest advanced by the Pakistan army, for example, extends well beyond competition over territory, and presents India as an existential adversary.[9]

Finally, grand strategy requires tying together these three elements—resources, interests, and adversaries. Strategy is ultimately the *means* of using one's resources to advance and secure one's interests. India's grand strategy today and for the foreseeable future will involve how it controls, enhances, and utilises its military, economic, diplomatic, and information resources to strengthen the Indian republic, preserve India's unity and sovereignty, and increase public prosperity, security, and the rule of law, while securing these objectives against inimical non-state actors and regional adversaries.

A Strategy for a Non-Strategic World

Although India has had a grand strategy, the world is becoming a less strategic place. This is not because states have less power.[10] Quite the contrary. The state is perhaps more powerful today than at any point in history. In most countries—both advanced and developing—the state's role increasingly extends into virtually every aspect of daily life. The state retains a monopoly on legal violence. There are fewer ungoverned spaces. The state bears ever greater responsibility for public welfare, providing health, education, basic utilities, infrastructure, energy flows, and retirement benefits—and even acts as a lender or insurer of last resort. And, despite the lowering of international trade barriers and market liberalisation, the state has unprecedented regulatory authority over the private and non-profit sectors.

The world is become less strategic for three very different reasons. One, in an era of greater international interdependence, engagement, and peace, adversaries are more difficult to identify. Two, with the spread of democracy and proliferation of information and communication technologies, the public debate over the means of pursuing the national interest has become more cacophonic. And three, with the decline in traditional security concerns, increased globalisation, the rise of welfare states, and the advent of professional lawyers and diplomats, the tools at a state's disposal to exert influence have become more varied. Rather counterintuitively, grand strategy is becoming harder even as the state is becoming stronger.

Certain changes to India's strategic circumstances are to be anticipated. In terms of *resources*, India will almost undoubtedly have more in the near future than it has today. Economic growth will almost undoubtedly continue, fuelled by a growing working-age population and greater opportunity, although it remains to be seen to what degree. Economic growth will mean a larger revenue base for the government. This, in turn, will result in an increased ability to spend, whether on diplomatic efforts, foreign assistance and loans, military preparedness, intelligence, and research and development. A rising middle class will also enhance India's appeal as a market, increasing its international attractiveness and leverage. The objective of intensified industrialisation—if achieved—will lead to greater exports. Overall economic growth and industrialisation will remain necessary elements for India's grand strategy in the 21st century.

The broad contours of India's national *interests* are unlikely to change, barring an unforeseen structural change either to India as a state or the nature of the international system. But what about *adversaries*? Domestically, the broad trend lines concerning separatism, insurgency, terrorist activity, and overall violence in India have been positive of late. Separatists in Punjab and Mizoram have been successfully dealt with. Insurgents in Jammu and Kashmir have largely failed in their objectives, even if separatist sentiments have not been fully extinguished. Even Naxalite violence has declined, although the results have varied considerably state by state. This does not mean, however, that such positive trends are irreversible. The end to a fragile ceasefire with separatists in Northeast India and periodic acts of dramatic violence by Naxalites hint at possible future reversals. While there has been a recent lull in terrorist violence in urban centres, this too is tenuous.

Therefore, while there are reasons to be cautiously optimistic about India's internal security based on the recent past, there remains the prospect—however remote—of greater violence at home. Examples include the sudden explosion of civil strife in more developed societies than India—such as in Iraq, Syria, the former Yugoslavia, Ukraine, or parts of Latin America—as well as the rapid rise of new extremist groups (such as the Islamic State). India's successes may in fact make it a more attractive target for those intent on threatening Indian values. And India's skewed gender ratio—resulting in over twenty million single men, or 'bare branches'—could have serious consequences for Indian security.[11] Economic growth alone does not guarantee a peaceful and harmonious society.

Internationally, India's ability to secure itself at the strategic level (as opposed to the tactical level) has improved significantly after it demonstrated an existential nuclear deterrent capability.[12]In other words, the prospects of India becoming embroiled in a major international war have sharply diminished since 1998. Yet India must continue to guard against—and potentially counter—the use of coercive force by regional adversaries. The nature of security threats will undoubtedly change, as an outcome of various technological developments. New threats could arise from developments in unmanned warfare, cyber conflict, and the targeting of critical infrastructure. Greater resources, more leverage, and better planning will naturally be required to address such contingencies.

Enhancing India's Grand Strategy

By 2025, India will have an economy of between $3.5 and $5 billion, depending largely on the success of economic reforms and planning in the near future. A sub-par growth rate of roughly 5per cent per year will position India closer to the lower end of that spectrum, while a healthier rate of 7.5-8 per cent annual growth would enable India to reach the higher end. There is no reason to believe that India will not have deepened and improved relations with most major economies in this process of growth, particularly given the absence of major points of conflict between India on the one hand, and the likes of the United States, Europe, Russia, Japan, Southeast Asia, Africa, and Latin America on the other.

Still, four major uncertainties will remain with respect to India's strategic environment. The first is whether this process of development can be managed while mitigating social upheaval. The second is whether India will successfully leverage its economic growth to better integrate its smaller neighbours, such as Nepal, Bhutan, Bangladesh, Sri Lanka, and the Maldives, for mutual benefit. The third is to what degree will India become part of global supply chains, and what this means in particular for its integration into Asia more broadly. This will largely depend on the nature of India's future growth. Finally, it remains to be seen how India is able to manage tensions with Pakistan and China, even if it cannot fully resolve its differences with these two neighbours.

India's growing resources, its continuing interests, and its evolving threat environment suggest several areas that are deserving of greater attention. Of primary importance, given how much else depends upon it, are policies that stimulate economic growth, promote industrialisation, and lift some 300 million Indians out of absolute poverty. This process would expand India's resource base considerably, increase its global influence, and further empower both the Indian state and society. Better project management, faster clearances, lower barriers to investment, better land acquisition, and increased agricultural productivity offer one attractive path to achieving this objective.[13] Yet, some question whether such developments are feasible.[14] In either event, as India grows, a combination of economic and diplomatic policies will have to be devised to integrate India's neighbourhood more closely with its own economy. This will help expand India's regional influence, create mutually-beneficial and less adversarial relations with its neighbours, and thereby enhance India's regional security environment.

In terms of domestic security, police and judicial reforms will be of primary importance. They will be necessary to address domestic security challenges, including improvements to law and order. Beyond that, a number of wide-ranging defence reforms are required to better prepare the Indian military to meet various contingencies in the 21st century. This involves changes to command structures, acquisition, training, and doctrine. Other important steps will involve better information. This might include better contingency planning, domain expertise on adversaries, a better understanding of opportunities and influencers in the international system, and mastery over the next generation of security challenges that are an outgrowth of various technological developments. India's industrialisation and security reforms may be a first-order priority, but increased diplomatic capacity as part of wider public sector reforms and more sophisticated information collection and dissemination will increase and broaden India's power potential.

All of these steps, while vital, should not be mistaken for a grand strategy. A strategy, after all, is a means to an end, and it will depend ultimately on India's leadership. India's leaders—whether political or bureaucratic, and of whatever political persuasion—would certainly benefit from having greater resources, a more varied toolkit, and a clearer understanding of India's challenges and adversaries. But they will have to contend with the inherently more difficult circumstances of a non-strategic age, as means proliferate, policies are more fiercely debated, and adversaries become less clearly defined.

In the Mahabharata, Vidura, counsellor to his brother, King Dhritarashtra, lists the qualities of wise men: self-knowledge, exertion, forbearance, and adherence to duty.

आत्मज्ञानंसमारम्भः तितिक्षाधर्मनित्यता।
यमर्थान्नापकर्षन्तिसवैपण्डितउच्यते।।

A wise king, he argues, must be able to discriminate between right and wrong, and he must be able to control allies, neutrals, and enemies through gifts, conciliatory gestures, sowing disagreement, and ruthlessness. As these passages show, strategic instinct—what was later described as *chanakyaniti* or *kautilyam*—has been ever-present in India. But as Dhritarashtra learned as a result of his own follies and shortcomings, even the sagest advice, when left unheeded, can result in misfortune.

The outlines and limitations of an Indian grand strategy for the 21st century are readily apparent. And judging by the positive developments of the past quarter century, India has no need to fear imminent or dire misfortune. But the world is changing, and changing fast. It will be up to India's leaders to effectively utilise the resources at their disposal to advance the national interest in the face of rapidly evolving global circumstances.

Endnotes

1 George K. Tanham, 'Indian Strategic Thought: An Interpretive Essay,' (Santa Monica, CA: RAND, 1992); Stephen P. Cohen and Sunil Dasgupta, *Arming Without Aiming: India's Military Modernization* (Washington: Brookings Institution Press, 2010);

Harsh V. Pant, *Contemporary Debates in Indian Foreign and Security Policy: India Negotiates its Rise in the International System* (London: Palgrave Macmillan, 2008).

2 V.P. Menon, *Integration of the Indian States* (Hyderabad: Orient BlackSwan, 2011); Srinath Raghavan, *War and Peace in Modern India: A Strategic History of the Nehru Years* (Ranikhet: Permanent Black, 2010); Sanjaya Baru, *Strategic Consequences of India's Economic Performance* (New Delhi: Academic Foundation, 2006); Srinath Raghavan, *1971: A Global History of the Creation of Bangladesh* (Cambridge: Harvard University Press, 2013); George Perkovich, *India's Nuclear Bomb: The Impact on Global Proliferation* (Berkeley: University of California Press, 1999); C. Raja Mohan, *Impossible Allies: Nuclear India, United States, and the Global Order* (New Delhi: India Research Press, 2006).

3 Shyam Saran 'China in the Twenty-First Century: What India Needs to Know about China's World View,' Second Annual K. Subrahmanyam Memorial Lecture, New Delhi, August 29, 2012.

4 Richard K. Betts, 'Is Strategy an Illusion?' *International Security*, Vol. 25, No. 2, Fall (2000): 5–50.

5 Edward Luttwak, 'A Damned Nice Thing,'*London Review of Books*, Vol. 36, No. 24, 18 December (2014):15-16; David Stahel, *Operation Barbarossa and Germany's Defeat in the East* (New York: Cambridge University Press, 2009); Edwin E. Moise, *Tonkin Gulf and the Escalation of the Vietnam War* (Chapel Hill: University of North Carolina Press, 1996).

6 'Cabinet Committee on Security Reviews Progress in Operationalizing India's Nuclear Doctrine,' Press Information Bureau, January 4, 2003. (http://pib.nic.in/archieve/lreleng/lyr2003/rjan2003/04012003/r040120033.html).

7 Devesh Kapur, 'And Now, (Modestly) Good News,' *Business Standard*, April 9, 2012.

8 Amrita Narlikar, 'All that Glitters is Not Gold: India's Rise to Power,' *Third World Quarterly*, Vol. 28, Issue 5, (2007): 983-99.

9 C. Christine Fair, *Fighting to the End: The Pakistan Army's Way of War* (New York: Oxford University Press, 2014); Aqil Shah, *The Army and Democracy: Military Politics in Pakistan* (Cambridge: Harvard University Press, 2014).

10 Susan Strange, *The Retreat of the State: The Diffusion of Power in the World Economy* (Cambridge: Cambridge University Press, 1996).

11 Valerie M. Hudson and Andrea M. den Boer, *Bare Branches: The Security Implications of Asia's Surplus Male Population* (Cambridge: Belfer Center for Science and International Affairs, 2004).

12 Ashley Tellis, *India's Emerging Nuclear Posture: Between Recessed Deterrent and Ready Arsenal* (Santa Monica, CA: RAND, 2001).

13 Arvind Panagariya, 'The Narendra Modi Economic Model Offers a Compelling Alternative to the Mess at the Centre,' *The Economic Times*, June 29, 2013.

14 Shyam Saran, 'Revisiting India's Growth Strategy,' *Business Standard*, May 12, 2015; Raghuram Rajan, 'Make in India, Largely for India,' Speech at the Bharat Ram Memorial Lecture, December 12, 2014, https://www.rbi.org.in/scripts/BS_SpeechesView.aspx?Id=930.

Indian Internal Security: Are we Sacrificing the Security of our Citizens at the Altar of the Security of the State?

Omair Ahmad

Defining National Security

India's security is a loosely defined term that allows a great deal of misunderstanding. For example, the term 'national security' is not defined in any legislation in India. Neither the 43rd Report by the Law Commission of India on Offenses Against National Security, presented in 1971, nor the National Security Act, 1980, have defined this term. What are we to understand about the mandate of an institution such as the National Security Advisory Board (NSAB), or the role of National Security Adviser (NSA) when 'national security' itself is not defined?

India is not alone in this confusion, and there are few states that have actually defined the term, although almost all states use the term. In light of the near-unanimity of the use of the term 'national security', and its misuse, the one major definition of the term comes from its limitation. In 1984 the International Commission of Jurists, the International Association of Penal Law, the American Association for the International Commission of Jurists, the Urban Morgan Institute for Human Rights, and the International Institute of Higher Studies in Criminal Sciences convened a meeting with leading experts in the field of human rights in Siracusa, Italy. They adopted a set of principles called, 'The Siracusa Principles on the Limitation and Derogation Provisions in the International Covenant on Civil and Political Rights', often known merely as the Siracusa Principles.

Section B (iv) of the Siracusa Principles refers directly to the term national security, and states, 'National security may be invoked to justify measures limiting certain rights only when they are taken to protect the existence of the nation or its territorial integrity or political independence against force or threat of force.' In doing so, the principles imply that 'national security' is limited to the protection of the existence of a nation, or its territorial integrity or political independence, against force or the threat of force.

The Siracusa Principles come very close to the definition of 'National Emergency', as defined in the Indian Constitution under Article 352, 'whereby the security of India or of any part of the territory thereof is threatened, whether by war or external aggression or armed rebellion'. This threat to national security, in the most extreme form, has only been claimed three times, during the wars of 1962 and 1971, and by Indira Gandhi's government declaring an internal Emergency in 1975. While the first two declarations of National Emergency have been fairly free from controversy, the last one is rarely accepted as legitimate, even by most supporters of the Indian National Congress party. This tells us something very important about national security in India. Except at times of war, it is extremely hard to threaten the national security of India, and most Indians will only accept that the idea of the basic framework of India is threatened, in the case of war with an external enemy.

If this is the case, then most of the laws and institutions devoted to national security are useless for most of the time, because the very thing that they are supposed to be securing is not really under threat. India is rarely under the threat of war with our external neighbours. Even if we have unresolved border disputes with Pakistan and China, and our engagement with the former is marked by continuing skirmishes along the International Border and the Line of Control, these do not threaten the sovereignty of India in any appreciable manner. Unlike many other states of the world, Indians today have the luxury of living in a state whose borders and political system are increasingly stable and cannot be easily threatened by external aggression. In fact, as the former Indian Prime Minister, Dr Manmohan Singh, stated, we live in a world where the redrawing of borders is not really an option.

National Security in the Current International System

Dr Singh's comments point to a profound change in the international system, where international conflict has declined precipitously over the last few decades. The US misadventure in Vietnam and the Soviet misadventure in Afghanistan were, potentially, the dying notes of the bugle call for international aggression, where great powers engaged in the affairs of lesser powers. The failures of both these wars clearly showed that even small countries could not be easily subdued any longer in the international system, even by the most powerful countries. This seems to be curious. The United States Army that went into Vietnam was far more powerfully equipped than the one that fought Germany and Japan during World War II, and yet the US had no problem in ruling (West) Germany and drafting its Constitution, or dropping nuclear bombs on Japan and ruling it thereafter for years. The Soviet conquest of Eastern Europe and East Germany, over which it drew an 'Iron Curtain', was equally effective—at least until 1991. What changed in the decades between these wars so much so that these superpowers, which were much more powerful by the 1960s and 1970s, suffered such catastrophic defeats?

Part of the answer lies in the idea of sovereignty, while the second part of the answer lies with internal security. The principle of national sovereignty was enshrined in the international political system by the treaties that made up the Peace of Westphalia at the end of the Thirty Years War in Europe in 1648. These treaties specified that sovereignty rested in the person of the prince, or ruler, of a principality, and that the ruler had absolute freedom vis-à-vis other princes of how he ruled the people in his principality. This rule was breached as often as it was observed, but it premised that national security was embodied in the prince, or as Louis XIV put it, a prince could say, '*L'etat, c'estmoi*' (The state, it is I).

The European colonial system was driven by this logic, with states inheriting parts and parcels of land as personal inheritances of the royal families that married, and merged both family trees and geographies. This system, though, was slowly being undermined from within as principles of individual human rights were espoused within the confines of the leading colonial powers themselves. The American and French Revolutions put the idea of the citizen as a participant at the centre of the state. The League of Nations, for the first time, discussed the idea of nations entitled to liberty, and the Universal Declaration of Human Rights enshrined the idea of the sanctity of human life. These advances shifted the idea of sovereignty, of nationality, away from the ruler to the ruled, or more properly from the unaccountable prince to the citizen as a participant in the nation.

The idea that a person existed for the glory of the state—and the prince—was turned on its head. In the post–World War II scenario the idea was increasingly accepted that a state was best judged on how it treated its citizens. The titanic struggle between the United States of America and the Soviet Union was as much a value-based struggle as an economic and military confrontation, with the situation of the members of the community under their administration as the principal propaganda point. It is therefore important to understand why the US lost in Vietnam, and why the USSR lost in Afghanistan. It was not that they were defeated in some catastrophic battle and signed a treaty in which they acknowledged defeat. No. They lost the battle for internal security. They could not keep the nations that they had conquered secure, because the nation was now the citizenry of Vietnam and Afghanistan respectively, not merely the government that ruled those countries. When significant numbers of the citizens in these countries rose against their rulers, the US and USSR could not guarantee internal security, which meant that they lost the battle for national security, and retreated from that failure.

The US in Iraq—Losing the Battle for Internal Security

The importance of this model of thinking was brought home to me in 2003 when I attended a talk by the then head of the United States Agency for International Development (USAID), Andrew Natsios, at the American Enterprise Institute. Natsios was speaking about Afghanistan and Iraq, and after glossing over the problems of Afghanistan ('the press are largely concentrated in urban areas, 90 percent of Afghanistan is rural, and it is peaceful...') he moved on to detailing how the United States-led Coalition Provisional Authority (CPA) was dealing with the rising insurgency in Iraq. He acknowledged that the CPA was struggling with the chaos as electricity, water, and other supplies were disrupted. In dealing with this, Natsios said, the US was moving away from the concept of 'line security' to 'point security'. He illustrated this by saying that it was impossible to secure the whole chain of electricity stations and supply lines. This was 'line security'. The US was therefore putting up generators at various 'points', and securing the areas that they supplied instead.

The audience at the American Enterprise Institute lapped this up, and applauded wholeheartedly, although it seemed like a fairly clear admission of defeat. Here again, was the defeat in the Vietnam sense. It was not that the US military was being defeated by superior firepower or its soldiers being killed at a higher rate than enemy soldiers, it was just that they were being defeated in their efforts to provide security to the people they were governing. They were losing the war for internal security. Under the Obama administration, the US acknowledged that this was a war that they could not win. Only the Iraqis could win this war. Thus the US military retreated, if in better shape than from Vietnam.

Lessons for India

India is unlikely to make imperial adventures abroad. The lessons from these examples have to do with our security situation within the country, primarily with regard to the Northeastern states, the militant wings of the Maoist parties operating in various parts of India, and the situation in Jammu and Kashmir. Let us begin with J&K as the troubles in that state dominate our headlines the most, largely because of the Pakistan connection. Casualty rates in J&K due to the conflict have fallen drastically over the last decade. In 2006 an average of 6 people were killed daily, with a ratio of 7 civilians to 5 militants to 1 member of the security forces. After the peace process with Pakistan began in 2003, this rate has fallen considerably, with conflict-related casualties coming down to less than 100 a year. In 2010, when police and paramilitary forces killed more than 100 civilians during demonstrations in Kashmir (one police officer died), the casualty rates due to purely internal disturbances outstripped that of encounters with militants. And yet the Disturbed Areas Act is applied across the whole of J&K, with the exception of Ladakh. Across India, the proportion of police to civilian ratio is just over 1 to a 1,000 people. In J&K, if one counts the paramilitary, which also fall under the police forces in the Indian administrative system, it is 10 times that amount. And of course this hides the fact that the police and paramilitary forces in J&K are often armed with Kalashnikovs or INSAS automatic rifles, and are massively concentrated in the Kashmir Valley, rather than in the Jammu region or in Ladakh.

What is threatened in J&K for which we need such a heavy deployment of troops? It would be difficult to suggest that the 'national security' of the Indian state is threatened. It is inconceivable that when a much weaker Indian state beat down the insurgency of 1989–90, that a much more robust state, with a much weaker insurgency—for the past decade the Indian military has estimated the strength of militants operating in the state of J&K at fewer than 200—is under any serious threat of political or military overthrow. Similarly the various insurgencies of the Northeastern states were defeated militarily more than a decade ago. The Maoist forces, or what is left of them, operating in Chhattisgarh and the various districts over India where they sometimes reveal their presence, are equally incapable of seriously threatening to take over—and hold—a district, much less a state. The idea of them actually threatening the political stability of the country is unrealistic in the extreme.

Like the US forces in Iraq, 'point security' is not threatened in these places, but 'line security', or the ability to impose peace on a wider population, still escapes the state in these areas. The problem, as Sanjib Baruah argues in *India Against Itself: Assam and the Politics of Nationality*, is not merely the military capability of insurgent units or the calls for 'independence'.[1] The military capability of the insurgent units is not a credible threat against the power of the Indian state—as has been proven again and again. Without that ability to threaten the state, the idea of any real independence is out of the question.

Why Militancy Persists

The worry, therefore, is why these calls of independence do not go away, or why the militants, who have often demonstrated a penchant for violence and criminality that has undermined their own legitimacy, are still considered, at worst, 'boys gone astray'. This is, as Baruah persuasively argues, because the militants base their demands on the ideas enshrined in the Indian Constitution. These ideas are based on the philosophical position which bases the sovereignty of the nation in the person of the citizens that populate it, not the geography of a 'nation' or its institutions. The Indian state, as a Republic which places all of its citizens—regardless of creed, gender or ethnicity, at the centre of its sense of self—has both a unique disadvantage as well as a unique advantage when it comes to dealing with dissatisfied citizens. The unique disadvantage is that the Indian Constitution promises the fullest possible freedoms to its citizens. If the state acts to constrain these freedoms—as it must when dealing with violence—it delegitimises itself.

In India the Armed Forces perform a ceremonial march-past every year on Republic Day. It cannot be that that these same forces are used to suppress or violate the rights that are the essence of the Indian Constitution which makes India the Republic it is. There is no surer way to undermine India's legitimacy than to use the coercive power of the Indian state to limit, rather than support, the freedom of its citizens. As long as insurgents, or even disaffected civilians, are able to demonstrate, or credibly claim, that this is the case, the calls for separatism will persist.

The natural, and obvious, corollary to this is that India has a very easy way to strengthen its legitimacy in areas where that legitimacy is under question. It merely has to live up to the promises enshrined in its Constitution. Bear in mind this does not just mean that the Indian state has to be better than its enemies. The fact that insurgent organisations may not follow the Rule of Law, or may be biased or abusive in their own right, does not offset any transgressions by the Indian state. The Indian state, through its Constitution, has made extensive promises to each and every one of its citizens, insurgent groups have not. Saying that the Indian state behaves, on average, better than insurgent groups does not help. Such comparisons inevitably show up where the state has failed in its duties. The argument that can be won is one that demonstrates that the Indian state, while nowhere near perfect, is expanding the zone of liberty for all of its citizens.

Unless this can be demonstrated, India will continue to nurture sullen populations that resent being governed by a state that does not put their rights and freedoms at the centre of its concerns.

The Insecure Rich and the Criminally Powerful

The idea of a disenfranchised and disaffected citizenry is not just present among the poor and marginalised populations. In actuality it is most visibly displayed by India's rich and powerful. There is no real record of exact number of security personnel hired in a private capacity, but in 2007, the then minister of home affairs, Shivraj Patil, estimated that at least 5,000,000 Indians were employed in this capacity. India has approximately 1,300,000 members on active duty in its armed forces, with another 1,000,000 in reserve. It also has a similar number of paramilitary forces. In other words India employs more personal security guards than the total military and paramilitary forces in active duty and in reserve. Obviously only the more prosperous Indians can afford to hire security personnel and this shows that the greatest threat they perceive, backed by the amount of money they spend, is that posed by other Indians.

An Indian state that is not able to deliver security of rights to marginalised citizens or security to its privileged ones, is one that is making key mistakes on how it defines and implements its national security policies. Part of the reason may be that the gravest number of casualties occur in what are euphemistically called 'riots'. As Steven Wilkinson showed in his landmark study, *Votes and Violence: Electoral Competition and Ethnic Riots in India*, the use of organised violence to polarise voters just before elections in constituencies where the margin for victory is small, is one of the most common reasons for such riots.[2] As successful examples of vote mobilisation and guarantors of electoral victory, riots have become a commonplace phenomenon, an illegitimate child of India's democratic process.

Politicians who achieve victory by the use, or threat of use, of violence have rarely been punished by Indian courts. Whether it was the Bhagalpur riots, the Nellie massacre, the anti-Sikh pogroms, or the Bombay riots, the guilty have not been brought to book. The one partial exception was the post-Godhra Gujarat riots, where the work of the indefatigable Teesta Setalvad led to the conviction of dozens of perpetrators and enablers of mob violence. Nevertheless a country that gives a state funeral to a politician like Bal Thackeray who was banned from politics for his role in the Bombay riots of 1992–93, is a country that rewards the practitioners of political violence with not just power, but even a sort of legitimacy. If such politicians come to power using violence and are able to command a police force that is supposed to be investigating their criminal activity, it is unlikely that any cases will be properly investigated. This has been, by and large, the fate of most criminal cases against politicians.

Conclusion

India faces specific and unique challenges of internal security. Much of this stems from the fact that 'internal security' is still understood as a term for the security of the state, not the security of its citizens. This confusion continues to lead the state to take actions that do not deliver complete security to its citizens and, at times, actively undermine the security of the very citizens whose rights and freedoms the state is charged with defending. Such strategies have left simmering insurgencies along India's borders, and within regions where people feel disenfranchised. While these insurgencies do not necessarily threaten the government of the country, or even of provinces, the experience of living in a zone of insecurity deprives the citizens living in these areas of the constitutional rights that the Indian state is supposed to deliver, all but guaranteeing a continuation of conflict, even if at a low level, over the years.

The lack of focus on citizen security has an effect on the privileged as well, who spend huge sums guaranteeing their security against their fellow citizens. The fact that some politicians use mob violence to strategically win elections, and therefore control state power that should be restraining such activity embeds the idea of living in insecurity as a 'normal' feature of Indian democracy. All of these developments militate against the fundamentals of the Indian Constitution, which identifies Indian citizens, and their freedoms and security, as the core idea around which the nation is built. The crude and unexamined use of 'national security' policies to continue using methods that undermine the security of the nation's citizens flies in the face of what India was meant to be—a Republic of free individuals with the maximum possible liberty for all. The only way to build a safer India, one in which our currently marginalised populations actually wish to belong and in which the rich, poor, and middle class all feel safe, is to define national security as a citizen-centric concept.

Endnotes

1 Sanjib Baruah, *India Against Itself: Assam and the Politics of Nationality* (Philadelphia: University of Pennsylvania Press, 1999).

2 Steven Wilkinson, *Votes and Violence: Electoral Competition and Ethnic Riots in India* (Cambridge: Cambridge University Press: 2006).

India's Imminent Prominence in Cyber Oceans

Samir Saran, Mahima Kaul

When the Edward Snowden revelations brought American control over global communications into sharper relief, the United States threw a curveball at the global Internet community. It proposed and backed a multi-stakeholder framework of governance to manage the critical logic layer of the Internet and offered to replace US oversight of key functions within the Internet Corporation for Assigned Names and Numbers (ICANN) to a body comprising all stakeholders. It was becoming apparent that while the net, as we know it, may well have been invented and seeded in the US, its continuing and overwhelming control of this common resource was untenable.

The US proposal was clever for two reasons. First, US corporations and US civil society groups (many funded by these corporates) are more than capable of managing core US interests even after Washington cedes control. Second, it was and is still quite improbable for a multi-stakeholder mechanism to replace US control of the functions of the Internet Assigned Numbers Authority (IANA), failing which the IANA transition process would continue to remain where it was. Indeed, this was precisely the outcome which loomed large as important digital nations such as India remained at a distance from this process.

Things changed dramatically when the Indian Minister for Communication and Information Technology, Ravi Shankar Prasad, in a video address to the ICANN gathering in Buenos Aires stated that, 'the Internet must remain plural, must be managed through a multilayered and multistakeholder system.' He added that 'its strengths will lie in partnerships between like-minded nations and stakeholders, built on a platform which supports and will sustain a future of equity and innovation and collaboration and inclusion.'

Nuances in India's Stand

Even as this announcement is studied, digested, and lauded, some nuances within the text need to be discussed further. First, it is clear that even as India has opted for the multi-stakeholder system of global governance, it is still pushing for reform of this system to ensure it becomes more plural, equitable, geographically representative, and democratic. This is something the minister's speech clearly highlighted. It is not business as usual for India and it will certainly not be business as usual for those occupying pride of place on the governance high table.

This model requires greater plurality and diverse representation that will challenge much of the group thinking that dominates this sector. Prasad was categorical in his pronouncement if the subtext of his speech is properly understood. India was not merely seeking to blindly support a system of Internet governance dominated by the Atlantic countries but was seeking an imminent rebalance towards Asia.

The second message embedded within Prasad's speech was that India is keen to engage with all forums. The fact that the Indian minister announced the policy shift at ICANN53 is a message in itself. That India went on to host ICANN57 in Hyderabad is evidence of a deeper engagement with a process from which India had hitherto distanced itself.

The development agenda and the framework for the digital economy that could change the lives of the 'next billion' must be crafted and co-developed by this billion, in their own neighbourhoods. The minister's assertion that India will host an international conversation that will articulate India's own motivations and objectives to the world and make the global community a partner in this mission, must be understood in this vein.

The Next Billion

The Indian state has both committed to transforming itself through digital means and at the same time building a global system that can accommodate and allow for such a transformation. Access, Voice, and Opportunity must not be more cumbersome for the 'next billion.' And, this also means more responsibility for the Indian government. By opting for multi-stakeholderism it has just signed up for a bagful of new responsibilities. The agency of the sovereign will now have to be secured by a variety of stakeholders who may be more acceptable in certain forums.

The government will have to invest in building capacity among them, building greater diversity among those who participate and ensuring greater representation of these stakeholders at key Internet governance debates globally. Without this, for India and many others, the global multi-stakeholder system will continue to reinforce existing disparities of the real world even in the digital world.

The third significant message within the speech was the quest of India to seek partnerships with key countries and institutions. And it is here that India will be able to carve a space significantly different from others—a space that a country of the size of India needs, the room a diverse and developing democracy must have. The needs of a billion people impose a very different set of responsibilities on a political system which must deliver to remain relevant.

This was a call to those on the governance high table, particularly the United States, to respond adequately to the Indian overture. That these two countries, the largest online communities in the democratic world, must cooperate is unexceptionable, essential, and inevitable. The details of this cooperation now need to be fleshed out and could be based on three key strands of association.

What the US Must do

The US has long considered the free flow of information and commerce a pre-condition to a healthy global economy. India, as it digitally connects, is looking to forge the right partnerships to ensure limitless economic opportunities for its citizens. The first pillar of the India-US cyber relationship should be to ensure that their consumers and producers are able to leverage the largest English-speaking digital markets in the world. For this, they need a digital space free from encumbrances of power politics and petty policy.

This would mean rationalising tax regimes, expanding Internet connectivity, settling issues of Internet jurisdiction, developing contemporary approaches to intermediary liability and operation, agreeing on data collection, data ownership and data management, privacy and freedom of expression, as well as developing an eco-system that would allow for investments in technology and infrastructure, crucial for the development of these digital markets.

A strong security partnership is the second aspect of the India-US relationship. Both countries believe strongly in the role of national governments in shepherding their societies through a host of new challenges. For both, strong nation-states lie at the centre of a multi-stakeholder system and, unlike European countries, neither is seeking to aggregate or dilute sovereignty. Therefore, the bilateral partnership needs to be built on a realist paradigm. From information sharing on crime, to attacks on critical infrastructure to countering terrorism, the India-US relationship can rise to become the backbone on which the Internet stands strong. For the US, this partnership should form the central 'I' of the Internet. For India, the US is already its chief digital interlocutor.

There should also be close collaboration on the logic layer of the Internet. Anyone who understands the Internet realises that there is a certain reality of the logic infrastructure that the Internet runs on. This is the dominance of the United States of America. Though the international community may manage ICANN or some other institutions, oversight rests with the US government alone. US courts have jurisdiction over the entities, and disputes between countries and Internet institutions are tried under US law.

Yes, WeCANN

The India-US relationship must deliver space to India on this front. Even as the all-important debate over how best to internationalise these institutions continues, the US must find ways to provide India the comfort that it seeks for its huge digital community. This could be by way of a bilateral deal around digital jurisdiction and territory, more Indian presence in the corporations involved with running the Internet—the 'i' family—as well as the eventual and desirable location of a root server in India.

The argument that 'if we give this to India, China will want it too' is disingenuous. The US policy community continuously reminds India that it must not side with a Russia or China, as it is different and democratic. Yet, the very same community is quick to create equivalence of these countries with India when the latter seeks unique treatment.

Carving out a place for India, proportional to its growing weight in the global Internet eco-system is crucial. If this does not happen, the celebrations around India supporting a multi-stakeholder system may be short-lived. The security and political hawks will strike back and prevail and the Indian state will find comfort in the old methods of the last century. The US must see this message from Ravi Shankar Prasad as an opening, a new opportunity to meaningfully engage India.

Even as Washington expects India to be a net security provider in the Indo-Pacific region, the country is offering itself as a key partner in managing the cyber oceans. This moment must not be lost. India has responded favourably to the post-Snowden Internet governance proposition, The US must now reciprocate.

Insurgency and Statehood: The Drive for Legitimacy in Northeast India

Namrata Goswami

Northeast India, has been in the news for long, not for its picturesque landscape and colourful ethnic diversity, not for the rivers that wind down its blue mountains, not for the sound of the hornbills that fly up to the turquoise sky, but for armed violence. This armed violence has resulted in thousands of deaths, with the hills pregnant with stories of despair and bravery, aspiration and apathy, hope and dejection. Over the years, violence has become a part of the folklore with songs sung and stories told across fires of the rebel youth who disappeared like thin air into the night, or the sound of an approaching army convoy, and along with it a sense of anxiety for the village folk.

Prominent amongst the insurgent groups have been the Naga armed groups who initiated the idea of an independent ethnically slanted homeland, carved out of Naga inhabited territories in India and Myanmar, into a separate independent state. In 1929 the Naga Club, which was formed in 1918 by 20 Nagas who had seen action in the European battlefields during World War I, submitted a memorandum to the Simon Commission, arguing that Nagas and the rest of India had nothing in common between them, hence, they should stay separate. In 1946, the Naga Club was followed by the Naga National Council (NNC). In June 1947, the NNC and then Governor of Assam, Sir Akbar Hydari signed the Nine-Points agreement, in which it was stated that Nagas will have full control of their land, resources, way of life, and customs. However, Clause 9 which stated that after 10 years this agreement could be extended or a new agreement arrived at, created a difference of opinion. The Nagas interpreted it as resulting in independence; the Indian state interpreted it as another agreement that included the Nagas in India. Angami Zapu Phizo thereby declared independence on 14 August 1947 and took to violence in 1955. This was followed by the Indian security forces moving into the Naga Hills and imposition of the Assam Disturbed Areas Act, later Armed Forces (Special Powers) Act, 1958 amended in 1972.

Leading the host of violent actors at present are the factions of the National Socialist Council of Nagaland (NSCN) which aim to establish *Nagalim* (Greater Nagaland) across Naga-inhabited parts of Northeast India and Myanmar. The NSCN was founded by Isak Chishi Swu, Thuingaleng Muivah and S.S. Khaplang on 31 January 1980. It then split into two factions on 30 April 1988—the NSCN (IM) led by Swu and Muivah and the NSCN (K) led by S.S. Khaplang. In 2011, a new group was formed as a breakaway faction of the NSCN (K) by Khole Konyak and Kitovi Zhimoni, called the NSCN (Khole-Kitovi) or NSCN (KK). Still another group, the NSCN (Reformation) led by Y. Wangtin Konyak and P. Tikhak was formed in 2015. Manipur has also been grossly disturbed by armed violence with the formation of the United National Liberation Front (UNLF) on24 November 1964. The UNLF's stated political goal has been secession of Manipur from India. The outfit believes that the accession of Manipur to India by King Budhachandra Singh on 15 October 1949 was under duress. Another significant Manipuri separatist armed group, the Revolutionary People's Front (RPF) and its armed wing the People's Liberation Army (PLA) has been engaging in an armed struggle since 1978. The RPF and the PLA are suspected of having been trained in Maoist guerrilla warfare by the Chinese in the 1960s and 1970s, and both outfits aim at violent revolutionary change to bring about a classless society in Manipur. Another armed group is the *Kanglei Yawol Kanna Lup* (KYKL), which has taken up social afflictions such as fighting corruption, drug trafficking, and sub-standard education practices. Still another group, known as the Peoples' Revolutionary Party of Kangleipak (PREPAK), was established in the 1970s with the objective of fighting for Manipur's independence from India. Manipur is also home to the Kuki National Army (KNA) and the Kuki National Liberation Front (KNLF) fighting for a separate Kuki homeland.

Assam has been plagued by insurgent violence since 1979 with the formation of the United Liberation Front of Assam (ULFA). The hills districts of Assam, namely, Dima Hasao and Karbi Anglong, also suffer armed groups like the Dima Halam Daogah (DHD) and the United Peoples' Democratic

Solidarity (UPDS) since the 1990s. The Bodo areas in Assam are disturbed by the existence of the armed National Democratic Front of Bodoland (NDFB). It is also important to note that most of these insurgent groups have thrived primarily due to strong external influences. Countries like China in the 1960s and the 1970s, as well as Pakistan, and later on Bangladesh have supported most of these outfits by making available arms, training, and most importantly, base areas for underground camps. Matters have, however, improved with Bangladesh since 2008 with the coming of Sheikh Hasina to power. The ULFA leadership including Arabinda Rajkhowa, the Chairman of the outfit, was arrested in December 2009 near the India-Bangladesh border. In 2010, Bangladesh handed over the leader of the NDFB, Ranjan Daimary, to India.[1]

Given Northeast India's location sharing international borders with Bangladesh, Bhutan, China, and Myanmar, the connecting bridge that the region can become via Myanmar to the financial prowess and capabilities of Southeast Asia has not been lost on India. For many years now, since 1992, India has had its own version of trade and infrastructure connectivity via its 'Look East' policy. Envisioned by former prime minister, P.V. Narasimha Rao as the much-needed thrust for greater connectivity with Southeast Asia, the 'Look East' policy has come a long way with India now a full summit partner with the Association of Southeast Asian Nations (ASEAN). In November of 2014, in the ASEAN summit in Myanmar, Prime Minister Narendra Modi changed the frame of reference of the 'Look East' policy to 'Act East' policy stating that 'A new era of economic development, industrialization and trade has begun in India. Externally, India's "Look East Policy" has become "Act East Policy"'.[2]

India has recognised the strategic significance of its Northeast with regard to its 'Look East/Act East' policy. First amongst the measures to augment connectivity were proposals to build the 'Asian Highway' and 'Asian Railway Link' and 'Natural Gas' pipeline. The proposed geographical niche for the Asian Highway is the Imphal (India)–Tamu (Myanmar) road going on to Kalemyo in Myanmar, from where a railway line goes onto Mandalay. A four-lane Asian highway is sought between New Delhi and Singapore linked to Kuala Lumpur, Ho Chi Minh City, Phnom Penh, Bangkok, Vientiane, Yangon, Mandalay, Kalemyo, Tamu, Dhaka, and Kolkata. Road construction has already started from Tamu to Kalemyo, Myanmar. There is a plan to construct a 1,360 km trilateral highway from Moreh (India) to Mae Sot (Thailand) through Bagan (Myanmar).[3] Moreh in Manipur is seen as the key to India's 'Act East' policy.[4] According to Manipur Chief Minister, Ibobi Singh, Moreh is the most strategic international trading point in the region'.[5] His view was reiterated by former external affairs minister Pranab Mukherjee in his visit to the region in June 2007.[6]

On 29 November 2014, Prime Minister Narendra Modi in a visit to the northeastern region of India tweeted about how he was eagerly looking forward to attending a wide variety of programs and connecting with the people of the Northeast. Invoking *Vaastushastra* (the Indian traditional system of harmonising energies for architecture) to highlight the importance of the northeast wing of a house for the prosperity of its occupants, Modi dreamt big for the region as India's gateway to Asia in the 21st 'Asian Century'. In a whirlwind tour covering Assam, Nagaland, Manipur, and Tripura, the prime minister coined a new acronym: NEZ, or Natural Economic Zone, and called for the region to be developed through economic corridors to Southeast Asia. Modi announced a slew of much-needed projects including scholarships for students, a national sports university, agricultural colleges, upgraded power and digital connectivity, and new railway lines. He addressed regional police chiefs, waved off the first train from Guwahati to Meghalaya, laid the foundation stone of the first railway line to Mizoram and inaugurated a power plant in Tripura. With a nearly US$10 billion budgetary allocation for the northeastern region, Modi's focus is on infrastructure, both inside India and on projects linking the northeast regionally, such as the road from Imphal to Mandalay in Myanmar. In his visit to Myanmar, for the 12th ASEAN–India summit on 12 November 2014, preceding the Northeast India visit, Modi had highlighted the significance of regional connectivity for economic prosperity through projects like the Kaladan-Multi Modal Transit facility and so forth.[7]

The impact of the Look East/Act East policy has been, however, limited—at best—due to the insurgent challenge and their ability to create parallel universes. This they have accomplished by setting up parallel government structures that tax people for safety, business, and entry, offer healthcare and judicial mechanisms, all the while utilising the money for insurgent weapons, salaries, clothes, and travel. For instance, the NSCN (IM), the NSCN (KK), etc, each have a full-fledged Government of the People's Republic of

Nagaland (GPRN) which have headquarters plus field offices where local people can go to for consultation.[8] The NSCN (IM)/GPRN, for instance, is a highly centralised political structure boosting cadre strength of 5,000 highly armed men and women.[9] The headquarters of the group is situated at Camp Hebron, near Dimapur in Nagaland, India. The GPRN has a president, vice President, prime minister, *kilonsers* (ministers) and ministries. Each Naga tribe (32 in all) has to elect a kilonser to the GPRN.[10] The military wing consists of the People's Army of Nagaland with the Chairman as the Supreme Commander, followed by the Defence Minister and the Chief of Army Staff. The army is divided into the Eastern Command, Western Command, Central Command, Northern Command, and the Southern Command. The five commands have one division and two brigades with four battalions. The GPRN is a government-like structure with separate departments run by kilonsers. These departments include departments of defence, education, finance, public relations, war victims' welfare, health, etc. There is a budget session, where the fund allocation of more than Rs 250 million per year is debated upon. The NSCN (IM) also has a parliament house at Camp Hebron known as the *Tatar Hoho*, where most of the debates on important issues are held. Similarly, the PLA, with cadre strength of 1,500 armed men and women identifies its struggle against India as a fight against political and economic exploitation of Manipur. The outfit is inspired by the Maoist ideology of Peoples' War, based on guerrilla warfare and the three phases of conflict: the strategic defensive, strategic equilibrium, and strategic offensive stages. The PLA also functions like a parallel government in Manipur by levying so-called taxes. This amount of extortion money is cut at source from different government departments, businesses, and individuals. Non-payment could result in physical harm and death.[11]

Significantly, there has been curtailment of extortions from individuals and government agencies since 2002 in Manipur, after the common people rose against it, but extortions from businesses continue. In order to make its presence visible, the PLA operates through three bureaus in Manipur: the eastern, western and central with the central bureau taking all the important strategic decisions with regard to the functioning of the PLA. Its armed wing is divided into four military divisions: the Sadar Hills (west), Sadar Hills (east), the hill areas of Manipur, and the Imphal valley. While its presence is rather weak in the hilly areas, it is quite visible in the Imphal valley. Its political wing, the RPF, also has a women's wing in order to reflect the views of Manipuri women. Significantly, the PLA has designated secretaries dealing with not only home, finance and foreign policy but also with regard to publicity and communication, social welfare, health and education. This extent to which the PLA has invested in social welfare issues like HIV-AIDS, fighting corruption, and human trafficking increases its legitimacy in society.[12] This legitimacy in turn creates the environment for targeted conflict escalation.

Given these parallel governments established for the purpose of questioning the legitimacy of Indian state institutions, as well as the monopoly of organised violence, there are four interrelated drivers for likely future scenarios for Northeast India. These are: ethnic exclusivity and colonial isolation; special laws; political representation and economic development; ceasefires and peace negotiations.

Drivers

Ethnic Exclusivity and Colonial Isolation

The basic issues leading to armed ethnic conflicts in the Northeast are identity, ethnicity, desire for political empowerment, and land. Added to this is the colonial residue of being treated as 'excluded, partially excluded' areas based on the Inner Line Regulation of 1873.[13] Due to the lack of a pre-colonial and colonial integrative policy with the rest of India, the hill tribes resisted the post-colonial Indian state's entry into the hill interiors. And out of these contradictions emanates what Johan Galtung conceptualised in the 1960s: the conflict triangle. According to Galtung, conflict, both symmetric and asymmetric, is best understood when seen through a triangle, whose vertices consists of i) contradiction, ii) attitude and iii) behaviour.[14] Contradiction refers to the actual or perceived incompatibilities of goals between conflicting actors and the conflict of interest inherent in the relationship between them; attitude refers to negative perceptions of the 'other', which is mostly informed by emotive (feeling), cognitive (belief), and conative (will) components. Behaviour includes threats, coercion, and direct physical attacks. According to Galtung, all three factors act simultaneously resulting in the dynamic nature of violence.[15] Interestingly, these factors are evident in the ethnic movements pertaining to the NSCN (IM), UNLF, ULFA, and the DHD.

Special Laws

The Armed Forces (Special Powers) Act, 1958 and amended in 1972 has been imposed on certain areas of Northeast India. While removed from Tripura in May 2015, and in some parts of Assam and Meghalaya, the act has created enormous social tensions with regard to its expansive interpretation of conditions of arrest and suspicion. According to the act, security personnel can shoot, arrest, and raid houses, on mere suspicion, and without having to prove without reasonable doubt, that someone is an insurgent, or someone may be supporting insurgencies. The lack of judicial purview heightens a sense of siege that affected societies suffer from. An example being, 'No prosecution, suit or other legal proceeding shall be instituted except with the previous sanction of the Central government against any person'.[16] For instance, this para from the act 'arrest, without warrant, any person who has committed a cognisable offence or against whom a reasonable suspicion exists that he has committed or is about to commit a cognisable offence and may use such force as may be necessary to effect the arrest'[17] would reveal to you why this act has such negative social consequences. There have been several visible protests against the act, the most famous being Irom Sharmila's 15 years' fast unto death against the act.[18]

Political Representation and Economic Development

Politics forms the core of the armed movements. Most of the propaganda of the armed rebellion revolves around issues of separate states, ethnic preservation, unique history, origin, and institutional structure. Studying the pamphlets and discourses of armed groups like the NSCN (IM) or PLA, we can get a sense of how political these developments are; mostly about better representation in political institutions, and that too based on ethnicity and tribal connections. Hence, for instance, in the Nagaland State Assembly, out of 60 seats, 59 are reserved and only one is a general seat. Politics is closely interspersed with economic development. Most of the northeastern states are dependent on central funds for their economic development. There is very little local entrepreneurial activity or other avenues to generate revenue. While Assam and Tripura are better off with oil, tea, and rubber production, yet the revenues earned have not visibly benefited the local people. Tripura tops the human development index,[19] while the other states are mired in local corruption, with few benefitting from any revenue generation through illegal means.

Ceasefires and Peace Negotiations

In order to manage and resolve armed conflicts in the Northeast, the Government of India has utilised the twin mechanisms of signing ceasefires with armed groups as well as simultaneously conducting negotiations. Ceasefires were signed with the NNC in 1964 followed by the Nagaland Peace Mission, though that ceasefire did not last for long and culminated in 1968. The Mizo National Front (MNF), which fought a 20-year insurgency against the Indian state entered into negotiations with the Indian government from the 1970s, with the latter at the same time resettling villages in order to cut the support base for the insurgency.[20] The Mizo Accord of 1986 succeeded in settling the conflict. The Government signed ceasefires with the NSCN (IM) and NSCN (K) in 1997 and 2001 respectively. Recently, on 3 August 2015, the Government and the NSCN (IM) signed a framework agreement to establish peace in Naga-inhabited areas.[21] This is a significant step forward given that the NSCN (IM) has agreed to give up the path of violence and instead enter dialogue to ensure that the dignity and unique history of the Naga people are ensured. While it remains to be seen whether the other Naga factions agree to accept this framework, the involvement of the Naga Hoho and other civil society actors would have the mitigating effect towards establishing an inclusive peace. A similar policy framework of use of force and simultaneous use of negotiations seems to be at play in the conflicts in Assam and Manipur, though the PLA and the UNLF have not yet responded to the negotiations/dialogue overtures.

The four interrelated drivers gives us the potential of three likely scenarios.

First, we have the rise of exclusivist parochial, protective narratives. With reinvigoration of exclusivist politics focused on protection of ethnic narratives, land, culture, and history, the demand for more institutional protection will give rise to an ethnic minority fear-ridden society and internally focused Northeast. We already see snippets of these in the demands of Manipur and Meghalaya for imposition of the archaic Inner Line Permit, a backward-looking legislation of 1873 to be re-imposed in the 21st century. So instead of opening up, and embracing the benefits of globalisation, and at the same time enthusiastically supporting the 'Act East' policy, there will be a backward slide within the Northeast, forcing those who want to make a better life migrate out of these states.

Second, armed conflicts will reside due to a successful conclusion of the Naga accord, with states wanting to benefit from the opportunities that embracing globalisation brings; better infrastructure, better investment climate, more opportunities, and a budding entrepreneurial spirit, where instead of blaming Delhi for their ills, people in the Northeast take their future into their own hands and make visible changes locally. This would lead to youths staying back and building up the Northeast by taking advantage of its location, climate, and natural advantages. Tourism, local industry, music, and folk culture will flourish, turning the Northeast into a magnet for outsiders, with specific locations being listed in travel sites like TripAdvisor and Lonely Planet as some of the most sought-after destinations in India.

The third scenario is that Northeast India suffers from internal stress of migrations from Bangladesh, internecine ethnic conflicts, political squabbles, and lacklustre development. This scenario results in more conflicts between local ethnic communities and outsiders with the former demanding stringent legislation against those migrating from outside. The political space for multiple voices constricts and there is an increase in intolerance for those other than ones' own ethnic community. This results in disorientation and investment drops, corruption increases, and multiple armed movements for ethnically slanted homelands. This scenario creates huge obstacles for the successful implementation of the 'Act East' policy with the Centre losing interest and investing more in open sea-based routes to Southeast Asia rather than the conflict-ridden land route via Myanmar.

Among the three scenarios, the second scenario has the highest potential for bringing about positive change in Northeast India augmenting development and progress. However, in the present context, the first and third scenarios are emerging as the most likely, given the constricted space for liberal discourse both from state and non-state actors. The future of peace and progress would therefore depend on how civil society, state and non-state actors find ways to work for the benefit of the societies they aim to represent, and create conditions of peace that can support the progress of these conflict-affected societies.

Endnotes

1 Subir Bhaumik, *Insurgencies in India's North East: Conflict, Co-option and Change* Working Paper (WashingtonD.C.: East-West Center,, 10July, 2007). Also see 'Bangladesh hands over NDFB Chief Ranjan Daimary to BSF,' *The Times of India*, May 1, 2010, *http://articles.timesofindia.indiatimes.com/2010-05-01/india/28287637_1_d-r-nabla-ndfb-anti-talks-faction* (accessed September 12, 2015).

2 '"Look East" has become "Act East Policy", says PM Modi at ASEAN Summit,' *The Indian Express*, November 13, 2014, *http://indianexpress.com/article/india/india-others/look-east-has-become-act-east-policy-pm-modi-at-asean/* (accessed July 16, 2015).

3 See *North Eastern Region Vision 2020*, Ministry of Development of North Eastern Region and North Eastern Council, Agartala, May 13, 2008, p. 275. Also see Namrata Goswami, 'Looking "East" through India's North East,' *IDSA Occasional Paper No. 2*, (New Delhi: IDSA, June 2009), pp. 5–30.

4 Field Visit by author to Moreh, Manipur, August 09–12, 2008. Moreh was showcased as the connecting link in interviews with local communities including the Kuki Hill Tribal Council, representing the major Kuki tribe in that area, the Moreh Chambers of Commerce, the Tamil Sangam, local policy makers, as well as security personal.

5 Graham Lees, 'Burma is the key to India's "Look East" Economic Strategy,' July 19, 2007, *http://www.worldpoliticsreview.com/article.aspx?id=941* (accessed August 28, 2015).

6 See 'Speech by the Minister of External Affairs Pranab Mukherjee,' in *India's Foreign Relations-2007 Documents, Part II*, ed. Avtar Singh Bhasin (New Delhi: Public Diplomacy Division, Ministry of External Affairs and Geetika Publishers, 2007), p. 1479.

7 'Remarks by the PM at the 12th ASEAN-India summit,' NayPyi Taw, Myanmar, November 12, 2014, *http://www.narendramodi.in/remarks-by-the-pm-at-the-12th-india-asean-summit-nay-pyi-taw-myanmar/* (accessed August 02, 2015).

8 Based on field insights by the author, 2007–2015.

9 A.S. Shimray, *Let Freedom Ring, Story of Naga Nationalism* (New Delhi: Promilla, 2005), pp. 150-151.

M. Horam, *Naga Insurgency—The Last Thirty Years* (New Delhi: Cosmo Publications, 1988), p. 23.

10 Speech by Thuingaleng Muivah, General Secretary of the NSCN (IM), Camp Hebron, Dimapur, Nagaland, July 27, 2007.

11 Field Visit to Manipur, March 2011.

12 Based on field interaction in Imphal, Manipur, March 2011.

13 The Inner Line Regulation of 1873 prohibited any British-Indian subjects from

entering Naga-inhabited areas without having prior permission thereof. The same policy continues till date, even after India became independent in 1947.

14 Johan Galtung, 'Theories of Conflict, Definitions, Dimensions, Negations, Formations,' https://www.transcend.org/files/Galtung_Book_Theories_Of_Conflict_single.pdf (Accessed September 12, 2015).

15 Ibid.

16 Sudha Ramachandran, 'India's Controversial Armed Forces (Special Powers) Act,' *The Diplomat*, July 02, 2015, http://thediplomat.com/2015/07/indias-controversial-armed-forces-special-powers-act/ (accessed September 05, 2015).

17 'The Armed Forces (Special Powers) Act 1958, Act 28 of 1958, 11 September 1958,' http://www.satp.org/satporgtp/countries/india/document/actandordinances/armed_forces_special_power_act_1958.htm (accessed September 05, 2015).

18 Iboyaima Laithangbam, 'Irom Sharmila's Fast against AFSPA Enters 15th Year,' *The Hindu*, November 06, 2014, http://www.thehindu.com/news/national/other-states/irom-sharmilas-fast-against-afspa-enters-15th-year/article6567476.ece (accessed September 12, 2015).

19 'Tripura Tops NREGA List, Mizoram Next', *The Telegraph*, April 25, 2016, http://www.telegraphindia.com/1160426/jsp/northeast/story_82249.jsp#.VyJAx_l97IU. (accessed April 28, 2016). Also see 'Tripura Beats Kerala in Literacy,' *The Times of India*, September 8, 2013. (accessed April 28, 2016).

20 Vasundhara Sirnate and Rahul Verma, 'From Insurgency to Electoral Democracy,' *The Hindu*, November 30, 2013, http://www.thehindu.com/todays-paper/tp-opinion/from-insurgency-to-electoral-democracy/article5406379.ece (accessed September 12, 2015).

21 Namrata Goswami, 'Nagaland: A Long Road to Peace,' *The Hindu*, August 06, 2015, http://www.thehindu.com/opinion/op-ed/nagaland-a-long-road-to-peace/article7504003.ece (accessed September 12, 2015).

India's Foreign Policy: Asian Dynamics

Rajeev Ranjan Chaturvedy[1]

India's foreign policy has been characterised more by continuity than change. Nevertheless, we are living in an interconnected web of interdependence. India, one of the fastest growing economic and regional powers, is reaching out and reaping some early fruits of its profitable engagement with the world. Furthermore, we are witnessing a remarkable transformation of India's foreign policy in recent years. Rising India's economic clout and recent changes in India's external interface have uplifted India's status globally. India now stands at a critical juncture, preparing herself to become a responsible stakeholder in the emerging global and regional economic and security architecture. The direction and key elements of Indian foreign policy are evident, which are mostly unrelated to the political ideology of the party in power, and driven mainly by India's national interests. This chapter examines contemporary vistas of India's foreign policy direction and its engagement with Asia. The scope of this chapter is limited to general trends and it does not delve into detail about bilateral relations with any specific country.

When any country contemplates a foreign policy framework, national interest becomes of the utmost importance. Therefore, it would be pertinent to begin with outlining various components of India's national interest. The core elements of India's national interests in its external interface could be mainly three:[2] securing the country against external and internal threats to its territory, populations, and vital economic interests; obtaining the external inputs necessary to achieve economic prosperity and inclusive growth; and playing an active role in international fora and global governance structures to secure a fair and equitable share of global public goods, ensuring their compatibility with India's national interests, and contributing to their development.

Keeping these components in mind, the following paragraphs discuss India's foreign policy directions. The previous sequel of this volume, *India Since 1947: Looking Back at a Modern Nation* (Niyogi Books, 2013) had discussed India's relations with the world up to the previous government. Therefore, this chapter focuses on the present and analyses the direction of India's engagement primarily with the Asian countries.

The Bharatiya Janata Party (BJP) came to power in a landslide victory in May 2014 under the leadership of Narendra Modi. It was little known to many Indian and outside observers of foreign policy, exactly what kind of approach Modi and his party had in mind regarding India's external engagements when he became India's Prime Minister. Mr Modi, however, has been 'the most effective, gaining the attention of different international power groups and having them compete for India's friendship. From getting the UN to declare International Yoga Day on 21 June to having the US President as Chief Guest for Republic Day to establishing a BRICS development bank to land swaps with Bangladesh',[3] Modi has demonstrated a remarkable performance on the foreign policy front in the first year of the NDA government. Most comments on the Modi government completing two-and-a-half years have made the point that the Prime Minister shines on foreign policy. Although he is being criticised by opposition leaders for his frequent foreign trips, wider agreement is that Modi has pursued India's foreign policy with an exceptional dynamism.

While there is no articulation of a foreign policy grand strategy by New Delhi, it is easy to identify the key elements of India's engagement with the world. The major powers want India to do well and succeed to become a responsible stakeholder on the global stage. Nevertheless, the performance of the Indian economy and a vibrant democracy will shape the global views of rising India in the years ahead. Like the former prime minister Dr Manmohan Singh, Modi also understands that the real challenges lie in achieving sustained economic and inclusive growth. Indeed, Modi has demonstrated his keenness to put economics first, and therefore, he has made national economic development the focus of India's global relations. In fact, economic imperatives are not new for Indian foreign policy makers. Economic considerations played a pivotal role in shaping India's foreign policy. As emphasised by Jawaharlal Nehru when he first articulated his vision of Indian foreign policy in a speech to the Constituent Assembly in December 1947: 'It is well for us to say that we stand for peace and freedom and yet that does not convey much to anybody, except a pious hope…What then do we stand for? Well, you have to develop this argument in the economic field.'[4] He understood that India's role in the world was likely to be achieved less by traditional balance of power politics or through strategic alliances and more by the rapid enhancement of its internal economic capabilities.[5] Nehru stated his interpretation of the relationship between foreign policy and economic policy:

> But talking about foreign policies, the House must remember that these are not just empty struggles on a chess board. Behind them lie all manner of things. Ultimately, foreign policy is the outcome of economic policy, and until India has properly evolved her economic policy, her foreign policy will be rather vague, rather inchoate, and will be groping.[6]

Hence, emphasis on strengthening the economy is nothing new. Moreover, Modi's emphasis is on five Ts—trade, tourism, talent, technology, and tradition. The challenge for Indian diplomacy would be to align India's national interests with these aspects and project India as a reliable and responsible stakeholder in global affairs. We are witnessing a new emerging world order, in which India needs to establish itself. Modi 'has shown a high level of self-confidence and ambition in envisaging India as a "leading power, not just a balancer"'.[7] Indeed, Modi has succinctly summed up his foreign policy as consisting of five elements: *Samvaad, Sammaan, Samriddhi, Suraksha,* and *Sanskriti* and *Sabhyata.*[8]

Immediate Neighbourhood

In order to achieve sustained economic growth, India needs a peaceful periphery. Hence, the primacy of neighbourhood in foreign policymaking is obvious. The Modi government has clearly indicated its priority for building stronger ties with its neighbourhood.[9] Prime Minister Modi was greatly admired for bringing much needed focus on India's relations with its South Asian neighbours during his first year in office. This was distinctly evident in India's recent foreign policy engagement in the neighbourhood. For example, the revival of the India-Nepal Joint Commission after a gap of 23 years, India's swift assistance after the tragic earthquake in Nepal, the Land Boundary agreement with Bangladesh, and the Motor Vehicle agreement between Bangladesh, Bhutan, Nepal, and India, are some good examples of 'neighbourhood first'. Furthermore, India's neighbourhood priorities were manifested in the first presidential address to parliament, which underlined the Indian government's 'determination to work towards building a peaceful, stable, and economically inter-linked neighbourhood which is essential for the collective development and prosperity of the South Asian region'. Speaking at the general debate of the 69th session of the United Nations General Assembly (UNGA), Narendra Modi aptly remarked, 'A nation's destiny is linked to its neighbourhood. That is why my government has placed the highest priority on advancing friendship and cooperation with her neighbours.' India's ability to manage its immediate neighbourhood is a critical component in accomplishing India's desire to be a responsible stakeholder in regional and global affairs.

It is important to note here that Modi has shown his zeal and vigour in engaging neighbours at the highest political level, which could be seen as an effort to build political connectivity. The previous government under the leadership of Dr Manmohan Singh was unable to put forward an overarching political framework to engage South Asian neighbours. Under domestic political compulsions, Dr Singh tried to woo all political allies, which hampered rare strategic opportunities that came his way. Political relations are as equally important as economic initiatives, and the current government is consciously making efforts to improve political connectivity along with economic and other aspects. In doing so, New Delhi is also actively engaging state governments in foreign policy manoeuvres and encouraging them to engage in a meaningful way. While there were consultations with state governments in the past, centralised foreign policymaking is facing resistance from various state governments. Hence, federalisation of foreign policy could be very helpful in advancing India's national interests.

The Indian government has renewed emphasis on seamless connectivity—economic, physical, and digital. Implementing overdue infrastructure projects to enhance connectivity, commerce, and people-to-people links seems among the top priorities of the current Indian government. Modi's neighbourly instincts have raised huge expectations, however, he needs to make sure that his overly personalised foreign policy moves towards a more institutionalised foreign policy in coming years. More importantly, 'during recent months there have been developments which, if unchecked, could well derail the benefits' derived from the works done in initial months. In fact, the Ufa fiasco, a display of muscularity and triumphalism after special insurgency operations at the India-Myanmar border and a serious crisis in Nepal due to an informal blockade have adversely affected India's critical relations with neighbours.[10] Empty symbolism and delayed actions have undermined relations in the past and any such repetition would prove detrimental to India's interests.

Extended Neighbourhood

India has enriched its engagement in its extended neighbourhood and has become an increasingly important economic, political, and strategic factor. Deeper engagement with the countries in the Asia-pacific region has become an 'integral and irreversible plank'[11] of India's foreign policy. India has long been expected to play an important role in the Asia-Pacific region but it is still addressing the consequences of years of relative neglect and disengagement of the region. Over the years, there has been steady and substantial progress in India's overall engagement with its East Asian neighbours under the rubric of Look East Policy (LEP). India, which has always been at the very centre of things in Asia, is repositioning itself in the evolving dynamics towards its east.

The LEP has shaped India's engagement with the Asia-Pacific region for over two decades, substantially deepening India's economic, institutional, and security relations with the region. Initially intended to develop India's economic ties with Southeast Asia, India's engagement with its eastern neighbours has since shifted to include Northeast Asia, Australia, and New Zealand. In recent years, Look East has acquired a strategic dimension with a significant naval emphasis. It can be expected that India will deepen its engagement with its eastern neighbours.[12] The nature of India's partnership in the east varies in content from country to country. An important feature of this partnership is a regular high-level political visit between India and the East Asian countries to discuss broader issues of regional and global security, and to firm up critical bilateral cooperation in the areas of defence, security, and economic engagements. India has not only institutionalised regular consultations on foreign and defence affairs at ministerial and senior official levels, but it has also established strategic partnerships of varying depths and intensities with a number of countries in the region.[13]

Certainly, India's deeper engagement with its East Asian neighbours will enhance India's economic and strategic space, much of which will hinge on the implementation of announcements made in the past and by the current government. The Modi government is changing the discourse by calling the LEP as 'Act East Policy' or AEP. The challenge for India in the coming years, however, would arise from changing regional balance due to increasing Chinese strategic and economic influence, and Chinese assertiveness and territorial disputes in the South China Sea and the East China Sea. Nevertheless, with its growing economic and strategic interests, India is likely to play a greater role in the east.

Maritime Neighbourhood

India is highly dependent on the seas. While Delhi is seeking to develop its blue economy, its significant reliance on the security of the Indian Ocean—combined with its need to monitor and, if necessary, check the naval activity of other powers—means that the country is compelled to reach deep across the ocean, far beyond its own littoral. In recent years, New Delhi has intensified its efforts to engage with the states in the Pacific and Indian Ocean region.[14] A new policy thrust in India's maritime neighbourhood is indispensable to India's national interest. Indeed, Modi has laid out a comprehensive framework for India's nautical engagement which includes deepening security cooperation with India's maritime neighbours; building multilateral cooperative maritime security in the Indian Ocean; focus on sustainable economic development for all through expanding cooperation on the blue economy; cooperation with extra-regional powers; and defending India's maritime interests.[15] The Modi government appears pragmatic by underlining the significance of maritime affairs in foreign policy discourse. Furthermore, India is decisive about taking a larger role as a valuable security partner and to promote regional mechanisms for collective security and economic prosperity.

Furthermore, protection of sea lanes of communications has emerged as a fundamental feature of India's foreign policy. Hence, the role of the Indian navy is increasingly becoming central to India's overall strategy towards maritime neighbours. The Indian navy and other defence forces hold regular training exercises and visits with almost all the countries of the East Asian region, including China. In some of these countries, India has set up defence academies to impart training on a permanent basis. India has also started supplying defence equipment and defence technologies to the countries of the region.[16] In fact, the Indian navy's outreach also 'includes provision of maritime security on request by neighbours. Agreements exist with almost all Indian Ocean region countries that permit Indian Naval ships, submarines and aircraft to avail refuelling and turn-around facilities at very short notice'.[17]While the Indian navy is gradually enhancing its capability, India still has to travel a long distance to become a credible and responsible maritime power in the emerging Asia Pacific security architecture.

India's policy initiatives and announcements also denote its pursuit of stable, rule-based, Asian security architecture. India has established or co-established its own multilateral institutions in the region, including the Mekong Ganga Cooperation (MGC), the Bay of Bengal Initiative for Multi-Sectoral Technical and Economic Cooperation (BIMSTEC) and the Indian Ocean Rim Association[18] (IORA).[19] The Indian government's prioritisation of the maritime neighbourhood is an attempt in the right direction to reinforce India's profound engagements with the countries in the Asia-Pacific. India's maritime neighbourhood policy, if implemented aptly, will significantly increase India's influence and will foster its national interest.

Global Role and Soft Power Diplomacy

India is taken quite seriously by major global powers due to its economic success and huge potential. While India is thinking globally, it also needs to act globally in coming years. With the economic rise of a democracy of 1.2 billion people, India will need to embrace a more proactive regional and global role in tune with its national power and to share global burdens and responsibilities on important global issues.

The Indian government is working closely with other Asian countries and several regional and global institutions on issues of common interest for better policy coordination. These issues range from climate change, technological cooperation, pandemics, terrorism, skill development, trade and services agreements, energy security, and many others. Such cooperations are likely to grow in coming years. Complex emerging challenges will pave the way for multiple partnerships, as well as regional and multilateral solutions. India, with its increasing economic development, would be able to take on larger responsibilities. Indeed, the rising economic and security profile of India will help her in playing a greater role in world affairs.

Another notable feature of India's increasing footprint is extending humanitarian assistance and disaster relief (HADR). The Modi government is continuing the tradition of India's foreign policy of HADR and is strengthening India's HADR capability. Delhi's swift response in recent disasters, for example, in the aftermath of the tragic earthquake in Nepal, is a case in point.

Promotion of Indian values, culture, and tradition is another important diplomatic tool to deepen India's relations with other countries. The interactions among civilisations, including the flow of ideas, culture, and institutions, among them, is increasingly recognised as a powerful force, which has shaped world history and still shapes the contemporary international order.[20] Between the fourth and fourteenth centuries (or perhaps earlier), Indian culture, religions, and political ideas played a significant role in the politico-cultural landscape of Southeast Asia. These ideas influenced the emergence of statehood and the inter-state system in Southeast Asia and the process of their transmission was largely peaceful, except for the expansionist Chola reign.[21] Indeed, indigenisation offers a more substantial evidence of the power of ideas. India's outreach and deeper engagements with the countries in the Asia-Pacific region is likely to grow because India is seen as a non-threatening power. Indian food, music, movies, and fashion are very popular among many countries. The Modi government has done a remarkable job through a rare display of its soft power diplomacy when the entire world, along with the United Nations, celebrated International Yoga Day on 21 June. Similarly, India is working on technological innovations in healthcare, traditional medicine, satellites for education, and other developmental cooperation, and sharing this knowledge with friends and partners. India's soft power diplomacy could make India's story more incredible in years to come if government encourages and uses these powerful tools along with building its hard power capabilities. In other words, India's 'smart power' approach will help India to advance its national interest.

The Indian diaspora has played and will continue to play a meaningful role in expanding India's footprint across the globe. Indeed, the diaspora community's involvement in economic, political, and cultural affairs is self-evident. The Modi government has also focussed to engage global Indians in a big way. This is clearly evident in Modi's interactions with the Indian community abroad, through various means including public meetings and connection through social media. Such focussed engagement could be very helpful in creating synergies for trade, investment, technology transfers, cultural exchange, and more importantly, in mobilising political support. Digital diplomacy has become a very effective means of communication. On occasions, the diaspora community has approached the Ministry of External Affairs (MEA) for assistance and due to quick and direct communications, timely assistance has been facilitated by the government.

Some Limitations

The scope of this chapter is limited to highlight the directions of India's engagements with Asia. While there could be debate over various measures and initiatives of Indian foreign policy, broadly it can be agreed that India's national interest guides and shapes foreign policy initiatives. Many good ideas have surfaced in the past and could not be implemented due to political reasons or limited institutional capacity of the MEA. The gap between good ideas and their implementation has created a wide impression of 'delivery deficit' about Indian foreign policy. There could be several reasons for such perception but the biggest shortcoming of India's foreign policy establishment is that India is served by the smallest diplomatic corps of any major country and this institution is miserably understaffed. While there has been a welcome priority to India's South Asian neighbours, India's foreign ministry's capacity remains weak. David M. Malone, currently the Rector of the United Nations University and a keen observer of India, wrote in his masterly work on contemporary Indian foreign policy that the MEA's

> headquarters staff work punishing hours, not least preparing the visits of the many foreign dignitaries laying siege to Delhi in ever growing numbers as India's importance has expanded...India's overburdened Foreign Service is, on average, of very high quality, but because it is stretched so thin, its staff spends too much of its time conducting India's international relations through narrow diplomatic channels, managing ministerial and other visits, negotiating memoranda of understanding of no great significance, and by other means that reflect only a fraction of the rich reality of international relations today and of official Delhi's actual international interests.[22]

There are indications that the MEA is taking steps to address this issue. Shashi Tharoor, who is currently Chairman of the Parliamentary Standing Committee on foreign relations, is a great supporter of institutional reforms. He has written extensively on this subject in his books and columns and rightly argues that 'the Foreign Service be strengthened, enlarged with the addition of new personnel, and reformed in significant ways'.[23] The MEA does not have enough people looking after the complex dimensions that define each of our neighbours and relations within Asia. We need a broader and more thorough understanding of interplay between domestic and external issues. If media reports are correct, political leaders and bureaucrats are sending signals of much awaited and critical institutional reforms in the MEA. Nevertheless, a considerable effort is needed to improve the software and infrastructure of our foreign policy establishment to prevent periodic derailment of well-intended policies.

Indian foreign policy seems to be taking the right approach to get external inputs necessary for India's development and its rightful place in global affairs, which will help the India story go very far. India's aspiration to regain its responsible great power status could become a reality if India manages a sustained high economic growth and its democratic and secular credentials are maintained. The current government has made a lot of promises and it needs hard work and coordinated efforts by concerned officials and other stakeholders to keep them. India and many Indians are bursting with optimism, but let us remind ourselves that foreign policy is an extension of domestic policy. Therefore, the Indian government must address enormous economic and social challenges at home, while expanding its global outreach.

Endnotes

1 Opinions expressed in this paper based on research by the author, reflect his personal views alone and not that of any institution with which he is associated.

2 This is based on the findings of an Indian Council for Research on International Economic Relations (ICRIER) project titled 'The National Interest Project'. This project examined India's national interest and relations with the outside world, in respect of both economic growth and security. The author was a part of the project team. Three volumes were produced based on the reports and papers of this project. See, Rajiv Kumar and Santosh Kumar, *In the National Interest: A Strategic Foreign Policy for India* (New Delhi: Business Standard Books, 2010).

3 Peter Ronald Desouza, 'Modi and his Chakravyuh', *The Hindu*, May 20, 2015.

4 Address by the Prime Minister Manmohan Singh, 'Indian foreign policy has had a basic consensus,' February 15, 2006, http://www.rediff.com/news/2006/feb/15guest1.htm.

5 See David M. Malone and Rajeev Chaturvedy, 'Impact of India's Economy on its Foreign Policy since Independence,' *Asia Pacific Foundation of Canada Research Report*, November 2009, http://www.asiapacific.ca/sites/default/files/Indian__Economic__and__Foreign__Policy.pdf.

6 Quoted in Sanjaya Baru, *Strategic Consequences of India's Economic Performance* (New Delhi: Academic Foundation, 2006), p. 58.

7 Rajiv Sikri, 'One Year of Prime Minister Modi's Foreign Policy,' in *Redefining Governance: Essays on One Year of Narendra Modi Government*, ed. Dr Anirban Ganguly (New Delhi: Prabhat Prakashan, 2015), p.130.

8 Ibid.

9 See Rajeev Ranjan Chaturvedy, 'India's Neighbourhood Policy Under Modi',' *FPRC Journal*, 2015/1 (2014): 89–95.

10 See, Shyam Saran, 'Put neighbourhood policy back on track,' *Business Standard*, November 10, 2015.

11 See Amar Nath Ram, ed., *India's Asia-Pacific Engagement: Impulses and Imperatives* (New Delhi: Manohar and ICWA, 2015).

12 For more insights and details on India's LEP, see Amar Nath Ram, ed., *Two Decades of India's Look East Policy: Partnership for Peace, Progress and Prosperity* (New Delhi: Manohar & ICWA, 2012); Amar Nath Ram,ed., *India's Asia-Pacific Engagement: Impulses and Imperatives*, (New Delhi: Manohar and ICWA, 2015).

13 See, for example, Ajay Kumar Das, ed., 'India–ASEAN Defence Relations,' *RSIS Monograph*, No. 28 (Singapore: Nanyang Technological University, 2013); Harsh V. Pant, 'India in the Asia-Pacific: Rising Ambitions with an Eye on Rising China,' *Asia Pacific Review*, 14/1 (2007): 54–71; see also Harsh V. Pant, 'China Rises, India Ponders: India's "Look East" Policy Gathers Momentum,' *The Fearless Nadia Occasional Papers on India-Australia Relations*, Vol. 1, Spring (2013).

14 See Rajeev Ranjan Chaturvedy, 'Shoring up Maritime Security Cooperation,' *Diplomatist*, Vol.2/, April (2014): 47–48.

15 See C. Raja Mohan, 'Modi and the Indian Ocean: Restoring India's Sphere of Influence,' *ISAS Insights*, No. 277, March20, 2015. Also see, Rajeev Ranjan Chaturvedy, 'South China Sea: India's Maritime Gateway to the Pacific,' *Strategic Analysis*, Vol.39/4, (2015): 360–77.

16 See S.D. Muni, 'Look East Policy: Beyond Myths', in *Two Decades of India's Look East Policy: Partnership for Peace, Progress and Prosperity*, ed.Amar Nath Ram (New Delhi: Manohar & ICWA, 2012), pp. 216–17.

17 See Arun Prakash, 'Maritime Security of India: Future Challenges', IDSA, November 26, 2013.

18 It was agreed at the 2013 IORA Council of Ministers meeting to change the name of the Indian Ocean Rim Association for Regional Cooperation (IOR-ARC) to the Indian Ocean Rim Association (IORA).

19 Rohan Mukherjee and Clara Marina O'Donnell, 'Challenges of a Multipolar World: The United States, India, and the European Union in the Asia-Pacific,' *Young Strategists Forum Series*, July 2013,http://www.gmfus.org/publications/challenges-multipolar-world-united-states-india-and-european-union-asia-pacific.

20 See Peter J. Katzenstein, 'A World of Plural and Pluralist Civilizations: Multiple Actors, Traditions, and Practices, in *Civilizations in World Politics: Plural and Pluralist Perspectives*, ed. Peter J. Katzenstein (New York: Routledge, 2010).

21 See Amitav Acharya, *Civilizations in Embrace: The Spread of Ideas and the Transformation of Power* (Singapore: ISEAS Publishing, 2013).

22 David M Malone, *Does the Elephant Dance: Contemporary Indian Foreign Policy* (New York: Oxford University Press, 2011): pp. 299–300.

23 Shashi Tharoor, *India Shastra: Reflections on the Nation in our Time* (New Delhi: Aleph, 2015): p. 60.

SOCIETY AND CULTURE

The Indian News Media: The Future of the Numbers Game

Kajal Basu

The global newspaper industry continues to shrink in its most established markets, but is growing well in countries such as China and India as expanding literacy, economies and population spur consumption. The two countries combined will account for an astonishing 57.3 per cent of global average daily unit circulation print in 2019, up from 49.7 per cent in 2014.

Chris Lederer[1]

In June 2015, India and China were invited into an imperialist(ish) postcolonial(ish) club comprising the modern-day vanguard of global journalism: trade bodies centred in the West but speaking for almost all of the rest of the world. It is a club concerned overwhelmingly more with news revenue than with news content, product marketing more than information sourcing, and 'relevant journalism' defined in terms fiscal rather than informational.

Given the long history of Orientalist disparagement of offbase journalism—journalism in the world apart from the West—the invitation was an elevation of status, a handing-over of the baton of 'relevant journalism' to two erstwhile outliers with a single shared quantitative distinction: massive and burgeoning overpopulation: India 'in the 'serious' books of distinguished Indologists, who have got it all wrong'[2] and China and its 'complete indifference to the idea of quantity and a total disregard for any quantitative measurement in Chinese philosophical thinking.'[3]

Both analyses are based on contexts long obsolete: equally, both notions remain stubbornly embedded in the West's sociological schematics. In India, the sheer numerics and the fallible human agency which collects data from primary sources continue to raise flags about both the national database and the metadata, even as the logistics of data-gathering continue to invoke awe worldwide. Alternative measurements often still tend to implicate China's statistical database, although its National Bureau of Statistics embarked on refining data-gathering and sequestering the results two decades ago, starting with a switch in 1995 to an international system of accounting.[4]

All the more reason to test the dubiety of demicontinent-size Big Databases, and to view national analytics, goal-setting and policies that rely on them as malformed, malfunctioning and, as has been well-documented, unprescient in the long-term. Finally, not least, as the news-consumption trade agencies and predictive global audit firms have so optimistically done, to base qualitative prognoses and prognostics, trend-forecasting, and, even, 'hopecasting', on vast repositories of noisy data:

> I may be completely lacking in power to change my reality; but I'm invited to partner with a God—the God—who has more than enough power. And (this is a BIG deal), God seems to want to partner with us.
>
> Mark Oestreicher[5]

»»»»»

Trade bodies, faithful to corporate empirics, and government, hobbled by Big Data analytics methodology, differ both in terminologies and in databasing. The statistics of both are *in superficie* mindboggling. From one viewpoint, it appears to be a standoff between a private sector datamart with a tight market focus and a government datalake indiscriminatelypacked with all manner of data and their attributes.

The five years from 2008–13 were a rollercoaster ride. From 2009, the Indian print media grew by 1.86 per cent: in 2009–10 by 10.1 percent, in 2010–11 by 8.24 per cent, in 2011–12 by 7.33 per cent, and in 2012–13 by 8.48 per cent.[6] The growth rate averaged out at 7.20 percent—mostly boosted by the spike of 8.15 per cent between 2009 and 2010—but it crashed thereafter: 2009–11, 4,853 newspapers were added. Or 202.2 a month. Or 6.74 a day. Or one newspaper every three-and-a-half hours or so.

The Indian print media grew at 8.35 per cent in 2014. It was projected to grow at the rate of 8.01 per cent in 2015, 7.94 per cent in 2016, 8.075 per cent in 2017, 7.86 per cent in 2018, and 8.05 per cent in 2019. The projected half-decadal growth rate (2015-2019) averages out to 7.987 per cent.[7]

The Registrar of Newspapers for India (RNI) statistics paint a different picture. In 2008–09, the total number of newspapers/periodicals registered with the RNI was 73,146, (including 8,588 newspapers). Of the total, only 11,752 (or 16.06 per cent of the total) submitted their Annual Statements. In 2014-15, of the 1,05,443 registered N/P (including 14,984 newspapers), only 23,394, or 22.18 per cent, filed their Annual Statements. The oddly-diminutive average rate of Annual Statements submission with the RNI, at 18.73 per cent, is a more reliable indicator of the state of India's print media than year-upon-year differential growth rates in N/P numbers, because the submission to the RNI of every publication's Annual Statement is a statutory requirement under the Press and Registration of Books Act, 1867 and the Registration of Newspaper Central Rules 1956. Any publisher who does not is either napping, has no need for advertising from the government's Directorate of Advertising & Visual Publicity (which are the lifeblood of any number of small newspapers and periodicals), has downed shutters, or has fulfilled whatever temporary, extralegal need there was for registering, in the first place, and is done with journalism. More importantly, an unregistered newspaper/periodical is deemed by the government as unfit for the RNI's one statutory function that impacts directly on the pockets of publishers—the issuance of Eligibility Certificates for the duty-free import of newsprint in line with the policy of the Union Ministry of Commerce.

Newsprint costs constitute the bulk of production expenditure—ranging from 55–65 per cent[8] to 'between 40 and 60 per cent'.[9] Black-market newsprint also being a sure-fire commodity with a burgeoning market in India, led the Office of the RNI to recently affirm: 'RNI does not have any authorised agent/indentor, nor authorizes/allows third party to import newsprint.'[10]

The RNI has also drawn up a list of defaulters, which is being sent to the district magistrates to verify. If these publications do not exist, then the titles can be freed up and given to those who apply for registration...Identifying newspaper and publications that exist only on paper will also help corroborate if these are beneficiaries of state government advertisements.[11]

All this heavy lifting by the incumbent government suggests that newsprint sales in India are growing apace, which, in turn, is not necessarily good for a governance methodology that attracts combative analysis in direct proportion to media muscularity. In fact, however, signs that the Indian media is in the pink of health serve mostly to camouflage a visceral consumption that is eating away at the corpus. The newsprint sales figures and projections for the future seem, in their lack of appraisive consensus, designed to assure confusion rather than certainty about the true state of things.

At one end is the nervy voice of the trade bodies, handing out clearly disposable data. India's demand for paper is expected to rise by 53 per cent in the next six years, primarily due to a sustained increase in the number of school-going children in rural areas and increase in the regional newspapers.[12]

But the ground reality disagrees. In India, newsprint consumption has plateaued and is peering down the edge. The Indian government's Newsprint Control Order, 2004 (and its predecessor, the Newsprint Control Order, 1962) studiously avoid mentioning this attenuation, or even lightly acknowledging that reduction in newsprint consumption must entail a proportional thinning of the News in Print (NIP). Government's policies and actions vis-a-vis the paper industry have traditionally been centred tightly on the print news media, which today accounts for 19 per cent of paper consumed in India. Over the years, newsprint has been used as a press control device, first under the Essential Commodities Act, 1955; then the Newsprint Control Order, 1962; next, the Newsprint Control Order, 2004. Each reworking of Acts has brought a tightening of the noose. Just when the press had assumed that no legislation more restrictive could possibly top the 2004 redaction and replacement, the government, on 2 May 2016, colour-coded the paper and pulp as 'Red' on the four-colour Comprehensive Environmental Pollution Index (CEPI). As the quaternary in the CEPI, the industry is in for significant grief, including the docking of a slew of import permits for machinery as well as wood pulp. The newspaper industry seems surprisingly unperturbed—which means that it probably is. The question is: *Why* is there not a whisper of protest from the usually-hyperreactive newspaper industry?

As of 30 July 2014, India had 99,660 registered newspapers. However, running *with* the data instead of *against* it brings us to this: Newspaper circulation in India shot up from 98,841 (in 2007) to 109,937 (in 2011)—an increase of 11.23 per cent.[13] As of 30 December 2011, about 1.221 billion Indians shared among them 82,237 registered newspapers. It worked out to 1 newspaper: 14,835 Indians, of whom 74 per cent, or 10,978 were, technically, literate enough to read.

Between 2011 and 2014, literacy in India grew by 1 per cent, adding 190,000 'literates' to the population. This should axiomatically have added 1 per cent to India's Gross Domestic Product, but it did not: What does, contrarily, is that in these 31 months, or two years and seven months, the RNI registered 17,423 newspapers. It is, on the face of it, an impressive figure: an average of 6,744 newspapers added each year; or 562 newspapers each month; or almost 19 every day; or 2.5, give or take, every three hours. This is the sort of growth stat that any assembly line anywhere in the world would kill for—but for the fact that in the Indian newspaper industry, numbers flat refuse to match with other numbers. Thus, each trade body and every audit firm ends up creating its own off-key database. And full-fidelity analytics goes to pot. In other words, when the numbers do not gel, the narrative falters.

So, exactly *who* bought more newspapers, and *where* in the world? According to trade bodies and audit firms worldwide, China and India were the cash cows, no matter the impoverished hyperlocal economics.

»»»»»

> For newspapers, China and India are two massively important engine-rooms of growth, accounting for almost 50 per cent of total global newspaper sales volumes between them. Strip these two influential markets out of the figures and the global newspaper business is in decline, accelerating in 2013 to -4.0 per cent year-on-year.[14]

But was this really the case? It is a matter of record that Indian and Chinese newspapers posted decent growth—just as it is undeniable that newspapers did not 'grow globally'.

Larry Kilman, then the deputy CEO of WAN-IFRA (World Association of Newspapers and News Publishers), led a team of 19 'newspaper executives' picked from 15 countries to imagine, after accommodating 66 trends (or 'uncertainties') into their deliberations, a future that professional future-planners and theoretical futurists think is too distant and changeable by guerrilla variables for prognostics and prognoses. There was a list of subordinate trends, too, including 'the trend towards hyperlocal newspapers... and the uncertainty about whether online-only companies might become newspaper competitors'. Both issues, of critical significance to understanding the nature of journalism in India and China, were sidelined as unimportant. The team had 'a still-woolly notion of the chain of causality', which helps to explain why they then stood causality on its head 'by pretending that it was already the year 2020, and from that future vantage point, they crafted four stories...'. The four past-building scenarios were all named after James Bond films. This is not to suggest that this playfulness lies at the root of the unevidential statistics of future-casting news media trade bodies. But the inference is difficult to dodge.

PricewaterhouseCoopers LLP, delivering its analytics and projections with blunt confidence and an auxiliary verb, holds that China and India 'combined *will* account for an astonishing 57.3 per cent of global average daily unit circulation print in 2019, up from 49.7 per cent in 2014'. (*emphasis mine*) A 'key insight' of PwC's pits the '(a)verage daily newspaper circulation print', in 2019, of China (1,79,577,000,000) and India (1,53,213,000,000) against the "rest of the world" (2,47,942,000,000).[15]

Is this prediction reliable? The PwC's metadata is as opaque as its self-confidence is assured. What are absent are accessible values that lead up to PwC's remarkable projections. India's NIP circulation of 4,61,086,922 (2014) would have to be ratcheted up by 3,300 per cent to come within touching distance of PwC's ambitious 2019 circulation figure. That's 660 per cent each year, or 55 per cent a month, or 2.29 per cent every hour upon hour. This is an overestimate so absurd that the answer to why it happened at all probably lies not in busted maths but in fears and anxiety about a future perceived as inescapably apocalyptic.

»»»»»

It was June 2015 when trade bodies sought to tackle a critical event: the unprecedented, unforeseen overtaking in 2014 of global newspaper advertising revenue by revenue from circulation. But it was a bad tackle: shifting the goalposts, redesigning the game, and ditching conventional wisdom—all at once. One day, it was, 'Advertiser pays'. Then, suddenly, it wasn't, because the advertiser refused to play ball. Since it is fundamental in marketeering that someone has to pay, just as it is aphoristic that to keep afloat, one requires a lifejacket, the trade bodies grabbed for the only visible straw: 'Readers pay'. And, just like that, a new doctrine was born. Market pundits and media wonks, not exactly skilled at multivariate econometrics, coined an instant terminology: 'reader revenue'.[16]

This rejigging took on aspects of a feeding frenzy, as trade bodies rushed aboard. 'The basic assumption of the news business model—the subsidy that advertisers have long provided to news content—is gone. We can freely say that audiences have become publishers' biggest source of revenue'.[17]

WAN-IFRA might or might not have the interests of information-based, exposé-orientated news journalism at heart. But its unreconstructed public announcements, avowals, and prescriptions seem not to be the result of serious brainstorming.

> A profound shift in the newspaper business model, evolving for years, is finally here: global newspaper circulation revenues have surpassed newspaper advertising revenues, meaning that audiences have become publishers' biggest source of revenue. In 2014, newspapers generated an estimated 179 billion dollars in circulation and advertising revenue. 92 billion came from print and digital circulation, while 87 billion came from advertising.

The aforementioned extract is a study in how not to deliver data. First, there has not (yet, at least) been, years in the making, a 'profound shift in the newspaper business model'. Profound shifts are tectonic. They tend to leave indelible marks. In the world of numerics and analytics, profound shifts usually come with built-in replicability. This has not happened.

Second, just because in 2014 their cumulative spend on newspapers happened to surpass advertising revenue, readers did not 'become publishers' biggest source of revenue'. In fact, if 'circulation revenue' was divvied-up between production costs (the total expenditure on bringing out the newspapers), taxes, and loan repayment, the net profit from 9/10th of $100 billion would probably fall below the industry's Plimsoll Line.

Third, if intercontinental trade bodies such as WAN-IFRA elect to run with the concept of 'Total Readership' (which was, controversially, adopted by the Media Research Users' Council for the Indian Readership Survey in 2008)—and why not: it links well with the ball-in-the-air idea of 'circulation revenue'—we are in for interesting times. It had even been proposed that 'Total Readership' entirely replace 'Average Issue Readership'. This sparked a debate about the new index and measurement needs of the Print industry. During this debate a better method to capture print readership in a better way was advocated.

To offset the collegiate optimism in trade circles about 'circulation revenue' making good advertising's debilitation *in perpetuum*, PricewaterhouseCoopers sent out a clear admonition: 'Growing circulation does not mean growing print circulation revenue.'[19] PwC's analytics (2010–2019) show that while global newspaper circulation will continue to rise, 'circulation/reader revenue' will tumble—from $67.6 billion in 2015 to $65.7 billion in 2019. There is a sound rationale for not celebrating, says the PwC.

> Average daily unit circulation print is forecast to rise at a 1.0 per cent CAGR [Compound Annual Growth Ratio] over the forecast period, from 552.7mn in 2014 to 580.7mn in 2019. But the replacement of premium-paid titles with lower-cost equivalents in emerging markets means that print newspaper circulation revenue will continue to fall at a-0.7 per cent CAGR.[20]

An utterly out-of-character, frothy optimism seems to have gripped even hard-bitten global consulting firms.

> Over the next five years, we expect combined spending on print newspapers and print consumer magazines to fall a cumulative US $14 billion, or 1.5 per cent compounded annually, less than half the decline of the past three years. Looking at just the last three years of the forecast period, we project the decline to be a relatively modest 1.0 per cent compounded annually.[21]

It is not enough to insist—as the news consumption industry and trade organisations never cease to—that 'digital newspapers' (a technological oxymoron) are poised to take up print newspapers' slack. They are not, and are neither prepared nor steeled for. In 2016, newspaper advertising revenue is projected to drop by 6.5 per cent, and ad revenue from magazines by 7.7 per cent—an averaged drop of 7.1 per cent. Meanwhile, Internet advertising is projected to grow at 12.2 per cent.[22] But while Internet advertising originated as a tributary of advertising-in-print, it is no longer entirely identifiable as a dependent.

Cyber adspend and print adspend are becoming separate entities, once connected, now estranged. For more than a decade, that slow-moving turtle, print newspapers inc., carried the cyberworld on its back. It still is, bringing home 93 per cent of newspaper revenue, relegating cybernews to 7 per cent. It is so wide a differential that to attempt to examine and explain the one from the vantage of the other using interchangeable numerics is a fool's errand.

In India, however, the picture seemed a little different than—or skewed from—the global norm, for no particularly noteworthy reason. It just was. Take, for instance, the circulation of *The Times of India.*

From 2010 to 2011 alone, *The Times of India*'s 'paid circulation' (PC) went up by 694,447 copies, or a whopping 20.45 percent. In the coming years, however, the TOI's circulation plummeted. From 2011 to June 2015, it tumbled by 25.4 percent, losing 1,040,275 copies in paid circulation.[23] *The Hindu* lost likewise. Between 2011 and June 2015, it lost 238,707 copies, or 15.9 per cent.

The regional language newspapers, the linchpin of the Indian newspaper industry, had equally dismal showings. *Dainik Bhaskar*, for instance, lost half its bulk from 2008 to 2011.But its most signal gain was from 2011 to June 2015, when the English-language newspapers were flailing: Its paid circulation vaulted up by 253.3 per cent.

Malayala Manorama, the Kerala state flagship, wasn't doing too badly, meanwhile. In fact, it never flagged between 2008 and June 2015. More remarkably, between 2011 and June 2015, its PC went up by 9.3 per cent.

This in no way suggests a huge differential between the English-language and regional language newspapers, with a corrective historical impulse reserving an especial hiding for the former. While the Hindi-language newspapers have generally weathered the inclement economy better than the English-language newspapers, across-the-board, the losses were conspicuous because they were striking and the gains were few and wintry.

Even as the Indian press' fortunes rose and nosedived in 2010–2014, the global take seemed steadier—but set at a very low quantitative bar. Global print newspaper circulation revenue just about held their own at 0.38 per cent growth in 2013–2014 ($89,906 million). In four years, earnings worldwide fell by 0.27 per cent.

»»»»»

What we have already ended up with are not secular and reliable data analytics with regard to news, mediums of news consumption, rates of news consumption, and real-world prognostics for the future, but with regurgitated bezoars of factoids and bunches of unreconstructed and often tweaked data. In this context, at least, all indicators point towards what Jim Gray described as 'an exaflood of unexamined data'.[24] Essentially, Gray was describing a hypothetical binary blowout of biblical proportions, which could carry enough force to reduce databases to disorganised dataspaces.

It is only a matter of time before a Big Data exaflood hits India—a chaotic Big Data exaflood. As of today, India will have to brave the deluge without floatation device or paddle.

Endnotes

1 Chris Lederer, quoting from 'Global Entertainment and Media Outlook 2015-2019', PwC, Ovum. Available via subscription/on-professional-request at www.pwc.com/outlook.

2 François Gautier, 'How Foreign Journalists View India'; available at https://francoisgautier.me/2015/03/17/how-foreign-journalists-view-india-the-excessive-media-coverage-of-the-nirbhaya-rape-or-the-so-called-vandalizing-of-delhi-churches/ (accessed May 27, 2016).

3 Amaury de Riencourt, The Soul of China (New York: Coward McCann, 1958).

4 Iacob N. Koch-Wesser, The Reliability of China's Economic Data: An Analysis of National Output, US-China Economic and Security Review Commission Staff Research Project; 28 January 2013.

5 Mark Oestreicher, *Hopecasting: Finding, Keeping and Sharing the Things Unseen* (InterVarsity Press: Illinois, 2015).

6 *Indian Media and Entertainment Industry Report 2015* (New Delhi: FICCI-KPMG, 2015).

7 Ibid.

8 K.K. Sruthijith, 'Newsprint price hikes forcing publishing cos to rejig practices'; 12 March 2008; available at http://www.livemint.com/Companies/

5nUNiHL3HBuPJ2vEBGXX4M/Newsprint-price-hikes-forcing-publishing-cos-to-rejig-practi.html (accessed 26 May, 2016).

9 WAN-IFRA India 2014, 22nd Annual Conference, New Delhi; 17-18 September, 2014.

10 Rolling ticker on RNI website http://rni.nic.in/#; accessed on 27 May, 2016.

11 *Registrar of Newspapers for India,* May 2016.

12 *Paperex 12th Edition Press Release*; October 2015.

13 (*World Press Trends 2012*).

14 *Distripress Circulation Monitor September* (Zurich); Wessenden Marketing (Surrey, UK, *2014*).

15 PricewaterhouseCoopers, 'Newspaper publishing: Key insights at a glance,' Outlook insights: an analysis of the Global entertainment and media outlook 2015–2019, https://www.pwc.com/gx/en/global-entertainment-media-outlook/assets/2015/newspaper-publishing-key-insights-4-china-and-india.pdf.

16 Ken Doctor, 'The newsonomics of zero and The New York Times'; NiemanLab. Available at http://www.niemanlab.org/2013/02/the-newsonomics-of-zero-and-the-new-york-times/?relatedstory (Accessed on 14 May 2016).

17 Larry Kilman, WAN-IFRA Secretary General, presenting World Press Trends 2015 to the 67th World Newspaper Congress, 22nd World Editors Forum and 25th World Advertising Forum in Washington, DC, 1 June 2015.

18 WAN-IFRA, Available at http://www.wptdatabase.org/world-press-trends-2015-facts-and-figures (accessed 23 May, 2016).

19 PricewaterhouseCoopers, 'Newspaper publishing: Key insights at a glance,' Outlook insights: an analysis of the Global entertainment and media outlook 2015–2019, https://www.pwc.com/gx/en/global-entertainment-media-outlook/assets/2015/newspaper-publishing-key-insights-4-china-and-india.pdf.

20 Ibid.

21 *McKinsey & Company Global Media Report 2015: Global Industry Overview.*

22 WARC (formerly World Advertising Research Center).

23 Audit Bureau of Circulations (India).

24 Jim Gray, Address to the US National Research Council's Computer Science and Telecommunications Board (California, 11 January 2007). An 'exaflood' is defined as an all-flattening data deluge of a thousand exabytes (1 exabyte = 1,000 petabytes; 1 petabyte = 1,000 terabytes; 1 terabyte = 1,000 gigabytes; 1 gigabyte = 1,000 megabytes).

Environmentalism Today

Sopan Joshi

The term 'environment' may refer to the physical conditions around us, but it means different things to different people.

School-going children get exposed to this idea in a didactic manner, as part of efforts to sensitise them. The environment is something to be saved, because it is full of things like plants and animals, which are beautiful. The lesson of environmental protection is imparted in the manner of a moral lesson. Honesty is the best policy, respect your elders, complete your homework, brush your teeth at night, and save the environment.

Grown-ups don't have it much better. It has become a custom to designate special days to raise awareness about important environmental themes, in the manner of the United Nations. So we have the World Wetlands Day (February 2), World Wildlife Day (March 3), International Day of Forests (March 21; also World Wood Day), World Water Day (March 22), Earth Day (April 22), Environment Day (June 5), and so on and so forth. If you can think of a valuable part of the natural world, it probably has a day dedicated to it. There is Mountain Day, Soil Day, Elephant Day, Wind Day, and Honey Bee Day, to name a few.

Environmentalism in India began in the 1970s. It was a response to deforestation. Naturalists were concerned about widescale deforestation to support the demands of industrialisation. They found political support in the form of the then prime minister Indira Gandhi. The Wildlife (Protection) Act was passed in 1972 and the Forest (Conservation) Act in 1980.

The early 1970s saw the rise of another form of action against deforestation. In the higher reaches of the Garhwal Himalaya, ordinary citizens had protested peacefully against a sports goods manufacturing company that had received a Forest Department permit to cut trees in the forest nearby. This came to be known as the Chipko movement. Villagers were aware that their existence depended on the forest. When that was threatened, they asked for control over their physical environment.

Since then, forest management has become a highly contested subject, with many sides pulling it in different directions. The government itself is divided. Industrial development requires the exploitation of natural resources, but this is destructive of the environment. Coal is essential for generating electricity in a power-scarce country. Yet India's coal deposits are in areas that have its most dense natural forests. And this area is also the home of some of the most vulnerable people who live on the margins—or inside—the forests: the Scheduled Tribes.

People of these tribes feel cheated when the government kicks them out of their homes and farms in the name of forest conservation, while it is only too willing to hand over the forests to industry. They assert that they have lived along with forests and wildlife since time immemorial. The government, meanwhile, struggles to control illegal poaching of endangered animals, like the tiger and rhinoceros. Degraded habitat often sends out leopards into nearby settlements and sometimes even into the cities.

From coal and sponge iron, to bauxite and other minerals, mining is increasingly the greatest conflict of interest within the government. Forest protection is crucial not just for wildlife conservation, but also because forests serve as the catchment of rivers. From the delineation of eco-sensitive zones to 'no-go' areas for coal mining, the environment-versus-development drama plays out every day in India. Each day, the line needs to be redrawn in the face of one or another kind of pressure. This is among the most political issues in India, even if it does not get the focus and importance it deserves.

In this contest, environmental conservation is usually the loser to the needs of economic growth, which jeopardises our future. Because, unlike in industrialised countries, India has a large number of people who depend directly upon natural resources to earn their livelihood. Numerous non-timber forest products form the basis of food security for millions of tribal people. These products also have elaborate markets that feed into, among other things, medicinal remedies.

Haphazard industrialisation is also contaminating our water sources and the air. There is an elaborate legal and regulatory framework, beginning with the Environment (Protection) Act of 1986, a very powerful law built on the right to life. But this framework is routinely flouted. Regulation and enforcement is in the hands of governmental agencies. Across the world, environmental regulation is a very difficult discipline. In India, it becomes particularly messy, because of our peculiar history.

After India's independence in 1947, the government took up industrialisation as a priority. Government-run corporations have been among the polluters, too. The mindset of government agencies and officials is to promote industrialisation, which creates a bias and compromises their ability to regulate. They do not have the objectivity and the culture of effective regulators and enforcers. Polluting industrial units almost always get away with terrible environmental performance. Even when they are pulled up, the enforcement is ineffective. Allegations of corruption are quite common. As a consequence, industry does not need to take good environmental practices very seriously. Sensible environmental management requires investment of funds and infrastructure, which reduces profitability and competitiveness.

Nowhere does the ineffectiveness of environmental regulations show as starkly as it does in the management of cities. The air quality of most large Indian cities is poor. The national capital Delhi is among the world's most polluted cities on ambient air quality parameters. The increasing number of private vehicles is a chief factor in this, given that there are no large industries in Delhi. Polluted air is among the biggest reasons for morbidity and premature mortality in our cities. Children and the elderly are the worst affected.

Actually, Delhi's ambient air quality registered a significant improvement after the supreme court's activism beginning in the late 1990s. The city was forced to invest in the world's largest fleet of buses running on compressed natural gas. Those gains, however, are a thing of the past. Increasing private vehicles have created several problems. Air pollution due to vehicular emissions is only one. The capital's traffic is turning unmanageable. No number of flyovers and widened roads can deal with the exponential increase in vehicles. The traffic police often expresses its helplessness.

Traffic snarls and poor air quality is becoming common across urban India. In smaller cities, the increase has been among two-wheelers, more than cars. Parking of vehicles is becoming an extraordinary problem in cities, as almost all vehicles are parked on public land. Roads get narrowed due to parked vehicles on either side—and in the case of some small cities, right in the middle of the road. Parked vehicles encroach on to public areas, like footpaths, parks, and playgrounds. Cities now report frequent cases of road rage and clashes among citizens over parking slots.

How do other countries manage urban mobility? Only by investing in public transport and by deterring private vehicles. They narrow down roads for cars and make parking extremely expensive. This leaves no choice for citizens but to use public transport. Bulk transport both speeds up mobility and controls congestion and vehicular air pollution. However, this can happen only with large investments into public transport infrastructure.

Indian cities reflect a dire lack of public transport planning. Even cities like Mumbai and Kolkata, which earlier had extensive public transport networks, have not invested in these adequately to keep up with the demand. In the smaller cities, public transport is entirely missing. It is left to unregulated private operators, who ply ill-maintained diesel vehicles that spew black smoke and are sources of great inconvenience to the desperate citizens who have no option but to use them. The tiniest amount of comfort and dignity in transport comes at a steep price.

Walking and cycling are made difficult in our cities. Pedestrians and cyclists form a bulk of the fatalities from road accidents in India, along with two-wheeler riders. Walking and cycling are good ways to lower congestion and air pollution. So not promoting them actually feeds into a vicious cycle, wherein everybody wants to get off public transport and have their private vehicles. Efforts to control cars become very difficult in our cities, even when the air quality is bad enough for it to constitute a public health emergency.

The danger is only greater in water. The rapid increase in the use of personal water purifiers reflects a decline in trust towards municipal utilities. Their water supply networks are usually poorly maintained. This sometimes causes sewage to leak into the drinking water supply. But such problems exist only for the class of citizens who have access to municipal water supply lines.

A large number of the residents of our cities live in slums, which have no regularised water supply. Private water suppliers cater to them; this has become a lucrative business at the fringes of our cities. Private companies get water from a public source or a tube well, and sell it to people who have no other source of water. Because of poor supply by utilities, groundwater exploitation is rampant, resulting in a dangerous lowering of the water table. Therefore, tube wells need to be deepened every now and then.

This means municipalities have no real calculation of the amount of water used in their jurisdiction, which, in turn, means they have no idea about the amount of sewage generated. The rule of thumb here, used across the world, is that 80 per cent of water used in a city ends up as sewage. No government in India has even a credible estimate of the amount of sewage generated. There is no way to catch this sewage and treat it before releasing it into water sources. No wonder most water bodies are highly contaminated with untreated sewage.

The Yamuna River in Delhi is the most expensive stretch of river—22 km long—in the country, in terms of the amount of money spent on cleaning up its water. Delhi, in fact, has more than one-fifth of the total sewage treatment capacity in India. The city has more than 30 sewage treatment plants. But the river is so polluted that its colour shows as black even on Google Maps. Just upstream of Delhi, at the Wazirabad reservoir, water is greenish-blue. Delhi takes out all the water from the river for its consumption and it dumps untreated sewage into the river. So, effectively, the river is nothing more than a sewage conduit. There are no fish or other forms of aquatic life in this water, which is sent downstream for other cities and towns to clean up for their use.

The Ganga is in a similar condition, as are most rivers that have cities built on their banks. Cities can afford to pollute their rivers and ponds because they can source their water from faraway reservoirs and dams. Delhi, for example, gets water from the Bhakra dam in Punjab, from Garh Mukteshwar along the Ganga, and from the Tehri dam. Delhi has been demanding the construction of the Renuka dam in Himachal to augment its water supply (which will then produce more sewage, hence more water pollution). People of the area where the dam is planned are opposed to it, because it will take away their productive land and render them homeless, with no alternate source of livelihood. All cities follow this model, which means they have no interest in maintaining their water sources, which turn into receptacles of untreated sewage.

This is the condition when only half of our population has access to toilets. Government after government has committed funds and resources to ensure that all citizens eventually have access to toilets. There is a great need to end open defecation. Besides being a source of great discomfort and indignity to people who have to defecate in the open, this is a source of several water-borne diseases that stunt children and kill them. Suppose everybody gets access to toilets with adequate water supply—which doesn't exist right now. How will our rivers and ponds cope with twice the burden of untreated sewage? When our cities fail to treat the existing sewage load, how will they deal with double the amount?

Our cities are locked in this cycle of pollution and wastefulness. They also turn into water-logged areas during the monsoon. About 70–90 per cent of India's total rainfall occurs during the three months of the Southwest Monsoon. Which means there is suddenly a lot of water in open areas of the city. Traditionally, all cities and towns and forts in India were designed to harvest the seasonal bounty of rainwater. Now, with the water sources either polluted or encroached, this water has nowhere to go. So it floods residential areas.

The wetlands in eastern Kolkata used to function as the city's flood control system earlier. In recent years, large portions of these wetlands have either been converted into planned real estate or have been encroached upon. The rainwater cannot find its way along the slopes to these wetlands anymore. So it floods residential areas and causes seasonal distress.

The spanking new and prestigious Terminal 3 of Delhi's Indira Gandhi International Airport is built on land that earlier had several ponds, which harvested the rainfall. Now, the water has nowhere to go. This means it floods the airport each year. In seasons when rainfall is high, the water has entered inside the terminal building.

As paved areas increase, the surface available to the water to seep into the ground is getting curtailed. This adds to water-logging. If Indian cities cannot be bothered about cleaning their polluted water sources, they will have to still open them up if they want to prevent seasonal flooding.

Environmental conditions in India ask very political questions of the planners and managers of the government. These problems cannot be solved by having a special day in the calendar dedicated to them. If we have a World Sewage Day, or a World Flooding Day, we will not create a better world. The only way is to study the problem and show readiness to take difficult decisions. Because when it comes to environmental matters, the low-hanging fruits are all gone.

Hindu India and the Subaltern Voice

Daipayan Halder

In the competitive cacophony of the 24/7 news cycle, the Dalit voice is often dismissed in the brief columns of inside pages in mainstream daily newspapers. Unless of course, the issue takes on a political hue and the Opposition benches get an opportunity to target the ruling BJP-led government as an essentially upper caste construct that puts more value on the holy cow than the untouchable Dalit. One such opportunity presented itself in July 2016.

On 11 July 2016, few Dalit youths from Mota Samadhiyala village in Una taluka of Gir-Somnath district in BJP-ruled Gujarat were flogged by cow protection vigilante groups when they were skinning a dead cow. The accused thrashed them alleging that they had killed the cow. After the video of the attack went viral, it sparked off violent protests across Gujarat.

The issue rocked not just the state assembly but also Parliament. But what was more damaging for the BJP that has been trying to shed its anti-Dalit tag in order to wean away Dalits from parties like the BSP is what *The Indian Express* reported on 27 July.

> In the wake of brutal thrashing of Dalits in Una, at least 1,000 people from the community in Banaskantha district have so far expressed their desire to convert to Buddhism, stating that there was no point in continuing with Hinduism, if they are not treated as equals. These Dalit community members have even filled up the forms giving their consent for the religious conversion, which will soon be submitted to the government authorities.[1]

Very worrying news, no doubt, for a party that believes in the supremacy and spread of Hinduism.

The incident yet again brought to mind the condition of India's untouchable millions. While almost all political parties in the country vie for their votes (Dalits, as they are called, make up 16.6 per cent of the total population of India according to the 2011 census), the condition of the average Dalit remains as problematic as before—run down, at the village level, by the local landlord and the police, and at the national level, by the bureaucracy and the political class.

For India to realise its potential and sit at the high table of the world's top superpowers, it is important that we as a society right this historic wrong and bring Dalits to the national mainstream. For no country can prosper till such time as all sections of its society are truly empowered.

It is one thing to be poor in India. Quite another to be casteless poor. The ancient text *Purusha Sukta* (hymn 10.90 of the *Rig Veda*) explains the origin of the four varnas from the mouth (Brahman), arms (Kshatriya), thighs (Vaisya) and feet (Sudra) of the P*urusha*. And those that came from the feet have remained there! Even as India makes giant strides in science and technology they are trampled upon by the higher castes for generation after tormenting generation.

Ask Bant Singh. When his minor daughter was raped by upper caste men in 2000 in Jhabhar village in Mansa district of Punjab, he dared to take them to court, a rather bold step for a Dalit back then. The trial led to life sentences for three culprits in 2004. It was one of the earliest instances of a Dalit from the region complaining against upper-caste violence and managing to secure a conviction.

Such cases have been filed before. But justice had always been a far cry, as even judges displayed caste bias. If we go back more than a decade we come across the example of Bhanwari Devi. On 22 September 1992, this grass-roots worker was gangraped in front of her husband, for trying to prevent a child marriage. The trial judge acquitted the accused saying 'rape is usually committed by teenagers, and since the accused are middle-aged and therefore respectable, they could not have committed the crime.' If that wasn't enough, he went on to say: 'An upper-caste man could not have defiled himself by raping a lower-caste woman.'

So Bant Singh's case could have been a reason for cheer. But on the evening of 7 January 2006, when he was returning home through wheat fields after campaigning for a national agricultural labour rally, he was attacked by a gang, sent by the same men who had earlier raped his daughter, and who had links with the Congress party.

Bant Singh was beaten to pulp and left for dead. He somehow managed to survive after both his lower arms and one leg were amputated since gangrene had set in—as the doctor at the hospital he was taken to ignored his case, allegedly because of his caste. The doctor was later suspended and Singh became a singer and campaigner for Dalit rights.

Amost 10 years since then, all this may seem old history. Except, things are the same. *The Huffington Post* reported on 22 June 2015, this year that despite cracking one of the toughest exams in the world, two brothers from Uttar Pradesh are battling casteist stigma in their village. Raju and Brijesh Saroj, sons of a daily wage worker, Dharamraj, are among those students who had placed in the top 500 ranks in the competitive entrance examination for the prestigious Indian Institute of Technology (IIT). Even though big political leaders have pledged financial support to these teenagers, they returned to their village in Rehua Lalganj, Pratapgarh, only to have stones pelted at them.

'There were five or six stones thrown at our home. We informed the police,' Raju told *The Times of India*. This isn't the first time the brothers (and their family) have been mistreated by the villagers. From their drainage supply being cut off to reducing their access to the public toilet, the family has faced plenty of stigma and harassment.

More recently, *TwoCircles.net* reported that death threats have started pouring in against protesting Bhagana Dalits by the Khap Panchayats of their village, nearly a week after 100 families of the Dalit community from Haryana's Hisar district converted to Islam.[2]

> The protesting Dalit families from Bhagana village, Hisar 'accepted' Islam during a protest demonstration at Jantar Mantar in the national capital in what their leaders termed as a mark of'protest' against 'perpetual persecution and torment at the hands of the upper-castes Hindu Jats'. The protesting Dalits had recited 'Kalma' and later offered 'Namaz' in congregation.
>
> 'The Khap Panchayat of our village has told us that we will be slaughtered if we try to go back to our villages as Muslims. We have

> been asked to abandon our property in the village after our conversion to Islam,' President of Bhagana Sangharsh Samiti, Virender Bagoriya told *TwoCircles.net*.[3]

From 2014, a new central government is in place, a government that came to power with the slogan: *Sabka Saath, Sabka Vikas* (Together with all, Development for all). Though Hindu Right wing, the government is headed by Narendra Modi who belongs to the Other Backward Classes (OBC), so one would have expected some change in how India's untouchables are treated.

The Vishwa Hindu Parishad (VHP) leader Ashok Singhal laid bare his 'Hindu' heart at the 2014 World Hindu Congress, soon after the Bharatiya Janata Party (BJP) stormed to power. 'Eight hundred years after it [power in Delhi] went away from Prithviraj Chauhan, it did not come into the hands of a proud Hindu," he thundered. Singhal was referring to Prime Minister Narendra Modi leading the BJP to victory in the 2014 Lok Sabha polls. What is interesting is Singhal did not regard Atal Bihari Vajpayee's reign either from 16 May to 1 June 1996, or from 19 March 1998 to 19 May 22 2004, as 'Hindu rule'.

A government headed by an OBC has today become the biggest source of strength for a Hindu supremacist organisation in a way two previous governments headed by a Brahmin (A.B. Vajpayee) could not be. This has to do with the fact that Modi has a 'Hindu strongman' image which the milder-mannered Vajpayee, who never flaunted his chest size, didn't, and a much wider acceptance among the rank and file of both the BJP and the Rashtriya Swayamsevak Sangh (RSS) as well as the rest of the country. But there is more to this.

For a while now, the Parivar has been trying to woo those whom Manu, the progenitor of caste, had kept aside as 'children of a lesser god'. To bring in the numbers during the Lok Sabha and later in Assembly elections, the BJP went after those whom Manu had kept at the bottom of the ladder.

Electoral compulsions forced the Parivar to change track though many of its members have kept caste alive in their minds and manners even in the 21st century. A recent news report says the BJP in the post-1990s era managed to attract only one in every ten Dalit voters. However, in the last Lok Sabha Election (2014), one in every four Dalits voted for the party. The ratio is even higher for the National Democratic Alliance (NDA) coalition where nearly one in every three Dalits voted for it.[4] The BJP has surpassed both the Congress and the BSP in attracting a larger share of the Dalit vote.

Inequalities in the Hindu caste system have forced millions of Dalits to trade gods. If the Hindu right wants to keep its flock together, it needs to address this problem. And the Sangh seems to be taking baby steps to correct this historic wrong.

It is no secret that the Parivar has not always been a meeting ground for egalitarian minds. In 2006, five Dalits were held for skinning a cow. Within three hours, a mob of a few thousand gathered near the police station where the 'culprits' were sheltered. As policemen reportedly watched in silence, the mob burnt two of them alive and lynched the other three. The Sangh Parivar had mobilised villagers from the surrounding areas to 'kill the cow-killers'. This happened at the police post of Dulena in Jhajjar district in Haryana.

It is delicious irony that eight years later, the BJP had to woo Dalits in Haryana and elsewhere to get the required numbers and wrest power from the United Progressive Alliance (UPA). The party even took the support of controversial Dera Sacha Sauda chief Gurmeet Ram Rahim Singh, to whom Dalits flock in large numbers.

Since then, the RSS has intensified efforts to find a common Hindu thread to unify all groups under one Hindu identity. A newspaper report on 22 September says three top RSS leaders have sought to attribute the genesis of Dalits, tribals and many other groups to 'Muslim invasion' in medieval times.[5] They wrote this in their forewords to three books, authored by the BJP spokesman Vijay Sonkar Shastri and released by Mohan Bhagwat recently—*Hindu Charmakar Jati*, *Hindu Khatik Jati* and *Hindu Valmiki Jati*.

The Sangh leaders said these castes had come into existence due to atrocities by foreign invaders and did not exist in the Hindu religion earlier. According to Bhaiyyaji Joshi, who sits pretty at the number two position as general secretary in the RSS hierarchy, 'sudras were never untouchables in Hindu scriptures' and 'Islamic atrocities' during the medieval age resulted in the emergence of untouchables, Dalits and Indian Muslims.

Joshi said:

> To violate Hindu *swabhimaan* (dignity) of Chanwarvanshiya Kshatriyas, foreign invaders from Arab, Muslim rulers and beef-eaters, forced them to do abominable works like killing cows, skinning them

> and throwing their carcasses in deserted places. Foreign invaders thus created a caste of *charma-karma* (dealing with skin) by giving such works as punishment to proud Hindu prisoners.[6]

Researchers on caste may shudder at such deliberate distortions of history, but to stop large-scale conversions to other religions, the Parivar feels it needs to manufacture a saner past.

It would be unfair, however, to only blame only the Hindu Right for atrocities against the Dalits. The political Left in India that talks about classless, casteless society has treated Dalits no better.

Most of those familiar with Kolkata—and the bhadralok ethos it celebrates—will tell you that in this city, atrocities based on caste bias are but stray incidents. Any display of caste discrimination is generally scoffed at and three decades of Left rule have, among other things, done away with the twin evils of class and caste. *People's Democracy*, the CPI (M) mouthpiece, informs readers with unfailing regularity of the communists' success in providing succour in Bengal to the socially marginalised.

Don't fall for that. On the surface, yes, it is different in Bengal. There is no Ranvir Sena to maim, kill, rape and burn the Dalit populace. Dark-skinned cows are not rejected because they may belong to lower castes, or white-skinned ones venerated as Aryan symbols. Caste politics hasn't reared its ugly head to the extent it has in some other states, notably in the northern ones.

The atrocities and inequalities in the rule of the Left Front are different. Urban Bengal has always had a tradition of 'unorthodoxy'. So caste discrimination does not always assume epidemic proportions. But that has not put a stop to the caste crimes here. It's another matter that they mostly go unreported. Truth be told, the government of the proletariat has been guilty not only of criminal negligence to the Dalit cause, but of atrocities against them as well.

Flashback to the late 1970s: an about-to-retire head of the Sanskrit department of a reputed university in Kolkata reacted strongly against an application for a lecturer's post in his department. Reason: the applicant was a namasudra (a scheduled caste). Surely a sudra can't be allowed to teach Sanskrit in a university, the professor fumed. Reservation for SC/STs and OBCs was still a distant dream. The candidate, a first-class degree holder, had applied purely on the basis of merit. The professor, a Left ideologue, garnered tacit political support to scrap the application. No reason was cited for the refusal.

All that the applicant got to know was that 'a more deserving candidate' has been selected.[7]

In November 2004, students in a primary school in Birbhanpur village in West Bengal's Bankura district refused to accept mid-day meals. Reason: the cook was a baghdi woman, an untouchable. With op-ed hacks from Kolkata newsrooms crying 'Disgrace', politburo member Biman Bose issued a statement 'The matter has to be resolved through detailed discussions.' When a similar incident took place in Purulia district's Dumuradi village around the same time, a quick solution was offered by the village education committee: hire another cook, an upper caste this time.

Soon after, the Howrah Municipality Corporation evicted several hundred Dalit families, mostly from the Balmiki community, from Belilius Park, Howrah. These families are mostly engaged as *safai karmacharis* (sanitation workers) with the corporation. Citing environmental degradation, and without providing any alternative, the government razed their houses and it was reported that the police even took away their belongings.[8]

After the mid-day meal incident, *Anandabazar Patrika* ran a series on the plight of Dalits in Bengal villages (panchayats in most of these were under direct Left control at that time). The findings were alarming. In village after village, the survey finds that Dalit families were marginalised; Dalit children were made to occupy separate seats in schools and denied access to libraries and other facilities.

So while comrades Prakash Karat and Sitaram Yechury proudly declare in Delhi, 'Where ever the Red flag flies, we will destroy untouchability', the Dalits live a life of shame and suffering in West Bengal's villages.

Let us now examine if a new faith brings with it a new life for the Dalit. Mohammad Saleem Adil, a 47-year-old lawyer based in Delhi, says it can. A decade-and-a-half ago, Adil was Satbir Jathav, a Dalit who had been enduring years of social discrimination. Then he decided to embrace Islam.

'There was a need to connect, to not be persecuted for being born an untouchable,' he says. 'This was possible, I found out, in the same lifetime, but only by discarding Hinduism. I was an outcast all my life. Then, after converting, I felt like I finally belonged.'[9]

Thousands of miles away, in the Burdwan district of West Bengal, primary schoolteacher Jyoti Mondol embraced Buddhism around the same time. The 35-year-old's reason: in a neighbouring shanty, a Namasudra family was publicly beaten up by locals for allegedly skinning a live cow.

'Economically they were much below me,' he explains, 'but socially we belonged to the same strata. I could not sleep for nights after that incident. The conversion was like a rebirth; I felt at peace with myself. The stigma of being a lowly-born was no more.'[10]

All Dalit conversions, though, are not knee-jerk reactions to caste inequities or discrimination. Dalit intellectual Chandra Bhan Prasad cites the example of the backward castes of Meenakshipuram in Tamil Nadu, who for seven long years discussed the issue of conversionbefore giving up on Hinduism.

'In 1981, to free themselves from untouchability and police harassment, 150 Dalit families from this village in Tirunelveli district embraced Islam; Meenakshipuram became Rahmat Nagar,' he recalls. 'With conversion came wealth and several of them got jobs in the Gulf countries.'[11]

There are other instances. From being an entirely marginalised community of toddy tappers and coir weavers who were not allowed into upper-caste Hindu temples and whose women were supposed to leave their breasts uncovered, the Nadars of Tamil Nadu gained immense socio-economic mobility by embracing Christianity in large numbers in the late 18th century.

This was the community that would engender achievers such as the late Tamil Nadu chief minister K. Kamaraj, the Amritraj brothers of tennis and Shiv Nadar, founder of the HCL group of companies.

There is another side to the conversion argument, one advanced most forcefully by the Hindu Right. This is that moving to another faith brings about no discernable change in the way society treats Dalits: whether you are a Dalit Buddhist, a Dalit Christian or a Dalit Muslim, you were, are, and will remain a Dalit.

'The Hindu right-wing argument is that Dalits learned the futility of conversions long before the advent of "foreign" religions like Islam and Christianity,' says social anthropologist Bibek Sinha.

'Those who converted to Buddhism to escape social ostracism reconverted to Hinduism to avail of the benefits of becoming *dwija* [twice-born] through good karma in the present birth.'[12]

Journalist and minority rights activist Anis Jamee says 'foreign' religions like Islam and Christianity have been, over the years, Indianised.

'Even after you convert, your caste identity remains with you.' But Sinha prefers to focus on the benefits. 'Christianity offers the most goodies to the Dalit,' he says, 'and with proselytising comes the exposure to Western education.'[13]

'The inequalities are not as stark as in Hinduism, and untouchability, the worst of human indignities, is definitely not followed in other religions,' contends Prasad.

> 'The fact is that most Dalit converts today are happy with the new faith they have embraced. In 1956, over 5 million Dalits, led by Ambedkar, renounced Hinduism and became Buddhists to escape from the caste system. Ideally, Hinduism should be cleansed from within. But that is another story. Till then there are other gods to turn to.[14]

It is tempting to be carried away by Sinha's optimism. However, fact remains, 'foreign' faiths have not been able to do away with the curse of caste and conversions have remained mostly a dubious game of assimilating numbers by peddlers of religion.

The proponents of Hinduism have to find an answer to this century-old problem. In its *Ghar Wapsi* programme, the RSS says those who converted to other faiths can reconvert and choose the caste they want. The problem with this is the RSS does not want to shake the superstructure of caste. So while a few may reconvert and become neo-Brahmins or neo-Rajputs, many others would still live lives of indignity. Diluting the idea of caste in Hinduism is the only long-term solution for a more equitable society. At this point it may seem wishful thinking, but for Hinduism to survive and not implode and for India to emerge as a world power, this is the only way out.

Endnotes

1 '"Pained" by Una episode, many Dalits plan to embrace Buddhism,' *The Indian Express*, July 27, 2016, http://indianexpress.com/article/india/india-news-india/pained-by-una-episode-many-dalits-plan-to-embrace-buddhism-2937625/.

2 'Bhagana Dalits get open death threats from Haryana Khap Panchayats for

converting to Islam,' *TwoCircles.net*, August 17, 2015, http://twocircles.net/2015aug17/1439785551.html#.V6r_gPl97IU

3 Ibid.

4 Rahul Verma, 'Desperately seeking Ambedkar,' *Indian Express*, April 30, 2016. http://indianexpress.com/article/opinion/columns/desperately-seeking-bhimrao-ambedkar-dalit-voters-narendra-modi-bjp-congress-2776888/

5 'Muslim invasion created Dalits and tribals in India, says RSS,' *India Today*, September 22, 2014, http://indiatoday.intoday.in/story/rss-mohan-bhagwat-hindu-dalits-tribals-muslim-invasion/1/384343.html.

6 Ibid.

7 Personal communication to the author.

8 Author's personal research.

9 Personal communication to the author.

10 Ibid.

11 Personal communication by Chandra Bhan Prasad to the author.

12 Ibid.

13 Personal communication to the author.

14 Personal communication by Chandra Bhan Prasad to the author.

New Time in Mofussil India

Abhay Mohan Jha

As times change in rural Bihar, so does the social texture of the village.

At first glance, you would feel you are still north of the Indian border, in Nepal's Madhes, with the sight of mutton, fish, chicken, and pork being fried by the village roadside, with the green expanse of paddy fields in the background. But this is the village where I was born and have spent most of my life, in Bihar's West Champaran district. The flow of liquor washing down fried meat might be a common sight along the Indo-Nepal border, but in Champaran and similar villages it signifies a major socio-economic change. The clientele at such meat-and-drinks joints in villages in this part of the country is neither bourgeois nor *kulak*—the working-class proletariat has the disposable income and can choose to spend their earnings drowning in alcohol now, if they wish.

This was unimaginable even a decade or two ago, with low wages and little work. After finishing college in Delhi in 1985 I came back home (on the edge of Bettiah, the headquarters of West Champaran district) and took up farming. A strapping young landless labourer on my farm left for Punjab after the *rabi* (spring) harvest to keep the hearth fire burning at home, during the lean months of monsoon joblessness. I inquired about this chap when I returned for the *kharif* (autumn) harvest to my farm, 40 km from Bettiah. He was still away in Punjab, and his wife had piled up a huge debt. As I came back from the fields one afternoon, I found a stranger wearing a shirt with trousers, goggles firmly in place above the bridge of his nose, a transistor radio slung across his shoulder, all accentuated by a grin across his face. I looked hard, but my eventual recognition was only prompted by a jibe from a woman on my threshing-floor: '*Siyaraoohey baa, rang badeley baa*!' (It is the same fox, he has just changed his colours).

Beneath the newly acquired swagger of this Punjab-returned farmhand was concealed an emaciated body. Within a day his acquisitions were pawned off, since his savings could not clear his family's debts. The next day he was back on my fields, harvesting paddy with his wife. A few days later, the bread-earner was bedridden. As I came to learn from other migrant workers, the opium-laced diet typical of Punjab's farms was taking its toll. My mind went back to Britain's colonisation of China, where opium from Patna and Malwa (in modern-day Madhya Pradesh) served the imperial design. Here I was seeing a hardy farmhand withering after a work stint in the hub of India's 'green revolution'. I remember engaging the workmen returning from Punjab in a debate. By then, wages had shot up in Champaran too—at times higher than the fixed minimum wages. But I could not reason with the psyche of the opiate.

Recalling the case of the dying migrant worker, I now realise that such workers were probably unsuspecting victims, whose employers were able to extract long hours of work with the help of opium. The higher wages were all that these migrants fell for. Back in Bihar, even though wages had risen, it fell short of Punjab, both in terms of man-hours per day and the money earned at the end of such toiling days. The case of such migrant labourers from Bihar, if analogy permits, now seems uncannily similar to the naive Indian athletes failing dope tests ahead of the New Delhi Commonwealth Games in 2010.

Benevolent Feudalism

The traffic out of the Bihar villages only multiplied and it spread farther—to Gujarat, Mumbai, Delhi, and even Jammu and Kashmir. The burgeoning of the kidnap-for-ransom industry in Champaran—where payment could be as little as a few lungis, some fowl, or goats—acted as an impetus to this flight of labour. However, things were changing; now, work was not limited to the farmlands outside Bihar. With industrialisation, the farmhands of Champaran and indeed much of the state were becoming factory workers. The newer migrants learned to work harder, earn, and save more. They also added value to their basic skills: some graduated to working factory tools from farm tools, others sharpened their skills as carpenters, masons, or electricians.

They even learned their working-class rights, as I discovered on a visit to a factory in the industrial hub of Delhi's Mayapuri one afternoon in 1983. I needed to get the cultivator I had just purchased for my tractor back home, loaded and sent to a transport agency. 'Lunchtime *hai, sardarji*,' the migrant Bihari labourers from Chhapra declined the factory owner's request to load the implement in unison, only to relent on hearing my request in Bhojpuri: '*Chala, chala, jaiware ke maal baa!*' (Come, come, it's a neighbour's stuff).

I remember the days when there were only two tractors in my village and over a hundred pairs of oxen to till the land. Today, there are only two pairs of oxen, while the number of tractors has gone up manifold—though not for agrarian purposes. The transportation of sand, cement, and steel has opened a new income avenue in this liberalisation-fuelled construction boom in the hinterland. This is true of most villages in Champaran. At a village in Inarwa, right on the border with Nepal, I recently discovered that people with half an acre of land, or even less, owned tractors. The economic boom in these parts, however, tells another story. It is not difficult to see how cross-border transportation—smuggling—of paddy and pulses has metamorphosed the economic condition of the peasantry in the border villages.

In my younger days, when I would invariably spend holidays from boarding school in my village, I found an abundance of labour available. The men and women were happy to be family retainers. Wages were low, but entire families were ensured a full meal. When I got back from college, the older generation of workmen and women had grown old, yet would still drop in and help around. They cared and were cared for. To re-jig historiography, it was benevolent feudalism. Then there was a generational shift, with the children growing up and forsaking farm and domestic work, either emigrating or taking up other skilled vocations—supervising, say, at a brick kiln.

For me, becoming a journalist after almost a decade of farming opened a new window to understand the changes that were taking place in our villages. Since childhood, I was conditioned to understand that only the patriarch of a village's landed elite would don the headman's mantle. Slowly, though, I came to realise that political power in the villages was not restricted to the upper-caste elite. The moneyed businesspeople—grain merchants and moneylenders—in the villages too commanded clout. Power equations were defined by the strength of one's economic standing.

At the end of the 1980s, the upheavals surrounding the recommendations for reservations for the other backward classes (OBCs) by the Mandal Commission also brought to the fore the caste divides in rural societies. However, while the social fabric was put under strain, there was no real transformation or development on the political and economic front. True, the 'backward' classes emerged as formidable political forces that changed the power matrix in Patna, and job reservations brought benefits to some. But the majority of hitherto-deprived people were destined to be vote banks in the churning of politics.

A miniscule minority of the sections empowered by the implementation of the Mandal Committee recommendations—by virtue of the better socio-economic status that gave them better education—were able to gain from job reservations. However, a vast majority still stood deprived due to an economic condition that denied them access to better education, if at all, and its concomitant benefits of jobs reserved. This 'creamy' and 'non-creamy' dichotomy within the Mandal-enabled castes was, thus, unable to benefit the entire targeted sections of society and the identification of castes termed as 'extremely backward' from the panorama of castes earlier clubbed together as 'other backward classes' can only be seen as an acknowledgement of inequitable distribution of caste-based benefits.

The issue of caste-based reservations did act as a political adhesive, where even those who could not benefit from job reservations became easy vote bank recruits. Over time, with the shifting of state power to OBC leadership, young 'caste' men showing leadership qualities during polls and endearing themselves to caste leaders in power benefited in another way: various income-generating government avenues such as, say, a ration-shop dealership in the village coming their way. Political patron-client relationships thus became increasingly cemented by caste alliances.

Hubby Politics

To my mind, the real shift happened in the early 1990s, when a constitutional amendment strengthened the Panchayati Raj institutions. This decentralisation of power brought about real changes at the base of the political pyramid, a process pushed further by the current chief minister of Bihar, Nitish Kumar, who brought in political reservations for the so-called extremely backward castes (EBCs) and women across the caste divide through grassroots democracy. This, together with the flow of development funds to the village panchayats, promised to transform village India completely.

Transformation did happen. Women and EBCs have come to wield power at the grassroots. Yet true to Indian democracy's inherent failings, a whole new breed of power brokers emerged to hijack development. Grassroots democracy, as seen and felt by villagers today, has become a tool by which to grab the spoils of office through spouses. Thus, the Panchayati Raj lexicon has become richer with words such as *mukhiyapati* (aka MP) and *sarpanchpati* (aka SP), referring to the husband of the *mukhiya* or *sarpanch*. In fact, the hubbies have formed their own cabals. '*Cabinet ka meeting kab rakhajaye?*' (When should we hold a cabinet meeting?), I recently overheard my village head's husband ask the spouse of a woman ward member.

Rajiv Gandhi famously quipped at the Congress party's centenary convention at Bombay, in 1985, that 85 paise of every rupee sent from the Centre do not reach the villages. Ask the villagers today and they will tell you that the money does reach the panchayats, but it still eludes the beneficiaries until they please the elected Panchayati Raj functionaries—and their spouses. Talk to the elected representatives who have a mandate to bring in change and development, and they will talk about a rankly corrupt bureaucracy holding them to ransom. Either way, real politics is at play in the villages.

In this way, the decentralisation of power has arrived at the grassroots along with its handmaiden of corruption, both spurning the clamour for politics in the villages. The silver lining is the empowerment of women that is happening steadily, despite the male 'remote control'. With women stepping out of *purdah*, the exposure to various opportunities—as, for instance, nurses and teachers—has given rise to a new awareness, resulting in a conscious effort to educate young girls. Girls in Bihar's villages are now enrolled in schools in increasing numbers, their dreams widening with prospective role models from across the vocational vista, from the crisp sari-clad, handbag-carrying teacher in the village school to the lady doctor treating them at the village's primary health centre. In turn, the employment of women in government institutions and elsewhere has changed the village male's mindset too. Thus, women taking up jobs are finding ready support from family patriarchs—unimaginable just a generation ago.

Yet, there are ironies. Each time that I step towards town from my village, I am unable to cease marvelling at a ladies' beauty parlour that operates from a wooden kiosk at the edge of my village. Is it television that brings such things about? Or Bollywood? Perhaps both and also, possibly, the exposure to metros? The trickle of clients beyond the curtained door only brings to mind the cliché of beauty being skin-deep when you realise that just adjacent to where these women drop in for grooming, scores of village women trudge along the railway tracks, pre-dawn or post-dusk, to defecate. The mismatch between the lack of toilets and the clamour for toiletries is painfully striking.

Leaving and Returning

Similarly, exposure to the outside world has sparked off dreams among young villagers. The penetration of the media to the back of the beyond has certainly been a catalyst. Corporate bigwig Indira Nooyi might still not catch a young village girl's imagination, but Sania Mirza, Saina Nehwal and the women journalists that she sees on the television at home sparks ambition. The sight of girls playing football in Bettiah, or even more remote Narkatiaganj, is no longer surprising.

Taking a few classes at a media course in a Bettiah college some years ago, and more recently conducting a workshop at a media college in Patna, I was struck by the number of girls from semi-urban or rural backgrounds aspiring to be journalists. Another thought struck me even more forcefully: While some of the top women anchors and reporters in national television have 'mofussil' Patna backgrounds, an even larger number of girls from rural up-country Bihar are joining the media today. A random background check of women print and television journalists in regional publications and channels will only confirm this.

Child marriages are not as common as they were earlier. Increasing exposure has also changed the contours of sexuality in villages, with courtship, romance, and elopement becoming recurrent 'aberrations'. Covering the Panchayati Raj polls in 2006, I was stopped in my tracks, transfixed, at a sight straight out of New Delhi's Lodhi Garden: Here, in Champaran's rural wilderness, young couples were on dates, cosying up under the *Sheesham* (North Indian Rosewood) trees next to a wheat field. '*Punjab-return baran san*' (they're Punjab-returned), a local scribe winked.

From where there was once negligible generation of wealth, villages in my part of the country are now flush with income, both hard-earned and otherwise. And, the affluence has seen a shift from the consumption of toddy to alcohol, as the meat-and-liquor stalls lining the rural landscape in Champaran testify. The packaging of 'country liquor' in easy-to-carry, disposable plastic sachets affords the brew easy shelf space in village kiosks, where the distinction between the legal and illicit evaporates. Consumption, too, is taking its toll.

A perusal of local Hindi dailies, having multiple editions that cover a part of (or all of) a district, would from time to time show small, single-column reports about deaths due to consumption of illicit liquor. The ready availability of liquor sachets, many villagers suspect, is not only though government-controlled depots. The news reports of liquor deaths point a finger to the illicit hooch feared to have penetrated the vast rural market. Even otherwise, with drinking becoming a lifestyle among rural youths, it is assuming life-threatening proportions, with many a village youth becoming addicted to the stuff.

But in the rancid stench of cheap liquor and resultant death, a new awakening is taking birth. As one young villager was sinking after wasting himself with liquor recently, women in my village took to the streets, brooms in hand. They raided the hooch-sellers in the village. The liquor shop's patrons—the women's husbands—took to their heels.

In the churning of democracy, I sense an energy in the sight of these demonstrating women. Equations are changing in the villages of Bihar not only due to the arrival of government funds and decentralisation of power. Better earnings and prudent savings by the new generation of both the skilled and unskilled who dare to venture out have also given them the wherewithal to invest in land, just as the traditional elite see their children settling in the cities, where the funds for their entrepreneurial enterprises or the buying of apartments come from the alienation of ancestral estates.

Land for Education

The 1980s and 1990s saw the shifting of many rural families in West Champaran to either Bettiah, the district headquarters, or to the towns of Tamkuhi or Padrauna in Uttar Pradesh, in the wake of the terror unleashed by the 'kidnap mafiosi'. A whole new generation's umbilical cord with the village was thus severed, with the children who grew up in towns refusing to take up agriculture or other traditional vocations of the village economy. Tales abound of families selling portions of their village land to secure a job for their progeny, preferably in the government. Many of the younger generation have also chosen to become, for instance, small traders in mofussil towns. The shifting of base has inevitably entailed the setting up of urban homes, the venture finding investment—more often than not—from the sale of ancestral village land.

More recently, there has been an awakening among rural families to the need to provide better higher education, preferably technical education, to their children. Go to any village and ask: Dozens of boys and girls, you will learn, are enrolled in engineering colleges in places as far away as Chennai, Bangalore, or Jaipur. Many are enrolled in courses of computer applications. While the availability of educational loans has facilitated such education to some, many have paid capitation fees by selling agricultural land.

Factors such as these are resulting in a stark change in patterns of land ownership in the villages. In this silent transformation, enterprise rules the market, not caste. The opening-up of the market since India took to liberalisation in the early 1990s has fuelled young dreams, and better education has helped to realise ambitions. Last year during Chhath, a deeply traditional and religious festival, I was amused at the unusually loud, continuous bursting of crackers. '*Ladka-sab England Italy se aaya hai*' (The boys have returned from England and Italy), a nephew quipped, even as I spotted another expatriate youth filming the *puja* with his new handheld video camera. The boy was home from the UK; another, back from Germany, was handing out crackers to children.

There could not be a louder statement of change.

This piece was first published in Himal Southasian. *It is reproduced here with the permission of* Himal Southasian *and the author.*

The Alchemy of Multiple Identities

Abdullah Khan

The 'idea of India' for most Indians is a country with more than 5,000 years of glorious history which once extended from present-day Afghanistan and Pakistan to the southernmost part of India and which has shrunk geographically, for various socio-political reasons, to become the India we know now. Unlike many international historians and political scientists, they don't see it as a political entity created in 1947 after the British left the Indian subcontinent.

But, 'Indianness' is perceived differently by different sets of Indians and their perceptions are moulded by their religious, regional, linguistic and other identities. This essay discusses the issues of Indian identities in the modern context from the points of view of two major religious communities, Hindus and Muslims, who make up almost 94 per cent of the total population. It also gives hints of how Indians will look at various aspects of their identities in the near future and how the issue of multiple identities will decide the fate of the republic of India.

The Majority

Sanatan Dharma or the eternal religion is the most commonly used word by the Hindus to describe their religion. This is based on the belief that the religion existed since time immemorial and the Vedic Age was the continuation of the Indus Valley civilisation. They also believe that they are the native residents of this land. The theory of Aryan invasion does not find many takers outside the academic circle. Yes, South Indian Hindus, especially those associated with the Dravidian Movement see themselves as the native inhabitants of this land and consider the north Indians as Aryans.

The modern day *Indian* Hindu identity is roughly based on an interpretation of Hindu nationalism during the freedom movement at the end of the 19th century when Indianness was equated with Hinduism. In order to fight the British imperialists, Indian freedom fighters used the past glory of the Hindu religion to motivate themselves and their fellow revolutionaries. For example, if you read Bankim Chandra Chattopadhyay's *Anandamath*, it clearly indicates that the Hindu religion is an integral part of Indian identity. But, at the same time, a majority of freedom fighters considered Muslims as their fellow Indians and sought their help in evicting the British from India.

At the beginning of the 20th century, after the birth of communal organisations like the Muslim League, Hindu Mahasabha and Rashtriya Swayamsewak Sangh, the Indian Hindu identity had taken a new form as Indian Muslims were perceived as outsiders. Partly, this was a reaction to the vitriolic communal campaign unleashed by the Muslim League for the creation of a separate homeland for Muslims. And, partly, it was the culmination of religious nationalism pursued by the Hindu right wing who viewed 800 years of rule by Muslims as slavery.

The bloody partition saw the wave of migration of Hindus and Sikh from the newly created dominion of Pakistan. And their traumatic experience during the post-partition riots shaped their views about India and their Indian identity. They believed that India is a country created for the Hindus in the same way that Pakistan was carved out for the Muslims. But, unlike the Muslim League, Mahatma Gandhi and Nehru envisaged India as a country with secular principles. A majority of Hindus ultimately bought the secular proposition offered by the Gandhi-Nehru duo and that helped to maintain social harmony between the Hindus and the Muslims.

In the post-Independence years some minor issues like support by many Muslims to the Pakistani cricket or hockey team caused resentment among moderate Hindus. When they heard that firecrackers were being lit in celebration after the Indian team's loss to Pakistan, they felt that those celebrating (the Indian Muslims) were definitely not Indians and should be deported to Pakistan. But, now after the sharp decline in the numbers of Indian Muslims supporting the Pakistani team, the scenario has changed.

Fast forward to 1986, the Ayodhya movement and Babri Masjid-Ram Janambhoomi controversy vitiated the atmosphere of India and we saw the rise of militant Hinduism with slogans like '*Garv se kaho hum Hindu hain*' (Say with pride that we are Hindus). Prior to that in 1985, the government's role in the Shah Bano case—where the Supreme Court ruling in a triple talaq case was overturned by the Congress government led by Rajiv Gandhi, by passing the *Muslim Women (Protection of Rights on Divorce) Act, 1986* in parliament, on the behest of Muslim clerics and conservative sections of Muslim society—sent wrong signals to the Hindu community. They began to believe that Muslims were above the law and even a Supreme Court judgment was not binding on them. That helped right wing Hindu organisations to whip up a frenzy against Muslims and in convincing people that Muslims are unreasonably appeased by the establishment.

Though this aggressive form of Hinduism was adopted by a minority of Hindus, that too in the northern and western parts of India, but they were enough in numbers to disrupt the precariously balanced equilibrium of peace and harmony. Religious or national identity doesn't always come alone but are mostly amalgamated with other aspects of one's identity. For example, the rise of the Shiv Sena in Maharashtra saw an ugly version of identity politics where a toxic cocktail of Hindu chauvinism, Marathi pride and nationalism was served to the unsuspecting public that resulted in attacks on Muslims, North Indians and hatred against Pakistani artists and sportsmen.

The ideas of Indian and Hindu identities, however, are different in eastern and southern parts of India. West Bengal, the biggest state in the eastern part of India, had been a citadel of communism and their perception of social division is mostly based on class divisions. Therefore, we rarely hear about Hindu–Muslim conflicts from that area. Another example is Bihar, where in the wake of the post-Ayodhya riots all over the country, the Hindus and the Muslims maintained complete harmony. Meet a modern day Bihari and he will emphasise more on his Bihari identity than his religious or any other identity.

In the south, people's identities are aligned more to their linguistic and regional identities than anything else. Therefore, a Tamilian or a Malayali is proud of their linguistic and cultural heritage, irrespective of their religious beliefs and that pride doesn't affect their association with their national identity.

The Hindu society is also divided on caste lines and the people at the bottom of the caste pyramid view their religious and national identities in terms of their social position. They are more aware of their caste identities than their religious identity. In short, there is no general trend and common thread which binds all Indian Hindus when it comes to the idea of identities.

The Largest Minority

During the run-up to the Indian general election of 2014, a Bihari politician, known for his hate speech and boastful proclamations, publicly announced that anyone opposing the election of Mr Narendra Modi, then Chief Minister of Gujarat, to the premiership was a traitor and should be sent to Pakistan. Obviously, his targets were non-Hindu voters, especially Muslims, and those Hindu voters who saw Mr Modi as a right wing Hindu leader whose electoral success might be detrimental to the integrity of this maddeningly diverse country. This was not the first time that a political leader had tried to associate the idea of national identity with support for a particular person or a particular event or a particular cricket team. In the past too, we had slogans like, 'India is Indira. Indira is India.' The game of cricket is still used to measure one's degree of patriotism, Muslims specially have to prove their national affinity time and again, by loudly proclaiming their undying support for the Indian cricket team. And what that politician said is not something new which happened in India, since the day India become free from British rule, Indian Muslims, especially north Indian Muslims, have to prove their national credentials time and again.

The unfortunate event of partition of the Indian subcontinent and the creation of Pakistan in 1947 was supposedly on the lines of religious identity. But, despite bloody communal riots on both sides of the border and subsequent cross-border migration, India was left with a sizeable Muslim population. In contrast to Jinnah, Nehru's vision of India was as a secular nation accepting its religious diversities. But, the leftover bitterness of the Hindu–Muslim conflicts of 1947 still haunts the nation and tries to disturb the solid foundation of the liberal ethos of the country. Even, in the 21st century the echoes of partition stories impact our country's social and political thoughts. And ordinary Indian Muslims find it difficult to answer the questions about their identities raised by the Hindu right-wingers.

The questions that are most commonly asked to an Indian Muslim are: 'Tell us what's more important to you, being an Indian, or being a Muslim?

If you had to decide between one or the other, which one would you choose?' Most of them find it very difficult to come up with a good answer. Many years ago Maulana Wahiddudin Khan, a famous Islamic scholar, had given the answer to this question in his celebrated journal *Ar-Risala*. According to him, a person can be both Muslim and Indian at the same time. If a person was born to Muslim parents, so he was a Muslim. In the same way, if he was born in India he was an Indian. In fact, in the precise moment of his birth he automatically acquired both identities. In other words, he tried to underline the fact that both national and religious identities are significant, explaining how a person is capable of belonging to multiple communities at the same time.

But not everyone would be convinced by the aforesaid answer. This is partly because of a misplaced notion that all Indian Muslims are culturally and socially the same. In actuality, Muslims are as diverse as their Hindu counterparts. Despite having a singular religious identity, they happen to follow different sects and sub-sects. Their languages and culture are maddeningly diverse. A Tamil Muslim doesn't have much in common with a Kashmiri Muslim. Go to rural areas in northern and eastern parts of India where Muslims are substantial in number, and you would be surprised to find the Muslim society, is divided along caste lines.

In 1970s and 1980s, a cricket match between India and Pakistan used to be a cause of social tension between Muslims and Hindus. A Hindu would presume that a Muslim would always support the Pakistani team and a Muslim would complain whatever he did, a Hindu would never believe that a Muslim would ever support the Indian team. In other words, the Indian and Pakistani teams were treated as a Hindu and a Muslim team respectively. But, it was also true that many Muslims in North India who had their relatives in Pakistan openly supported the Pakistani team and even burnt crackers when the Indian team lost to Pakistan.

Then in 1984, a lanky man from Hyderabad created some sort of a blitzkrieg with his bat by hitting three consecutive centuries in his first three matches in a test series against England. He was Mohammad Azharuddin, who later went to become the captain of the Indian team. With the ascent of the cricketing fortunes of Azhar, the number of Muslims supporting Pakistan dipped and a majority of Hindus started to believe that an Indian Muslim can be a fan of the Indian cricket team. Then the rise of Irfan

Pathan, Yusuf Pathan, Mohammad Kaif and Zaheer Khan gave them new heroes and role models.

The advancement in education and improvement in social indicators also made Indian Muslims assert their Indian-ness. Even the right wing Muslim organisations began to lay claim on patriotism citing the examples of Brigadier Usman and Lance Naik Abdul Hameed, who laid down their lives while fighting against India's arch enemy Pakistan.

Things took an ugly turn when in 1992, a disputed mosque was demolished by a frenzied mob. This event left a permanent scar on the psyche of the Muslim community and then the 1993 riot happened in Mumbai, a city which was cosmopolitan in the real sense and had not seen any communal conflict during the previous 100 years. The Congress government came out of inertia only after hundreds of people were already dead in the carnage. The commission set up by them gave a report indicting many politicians and police officers for fanning the riot and shirking their responsibilities but no action was taken. Almost 10 years later, the Gujarat riots reinforced the perception among a majority of Muslims that they had been denied justice time and again, also the politicians responsible for their miseries would never be punished. Instead, their direct and indirect involvement in the violence against Muslims became some sort of political qualification for them. The disenchantment among Muslim youth provided a good opportunity to anti-national forces to recruit them and use them against India.

The opposition to the hangings of Afzal Guru or Yaqoob Memon from various Muslim organisations was an outcome of loss of faith in the justice system of the country. It was of course not a support for anti-national activities but support for the persons who had been wronged by the powers that be. They believed that justice was not done to these two Muslim men. Wherever Muslims believed that an individual was really involved in terrorism or anti-national activities, the communities not only distanced themselves from those persons but also condemned their acts in the harshest terms. For example, Mumbai's Muslims denied Ajmal Kasab burial in their graveyard. .

The thumping majority of the right wing Bharatiya Janata Party alienated the Muslims further as they began to see the new government as some sort of existential threat for them. The opposition party in order to win over the minority voters had also been involved in fear mongering. But after ascending to power, Prime Minister Narendra Modi spoke in a tone which was reassuring, and many Muslims began to believe that all the communal rhetoric during the election would come to an end and the new dispensation would take care of all Indians. The prime minister more or less kept his promises by not raising communal issues but the minions in his team did not. First 'Love Jihad' and 'Ghar Wapsi' and then the beef ban and raking of other communal issues made the minorities suspect the real motives of the current government. They began to feel that there are discreet attempts to turn India into a Hindu nation.

Despite the changed political scenario, today's Muslims have no doubt about their identities. They see themselves as Indian only and ready to take part in the progress of the country, eager to partake in the fruits of development. The stories unfolding in Pakistan have also made them realise that Mohammad Ali Jinnah's idea to carve out a homeland for Muslims from British India was a big mistake. They are eager to educate themselves and make themselves capable of competing for the opportunities available.

The Future

The biggest question is whether an individual Indian, Hindu or Muslim or anyone else, will be allowed to do what he wants to do in the charged political, social, and economic environment of 21st-century India or he has to carry the baggage of collective identity as imagined by the extremist elements of his or her community. It is frightening to see that India is tending towards jingoism and communalism despite its youthfulness and modernity.

One should remember that a major chunk of Indians live below the poverty line and have little access to proper sanitation, health or education. They must be brought into the mainstream and made to believe that they are as much part of this country as others are. Otherwise, they are prone to incitement by every kind of extremist forces.

The rise of Islamic State and similar terror philosophies using Islam has sent the warning signal across the world and India should be careful that these monsters with their ideology of hate and violence should not extend their reach across India. Vigilance by the intelligence agencies alone is not enough to ensure this. The government has to clamp down on individuals and organisations which are in the business of spreading hatred across the communities including right wing Hindu organisations. The message from the present government should go those people and organisations that their sinister plan to disturb the harmony of the country will not be accepted. The message should especially go to those individuals or organisations, which see themselves as ideologically close to the ruling party.

Members of the Muslim community should also remind themselves that radicalism is not the solution to their problems. If any injustice has been done to them, they should fight with the establishment within the democratic framework of the country. To serve the broad-aimed 'Idea of India', the Hindu community should look at the shared cultural heritage of India. With such collective efforts, the equilibrium will always be maintained in the social sphere.

The best thing about India is that a large chunk of our population, Hindus, Muslims and others, think that violence and hatred will take our country nowhere and peace and reconciliation is the only way for the nation to prosper.

The Final Word

To preserve the idea of India which was shaped by Mahatma Gandhi and Jawaharlal Lal Nehru's ideas of secularism and inclusiveness, both Hindus and Muslims have to come forward, shed their differences and strike a reconciliatory note by discovering a new ethos which is not based on identity politics. They have to stop looking at history from the lenses coloured with religious prejudices and have to accept India as a modern country, created or recreated in 1947 and anyone who lived or was born in this country post-Independence is an Indian, irrespective of his other identities.

Let us hope this toxic cocktail of so-called modernity, corruption, crony capitalism, pseudo-secularism and religious fundamentalism in India makes way, in the next couple of decades, for a more equitable and just society where human values and honesty are cherished as the greatest of virtues and where talents and merit are rewarded.

If that happens, India with a huge pool of natural and human resources, will emerge as a real superpower, which will be capable enough to maintain sanity on its home turf and beyond its borders. As 'identities' can be played in more vicious ways, it is time to look back on our own basic identity that was never bereft of humanity and progressivism. Let us reclaim our basic human qualities and shun the 'insanity' around us.

Indian Cinema: Forever in Search of its Golden Era

Pallavi Rebbapragada

When God speaks to people in their heads, does he do it in Amitabh Bachchan's voice, who is as—if not more—omnipresent? When goal posts seem unreachable, do they picture Shah Rukh Khan as coach Kabir Khan from *Chak de India* (2007), urging them to stand up and snatch their moments from all those who didn't believe in them. Is it possible that they take him seriously because he too walked into an empire as a commoner and rose to become its king? Nawazuddin Siddiqui is a lesson that a heartland-bred man, largely viewed as cheap labour in big bustling cities, has as much 'swag' to change the way a country entertains itself. As Phaizal in *Gangs of Wasseypur* I & II (2012), when he seeks a bloody revenge on the man who destroyed his forefathers, a raw rural and yet relatable energy is invoked. Vidya Balan, who holds a masters' degree in Sociology portrays what society perceives as an ideal woman in *Parineeta* (2005) and even what is considered its filthy opposite in *The Dirty Picture* (2011). With an effortless intelligence, she chooses to portray complex characters with the kind of strength women keep searching for everywhere, except within. Priyanka Chopra convinces the audience too; her broad smile is as inspiring when it's pretending to be a 19-year-old autistic Jhilmil in *Barfi* (2012) as it is when she sings about feeling 'exotic' with Pitbull and or just being herself in a shimmery plunging gown at a formal dinner at the White House. The abundance of her in the media is proof enough that self-belief has an ambassadorial capacity to it. That is Indian cinema today. In the industry that makes between 1,500 and 2,000 movies a year and grosses over $2 billion a year at the box-office, there's greater consciousness that actors are real people, just making honest and elaborate attempts to portray other real people.

On one side, the belief that stars didn't fall from the skies has set in; on the other hand, even if they're lying on the ground they are still brighter and shinier. One industry that is capitalising on the precarious new nature of stardom is that of advertising. The media and entertainment market in India is pegged at Rs 60,000 crore, of which advertising and promotion contribute roughly half and of this Rs 30,000 crore, celebrity endorsements account for nearly 10 per cent. A serious wave of campaign branding started with the Ministry of Tourism's Incredible India campaign in which Aamir Khan was seen urging Indians to be sensitive towards tourists—with simple do's and don'ts like keeping cities clean and cultivating a faithful friendliness towards international visitors. A brand of course correction has been styled by Khan, who televised social problems in his show *Satyamev Jayate* and stars in movies like *3 Idiots* (2009) that raised consciousness about the increasing social expectations from engineering students and and *PK* (2014) that questioned the purpose of outdated religious dogmas. It is essentially the same reformative voice that transcends through make-believe cinema reels and reality television. If Shilpa Shetty is seen stretching on yoga mats in neon spandex, endorsing her support for the Modi government's emphasis on reviving yoga as a way of life, Hrithik Roshan in Mumbai, Ravi Kishan in Bihar and Nagarjuna in Hyderabad were seen sweeping the streets in support of the 'Swachh Bharat Abhiyan'. Whether they are reinstating their presence in the media or earning goodwill points, the new norm is that celebrities ought to be socially responsible and till they are in the limelight, must also be exemplary in their ways.

One reason for this is greater visibility and documentation of their independent opinions, not necessarily about their films. From Sonam Kapoor's Instagram handle to Karan Johar's Twitter account, cinematic nuances are a mere drop of what is being generously dispensed. From hasty decision-making about attire to a borderline sexist/racist remark that is subjected to scrutiny; even their romantic failures aren't merely gossip, because the average young Indian is possibly going through similar situations. If open letters expose their humanness, motivational videos where they speak of rejection, loss and other more easily understandable truths make that humanness glorious. Either way, the spotlight is always on them and they are ordinarily and intriguingly next-door.

Along the journey towards realism in movie-making, two ends of the same road—one critical, the other commercial—came closer. When Anurag

Kashyap made *Dev D* in 2009 and showed a girl dragging a mattress into Punjab's fields so that she could comfortably make love, and also sending her lover nude pictures of herself, it struck a chord with a young India that's modernising alongside hypocrisies big and small. This started a trend of critical-commercial hits.

At an earlier time in Indian cinema, it was possible that the audience realised a movie's brilliance once it was off the screens. Case in point: *Jaane Bhi Do Yaaron* (1983), a National Film Development Corporation of India film that was very unlike the Bollywood of its time. It was made by a bunch of film enthusiasts on a shoe-string budget (Rs 7 lakh roughly), a pittance compared to what big banners like Subash Ghai's Mukta Arts or Yash Chopra's Yash Raj Films were splurging on theirs. Cathartically, it commented on the helplessness of the masses against a state scarred by corruption and bribery. Today, the intent behind such art-in-motion is more common. One reason for this could be the expansion of critical debates around each movie. Earlier, a designated review column in newsprint or a television show—conferring one to three stars—was all that the reader consumed before the movie, if at all. Today, each new release comes under several scanners for the message it is sending. In 2014, Vishal Bharadwaj made *Haider* tell the story of all those seeking closure on the disappearance of their loved ones from the Kashmir Valley and in the same year, Vikas Bahl's *Queen* showed a young girl naively distancing herself from the pain of being dumped hours before her wedding. In *Queen*, the protagonist Rani decides to go on her honeymoon alone and her experiences with the people she meets lend her a sweet, simple, yet very irrevocable belief that happiness isn't the conventional presumption of it. The clarity with which women's issues are being addressed is made of crystal, a rainbow of shades flowing from it. In Sanjay Leela Bhansali's period film *Bajirao Mastani* (2015), the character of Kaashi Bai was a complete devotee of her husband. But, after he takes a mistress, she urges him to never enter her room. In *Piku* (2015), a 30-something girl played guardian to her ill, ageing father, who in turn advised her not to get married and find men to occasionally satisfy her instead; a mature reorientation towards casual sex. *Daawat-e-Ishq* (2014) juxtaposed a love for biryani and kebabs against the social problem of dowry in cities like Hyderabad and Lucknow. Tastefully, a playful Gulrez sets out with her clueless-helpless father to con the next family who asks her for dowry and run away to America to fulfill her dreams at their cost. Innovative ways to fight a system are what women in cinema are holding onto. In 2010, *Turning 30* told the story of Naina. Like every other urban woman, she too is plagued by the fear of turning 30, even as her life is still a tussle between nursing a broken heart and managing tough and unreasonable bosses. She has two close friends, one denying her husband's affair and another who experiences the trauma of heartbreak in her lesbian affair. The pain painted in the movie isn't abstract and arises from very specifically universal themes.

Bollywood has moved away from song-and-dance around trees and waterfalls; the Govindas and Mandakinis of the late 20th century have to rethink their game. But, the path away from big-budget celebrations in palatial homes and Swiss valleys can't lead India to a dull humid kind of silence. There's a difference between theatre and cinema and like Munna Bhai made Gandhigiri mainstream by lending a cool, casual vibe to it, the artistic strength in cinema too needs to be repackaged for the masses.

In 2008, Dibakar Banerjee gave the world a black comedy in the form of *Oye Lucky Lucky Oye!* In the film, Banerjee differentiates between show and tell. He adopts the former to share a story of an unusual conman who battles his own inadequately parented past by stealing his way through life. The noir filters inside Banerjee's brain became visible in the way he made the protagonist steal happy photo frames from people's drawing rooms and hang it in his own; there's a dark charm in staring at lives that seem happier than one's own, it is both hatred and a casual attraction towards some degree of loss (and Facebook is all about this). The music featured quirky Punjabi rap with lines like '*Odi kothi sector chaar*' (she owns a bungalow in Chandigarh's sector four) and '*Jaati Kanede Maasi Kol*' (she visits her aunt in Canada). Interestingly, the film also returned north Indian folk gems like *Enna Akhiyaan* and *Tu Raja Ki Raj Dulari* to public memory. Filmmakers are now realising the merit in representing India's many musical moods.

Not just regional music, but regional cinema too is making its way into Bollywood. Cable providers thrive on dubbed regional fare. Satellite rights of the film that would have sold for a little less than Rs 10 lakh a decade ago, now go for a minimum of Rs 1-2 crore. Data from the Broadcast Audience Research Council India (BARC) for June 2016 across the top movie channels like Sony Max, Star Gold and Zee Cinema shows at least one regional film features among the top five programmes in the Hindi movies category every week. This includes films like *Baahubali, Bengal Tiger, The Return Of Rebel* and

Kanchana: Muni 2. Rajinikanth, a 70mm demigod, with his recent release *Kabali*, hit nearly 1,000 screens in North India. The game could have been bigger but the country is under-screened. As the multiplex industry sees it, cinema is now about: lights, camera, acquisition.

Mexican multiplex chain Cinepolis is gearing up to invest Rs 400 crore to open 160 cinema screens in 60 Indian cities by the end of 2017. India is the second largest market for Cinepolis after Mexico. The fourth-largest cinema exhibitor in the country has entered into a strategic alliance with Rathi Group of Cinemas for operation of 10 single screen theatres. These theatres will be in Nagpur, Raipur, Bhilai, Durg, Akola, Yavatmal, Paratwada and Amravati.

Inox Leisure, the second-largest cinema exhibitor in the country after PVR, will be spending Rs 800 crores in the next 3-4 years to add 312 screens. Meanwhile, Carnival Cinemas, a part of the Mumbai-based Carnival Group, plans to scale up its presence in tier II and III cities and add 700 screens by March 2018 to reach a target of 1,000. The investment is estimated to be around Rs 850 to 900 crore and the company is looking at Madhya Pradesh, Bihar, Jharkhand, Uttar Pradesh, Punjab, Rajasthan and the North East. At the root of all expansion rests the mammoth commercial success of movies. Bollywood has upgraded from Rs 100 crore to Rs 200 crore and this affects multiplexes positively. Typically, a Rs 100 crore film runs for 5 to 6 weeks, a 200 crore film goes on for 8 to 10 weeks, and these films keep the theatres packed even on weekdays. In the past few years, the distribution game has corporatised. Producers are now dealing directly with major multiplex companies for distribution deals, while single-screen theatres continue to be handled by individual distributors. Multiplex companies now benefit from control over distribution surpluses. The growth of regional cinema also triggers multiplex expansion. In tier II and tier III cities, the footfall for vernacular cinema is more than 50 per cent higher than Hindi or English movies.

In 2016, *Sultan* became Salman Khan's 10th film to enter the Rs 100 crore club. These movies were mind-bendingly cheerful mood lifters, if not more. His kind of cinema may not appeal to all, but it certainly floats on hype and sails through. A little before Sultan's worldwide release, Razi Muhammad's *Velutha Rathrikal* (2016), was screened at the 16th edition of the New York Film Festival. This reinterprets Dostoevesky's *White Nights* in an alternate gender context. The latter may not have earned a fortune, but managed to find an audience who cares about alternate cinema. Shaunak Sen's *Cities of Sleep*

(2015), which awakens the viewer's consciousness to how the homeless sleep in Delhi, Rinku Kalsy's *For the Love of a Man* (2015), based on ardent fans of Rajnikanth, have fought and won their silent wars. Art isn't always escapism in exchange for money. A greater democratisation of content is visible from the popularity of short films on YouTube, like Devashish Makhija's *El'ayichi* (2015) and Sujoy Ghosh's *Ahalya* (2015). The former had 366,542 views as on 15 July 2016 and the latter 5,890,665 views on the same date.

Even the reality that is a biopic, which was earlier about giving the audience a peek into the life of public figures like Gandhi and Bose, has started weaving gripping human tales around lesser-known heroes. The bravery of a young flight attendant Neerja Bhanot (Sonam Kapoor) who died while saving lives during the hijacking of a Pan Am flight in Karachi in 1986 has been shown in *Neerja* (2016). *Paan Singh Tomar*, starring Irrfan Khan depicted the life of a steeplechase runner who represented India at the 1958 Asian Games in Tokyo and was later forced to become a bandit in the eponymously-titled work. Even period cinema, which was earlier sworn to Mughal splendour or told whatever was recorded in partition scholarship, has diversified. *Bombay Velvet* (2015) brought back a Bombay of the 1960s with its run-down jazz bars, where the aesthetic of fedoras, silk-gloves and fascinators was shown. *Detective Byomkesh Bakshy*! (2015) detailed the Calcutta of the 1940s right down to the last poster on the tram depicting a city where femme fatales and oriental gangsters were on the loose. Such diversification into more advanced eras of the past allows the script writer to make interesting creative departures.

If *Band Baaja Baaraat*'s (2010) Shruti Kakkar played by Anushka Sharma inspired a generation seeking solace in enterprise; *Vicky Donor*'s (2012) Vicky played by Ayushmann Khurrana made an issue like sperm donation a subject so commonplace that a family could discuss it casually; *Rocket Singh* (2009) has a turbaned Ranbir Kapoor fighting his way out of mediocrity with his unconventional management strategies that continue to solve corporate India's daily dilemmas.

The export quality of movies for NRI audiences has been taken very seriously lately. *Salaam Namaste* (2005) took a young couple far away from the baggage of large families and the predictability of marriage and introduced the concept of live-in relationships into mainstream Bollywood. *Love Aaj Kal* (2009) romanticised long-distance relationships that break up due to career choices, with a fresh kind of melancholy. Weaving a powerful sentiment around a city or a town is what Bollywood is getting right. If *Masaan* (2015) took viewers into the lives of those who work in the cremation grounds of Benares, *Kahaani* (2012) followed the struggle of a woman walking the streets of Kolkata in search of her lost husband. Places in India —through accents, food, festivals, streets and transport—are being graphically refreshed in memory. Such movies don't lie by playing up the flashy and suitably clean parts of an area. They show every bit of it—from open wiring to splatters of *paan*-stained spit—and make the people want it for what it is.

Post the gangster-era of dark and murky Ram Gopal Varma films where guns, cuss words and smoke resided, alternate cinema met with commercial success in the case of *Dev D* that captures the sexual mess of Indians that they'd never talk about. Anurag Kashyap has ever since led a revolution of mainstreaming alternate expression, such as in *Gulaal* (2009) where student politics is laid bare and *Black Friday* (2007) that put the conspirators behind the Bombay blasts under the scanner, one dialogue at a time.

The frequency of bold cinema at the box office has met with adversities. *Black Friday* was banned by the Censor Board due to reasons purely political and nearly nine years later, another movie co-produced by Kashyap met with a similar fate. In 2016, under Pahlaj Nihalani's chairmanship, the Central Board of Film Certification (CBFC) ordered 89 cuts on *Udta Punjab*, especially on the references to Punjab and its politics. The opening dialogue in the trailer is 'Punjab youth is in drug addict [sic], if this is not stopped, Punjab will soon become like Mexico', where cartels, trafficking and mafia are key national concerns. Taking a dig at Nihalani's oligarchic ways, Kashyap tweeted 'I always wondered what it felt like to live in North Korea…*Ab to plane pakadney ki bhi zaroorat nahin*….' He dragged the censor board to the Bombay High Court and demanded a copy of the order passed by the censor board's review committee on 3 May 2016. The film was finally released with one cut and three disclaimers.

What became clear through the incident is that if film is cinematic exaggeration, then investigative reports on the drug crisis that are now being front-paged more than ever, too must've been planted and peddled by the opposition? Hard news about the police cracking down on drug abuse victims, seizures of thousands of kilograms of poppy husk from police districts, deaths of those under trial and the rising voices of NGOs working towards relief was running parallel to opinions and discussions on a piece of cinema. It was also a curious case of publicity, at once negative and positive. As the Censor Board is doing its bit to curtail cinematic freedom, a string of short films that have broken and fallen on the surface of the Internet are determined to expose uncomfortable hypocrisies matter-of-factly.

Even ordinariness evolves. In 1994, *Hum Aapke Hain Koun* saw plenty of box-office success. The plot, if there was any, involved an ultra-rich family that owns a cricket field and a swimming pool, counting its blessings—a marriage and a birth—and mourning the death of a young daughter-in-law. What makes a society attracted to such a cheerful packaging of banality? Is it boredom or collective frustration? Art may seem simple, but the perception of it is mysterious. The repetition of such fortune for a film of such characteristics doesn't seem possible because the audience isn't singular in taste and is easily bored. Today's Bollywood is moving away from Rajshri's selectively unreal and stopping shortly before Madhur Bhandarkar's painfully real.

There are many kinds of cinemas. Mostly, there are three kinds of cinemas. One is the cinema of internet trivia and memes that is cooked, shared and consumed each day. The other is the cinema of news that intellectualises and politicises and raises awareness about issues like censorship and the dangerous nonchalance of misogyny, gun violence and other anathemas of the time. The third is the cinema that lives on in hand-painted images of Sunny Deol, Aamir Khan and Aishwarya Rai at juice shops and salons and in dialogues from yesteryear that still serve as legitimate references. These celebrities have grown older than the arty versions of them, but they thrive on in memories and symbols signifying both nothing and everything. Indian cinema isn't just corresponding to the changing socio-cultural and economic reality of its country; it is also preceding it in a way that it's hard to tell which came first.

Money and Mindsets: Sports in India

Shamya Dasgupta

Sports in India is clearly divided between cricket and 'other sports'. Not unlike, say, Brazil, where football has utterly dominated the nation's consciousness. But football is a global sport, a sport for and of the masses. It's funny how cricket, with its elite origins, and its association with the British Raj, has found a home in the Indian subcontinent. But it has, and how—'an Indian game accidentally discovered by the British', Ashis Nandy called it in his *The Tao of Cricket*.

It hasn't always been this way. Truth be told, cricket still isn't a truly national game. Take India's northeast, or large belts in Chhattisgarh, Jharkhand, and Madhya Pradesh, or chunks of Rajasthan and Gujarat, the mountainous tracts of Himachal Pradesh, and Jammu & Kashmir, the coastal states of Goa and Kerala, the islands in the Arabian Sea and the Bay of Bengal, and you'll realise how much of India has little or nothing to do with cricket.

Then again, the parts that follow the sport intensely form a significant chunk. More crucially, a big part of the commercial revenue in the field of sports is generated in—and goes to—cricket. To repeat, *it wasn't always so.* Before and after 1947, cricket jostled with hockey or football for national attention. Cricket's 'elite' status meant that the big cities of Mumbai, Calcutta, Delhi, and Madras were its primary playing fields, with Bangalore, Hyderabad, and Pune in the picture too. Prior to Independence, and for a while afterwards, the rich and royal played a big part in making the game popular—they were the patrons, turning out in whites themselves, arranging tournaments and financing the prominent players of the time. The works of Ramachandra Guha, Boria Majumdar, Mihir Bose and other historians of the sport have detailed those times and the gradual change in the game. Suffice it to say that cricket was played by (a) the rich, (b) the urban, and (c) the extremely talented, who managed to impress, either by playing for the princes and nawabs or at the Pentangular and other such tournaments in Mumbai.

Cut to 2011, and the winning Indian team at the World Cup had a Rajput from Ranchi as its captain. There were players in that team from New Delhi and Mumbai, of course, but also from Ghaziabad, Kothamangalam, Ikhar, Shrirampur, Najafgarh, and Aligarh—how did that come to pass?

There are many attempts to explain how and why India became such a cricket-obsessed nation—the most compelling of them, to my mind, being that the decline of hockey in the 1970s and the Indian cricket team's World Cup win in 1983 were decisive factors.

Back in 1964, when India won the seventh of their eight gold medals in hockey at the Olympic Games, the team was so dominant that other teams were practically competing to lose to India in the final. The World Cup was quite a different story—the only time India won was in 1975, in the third edition of the tournament. That was also the last significant victory at the highest level by the Indian hockey team; the Olympic gold in 1980 blighted by the absence of many of the top nations, who boycotted the event because it was held in Moscow in protest against the Russian military presence in Afghanistan.

After 1975, hockey slid down the pecking order. Key among the reasons for the decline were (a) loss of the next generation of players to militancy in Punjab, the most important centre for the sport in India, and (b) the move away from turf to synthetic surfaces. Due to a combination of reluctance and apathy, and lack of foresight as well as financials (and, of course, politics) on the part of the administrators, Indian hockey did not adapt quickly enough. India ruled the sport chiefly because of the players' dribbling skills, something the slower grass fields facilitated. Synthetic grounds, made of AstroTurf, were better suited to speed and strength and long passes—teams from Europe and Australia went up the ladder, and, over the years, India and Pakistan fell so much that when the Indian team failed to qualify for the 2008 Beijing Olympic Games, not many people even noticed.

By then, of course, India had become champions of the brand new Twenty20 format of cricket—in 2007.

Now, whether it's the subject of hockey, cricket, or even of sport in general, in India there is a 'Before 1983' and 'After 1983'.

Before 1983, Bombay was the centre of cricket in the country. There was not much money in playing for the Indian team, but the two 1971 wins under Ajit Wadekar in the West Indies and in England, and Sunil Gavaskar's rise had attracted eyeballs. It wasn't as if India didn't have great cricketers before Gavaskar. Lala Amarnath and CK Nayudu, Mohammad Nissar and Amar Singh, Vijay Hazare and Vijay Merchant, Vinoo Mankad and Dilip Sardesai, Vijay Manjrekar and Subhash Gupte, M.A.K. Pataudi, and B.S. Chandrasekhar, Bishan Singh Bedi, Erapalli Prasanna and S. Venkataraghavan...there have been big-name players over the years. Yet, the national team was, at best, losers abroad and achievers of draws at home—before 1971.

That was also the year that India's first true-blue superstar broke onto the scene—Gavaskar. India was still an average cricketing country. England and Australia ran the show. West Indies had already emerged as the supreme performers, the world-beaters. South Africa may or may not have been a force, we'll never know. India, Pakistan, and New Zealand were the outsiders. To be fair, Pakistan had made a bigger splash internationally than India, before we came to 1983.

The captain of the Indian team in 1983 was a 24-year-old buck-toothed, Punjabi/Hindi-speaking Jat from Chandigarh. Kapil Dev had, since starting out in 1979, made a name for himself as one of the premier all-rounders of the game, but he wasn't Imran Khan or Ian Botham. And the team he led had gone and lost against a rag-tag bunch of amateur cricketers—farmers and salesmen—going under the name of Minor Counties Select XI, in the lead-up to that 1983 World Cup in England. In both the 1975 and 1979 World Cups, India had been dismal, and there was no doubt 1983 would be the same. Except, it was not.

That changed everything. The story, possibly apocryphal, is that N.K.P. Salve, the boss of the Indian cricket board at the time of the World Cup, was denied a handful of tickets he had asked the authorities for at Lord's for the final. In somewhat Bollywood-ish fashion, he swore revenge, and thus was planted the seeds that led to the 1987 World Cup being hosted in the Indian subcontinent. Then, chiefly courtesy the machinations of Inderjit Singh Bindra and Jagmohan Dalmiya, the power centre (read financial hub) of cricket shifted Indiawards.

It started with small TV deals, long-term arrangements with sponsors—ITC to start with and then Sahara and Star—and the projection of top-drawer

Indian cricketers as superstars. The public lapped it up. Between 1983 and 1987, India had also won the World Championship of Cricket in Australia, a mini-World Cup of sorts, and here, for star-crazed India, were a group of boys who were, truly, world champions.

Hockey was fading, Viswanathan Anand was some way away. We liked thinking of Vijay Amritraj as the 'A' in the ABC of tennis, with Bjorn Borg and Jimmy Connors but he was, in truth, 'P' in that pecking order—No. 16 in the world is as good as he ever got. P.T. Usha too was some years away and, in any case, she ruled Asia not the world. And Michael Ferreira was a champion in a sport few cared for, at least at the time.

Yes, cricket was a small sport. It still is, limited to a handful of top-performing nations and spreading, in fits and starts, to other parts of the world where, again, it's the expatriates from the subcontinent who do most of the organising and playing.

As cricket in India rose, Sachin Tendulkar appeared on the scene, taking the buzz around the sport to a whole new level. Tendulkar was a true middle-class hero who went out and dominated the world, his short stature adding to the David vs Goliath imagery. And Tendulkar meant money. For the Board of Control for Cricket in India (BCCI). For TV stations. For sponsors on the lookout for someone to sell their products. Match fixing hit cricket in the late 1990s—around the middle of Tendulkar's 24-year-long career. It has continued, but people have moved on. Cricket survived, nay thrived. Indian Premier League (IPL) came in 2008 then; much more cricket, much more money. That, briefly, is how we got here, to a time when cricket drives large parts of India. *Bollywood and cricket*, say people from beyond our shores—cinema of the sort they haven't seen anywhere and a sport they are largely clueless about.

And the *other sports*—what happened to them?

Well, truth be told, mainstream India is not culturally aligned to sport. It is not in our everyday horizon, and it has never been seen as a viable career alternative, unless we talk of the people with money, who can play tennis, or become shooters, or golfers. Cricket is an exception. Yet, against the odds, Indians haven't done too badly in non-cricket disciplines over the years.

'A billion people and so few Olympic medals,' the media moans every four years. That's when India wakes up to the existence of sports like boxing, wrestling, shooting, weightlifting, badminton and gymnastics for a couple of weeks. But, except for a spot of armchair opinionising and, these days, Facebook updating, we simply don't care.

That's one part—social and cultural indifference.

Next, the bigger issue: administrative apathy. Successive governments have done precious little for Indian sports. Mani Shankar Aiyar, the Union Minister for Youth Affairs and Sports between 2006 and 2009, was the only one to actually call his appointment a punishment posting, but others before and after him—with the exception of Ajay Maken and the well-intentioned but ineffective Sunil Dutt—have looked at the job no differently. Add to that the fact that politicians of all hues helm the major sports federations. Think back only to the shambolic Commonwealth Games of 2010 to understand what that means for Indian sport. All of this is true from 1947 onwards. Indian sportspersons, when they do well, do well in spite of the system not because of it—a cliché but undeniably true.

The people who run these sports blame cricket for cornering all the sponsorship money. The fact is, money will go where returns are assured. Cricket, run by a non-governmental body, has managed to crack the code. And the people who put in the money have, over the years, got that money back. That's why every inch of every player's kit has a sticker on it and hoardings dot cricket grounds for international and IPL matches.

It is a hard question—will performance follow the money? Should the moneybags put the big bucks in to stimulate the system? Organisations like the Mittal Champions Trust and Olympic Gold Quest have done some good work in recent years, doing what the federations should have been doing: getting sponsors to put in money and using that money to support top-notch athletes (along with a big focus on the lower levels), helping them train and prepare. There's hope there, but it's something the sports ministry and its affiliates should be doing.

Speaking of the government, there is one important role it does play.

A child from a low-income household with talent in a sport might just find himself or herself sent off to the nearest government sports coaching centre. A far cry from what that child would have been told in a middle-class home. Then, step by step by step, the youngster becomes an athlete. Not to become the best in the world or compete with Usain Bolt, but to land a sports-quota job in one of the many public-sector setups. The family is secure. The athlete has served his/her purpose. India's medals tally at the Olympics is stuck where it was.

There is no gain in quizzing the wisdom of the sports quota, the incentive it gives players to compete. Yet, once they have reached a certain level of excellence, what structures exists to boost them to the next one?

Things have been a little different in more recent years. The rise of the Indian boxing contingent coincided with the emergence of a number of world-class shooters and the sustained top-drawer performance of a number of wrestlers. These were the athletes that brought home six Olympic medals in 2012 as against seven individual medals in the 22 Olympic Games appearances before London—Sushil Kumar, the wrestler, a part of both honour lists.

Away from the Olympics, too, shuttlers like Saina Nehwal and P.V. Sindhu, a number of chess players (led by Anand, India has over 30 grandmasters now), the tennis players (Leander Paes is still winning the occasional Grand Slam doubles title and Sania Mirza recently became the World No. 1 women's doubles player), stalwarts like Pankaj Advani and others have done their bit to keep India on the map. Again, despite the system, not because of it.

I spoke at length to Abhinav Bindra on this subject. India's only individual gold medallist at the Olympic Games, Bindra has often spoken out against the sports administration in the country, and is a classic example of someone who has risen to the top by shunning all federation help. That he is from a wealthy family, of course, gives him an advantage others can only dream of.

That said, here's Bindra summing up the situation:

> We need world-class sportspersons and world-class administrators—it has to go hand in hand. We have to leave politics out of sport. The running of sport has to be done with the point of view that the athlete is the priority. The athlete is supreme, his interest is supreme; everything else is secondary. I am sure there is politics everywhere around the world. It happens. But what also happens is that the athlete remains the priority. And, listen, sports administration is hard work. If you want to do it well, it takes a lot of work. You have to give your athletes the best possible chance to do well at a given event. In our country, people with no idea about sport take decisions about the careers of athletes.

Look at the Indian boxing story to understand this. A series of unfortunate incidents, all handcrafted by the people who run the sport, led to the Indian Boxing Federation being blacklisted by the international governing body.

The nonsense went on for well over four years, and a resolution of sorts was reached after the 2016 Rio de Janeiro Olympics had gone, with little change in the goings-on here in India. And here we are talking about a sport that was on the rise, one where India was bringing home the medals on a pretty regular basis. Did you sign any petitions on *Change.org* about this?

On the other hand, the boxing story is also proof of what could happen if politicians had the right intentions. Haryana, which has emerged as the pre-eminent centre for the sport over the past decade, has managed to make becoming professional athletes lucrative. Infrastructure in towns and cities has been put in place, achievements are rewarded, job security has been provided—the athletes can actually focus on being the best. The results speak of it too, especially in boxing but also in other sports: athletes from the state won almost 40 per cent of India's 101 medals at the 2010 Commonwealth Games in New Delhi. Something must be right there.

To return to cricket, yes, it is the No. 1 sport in India, and that's because, despite all their faults and politicking and alleged corruption, the BCCI runs the sport professionally, takes care of its players, ensures games take place across the country, around the year, and across age levels. It has the money and the performances. Most importantly, fans of the sport haven't given up on either the BCCI or the national cricket team, even if their support for the sport can be called into question in view of the empty stands for non-glamorous domestic matches.

Is there a way to fix the system for non-cricket sports too then? Of the many proposals and theories going around sporting circles, the most workable ones call for athletes to be put in charge. No, it's not a cure-all, certainly not; there are enough instances in sporting history, in India and beyond, to prove that athletes are as corruptible as the next person.

But athletes bring with them credibility, because they intimately understand the needs of the game. And they bring with them accountability, because they are tied to the ecosystem, the community of that sport. The Karnataka State Cricket Association, where Anil Kumble, Javagal Srinath, and other prominent cricketers worked to promote the sport and improve the infrastructure in their short tenure, is a case in point. Olympic Gold Quest is also manned by prominent former athletes—it was they who stepped in when, before the London Olympics, M.C. Mary Kom was dissatisfied with the facilities at the National Institute of Sports in Patiala, and got for her

Charles Atkinson, the revered British boxing coach, and arranged for her to train in Pune. The result of that focus was an Olympic bronze medal.

Athletes, it stands to reason, will put athletes first. At the very least, they will know what sportspersons need to perform at their best, and that could be a start. In cricket too, even if the BCCI's work has been impressive in many ways, more cricketers in the top management can only help. The Karnataka story is proof of that.

Caught in the mix is another interesting development, true of the last four–five years: the emergence of leagues in a wide variety of sports, mostly based on the model of the IPL, which started in 2008. Once the IPL took off, and became successful with its combination of glamour, money, action, stars—and *Cricket and Bollywood*—it gave people something to think about. And thus was born a horde of wannabes: some with an eye at either a quick buck by putting together a league of IPL proportions with another sport, others putting in a genuine effort to push another sport to the forefront by, of course, putting together a league of IPL proportions.

Of the multitude of leagues, some have become successful, others less so, some sank without a trace. As such, the leagues that became successful stitched their plans around the obvious—city-based franchises, big-ticket stars—and the innovative. The Pro Kabaddi League is the best example of thinking outside the box, pulling out a sport with little or no traditional TV appeal, packaging it smartly and throwing it in the faces of unsuspecting viewers, who lapped it up.

Does the mushrooming of these leagues have cricket, and the BCCI, to thank for showing the way? I think so. Of course, the idea of the IPL, as confessed by the people who made it happen—Messrs Lalit Modi and others—was based on the English Premiership model (with a liberal dose of Indian-ness), and, again, it was the Indian Cricket League (ICL) that was the first to walk the path, before the IPL came into being. That the BCCI flexed their not-insignificant muscles and killed the ICL off is a story irrelevant to this discussion, but it was the ICL first and then the IPL that showed the way, and 'other sports' followed.

Purists don't like the IPL, and there's a good chance they won't like some of the things the other leagues have–except that unlike T20s, the other sports are single-format sports and there has been no tampering with the game itself. But the fact that these 'premier' leagues have created a buzz is undeniable.

They have helped popularise sports—including football—that weren't really the most popular around our country. They have, much like the IPL, helped the players, at least some of them, get richer. And they have created a legion of fans.

Elsewhere, in many urban parts of the country, distance running has caught on as the next cool lifestyle choice, followed some distance away by distance cycling. None of these might signify a tectonic change in our non-sporting society, but it seems clear that some reorientation is coming about. Watching sport, playing sport, thinking about sport—these are the first steps towards a revolution. Led by cricket, of course.

Other sports will also live, and occasionally thrive, as will their practitioners. But we cannot expect sustained glory. Not unless there's a sea change in how India as a nation views sport, both culturally and in terms of policy—we have only just about started taking baby steps in terms of public interest and private investors. The destination is at the end of a long, rather dark, tunnel.

Wielding the Scissors: Indian Censors and the Silencing of a Generation

Aditya Mani Jha, Rini Barman

On the evening of 1 August 2015, the Reddit India community, nothing if not vigorous, had worked itself into a state of remarkable frenzy. For the uninitiated, Reddit is the social network that takes freedom of expression the most seriously; to offend and to be offended are cherished rights for Reddit veterans. Those with less-than-thick skins are swiftly ejected and sent out to pasture.

The Redditors of India were angry and unusually vocal, even by their standards. The reason: Internet Service Providers all over the country had blocked access to some of the most popular pornography sites in India. Surprisingly, this development came less than a month after a supreme court ruling that explicitly refused to ban pornographic websites. This ruling followed a Public Interest Litigation that sought a blanket ban on porn. Speaking on the matter, the Chief Justice of India H.L. Dattu said:

> Such interim orders cannot be passed by this court. Somebody can come to the court and say 'Look, I am an adult and how can you stop me from watching it within the four walls of my room? It is a violation of Article 21 (right to personal liberty) of the Constitution.' Yes the issue is serious and some steps need to be taken. The Centre has to take a stand. Let us see what stand the Centre will take.[1]

Users reported how logging on to a porn website simply yielded a blank page or a variety of error messages, like 'Directory does not exist'. One Reddit user uploaded an error message that read: 'This site has been blocked as per the instructions of Competent Authority'. The 'Competent Authority' is a reference to Shovon Chowdhury's satirical novel of the same name, wherein a post-apocalyptic India is ruled (with an iron fist) by a despotic bureaucrat, the titular Competent Authority.

India has finally upped its Kafka quotient beyond the tipping point: life is now openly and notoriously imitating art. But this is not surprising, really, as we are going to argue in this piece. All you have to do is to take a long, hard look at the events of the last five years or so. Literature, cinema, comedy, and finally, the Internet: the wrath of India's trigger-happy censors has now pervaded every level of popular culture in India. This has hurt a lot of creators, financially and morally. Even worse, we are witnessing the alarming rise of self-censorship: publishing and media, in particular, are vetting content for possible 'red flag' areas. How did we get so lost?

L'affaire Wendy Doniger and its Aftermath

In February 2014, Penguin announced that it would pulp all available copies of Wendy Doniger's book *The Hindus: An Alternative History* (2009).[2] This decision came in the wake of a civil lawsuit filed by Dinanath Batra, an octogenarian former headmaster, who started a Hindu chauvinist group called Shiksha Bachao Andolan (literally, 'Save Education Campaign'), that has sued the authors of several textbooks, academic treatises, and other works in the past decade, for pursuing what it perceived to be an anti-Hindu agenda.

In an interview with *Time* later that month, Batra laid out his concerns about Doniger's book.

> Her intention is bad, the content is anti-national and the language is abusive. Her agenda is to malign Hinduism and hurt the feelings of Hindus. (...) Doniger says [in the book] that when Sanskrit scriptures were written, Indian society favoured open sexuality. The jacket of her book shows Lord Krishna sitting on the buttocks of nude women. She equates the *shivlingam,* worshipped all over India by millions, with sex and calls it an erect penis.[3]

Much like conservative Christian groups in America, Hindu chauvinist groups in India cannot stand the idea of Hindus and 'open sexuality' in the same sentence. The case of Deepa Mehta's film *Fire* is instructive—the cast and crew were not allowed to shoot in Varanasi because the film explored a lesbian romance. This is the first important tenet of censorship in India: life choices that do not fall in line with the censor's own worldview are quickly branded 'anti-social' or in the case of Batra and Doniger, 'anti-national'. This nomenclature is essential for the kind of impassioned breast-beating facade that must accompany the censor's claim that the book/film/song has 'hurt the sentiments' of a religious or ethnic group.

As the historian Vijay Prashad pointed out in a brilliantly argued piece in *The Guardian*,[4] the Doniger affair was the latest in a long line of scandals which were concocted to assert the supremacy of Vedanta Hinduism, a relatively orthodox and straight-laced version of the religion that naturally, hardliners like the RSS (Rashtriya Swayamsevak Sangh) prefer for political reasons. Doniger and several other scholars were attacked and censored because she sought to explore the Tantric tradition, which is not interested in imposing restrictions on a person's dietary or sexual behaviour.

Doniger was also a likely target for persecution because she is a Western scholar of Hinduism and there are those that wish to see Hindu scriptures and mythologies being interpreted only by Hindus. There is a rising perception among the right wing that the media and the intelligentsia are biased towards Western readings of Sanskrit texts. The case of Sheldon Pollock is instructive: there was, in 2016, an online petition to remove Pollock (one of the leading Sanskrit scholars in the world) as the editor of the Murty Classical Library, an ongoing project that seeks to translate classical works in Sanskrit, Urdu, Tamil and so on into English. Among the signatories was Professor Makarand Paranjape of JNU, who wrote an op-ed in *The Indian Express*, explaining his reasons for doing so. According to Paranjape, Pollock's appointment was proof of India's inferiority complex.

> Even as India has powered ahead in the latter spheres, its educational and cultural institutions have deteriorated. Regretfully, the politicisation of academics by caste, language and regional lobbies has eroded the credibility of our universities. The possibly related emigration and relocation of lakhs of gifted Indian intellectuals to Western countries has only exacerbated our sense of inferiority. Indian knowledge production, especially in humanities and social sciences, lacks global recognition. No wonder, Rohan Murty preferred the prestige and

> brand value of Columbia and Harvard for his Library. He is not the only one; many Indian business leaders have chosen similarly to endow foreign universities rather than Indian ones.[5]

Meanwhile the triumph of the censors was complete when Aleph, an Indian publishing house, followed Penguin's lead and decided to withdraw Doniger's *On Hinduism* from bookshops. Around the same time, Aleph's publishing partner, Rupa, published a translation of Narendra Modi's poems during the 2014 election campaign. Clearly, somebody at Aleph had decided to back the winning horse. Ravi Singh, co-publisher at Aleph along with David Davidar, resigned with a view to opening his own firm Speaking Tiger books, which began operations in 2015.

Singh's initiative led to a small moral victory for the champions of freedom of expression. In the wake of Aleph ditching Doniger and Singh's departure from Aleph, they lost a lot of authors who decided to jump ship with Singh and be a part of Speaking Tiger's line-up (some Penguin authors, like Siddharth Varadarajan had asked the publishers to withdraw their books by then). These authors included Jerry Pinto and Omair Ahmad. Ahmad's novels *Jimmy the Terrorist* and *The Storyteller's Tale* had previously been published by Penguin. After the pulping of Doniger's books, he asked Penguin to cancel his contracts and Speaking Tiger editions of his novels are now available in bookshops. In a statement later published by *Time Out* (Delhi), Ahmad expressed his disappointment with Penguin's actions.

> Penguin does not have the right to criticise Indian laws or the legal system when it has withdrawn without even fighting. What message does this give? That the biggest publishing firm in the world has such little respect for Indian courts that it will abandon the fight without standing up for its authors, and its own decisions, in court? If Penguin will not fight for its own decisions, its own authors, then what is its reputation, all its money and organisation really worth? And if its reputation is worth so little, then it is a shame to be associated with them, not a point of pride.[6]

Ahmad strikes at the heart of the matter here: Penguin decided to throw in the towel, which was surprising because most legal experts agreed that

Batra stood virtually no chance of winning the case against them. Courts tend to favour freedom of expression, unless the text in question is extremely inflammatory and can, in the opinion of the court, lead to riots. The thing is, most individuals do not find it within themselves to prepare for a prolonged battle in court. Moreover, the impact this has on their day-to-day lives often proves to be enough of a deterrent: they simply choose not to fight well-funded, well-armed organisations with vested interests.

This is what happened in the case of Tamil writer Perumal Murugan and his novel *Madhorubagan (One Part Woman)*. Murugan's transgression was his portrayal of the Kailasanathar temple in Tiruchengode in a negative light; special offence was taken at the 'promiscuous' depiction of its female devotees (The twin red flags of religion and sex were thus present here as well). Despite receiving support from a large number of writers and activists, Murugan eventually withdrew his books. In a heart-breaking letter that he wrote explaining his decision, he said: 'Author Perumal Murugan has died. He is no god, so he is not going to resurrect himself. Nor does he believe in reincarnation. From now on, Perumal Murugan will survive merely as a teacher he has been.'[7]

Even when a section of the Indian public fights against censors, what they tend to miss out on is the larger psychological ramifications of censorship. The censor board, when read in the context of the Italian theoretician Antonio Gramsci's treatise on hegemony, is a cultural institution that propagates the ideas of the dominant classes in a compelling way, so that the other classes bow down to their belief system. Their loyalty is 'consensual' because they are convinced that their best interests lie in aligning with the establishment. Within this framework, any form of dissent or an individual's freedom to oppose the dominant machinery is liable to invite conflict.

Censorship creates a climate of fear. Young people get the message that they must toe the line or be ready to face dire consequences. Conformism is never good news for a country's future, but unless the current penchant for censorship is reversed, that is exactly what we are destined to get.

Censoring Syllabi and the Revisionism Doctrine

On 9 October 2011, Delhi University's Academic Council decided to drop A.K. Ramanujan's essay 'Three Hundred *Ramayanas*' from the B.A. syllabus. Ramanujan's essay is a wonderfully written treatise on the many retellings of

Valmiki's *Ramayana* across India as well as Thailand and the rest of the South Asian region. For students interested in the mechanisms of folklore and oral literature, Ramanujan's essay has been an invaluable resource for a long time, which is why it was on the syllabus in the first place. And yet, the Delhi University Academic Council decided that the essay was a liability. Why?

Unsurprisingly, the precipitating factor was a sustained campaign led by right-wing organisations like the Akhil Bharatiya Vidyarthi Parishad (ABVP), the youth wing of the Bharatiya Janata Party (BJP). And the point of contention was the presence of characters from Hindu texts in sexual scenarios. In one of the *Ramayanas*, Sita sleeps with Ravana during her period of captivity. In another, Hanuman is depicted as a bit of a Lothario. Of course, what the ABVP and other organisations of its ilk fail to realise is that the essay only sought to provoke debate and academic enquiry—curiosity and tolerance for differing viewpoints being the twin bulwarks of a healthy academic environment. It suited their political posturing to paint this as an issue of religious sentiments, framing Ramanujan as some sort of a malicious prankster, rather than the sensitive and brilliant scholar that he was.

In a January 2012 press conference, ABVP president Rohit Chahal said:

> There are 300 versions of the Ramayana, but A.K. Ramanujan chooses to quote five examples that are bound to hurt our sentiments. They (Delhi University) want students to learn about those five. We have not read the essays that are going to replace this one, but we are very clear that we will not tolerate such subject matters becoming part of the Delhi University syllabus.[8]

Chahal conveniently forgot to point out that in 2008, his organisation had vandalised DU's History department, demanding the removal of Ramanujan's essay.

Censorship by hook or crook: that's the motto of 21st-century India. The behaviour of publishers like Penguin is better understood when you consider the reality that a fanatic fundamentalist group is more than willing to use violence to achieve its narrow-minded aims.

In the last 12 months, school and college syllabi across the country have undergone a booster dose of historical revisionism, designed to rewrite India's history and give it an almost comically exaggerated pro-Hindu slant. A brief look at the proposed re-writes tells you all you need to know about the callousness and the apathy that India's censors not only possess, but actually flaunt proudly. In a December 2014 *Hindustan Times* report, we came face-to-face with our new, censor-approved history.

The Emperor Ashoka's preaching of non-violence, for instance, 'weakened north India' and cowardice spread throughout the kingdom. During his reign, people were saddled with the economic burden of having to feed Buddhist monks. The Qutub Minar was not built by Qutubuddin Aibak, but by a Hindu king called Samudragupta; the monument's name was Vishnu Stambha. Dalits were 'the creation of Muslim invaders during the medieval period.' And of course, India is 'the most ancient country in the world. When civilisation had not developed in many countries, India's rishi-munis brought the light of culture and civilisation to them.'[9]

This is the worst kind of censorship, aiming to influence children, youngsters who may very well grow up to become adults peddling this ridiculous perversion of history. But then, the future of our children must be sacrificed to further the political future of India's censors.

Both Sides of the Aisle

Which isn't to say that censorship is the sole refuge of the BJP or right-wing politicians in general. On the contrary, most governments in India have been trigger-happy, as far as banning books and movies are concerned. Indira Gandhi famously claimed to have been defamed by a single sentence in Salman Rushdie's magnum opus *Midnight's Children*. Curiously enough, she sued the novelist in 1984, a full three years after the book was first published. By then, of course, it had won the Booker Prize and was already being talked about as one of the definitive novels about the subcontinent. Rushdie wrote about his encounter with Mrs Gandhi (and the lawsuit that followed) in May 2006, a full 25 years after the novel was published, in an article published by *Outlook* magazine.[10]

> This was it: 'It has often been said that Mrs Gandhi's younger son Sanjay accused his mother of being responsible, through her neglect, for his father's death; and that this gave him an unbreakable hold over her, so that she became incapable of denying him anything.' Tame stuff, you might think, not really the kind of thing a thick-skinned

> politician would usually sue a novelist for mentioning, and an odd choice of casus belli in a book that excoriated Indira for the many crimes of the Emergency.

Rushdie would ultimately come to a settlement, preferring not to take his chances in court, where Mrs Gandhi's actions during the Emergency would almost certainly have come into play.

In 2010, history would repeat itself. Mrs Gandhi's daughter-in-law Sonia Gandhi was the most powerful woman in the country, being the President of the Indian National Congress, which was in power at the time. The Spanish novelist Javier Moro's book *The Red Sari*, a 'dramatised biography' of Sonia Gandhi's life, was first published globally in 2008. But when Moro tried to get the book released in India in 2010, Sonia and the Congress's censors would not budge. They claimed that the book contained salacious and unfounded gossip about the Congress President. Moro and his publishers tried their best to negotiate with the Congress, but to no avail. It wasn't until 2015, when the Congress had been voted out of power that the book finally released.

Just months before the Moro controversy, the Congress had also forced the director Prakash Jha to edit portions of his political drama *Rajneeti*. It is worth noting that Jha's film was nowhere as closely hewed to reality as Moro's book (which—after all—was fiction but in the form of a 'dramatised biography'; this terminology is similar to another seemingly oxymoronic phrase, 'non-fiction novel'). Even a purely fictional allusion was deemed to be unsuitable for the audience.

Silver Screen Censorship

Although there have been quite a few feature films that have suffered years of oblivion due to the censor board (Anurag Kashyap's *Paanch* and *Black Friday* are the two best-known examples of this), documentaries generally have the toughest time in India, in this regard. Leslee Udwin's documentary *India's Daughter* is an example of a documentary becoming a victim of the Indian censors. The main reason for this was that Udwin had the temerity to interview one of the people accused in Delhi's infamous Nirbhaya gang rape case of 16 December 2012. In March, the Indian government asked YouTube to block access to the film: Indian viewers could not watch it.

Some critics said that a film made by a foreigner using Orientalist techniques to make sweeping statements deserved to be banned in India. Others, while admitting that a ban was probably overkill, opined that the film was certainly bad for India's image overseas.

The reason behind the ban on Udwin's film was actually quite mundane and in line with the events of the Wendy Doniger affair. Conservative elements do not like liberals raising their voices, neither do they like being shown a mirror. Udwin's film was guilty of the latter. In the film, a pair of particularly odious defence lawyers stated that a woman travelling with her boyfriend is to be blamed for the rape. One of the rapists stated firmly that the girl would have survived had she not resisted the violence meted out to her. For both of these scenes, the documentary received criticism from media persons, celebrities, and activists.

India's Daughter triggered another important development in July 2015. In a controversial move, journalists, academics, NGO members, and so on have been denied the right to interview prisoners, even for research purposes. Under the new regulations, you cannot carry a camera, a notebook or even a pen inside a prison. Even if you have special permission to interview a prisoner, you first have to deposit a security deposit of Rs 1 lakh.

'No private individual/press/NGO/company should ordinarily be allowed entry into the prison for the purposes of doing research, making documentaries, writing articles or interviews' said Joint Secretary in the Home Ministry Kumar Alok, in an advisory sent to all states and union territories. It is hard to believe that this decision is unrelated to Udwin's film and the public relations nightmare that the Indian government faced following its release.

As we have mentioned earlier, the student community suffers the most due to politically motivated censorship. In July 2015, Nakul Singh Sawhney's film *Muzaffarnagar Baaqi Hain* was about to be screened at Kirori Mal College (KMC), before the screening was cancelled due to another ABVP intervention. Predictably, the BVP claimed that the film was 'anti-national'. More than 40 ABVP members stormed the KMC campus, creating a ruckus, dubbing the teachers as 'Naxalites' and threatening the organisers of the screening. A screening supposed to encourage a dialogue about terror and its far-reaching effects culminated, ironically, in a show of terror.

Banning films is by no means an original or uncommon phenomenon in India. Militant groups in Manipur, for instance, have long since banned Hindi and English films, under the notion of protecting the youth from adverse external influences. It is interesting to note, however, that many people from Manipur travelled to Guwahati to watch the Hindi film *Mary Kom*, based on the boxing world champion of the same name and one of the most famous people from Manipur.

More recently, the Central Board of Film Certification (CBFC) banned Raj Amit Kumar's film *Unfreedom* for its portrayal of homosexuality, an 'unnatural passion', and its 'provocative' message about religion. This came as a huge disappointment to social activists, including LGBT groups, who were shocked at the hypocrisy of allowing crude, sexually suggestive songs, while not permitting the release of a film that sought to interrogate social issues.

In her 1992 book, *Censorship: The Knot that Binds Knowledge and Power*, Sue Curry Jansen stresses the need to analyse how social relationships influence censor committees, not so much vice versa. Revisiting the term, she writes:

> My definition of the term encompasses all socially structured proscriptions or prescriptions which inhibit or prohibit dissemination of ideas, information, images, and other messages through a society's channels of communication whether these obstructions are secured by political, economic, religious, or other systems of authority. It includes both overt and covert proscriptions and prescriptions.[11]

Most taboos and social codes are implicit; they already accomplish the task of censoring by the state.

Much before the child grows up to understand the polemical functioning of state censorship, he has already been reduced to an object that obeys and self-censors. A child, for instance, is never encouraged to question the monolith called 'Indian History'. And if he or she goes through their entire childhood without so much as glancing at a piece of fiery, rebellious, non-conforming art, the odds are that we will have yet another uncomplaining, unremarkable sheep on our hands.

Writing Back

Despite the many clamps on creative freedom that we discussed earlier in this piece, there have been encouraging developments as well. The piracy campaign engineered around *The Final Solution* (a documentary film on the

Gujarat riots of 2002, directed by Rakesh Sharma in 2004) was one of them. The idea at the core of the campaign was simple and ingenious; a free copy of the film was made available to anyone who promised to make five copies and distribute them online. Pro-democracy pamphlets and journals were piggy-backed along with the film. And let's not forget the fact that a massive number of online and offline petitions managed to get the ban against the film overturned.

The publishing industry, too, has made small but significant steps in this direction. In 2015, HarperCollins published *Bedtime Story*, a 1978 play by Kiran Nagarkar, which had been suppressed by right-wing outfits when it first came out. Shows were cancelled after threats of violence were made against the troupes that wanted to perform the play. Nagarkar, one of the greatest Indian writers alive, wrote a fresh preface for the 2015 edition and included updated stage directions.

Angaaray, a 1932 collection of Urdu short stories (and a play) that was banned in India by the British government, saw two independent translations in 2014.[12] The writers of this collection belonged to the Progressive Writer's Association and were acutely aware of the dangers of censorship. Young readers exposed to their words today will, hopefully, learn a thing or two about courage under fire. Wendy Doniger herself made a comeback to Indian bookstores in 2015, thanks to Speaking Tiger Books, which published *The Mare's Trap*, a collection of her writings on the *Kamasutra*. All of this is very gratifying for the Indian reader, whose confidence had been somewhat deflated after witnessing the prior treatment of Doniger, Murugan et al.

India certainly has a long way to go, as far as tolerance for dissent is concerned. For far too long, we have talked about ourselves as one of the most remarkable democracies in the world. It's time we walked the talk. As Salman Rushdie, one of the first and certainly the most illustrious victim of Indian censors, famously said: 'What is freedom of expression? Without the freedom to offend, it ceases to exist.'[13]

Endnotes

1 Krishnadas Rajagopal, 'Can't stop an adult from watching porn in his room, says SC,' *The Hindu*, July 9, 2015, http://www.thehindu.com/news/national/cant-stop-an-adult-from-watching-porn-in-his-room-says-sc/article7400690.ece.

2 Wendy Doniger, *The Hindus: An Alternative History* (New York: Viking Penguin, 2009).

3 Nilanjana Bhowmick, 'Sex, Lies and Hinduism: Why a Hindu Activist Targeted Wendy Doniger's Book,' *Time*, February 12 (2014), http://time.com/6601/sex-lies-and-hinduism-why-a-hindu-activist-targeted-wendy-donigers-book/.

4 Vijay Prashad, 'Wendy Doniger's book is a tribute to Hinduism's complexity, not an insult,' *The Guardian*, February 12, 2014, http://www.theguardian.com/commentisfree/2014/feb/12/wendy-doniger-book-hinduism-penguin-hindus.

5 Makarand Paranjape, 'The Problem with Pollock,' *The Indian Express*, March 21, 2016, http://indianexpress.com/article/opinion/columns/the-problem-with-pollock/.

6 'Pulped Fiction,' *Timeout Delhi*, February 2014.

7 'Author Perumal Murugan has died': Tamil writer withdraws all published work following protests,' Scroll.in, Jan 13, 2015, http://scroll.in/article/700217/author-perumal-murugan-has-died-tamil-writer-withdraws-all-published-work-following-protests.

8 'There are 300 versions of the Ramayana: ABVP,' *The Hindu*, January 19, 2012, http://www.thehindu.com/news/national/there-are-300-versions-of-the-ramayana-abvp/article2568550.ece.

9 Danish Raza, 'Saffronising textbooks: Where myth and dogma replace history,' *Hindustan Times*, December 8, 2014, http://www.hindustantimes.com/india/saffronising-textbooks-where-myth-and-dogma-replace-history/story-CauM4dmmsPGrjZ3APAvNxO.html.

10 Salman Rushdie, 'His Own Mt Sinai,' *Outlook*, May 8, 2006, http://www.outlookindia.com/magazine/story/his-own-mt-sinai/231147.

11 Sue Curry Jansen, *Censorship: The Knot That Binds Power and Knowledge* (New York: Oxford University Press, 1988).

12 Snehal Shingavi, ed, *Angaaray: The First-Ever English Translation of the Banned Short-Story Collection* (New Delhi: Penguin, 2014); Vibha S. Chauhan and Khalid Alvi, trans., Angarey (New Delhi: Rupa, 2014).

13 Ashutosh Varshney, 'The Political Rushdie,' *The Journal of the International Institute*, 10(3). Spring/Summer 2003, http://quod.lib.umich.edu/j/jii/4750978.0010.306/--political-rushdie?rgn=main;view=fulltext.

A Real Market for Dreams: Advertising and the Economics of a Good Deal

Anuraag

Advertising is not new to India. It goes way beyond the dawn of advertising agencies. From the catchy pitch of street-snack vendors to the whimsical but pitch-perfect calls of the ice-lolly hawkers, from the presentation of a sari salesman to the promise of a fresh-water fish seller—they all know that it's not enough that you have the spiciest peanuts or the freshest fish. You need to talk about it. And you need to talk about it to the right audience, at the right time, place, and perhaps most importantly, in the right tone. The roots of an enterprise that has since been the voice of every other enterprise lie deep. It's a voice that at various times has been everything from the sharp prudence of Lalitaji to the inclusive pride of '*Hamara Bajaj*'. From intimately personal to overwhelmingly national—this has been the voice of advertising that has sold everyone everything.

There's no escaping the ads. They are everywhere—all the time. They are the shiny colorful balloons put up by mega corporations and new startups alike, to catch your attention. And in order to do that the advertisers have been digging into their bottomless bag of tricks to get you to look at them, engage with them, listen to what they have to say, see the sometimes fantastical and occasionally realistic dreams they spin, to get you to acknowledge your deepest insecurities, anxieties, fantasies, and aspirations. Advancements in technology is giving brands and advertisers ever more tools to catch you at the right time and place. And by 'you' I don't mean someone vaguely like you, belonging to the same demographic or psychographic segment as it once used to mean, but you specifically with your idiosyncratic behaviour patterns and attitudes revealed by your media habits and online footprint. It enables them to reach out to you at just the right time, not by using a megaphone in a crowded market square but with a popup on your computer screen that is bound to catch your attention.

That's enough to get you interested, to draw you in, before you gladly reach for your wallet and enter into an economic transaction where you feel that you have got more than you gave. But is it only about economics? Is it about courting rational consumers who choose what's in their best interest only after due consideration? Who cares? Who even knows how to define 'best interest', as long as it feels like a good deal? And if you have to choose one stereotype about India that is most likely to be true, I suggest you go with the one that says Indians love a good deal. The essence of a good deal is the feeling that you got more than what you paid for. Advertising makes this possible. Take for example Amul, which sells dairy products made from the largest milk co-operative in India. Its butter brand is known as much for the quality of its product as for the iconic series of topical advertising that has been a commentary on the mood of the nation, in the process becoming a sort of collective subconscious of a country that may not even realise every morning that they are consuming a bit of harmless nationalism. Wrapped in the butter paper comes not just the dairy fats with a maximum retail price, but a sense of belongingness, collective identity, social awareness, and pride. That is what makes it a good deal. The happiness inside a bottle of coke, the unrelenting spirit in a bottle of Johnnie Walker, the grit and determination in a pair of Nikes—they didn't put any of that in their factories. Take away the stories and they are just sugar water, or alcohol water or just a pair of shoes. In all these cases, the value of the deal is incomplete without their narrative.

What makes the business of advertising particularly interesting in a country like India is that it is essentially a business of voices in a country that is unapologetically noisy. And by that I don't mean it's loud, which it is, but that it is so diverse in what makes it, that any attempt to represent it conceptually is almost always going to be a simplistic misrepresentation. It's not just a land of elephants and snake charmers but it does indeed have those elephants and snake charmers. It also has its space programmes and IT consultants lounging in their condos sipping single-malts on days that are not Tuesday or Thursday. It has abject poverty and about one-third of the world's poor live in India. It has deep-rooted corruption. It has international airports and globetrotting professionals. It has millions who have been exploited for generations and failed by the state. And millions who are confident dreaming of a future where they can take their place as citizens of the world. Constantly in churn, developing while simultaneously decaying, India has its own metabolism. In many ways the chaos of advertising mirrors the noise that India is. And going forward, it's only going to get noisier.

So what next? Where next? We've seen advertising, like any other human enterprise, undergo changes through the ages, adapting and evolving to suit the needs of the times. In every age we had the doomsday knell getting rung in premature enthusiasm. With the advent of TV, it was feared that the creative copy writers would forever cede their ground to the media buyers who could churn viewership data through their mighty computers and ensure that the message reaches the most viewers at the least cost. Then came the internet, and along with a bunch of other industries, it changed advertising too. Now you can be more specific in your targeting and get real-time feedback on whether your ads work on not. 'Digital' became so loaded a word that it started to suddenly mean a lot much more than it did. We've seen the ability to maintain, mine, and put Big Data to use in a way that turns advertising comparable to some sort of an Orwellian two-way screen establishing a direct link between the buyer and the seller. Change at this level may truly be unprecedented. And more than anything, it is reflected in the emergence of 'platforms' and the power they wield. Google, Apple, Amazon, Facebook are more than a discreet bunch of products and services. They facilitate interactions, including between buyers and sellers, while charging a fee for it. And their success or failure depends on maintaining an ecosystem where one side pulls in the other and vice versa. Their success lies in solving a finely balanced catch-22 that makes their platform indispensable. As a result, it's no surprise that the biggest revenues today for a Facebook or Google are from their ability to monetise their user base through various methods, including advertising. And while it impacts the way advertising 'is done' on those platforms (some ads on Google, for example, are just text based) the question to be asked is whether it changes advertising itself in a way that is fundamental and irrevocable. The modalities may change, the ontology remains. Then there is good old fashioned advertising by the platforms themselves. Fllipkart, Snapdeal, and now Amazon—the Indian online retail market has seen some of the fiercest competition and the most high-decibel campaigning in recent times reminiscent of the cola wars or the telecom subscriber land-grab of earlier years.

By this point, you must be getting an impression that the world of advertising is a hopelessly chaotic one. Some statistic about the number of commercial messages you receive before you've even started your day's work must be vaguely coalescing in your brain. You try and remember the number of TV channels you get at home and draw a blank. And the amount of content that is there on the internet is simply astronomical. So what does any of this mean for advertising? What does advertising do anyway? What does it mean to be shouting in this noise that India is today? Who are we shouting out to? Also, people hate advertising, don't they? They find it annoying and flip the channel, right?

Let us pull back for a while and see what advertising does or why it is needed. Simply put, advertising is merely the voice of brands. Brands exist because people don't like dealing with things that are not people. They resort to what we call anthropomorphism or personification. For centuries humans have attributed human-like motives to everything from animals to inanimate things like the wind, the sea, or the Sun. Most gods and goddesses across cultures and folk religions have indeed been anthropomorphic depictions of everything from forces of nature to heavenly bodies. Organisations, the collective human enterprise working as cogs in the economic machinery, needed a face with which to meet their consumers when they took their output to them. That's what brands were and still are. And people need brands—it's evident from how they love certain brands, while they hate others. They need brands not only for the practical purposes of being able to differentiate between competing products of varying quality standards but also because it humanises an economic transaction and the act of consumption. They have long-standing relationships with brands built on trust and loyalty. And as is true for all relationships, it's not just enough to do the right things, it's needed that the right things be said too. The job of advertising then is to nurture those relationships by saying the right things.

Advertising is often criticised for promoting consumerism and selling dreams that never match up to the reality. But to blame advertising would be like shooting the messenger. It has merely been a tool at the disposal of everyone, no matter what your ideology. It has served everyone alike whether a communist regime in need of propaganda or a cereal brand in need of a mascot that everyone must find cute. Advertising's job is to merely make brands look relatable, and desirable.

Desires! Ah! That's the bête noire of all those eager to blame advertising for creating a shallow, superficial, and meaningless world where the hedonistic pursuit of desires is all there is to it. Well, they are right. And I would argue there is nothing wrong with it. This is my argument.

It's the old existential proposition (which also happens to be true), that the universe is inherently without any meaning. Nothing means anything else. The illusion of meaning is the by-product of the human brain trying to understand the world by constructing logic out of causality using symbols and language. But this is somehow not very satisfying to many people. Because while growing up, both as individuals and as a species, our very survival depends on successfully learning to interpret causality through symbols, we find it difficult to see that it is just an adaptive mechanism awarded by evolution and the rest of the universe doesn't care or is incapable of caring. And indeed the need for the transcendental is present in all of us. It reassures us of our superior mental faculties that go beyond animal instincts. But those who frown upon 'materialistic' desires fail to see that all life is essentially a pursuit of satisfying needs in order to stay alive and procreate. Desires are needed. The distinction between wants and needs is an unnecessary one. We love to eat because we need to eat. We love to have sex because we need to have sex. Everything else is just a nice by-product geared at helping either homoeostasis or reproduction. Even the huge brain (it's just 2 per cent by weight but requires almost 20 per cent of our energy supply) and the consciousness housed in it (sorry to disappoint the dualists) that now seems to have its own needs, originally seems to have evolved only to aid those two.

Irrespective of whether you buy my point about aspiration management or not, it's safe to say that our country today is definitely no longer bothered either with Nehruvian socialism or the ascetic austerity of ancient India. It's okay now for people to dream and to work towards fulfilling those dreams. And for every desire that seems to be perpetually getting out of reach there is something that can be grabbed right now. Real economies are seldom about the choice between guns and butter but they are always about choices. Choices to make from options that are neatly arranged on a spectrum, much like a supermarket shelf in an aisle where there's always something to fit your budget while there are other things you'll be never be able to afford. And then there's technology, making sure that complex economies are able to realise their full potential by offering more and more choices at every level.

Take phones for example. Telephones were a luxury a few decades ago. They became consistently cheaper and then came mobile phones. However, it still wasn't the same for everyone. Before the advent of smart phones, every nifty feature in your phone meant that the price would be that much higher. Want a colour screen, music playback, camera, or email? Just keep adding to the price. Not anymore. Today the latest phone by Apple is not fundamentally different from an Android device selling at one-tenth the price. Sure the iPhone is bigger, faster, and arguably better, but the guy who's just got his first entry-level smart phone, which costs as much as two weeks' salary in a blue-collar job doesn't have the time for that argument when he's busy rocking YouTube on his 3G data plan. He's happy playing the latest Bhojpuri hit while sitting in his one-room accommodation that he shares with other migrant workers. Perhaps as happy as the Manhattan photographer listening to a podcast on his iPhone while doing yoga in Central Park. Different desires, same needs. So in the future, when economies grow even more complex and chaotic, the role of advertising is then to present that which is needed as ultimately desirable.

The role of advertising then is going to be that of the matchmaker—between brands and people. Finding the consumers for the brands who will love the brand for what it is able to give them—happiness. To make them feel that they are getting more than they are giving. To make them feel happy about the choices they make. It never was nor is it going to be a shallow endeavour, or an ignoble one. And it's not pointless either. Which brings us to a rather absurd but irrefutable conclusion—that it is possible to maximise human happiness by managing aspirations.

And that could very well be the defining role for advertising in a nation in transition—to be a matchmaker in a pluralistic market. Guiding the right consumers to the right platforms where they board different trains for different destinations. While India may never become a developed nation in its entirety, more and more people are going to be pulled out of poverty and into what is defined as the consuming class. Not all of them at once, and not all of them in the same way—the universality of human nature contrasted with the differences in the human condition. The differences will remain, as can be seen by a number of pointers. First, the once optimistic belief that the developing economies, bolstered by a confidence in their continued growth will reach the level of wealth and prosperity of the rich world has seen some adjustment on account of a faltering global economic outlook and the uncertainties brought about by a slowdown in demand from the rich world. There is a chance that the often hailed convergence may have to wait much longer than previously thought, if at all. While the fact that India continues to be an island of sustained growth in an otherwise gloomy scenario will produce just the kind of a fractured economic class system that is stratified while being simultaneously fluid. The second, is the growing evidence internationally that there is no such thing as one country anymore. No country is one country. At the very least it's two—as exemplified by the way the Brexit vote turned out in July 2016. And as we have already seen in the case of India—many. The diversity of India spans both space and time. While the differences among regions is clearly evident, so is the fact that we have people existing simultaneously in the 16th century as well as the 21st century.

This has an impact on how markets are shaped and how the players communicate. Earlier every category would have a very limited number of brands clearly pitted against each other which has now given way to an explosion of highly vocal brands in each category. From the many mobile phone makers to deodorant manufacturers. From telecom service providers to apparel brands. It's no longer a case of the big boys battling it out on a national stage and prime time television which itself has seen its prima donna status eroded with the advent of a slew of new and often fragmented media platforms. The global preeminence of Apple and Samsung in the mobile phones market means nothing to the proud owner of a Lava or Gionee smartphone in Jaunpur or Muzaffarpur. We will continue to see the rise of brands like Patanjali who have emerged indigenously and sent the multinationals and their billion dollar brands scurrying for cover. Rapidly evolving technology means that the earlier sales and distribution muscle of the large and established players is no longer as formidable a barrier as it once was to the newcomers who are today armed with the power of e-commerce. While technology continues to disrupt, so can advertising and communication. Paper Boat—a maker of soft drinks in various 'Indian' flavours, the kind that evokes nostalgia in grownups living in cookie-cutter times of their own childhoods and everything that was a part of it—has managed to break into a market dominated by established global and national giants based almost entirely on emotional appeal. Long-forgotten summer vacations spent at the grandmother's home amidst a gaggle of first and second cousins were dusted off and made vivid again in the memories of countless urban dwellers longing for simpler times and priceless pleasures. Take any category, and the ever-complex pluralism of the Indian market will mean that you will have a wide spectrum of consumers ranging from the matured and insouciant to the newly introduced and bubbling with wide-eyed excitement. The role of advertising will be tested in being the right matchmaker that finely tunes the tones as per the tastes.

Another area where we see advertising changing is how it is shifting from merely being a reflection of the social norms to actually becoming an agent of change. We have seen a number of brands and campaigns that challenge and question the norms in an attempt to establish what is often referred to as 'thought leadership' and be seen as someone who moves the needle on social discourse. This is a result of maturing markets and the disappearance of long- term competitive advantages from 'unique selling propositions' which can often be replicated with the aid of accelerated innovation. In the absence of tangible functional differentiations, brands often choose to stand for values and causes. One of the most visible of these has been the cause of gender equality and female empowerment that has seen a bevy of brands lining up to be seen as being the voice of the new Indian woman. Share the load, a campaign by a detergent brand Ariel, encourages society to stop thinking of laundry as being only a woman's job while brands like Tanishq (a jewellery brand) and Raga (by Titan, a watchmaker) have taken up issues like remarriage and women's independence. We've seen brands tackling old taboos on topics from menstruation to homosexuality. Going forward, the ability of brands to break the clutter and stand out will depend largely on their willingness to display both boldness and clarity of thought.

As to the question of how these changes will impact advertising itself, the answer will vary depending on whom you ask. To paraphrase Fairfax M. Cone, an advertising guru and one of the founders of Foote, Cone & Belding (FCB), advertising works best not when it's aimed at millions but when it's written from one person to another. And that quality of advertising may just be its biggest strength when tasked with selling a billion bespoke dreams.

LANGUAGE AND LITERATURE

View From Below: Utopia and Change

Udaya Narayana Singh, Rajarshi Singh

Problematising the Points of View

The 'competition of systems' that developed after the Second World War, divided the world in terms of bipolar ideologies. This resulted in the creation of three separate worlds, where the basket of the Third World contained poorer countries that tried to follow sometimes pro-western and sometimes pro-eastern lines, with some of them remaining uncommitted and non-aligned. Time did not stand still and the world went on struggling to find pathways through this quagmire. The basic problem of conceptualising both nature and the method of 'development' did not disappear in all these decades, although there seems to be a general agreement that everyone should somehow follow the path of 'modernisation.' With that we were presented with evidence from industrialisation of the West as a success story that many thought was the ideal to emulate. Some advanced similar arguments in favour of the Socialist regimes, and their model of development. As time went by, it was becoming clear that for each society, traditions must make way for the modern, which in turn was a pre-condition for globalisation. From designing or reconfiguring of our linguistic space to running an economy or a country, this was thought to be the inevitable direction.

Another aspect to consider is the concept of Utopia. The story of the Indian people is evidence enough of the transformative power of education. But somewhere in our narrative we stepped off the path and landed ourselves in the quagmire of un-education, where schooling and education are not effective anymore. The probability of first generation learners making their way out of illiteracy seems to increase every year. If we look into the short fiction that has emerged from Maithili and Bhojpuri, we find a common story of a simple farmer in a remote village of Saharsa or Purnea in Bihar—a rural state, rich in natural resources but burdened with marginal development during the 1920s. The farmer, an illiterate but perhaps wise man, works in the fields, growing maize, rice or wheat on a meagre patch of land that destiny provided to his family. News, views, and stories of a world war far away, and a nation-wide movement against the foreign rule seep through his mental space as he goes to the village market where traders bring in stories of the world. He comes to know that there may soon be a time when the white men would leave and the country would become independent. With this half-baked news and views, he begins to dream of a time when there would be power in their own hands, and when poverty would be alleviated. Despite being illiterate, he took it upon himself to provide for the formal education of his child to join a school located at a distance that one had to walk every day. The wisdom of investing in educating his children ultimately pays off. A time comes when not only his son, but others among his relatives also cross the hurdle of schools to join colleges in Bhagalpur, Darbhanga or Patna. Some become skilled workers as well. Such changes have been quietly happening in many villages since the 1940s and 1950s. While some remained in their villages to cultivate their land, others set out on journeys to discover other avenues of income. Geography and history did not remain confined to their schoolbooks, but became realities as they flooded the metropolitan cities of Mumbai, Kolkata and Delhi.

The farms of these families may still be there in the family, but is not the only source of income anymore. This is not merely a narrative of one family but the story of numerous Indians and their families living in different parts of India. India's Ministry of Statistics and Programme Implementation's *Migration in India 2007-08 Report* (June 2010)[1] based on the 64th round of the National Sample Survey (NSS), tells us that 28.5 per cent of Indians (about 325 million) are migrants, with 35 per cent of people in urban areas and 26 per cent of people in rural areas having moved from their place of usual residence.[2] This large-scale human migration pattern witnessed in post-independence India is based on an idea of collective utopia that keeps driving Indians from one space to the other in search of a better life and livelihood. In the process, cultural and linguistic admixture has changed the language dynamics of India. The findings of the People of India (POI) Project of the

Anthropological Survey of India (cf. Singh, Kumar Suresh & S. Manoharan 1993)[3] based on a survey of 4,635 communities (2,209 main communities, 586 segments and 1,840 territorial units) show a high degree of linguistic heterogeneity in India. It was suggested that it probably resulted from two factors: i) Culturally homogeneous communities becoming hetero-lingual in different linguistic situations, preferring the language of the present habitat in place of their original; and ii) Linguistically heterogeneous communities coming together within one cultural fold. The figure of 325 languages that POI showed as against the Census of India 1961 figure[4] showed 1,652 mother tongues included 350 linguistically homogeneous communities, (Scheduled Tribe 72, Scheduled Caste 52 and Other Communities 226). Linguistically heterogeneous communities within the states are 154 and across states 380 (Scheduled Tribe 37, Scheduled Caste 78, Other Communities 265). The study also showed that the highest numbers among 998 monolingual communities were found in Andhra Pradesh (204) followed by Tamil Nadu (198), Gujarat (136), Madhya Pradesh (126), Orissa (120), West Bengal (108), and Kerala (106). The question is how to manage this divergence.

Many wrong perceptions could be found here. It was thought in some post-colonial countries that the languages of the masters could be adapted to quick-fix all divergences in the community. Similarly, some smaller nations thought it wise to shun all intermediary processes of language development. Their languages jumped the stage of 'standardisation' to move on to the 'modernisation' bandwagon straightaway, where this transition prompted these yet-to-be developed speech forms to be used as languages of media, business and governance. Whereas political and economic development promoted personal growth and liberty, the ethno-historic link had to be sacrificed with an apprehension that any interest in or turn towards historicity would stilt all growth. All these resulted from the view from the above. But that this is not necessarily the best course of action, and that this is not all that 'natural' is being realised now, which we would say is the biggest transition happening in the current thinking.

Nature, as we know, is multi-scale; accordingly, scientific and philosophical perspectives vary with spatial and temporal resolution. While we delve into a multi-scale overview of primary education in India, it would be prudent to explore two philosophically distinct approaches to systems design—the *pragmatic view* which builds on ground realities, and associated restrictions, and the *utopian perspective* that introduces limitations and checks only after establishing a design independent of any restrictions of the current reality.

In *The Philosophers' Mail*, the School of Life group of thinkers talk about the 'Utopia Series: The Schools of the Future'[5] where they remind us that it is not prudent to call the concept 'utopian,' because that "is normally a way of saying it's pie-in-the-sky and not worth paying attention to. Far from it. Throughout the ages, a number of philosophers have put forward some highly provocative and interesting utopias, describing ideal arrangements of everything from schools to religion, government to holidays." They identify two fundamental tasks education should help us with when we grow up as adults: *working* and *sustaining good relationships.* And then, they would ask ordinary people systematically about the main problems in their work and home lives—and then work backwards to put adequate, thoughtful responses in place in the training years, and create a curriculum of the future. One may not agree that there should be courses on Economics of Profit and Loss, or Change in Society, Business Ideas, Consumption, or Relationships, but the point they make is evident.

What if these approaches and alternatives are not paid attention to while planning for our society or polity? In fact, an overemphasis on the uniform westernisation model led to what Eisenstadt (1964) called 'breakdowns of modernisation'.[6] In the post-cold war period, the predicted and promised development did not happen in many underdeveloped countries, resulting in trouble and turmoil. In the more recent period, the trouble began to be exported to the western world making the lives and living of the people in the developed countries difficult and unsafe. We soon find Gunnar Myrdal (1968) talking about the poverty of nations resulting in the Asian Drama.[7] That crises and instability grew from gross inequalities between countries of different worlds were becoming clearer now. The development in the world of communication made it possible for many under particular blocks to call the strategies of the powerful a bluff, and consequently there had been many unprecedented breakdowns of world order. This transition also saw the collapse of many existing political institutions and order, resulting in mistrust, corruption, unrest, and violence. The success and speed of these changes depended on the degree of suppression and exclusion from politico-societal participation of small groups or nations in having a better say. The bigger nation-states and the former colonial masters who believed that these smaller groups could be made use of to engage in a fight among and against a certain ideology are perhaps now realising the coming alive of the *Bhasmasura*-syndrome.[8]

View from Above

Logically, such views from above have to take a universalist position that there is a seamlessly single humanity in which differentiation is insignificant, whereas the practical problem is that such differentiation is neither insignificant nor wishful thinking. Any departure from equal treatment in multi-lingual and multi-ethnic societies such as ours where such treatments are forced in the name of religion or nation becomes suspect. The authority, the law, and the sacred usually become justifications or instruments of repression in such spaces wherever individualism tries to raise its head. When one sees a commotion or a disequilibrium from the above in a given socio-spatial space, it is usually (but not necessarily) the case that one person's or group's 'individualism' is becoming a matter of nuisance to others, or is in direct clash with other strands of 'individualisms', and hence the disharmony. Lord Ramakrishna's teaching of mutual respect and harmony or Emile Durkheim's idea of Sacralisation, i.e. 'that humans have a nobler, more spiritual side and that life has a higher purpose than pleasure or profit' (Goodhart 2012) try to apply a kind of balm that may bring in a temporary quiet, but such dissentions keep appearing again and again.[9]

At the same time, this is also true that with the decline of views on managing societies such as Liberal universalism and Marxist universalism, one could see the rise of another—in fact the end of the great empires, has coincided with an increase of another kind of model of governance based on nationalism, fundamentalism (religious or otherwise), and a new brand of racism, exerting a decisive pressure on social governance, resulting in events with tragic consequences for humanity—ranging from riots, dislocations, mass exodus to wars. What is more distressing is that we find this return to identity politics even when we are faced with a grave worldwide economic crisis today, as between the two world wars.

The problem is that such clashes of identities have no place for appreciating otherness and differences. In fact, it is a dangerous strategy to hold on to, especially in the field of education. For linguistic minorities and migrants, the threat that an alien language poses in the early schooling periods can be a great problem for their growth in later years. Further, the now popular 'Son-of-the-soil' theory is only an extension of this general feeling of intolerance. Whether we consider South Asia or Europe or pay attention to the song of America for the Americans, the theory remains the same. The terms such as 'ethnic minorities' or 'ethnico-national' or even 'linguistico-cultural' groups have all been a matter of debate during this time. The likely ill-effect of this has not been difficult to see, as there would then arise greater disequilibrium that would argue in favour of assertion of independence by the diverse social formations, or division of geo-political spaces within (the most recent being the break-up of the state of Andhra Pradesh into Telengana and Andhra) or across countries (Pakistan's western and eastern wings having become separate countries of Pakistan and Bangladesh) showing a clear sign of the increasing segmentation of modern societies. 'Multicultural and multi-ethnic societies thus pose problems which raise fundamental questions about the organization of our civilizations', says Henri Giordan (1993) in his discussion paper—'Multicultural and Multi-ethnic Societies' under the UNESCO Series on 'Management of Social Transformation'.[10]

View From Below

What should then be the view from below? How would that alter the course of planning and action in the sector of development of languages, culture and education? We believe that a view such as this might lead to an alternative way of configuring the speech communities and that, in turn, may lead to transitions into a better world.

Schooling or formal education is often used as a term instead of its generic counterpart, namely education, which is not confined to schooling. Although the term education itself presupposes a source of education—which on some occasions is a schoolroom, but could also be the world at large. Writing in the *Times of India*'s web-portal on 16 April 2003, Sandy Sundaram writes in a centre-spread essay titled 'Speaking Free' about the predicament of many multilingual and pluri-cultural families of India like her own in the following words:

> Father was posted in the 'true' Telugu districts; it was but natural that we siblings spoke purest Telugu. Grandma, being a true Tamilian, made sure we also spoke Tamil and tutors gave us the basics of English.

> Mother, being a very wise lady, engaged a Hindi tutor. To complicate matters, father went to Calicut and Mangalore, making us reasonably proficient in Kannada and Malayalam. This multi-lingual upbringing can be a boon and a curse. Curse in that: occasionally, amnesia would set in and one stuttered and failed to communicate; at others the words had an entirely different syntax...[11]

Such diversities are real.

If there is a positive encouragement to the plural ethos in planning for education through a set of organised state interventions, it would be an ideal move. It would go in the right direction in meeting the objectives for the development of minor and minority languages as argued in a UNESCO document on mother tongue education dated 1953. In civil societies, there should be no disagreement now that the linguistic minority communities also have a right to develop their own languages and writing systems. It goes without saying that such experiences of picking up languages teaches us the possibilities of a *world school* (literally, *Viśva-vidyālaya*—Indian translation of the term 'University') where the world itself is the source of education, which would mean that learners are not limited to a school and there is immense potential outside schools as well. Parallel to the world-school, is this related concept of *school of life*. For instance, although mathematics in schoolrooms is taught in isolation, most persons use mathematics and numbers for measurements or financial transactions. The school of life is cognisant of the long term practicality of knowledge dissemination, so as to map today's instructions for tomorrow's utility. Our Utopia, which we could tentatively call *Vidyaranya*, is a culmination of these two schools.[12] As we move forward the concept of *Vidyaranya* will help us problematise education in India.

Here we present a critique of existing philosophies of educational transformation and development in brief before outlining our utopia for a changed landscape. Presently prevalent approaches use the gap finding methodology of investigating and fixing the educational system. Inputs are noted, processes are outlined, outputs and outcomes are specified and a hypothesis of change is charted out. The defined outcomes and outputs and target of the effort are based on what should be and what is today, giving us the requirements to build a bridge to the ideal state. The limitation of the gap finding methodology lies in the heart of its ideal; an ideal built on the present realities. Although it is very pragmatic, the ideal is limited to the tensions of the present. We become very focused on making the best of what is available and yet we do not stop asking if indeed what is considered to be the best is the most appropriate and ideal possibility here. As the ideal borne out of constraints and realities of today drives us to busy ourselves with plugging the gaps and plumbing the leaks, we are prone to overlook the larger canvas of probabilities and possibilities. Problematising education through utopia encourages one to construct ideas without bounds. Beginning with a clean slate, the conditions of the present and past inspire us to investigate possibilities bypassing modes of previous failures. For example, we now know that a mechanised education system that follows the industrial model and strives to 'create' competent workers for different sectors is not apt for the heterogeneity and creativity that define India, filled with multiple knowledge avenues, both local and national. Furthermore, we also know that personalised education has successfully worked in Indian civilisation for a long time, and is often realised through the traditions of master and apprentice or environments where learners and teachers participate in the discovery of knowledge together, and where a whole tradition is established through these practices across many generations.

Consider the *Annual Status of Education Report* (ASER 2014),[13] a yearly citizen-led, household based survey of approximate six lakh children across 3 lakh homes from 577 rural districts of India that has showcased the limitations of our existing philosophy and implementation of the school education system, where more than half the children placed at the fag end of their primary education are still, for all practical means, close to being illiterate. In conjunction with multiple rounds of National Achievement Surveys, large scale achievements have shown the frailty of our education, thus prompting the need to think and deliberate outside its purview. If one were to continue following this path of failure, the possibility of succeeding becomes improbable as the years pass by. The utopia of *Vidyaranya*[14] considers invoking the rural mindset of trust while building its aims and educational futurescape to deliver. Let us elaborate on this point: What do we mean by the mindset of trust? A farmer in rural parts of India, despite having taken precautionary measures still trusts the weather and seasonal cycles to deliver. We trust medical professionals and doctors to diagnose our ailments and give the correct treatment in accordance with our ailment. The rural populace trusts banks similarly, where their wealth is stowed away with the belief that the bank will not lose their hard earned money. Quite similarly, rural people have a penchant of trusting schools and associate stakeholders. In contrast the urban space survives on implementation and gains (outcomes) in addition to trust - but not wholly dependent on it. *Vidyaranya* as the freehold forest of learning builds on this available quality of trust and harnesses it to better education across urban as well as rural parts of India.

India has over six lakh functional communities that have their own unique culture of commerce, society and learning;[15] they also have shared villages, regions or districts, i.e. physical spaces that are more than a matter of geographies for them as they share a common core of being as well. These cultural islands are connected physically via roads, railways and an information system (both digital and non-digital). Local concerns, local festivities, and the locally popular stories and legends bind them together. More so, they are also inclined to identify with a common region, and its linguistic, socio-economic, cultural and religious landscape. An aggregation of approximately 20-60 villages constitute a *Panchayat Samiti*—where residents of its member villages agree to adhere to the locally ratified ideas of peace, justice and prosperity. Such decentralised governance is not novel to Indian civilisation. This inspires us to propose a cluster of 10-15 villages forming a *Gram Siksha Samiti*, a non-formal grassroots level functional unit responsible for overseeing education in its member villages. Learners from these villages are participants in their own education, an education that is self- determined and directed towards the discovery of their selves. Our educational utopia could then be distributed throughout these roughly 60,000 local democratic units. Since each school belongs to these village-clusters, the principal of each such school is aware of the unique cultural milieu of the region. They know the stories and legends that appeal to learners the most, and have the maximum capacity to understand the contextual learning requirements of the students. The school need not put any restriction on age. It will be a place where the young and old can come together to learn together. There is much to be gained from such intermingling of experiences—the young receiving lessons from people who have lived through much time and change, and the old benefitting from the constant curiosity of younger children.

One of the first lessons to be learned in these *Vidyaranya* schools is fearlessness—the ability to question without reprimand and the art of listening. Notice that the current emphasis of educational techniques today focus on reading and speaking, whereas what we are recommending is to lay emphasis on listening and comprehending. In fact, it is seldom realised that 'Oralcy' is as important as 'Literacy'. The principals, in collaboration with the chiefs of the local *Gram Siksha Samiti,* are together collectively responsible for weaving local systems of knowledge with other knowledge systems that are more established. Such a net of information and thought allows for the integration of the organic and inorganic—knowledge that a learner internalises from a very young age from their surroundings and that which is foreign to their local environs. The principal will have to work with school teachers and the community who help children learn the basics and apply their learning to questions and problem areas of their own choosing. For example, a child may learn to create a right-angled triangle from a teacher, but a mason is an ideal source of knowledge when it comes to the application of Pythagoras theorem. Some players in elementary education did experiment with teaching science and practicals using local materials rather than depending on sophisticated laboratories. Thus, the schools we think could usher in change must have participation of the local artisans and skilled personnel. The participatory nature of this Utopian schooling helps create a learning environment that is not only learner centric but also culturally aware. This cultural awareness aids in the contextualisation of knowledge. Learners learn concepts through examples and case studies—in the classrooms, at the market, in the workshops and factories or mills in the region, or similar spaces that connect to their senses. And technology is used to enrich the knowledge system as a whole through the sharing of ideas and stories across people in these islands of learning through multiple channels of communication—between children, principals, teachers and communities across different *gram panchayats*. Groups of children, communities, and village clusters here work together as learning units, not only gaining from learning and solving problems as part of a group but also contributing their own experiences to the group. The principals of these learning units come together in groups of ten at conferences to share their experiences and challenges. They are mentored by a panel of the elected Council that oversees the conferences of principals. Their leadership is accessible to the learners as they are elected by and for those under their guidance. Each council in effect aids the learning atmosphere across 500 villages. The council facilitates the inquisitiveness and eagerness of learners.

They are also responsible for the discovery and continued development of teachers and community member-instructors who are not only capable and motivated but are invested and specially trained in listening to and observing as well as aiding in the learning of children. The council members themselves have to be equally driven problem solvers.

The learning environment aids in the discovery of the self and group identities. Only through the knowledge and understanding of oneself does external knowledge add to the wholesome development of individuals. The interaction of learners with specialists and technically qualified people in the community helps in the exploration of others and practical questions such as 'how to…', 'what to…' and 'where to…' While school teachers are responsible for basic knowledge development of children, including reading and numeracy, they are also key facilitators of knowledge discovery for individual students as well as groups of learners and communities participating together.

The democratisation of learning demands a system enabled to accommodate and respect the individual motivation of learners. The utopia of *Vidyaranya* is open and ready to accept varying values that people assign to learning and education. Learners may be motivated to participate in their educational exercise for a plethora of reasons; some participating to earn a degree, others to equip themselves with skills to earn a better living in time, social prestige, for the sake of knowledge, or simply for the love and happiness earned from gaining new knowledge. The senior students may also be involved in training and aiding the much younger learners and beginners. Members of this utopian educational system should not be constrained by any of these motivational purposes as the reason learners may want to participate in utopian learning could be as numerous as the number of learners.

The improbability of the *Vidyaranya* Utopia is not insurmountable; it requires a willing government and local governance clusters accepting of change, a society of learners, and 60,000 citizens who willingly take the responsibility of facilitating the development of learners; namely the principals and council or the *Gram Siksha Samiti* members from amongst a billion. The Utopian model of education and learning adapts knowledge and cultural contextualisation at the finer scale, learning from the learners themselves, making the effort participatory in nature. This participatory experimentation will be crucial to the democratisation of learning in India of the future times where the heterogeneous nature of learning and knowledge is utilised to its full potential, instead of constraining it with limited and myopic borders. The multiple levels of interconnectivity of *Vidyaranya*'s learning communities would thus create a network that is inherently intelligent and is prone to learning from the experiences of its participants. This bottom-up approach, or a 'view from below' would be capable of shaping or informing higher level policies through this network of information and knowledge flow. The network could have seven dimensions: (i) Space, (ii) Time, (iii) Personnel, (iv) Tools, (v) Behaviour, (vi) Politics and Economics, and (vii) Outcome or Quality. Each of these dimensions could then be expanded to include certain components. For instance, 'Space' could include physical space/infrastructure, technology solutions, facilities and functional classrooms, rural schools and indigenous solutions, facilities and ratio of users, texts and materials, instruments and labs as well as space for extra-curricular activities. Similarly, the 'Time' dimension could be expanded in terms of teaching load and estimation of time allotment, division of time at hand—units (year/half-year/ quarter/semester/ fortnight/week-wise monitoring), units of teaching and credit levels, matching/syncing seasons with contents, tests, gaps, schedules and self-assessments, computer time/browsing/referencing/virtual libraries, physical library hours/book or content reading time and time for social work. teachers, principals, administration/school management, policy and decision-makers, boards of examinations/evaluators/tabulators/exam managers, curriculum designers/system developers, tutors (school-level and private) will all come under 'personnel' as much as the parents/community leaders/ mentors, and the learners and self-learners themselves. Under the 'Tools,' the most important thing would be learning material—both conventional, or non-digital kind (books, distance learning units, activity-materials, exercises and self-checks/work-sheets) as well as digital materials (CDs, DVDs, A/V Materials—especially on tablets, pre-loaded machines, portals, searchable/ browser-based materials, and subject/language-based games), and then there are assessments (periodic self-check and formal assessments) and assignments (library based and activity based), besides the quality/M&E type-tools. The dimension of 'Behaviour' includes acute understanding of student profiles, understanding the motivation of learners, constant evaluation of teacher motivation and personal development and self-knowledge. Politics of inclusion and economics of participation are both important under the sixth dimension. In the 'Outcome or Quality' segment, the points are: Learner centric learning goals (outcomes), quality of teachers, tools, and facilities as well as outcome oriented pedagogy.

Concluding Remarks

Education aims to empower individuals to realise their freedom and opportunities. Although the universalisation of primary education is meant to foster the love for learning and knowledge amongst children, universalisation of a universal assumes the uniformity of children's attitude, behaviour and capacity to learn; clearly the single most prominent fallacy of universalisation. Considering that socio-cultural cognition is triggered by one's speech and is language-dependent, fostering locally influenced knowledge systems is a reasonable means of harnessing the individuality of every child. Utopian thought transformed into policies promoting the uniqueness of a child and made probable by the inclusion of restrictions have the potential of informing an efficient and useful child development platform. Instead of expecting children to align themselves with education and aligning education with business or industrial opportunities, it is appropriate to empower education to consider children individually so as to introduce democratic values.

Furthermore, homogenisation is not a desirable reality for the multi-lingual and pluri-cultural people of India. Hypothetically, despite the existence of a common medium of communication (through an enforced language policy) the existence and practice of multiple languages or speech varieties (stylistic and other variations) would essentially negate the adherence to 'one people, one language'. Persons from heterogeneous groups based on gender, regions of origin, caste and creed and other socio-cultural traits would invariably use multiple perspectives. Development and growth based on utopian ideals have the capacity to promote the spirit of togetherness while also promoting language and educational heterogeneity. Many language and multi-perspective policies are bound to be carefully drafted, and fraught with challenges of implementation. But given the potential payoff, the hurdles could be viewed as bumps on the road towards a reality where the nations sweat for their children today to enable them to achieve freedom and participatory service to their nation in the future.

Endnotes

1 Government of India. *Migration in India 2007-08 Report* (New Delhi: Ministry of Statistics and Programme Implementation, 2010).

2 http://blogs.worldbank.org/peoplemove/almost-a-third-of-indians-or-over-300-million-people-are-migrants

3 Kumar Suresh Singh, and S. Manoharan, *People of India, Vol 9. Languages and Script* (New Delhi: Anthropological Survey of India, 1993).

4 The Registrar General of India, *Census of India* (New Delhi: Office of the Registrar General & Census Commissioner, India, 1961).

5 'Utopia series: the schools of the future,' accessed at: http://thephilosophersmail.com/utopia/utopia-series-schools-in-the-future/.

6 Shmuel Eisenstadt, 'Breakdowns of Modernization,' *Economic Development and Cultural Change* 12 (1964): 345-67.

7 Gunnar Myrdal, *Asian Drama. An Inquiry into the Poverty of Nations*, 3 volumes (New York: Twentieth Century Fund, 1968).

8 Bhasmāsura is a character in Hindu mythology who performed a penance to obtain a boon from Lord Shiva. He requested the power to burn anyone whose head he would touch, into ashes (*bhasma*). When Lord Shiva granted the boon, Bhasmāsura tried to chase Shiva to touch his head so that he could gain Shiva's consort, Pārvatī.

9 David Goodhart, 'Last hope for the left.' Prospect, March-April 2012, http://www.prospectmagazine.co.uk/arts-and-books/haidt-weird-liberals-righteous-mind-america.

10 Henri Giordan, 'Multicultural and Multiethnic Societies.' Management of Social Transformations (MOST), Discussion paper 1 (Paris: UNESCO 1993. http://www.unesco.org/most/giordeng.htm 1993 [accessed July 7, 2016])

11 Sandy Sundaram, 'Speaking Free,' *Times of India,* April 16, 2003.

12 As we know 'Vidyaranya' (1300-1386) tried to combine all schools of thought, often mutually conflicting, into one text, the *Sarvadarśanasaṅgraha* and the Vijayanagara Empire was founded in the 14th century around the present-day temple town of Hampi, upon his prudent advice.

13 ASER Centre, *Annual Status of Education Report* (New Delhi: ASER Centre http://img.asercentre.org/docs/Publications/ASER%20Reports ASER_2013/ASER2013_report%20sections/aser2013fullreportenglish.pdf [accessed June 3, 2016]).

14 A reference is also made to the philosophy of 'Vidyaranya School' in Hyderabad which draws its inspiration from the ideas of the philosopher Jiddu Krishnamurti (1895–1986).

15 India has more than 638,000 villages and 238,617 gram panchayats (Census 2011).

Indian Poetry in English

Tabish Khair

Where is Indian poetry in English headed? No one can answer that question. A critic who claims to predict the future is a charlatan. And yet, one can look at the paths traversed by Indian poetry in English until now and perhaps guess the directions in which it will march, or stumble, on.

In a recent paper, Jahan Ramazani makes a valid point—and a point made less often in mainstream critical circles in the USA and UK than in those of postcolonial criticism—about the dominance of 'single-nation genealogies' in studies of modern and contemporary poetry in English.[1] Strangely, the case of 'Indian English poetry' can be seen differently: Indian English poetry has been far too readily and uncritically inserted into the moulds of 'transnationalism'. Perhaps this was inevitable, given its 'name'. After all, while critics talk (mostly) of English, American, Irish, Scottish, Canadian or, even, Jamaican poetry, we talk of 'Indian English' (or, earlier on, 'Anglo-Indian' and 'Indo-Anglian') poetry. Its very 'name' inserts Indian English poetry into 'transnational' networks, and while this insertion is correct and necessary to a point, it can also be misleading and unfair to the distinctive character of Indian poetry in English, if taken too far.

But this insertion starts quite early on. After all, as V.K. Gokak famously remarked, 'Indo-Anglian poetry was born under a Romantic star.'[2] One has to agree with this perception to a certain degree, for at least historically when the first significant Indian English poet (Henry Louis Vivian Derozio [1809–1831]) started writing, major British Romantics, like Lord Byron and William Wordsworth, were still alive. The Romantic star obviously twinkled in the West, and cast its light on Indian English poetry. But it did not twinkle in the same way as in the West. Far from it. Let us cast a look at an early poem 'The Harp of India' by Henry Derozio.

Derozio starts his sonnet by addressing, with a degree of apotheosis, 'the harp of India':

Why hang'st thou lonely on yon withered bough?
Unstrung for ever, must thou there remain;
Thy music once was sweet—who hears it now?
Why doth the breeze sigh over thee in vain?[3]

Forget about the 'Romantic' diction of the poem: it would be as anachronistic to blame Derozio for it, as it would be to rap the ghost of Lord Byron, who was alive when Derozio started writing, on the knuckle for poems like 'The Giaour' and 'The Corsair'. What is interesting is the fact that Derozio laments the silencing of the 'harp' of India. This lament fits into a growing Orientalist tendency in the 19th century to posit a glorious ancient past for India, and contrast it to the degraded present. This was in keeping with 19th-century theories of civilisation and degeneration and, later, social evolution, and it could cut both ways: it could be used to defend British colonisers (as restorers of India's ancient vigour) and it could be used to critique British colonisation.

As such, if Derozio's sonnet, written in English, is a fragment of the 'new' culture of colonised India, it is also—despite being written in English—a critique of present circumstances and, hence, at least potentially a critique of colonisation. This aspect is under-girded by the imagery of the second stanza, where the 'harp' of India is presented as having been bound by 'Silence' in 'her fatal chain', portrayed as 'neglected' and compared, perhaps with echoes of P.B. Shelley's 'Ozymandias' , with a 'ruined monument on desert plain'. If the 'ruined monument' is a partly Orientalist construct of the Indian past, the 'desert plain' is a potentially nationalist critique of colonisation.

The sonnet proceeds. The poet humbly acknowledges his inferiority to the great poets of the past ('many a hand more worthy far than mine'), notes that 'those hands are cold', and concludes:

...but if thy notes divine
May be by mortal wakened once again,
Harp of my country, let me strike the strain![4]

Note again: 'harp of my country', not harp of, say, the Muses. In the 18th century, the Black Caribbean poet, Francis Williams, wrote a Latin ode to welcome a new British Governor. In itself, an act of colonial 'mimicry', the ode however assumed a radical, independent perspective —the voice of the subaltern—not only in its direct critique of colour-based racism but also in the fact that it was addressed to a 'black Muse'. Similarly, Derozio's poem in English cannot be seen only or even primarily in the light of colonial 'mimicry'. The poem speaks in a voice that has not been derived simply from the discourses of the colonisers.

And yet, it remains a voice in English, and that returns us to the position of English in India. For the 'harp' of India was by no means 'silent' in the 1820s and '30s: many Indian languages were undergoing a blossoming because of diverse reasons. The greatest age of Urdu poetry was taking place in Delhi, and poets like Zauq and Ghalib were still alive. Could it be that if Derozio had been writing in a language other than English, he might have heard other harps playing more loudly than he seems to have?

And would these have been 'harps'? However, Derozio's choice of 'harp' is not only a vestige of the classical imagery of Romanticism or the consequence of his choice of language. If one thinks about the reasons why Derozio might have preferred 'harp' over the more obviously classical equivalent, 'lyre', one opens up a rich field of political possibilities. The choice of 'harp' carries another echo, and one that—for all we know—Derozio might well have retained consciously.

Let us try and place this choice in the political context of the early 19th century, a context that Derozio, writing and reading in English, would have some inkling of (and, say, Zauq, writing in Urdu, would not have been able to employ or use). The 'harp without crown' was the symbol of the Society of United Irishmen, founded in the 18th century as a liberal organisation working for parliamentary reform in Ireland, but greatly radicalised by the end of the century. In 1798, the Society of United Irishmen, allied with the republicans of revolutionary France, launched a major rebellion with the aim of ending British rule over Ireland.

This rebellion sent echoes all over the British Empire and remained a force in the 'international revolutionary circuit' for decades—perhaps also reflected, even after the chimes of the 1798 Uprising had grown inaudible, in the presence of Indian nationalist squads during St Patrick's Day parades in USA as late as the 20th century. In Calcutta (now Kolkata), then capital of British India, Derozio could hardly have been unaware of it in the 1820s.

So here we are: an Indian writer, employing English. With this combination come a set of problems, and a set of possibilities. Perhaps Derozio cannot always hear the music of other Indian harps—as was perhaps the case with Salman Rushdie in the 20th century, when he edited and introduced his anthology of the best Indian writing from 1947 to 1997, and managed to leave out all except two or three texts written in languages other than English (and dismissed Indian English poetry with airy brusqueness). But Derozio does not simply mimic the master's voice. He sets his own political agenda, shaped by his own relationship to English, to time and space. And he can employ his chosen or imposed language, English, to do things—for instance, consciously or unconsciously, suggest an international radical politics—that would not have been possible, or not in the same way, in Urdu, or Hindi, or Tamil. It is this that, I believe, Indians writing in English have to bear in mind.

Unfortunately, if praise or blame for its legible, anglophone 'transnationality' (as and only as mimicry) hobbled Indian poetry in English in the Commonwealth and pre-Commonwealth past, something similar seems to hold it down in the postcolonial present. For the postcolonial present has helped further and has coincided with a democratic privileging of the spoken word in literature, including poetry. From literature to the parole of linguistics, the written word has been sorely battered—and for good reason—in recent decades. As the man who 'didn't graduate' but 'immigrate' warned sometime back in John Agard's 'Listen Mr Oxford Don':

I ent have no gun
I ent have no knife
but mugging de Queen's English
is the story of my life...[5]

Not only the 'story of my life', but absolutely necessary for the 'story of my life' to be told in postcolonial contexts. This has been most comprehensively addressed by Edward Kamau Brathwaite's *History of the Voice*,[6] a major intervention in poetry criticism by an important poet. What it says adds to the discourse on postcolonial poetry, but it is particularly aimed at Caribbean poetry (as the subtitle indicates). It would be a mistake—and a mistake that I am sure Brathwaite would warn us against—to apply it simplistically to Indian poetry in English.

Brathwaite's discussion of 'nation language in anglophone Caribbean poetry' can be used more effectively in the context of Indian poetry in English, if it is not applied verbatim. It is true, as Brathwaite says of Caribbean poetry, that 'the noise that it makes is part of the meaning, and if you ignore the noise (or what you think of as noise, shall I say) then you lose part of the meaning.'[7] But this 'what you think of as noise' refers to two main factors in Brathwaite's essay: the 'oral tradition' and 'syllabic intelligence'. Oral tradition is clear enough as a description, and I will return to it later. But Brathwaite makes a crucial point about 'syllabic intelligence': he argues that the English that has been learnt by Caribbean speakers does not manage, because of transplantation and youth in the postcolonial context, to express the sounds of all Caribbean realities. For instance, he illustrates, this standard English has to be fractured and stretched and distorted to express the force and character of a 'hurricane' in the Caribbean, something that is both more common there and different from storms in England.

This applies to India too, though in slightly different ways. But the other factor, 'oral tradition', which combines to manufacture the kind of contextual 'syllabic intelligence' that Standard English lacks, is a completely different matter in India. There are 'oral traditions' in India, but they exist in languages other than English. English is and still remains a predominantly written language in India.

As I have pointed out in various articles, the English spoken by Indians who speak English from choice varies in its accent and is inflected by the 'idiolect' of the speaker. But it remains a largely textual and 'standard' English in its vocabulary and syntax, informed by the presence of largely textual versions of other Indian languages. On the other hand, at least 90 per cent of all Indians do not speak English at all, though a number of them speak standard versions of other Indian languages.

The standard postcolonialist discourse of 'creolisation' as well as the recent celebration of the 'spoken voice' in mainstream British and American poetry cannot be transposed to Indian poetry in English. No doubt there is 'hybridity', but it is a distinctive type of hybridity. As A.K. Mehrotra puts it in his introduction to *Twelve Modern Indian Poets*, most Indian English poets' 'idiolect is constituted differently: Ramanujan's is of English-Kannada-Tamil, Kolatkar's and Chitre's of English-Marathi, Ali's of English-Urdu, Mahapatra's of English-Oriya, and Jussawalla has in an interview spoken of 'various languages crawling around inside [his] head.'[8] Actually, the Indian English poet whose idiolect is confined to English/pidgin English is extremely rare. In his introduction, Mehrotra lists only one: Eunice de Souza. Bruce King's extensive survey of modern Indian English poetry reveals that only 4 out of 32 significant poets list English as the only language spoken at home.[9] However, one can imagine this factor changing—it has been slightly since the 1980s—in the future, at least in the larger cities of India.

Still, one cannot confuse this with either the interplay of dialect and Standard English in Toni Harrison or the interplay of Creole and Standard English in, say, Edward Kamau Brathwaite or Linton Kwesi Johnson. Indian writers are not only confronted with largely textual English, but also with its relationship to largely self-sufficient and textual traditions in other Indian languages. Given the class structures of education in India, English, when it 'relates' to other Indian languages is much more likely to relate to, say, textualised Hindi, Urdu, Marathi, or Tamil than to some vernacular dialect of those languages, or even Bhojpuri, or some aboriginal language. Moreover, the sort of displacement and deprivation that Caribbean poets had to confront to carve out their rich and vibrant literary traditions do not exist in the same form or the same degree (historically) for Indians who write in English.

But to say this is not to dismiss Indian English poetry. For literary voice is never a tape recording of some voice out there: it is always a creative construct. While it can be enriched by 'oral traditions' it does not depend simply—as Brathwaite's poetry indicates again and again—solely on the spoken voice. The written alphabet, as well as dots, spaces, commas, etc., on the page, all play a role in poetry. The very transnationalism of modernist poetry that Ramazani champions in his paper depended largely on these textual elements, on the fact that literature today is also 'written literature'. Moreover, in India we have a long tradition of literature in largely textual and standardised 'elite' languages: Sanskrit and Persian. To ignore this tradition is to deprive Indian English poetry of its heritage—and its voice.

No doubt, there was and is cause to fight for the spoken word as an essential element in poetry. And yet, it should be recalled that a simple celebration of the spoken word is not necessarily a mantra for change, freedom, 'speaking back', or even greater critical depth. One can argue that critics writing about literary languages in English have been guilty of what Jacques Derrida has termed 'logocentrism'. One does not need to buy the entire Derridaean package to recognise the dominant logocentrism of criticism that establishes a binary opposition between 'a pure, inner core or origin (in language, voice), and the externalized mediation of this core or origin (writing).'[10]This opposition also privileges the 'originary' or inner core over the externalised mediation, that is, voice or speech over writing.

A conservative critic talks about the purity of some version of standard English and how it remains true to the 'real rhythms' of the language; a radical critic finds some working class dialect or Caribbean Creole to celebrate. But even though these two kinds of critics are liable to come to blows over the language that 'matters', their basic assumption is the same: that literary language is a kind of tape-recorder. This is a misleading assumption. Literary languages do not simply imitate or mimic spoken language. However, they can, in some cases and under certain circumstances, give the impression of doing so. This impression is art and being art it is artificial; it is not simple verisimilitude or mimicry. This was as true of Mark Twain as it is of Salman Rushdie.

Critics who dismiss all or almost all of Indian English poetry, as Rushdie himself did in his anthology, are usually guilty of not reading Indian English poems as they demand to be read. With a few exceptions, usually of light verse, as I have indicated in my reading of Nissim Ezekiel's 'Irani Restaurant Instructions', the 'literary languages' of Indian poems in English present a particular combination of the written and the spoken.[11] In this they are not different in kind but in extent from literary languages in general. But this extent has to be registered and read. Indian English poetry cannot be praised, as Anita Desai praises Rushdie, for he 'finally brought the spoken language off the streets onto the printed page...Suddenly it was made apparent that the Indian writer had as distinctive and authentic a voice as the American or the Caribbean.'[12] Yes, the Indian English writer has a voice that is as 'distinctive and authentic a voice as the American of the Caribbean' writer, but this voice cannot be picked off the 'streets' of India because English is not spoken on the streets of India. It is spoken in the classrooms, offices, drawing-rooms, and colleges, though not all, of India. When spoken in the 'streets' it comes in different registers, and is shot through with differences of class and region. It cannot be picked off the 'streets' of India and turned, with minimal art, into a 'literary language.'

And that may be the reason why the poems that work most owe a lot to the conscious balance of the written and the spoken word that one finds in much of Modernist literature. This applies to Arun Kolatkar as much as to A.K. Ramanujan. For instance the 'poems' of Kolatkar's great work, *Jejuri*, need to be read on the page before and as they are spoken aloud. The spoken voice is not just the voice of, as is the case that follows, a 'small person'; it also needs to be spelt in small letters, for instance, to convey the effect sought by Kolatkar.

To conclude, the language of Indian English poetry has its own register, and one that reflects the position of English in India. To ignore this register may be possible for poets who write elsewhere (as is the case with Daljit Nagra's excellent *Look We Have Coming to Dover!*) or assume, as Vikram Seth magisterially does in *The Golden Gate*, another narrative space. It may also be possible to ignore this register for comic effect or short and limited contexts. But a poet who sets out to write about complex aspects of India in English cannot ignore this distinctively 'textual' (but not unrelated to the spoken voice) register of Indian poetry in English.

If one applies this perspective to the poems in the best anthologies of recent Indian poetry, such as those by Sudeep Sen, Ranjit Hoskote, and Jeet Thayil, one finds a tool that frees many of the poems from the straightjacket of postcolonial creolisation and Rushdian hybridity into which they are often fitted, or dismissed for not fitting. The best of Indian English poetry has always had to negotiate its own distinctive relationship to English, to other Indian languages and to the world: unfortunately, criticism has seldom followed in its wake.

When I imagine the year 2047, I suspect the role of English in India would have changed a bit further: English might be more of a spoken language in urban India, as has been the trend since the 1980s, despite the protests of the Hindu Right. But it will still *not* be a spoken language like it is in Jamaica or Ireland. The kind of lightly skipping Indo-urban English—with a thin globalised veneer—that is taking over popular Indian English fiction (in the Chetan Bhagat era) will probably make its presence felt in poetry too. But will it be good poetry—for poetry demands a more layered, nuanced use of language than fiction or prose? You can skip in poetry too, but only if you hear a deeper beat.

I have my opinions, but only time will provide the answers.

This article was previously published as 'Language in Indian Poetry in English' in Smita Agarwal, ed. Marginalized: Indian Poetry in English *(Amsterdam: Rodopi. 2014), and is reproduced here with the permission of the author.*

Endnotes

1 Jahan Ramazani, 'A Transnational Poetics,' *American Literary Review* XVIII /2 (Summer 2006): 332-59.

2 V.K. Gokak, *The Golden Treasury of Indo-Anglian Poetry* (1970) (New Delhi: Sahitya Akademi, 1985), p. 19.

3 Ibid. p. 53.

4 Ibid.

5 John Agard, Mangoes and Bullets. (London: Serpent's Tail, 1990).

6 Edward K. Brathwaite, *History of the Voice: Development of Nation Language in Anglophone Caribbean Poetry* (London: New Beacon Books Ltd, 1984).

7 Edward K. Brathwaite, *History of the Voice: The Development of Nation Language in Anglophone Caribbean Poetry* (1984) (London and Port of Spain: New Beacon Books, 1995), 17.

8 Arvind K. Mehrotra, ed., *The Oxford India Anthology of Twelve Modern Indian Poets* (New Delhi: OUP, 1992), p. 6.

9 Bruce King, *Modern Indian Poetry in English* (Delhi: Oxford University Press, 1987/1994), pp. 277–84.

10 Christopher Johnson, *Derrida* (New York: Routledge, 1997/1990), p. 40.

11 Tabish Khair, 'Indian English Poetry: Problems of Language and Prosody,' in *A World of Local Voices*, ed. Klaus Martens, Paul Morris and Arlette Warken (Würzburg: Neumann Gmbh, 2003), pp. 55-63.

12 Malashri Lal, *The Law of the Threshold: Women Writers in Indian English* (Shimla: Indian Institute of Advanced Study, 1995), p. 130.

The Indian Novel Today: Existing and Emerging Paradigms

Namrata Rathore Mahanta, Banibrata Mahanta

The idea of India was marked by a variety of tensions from the time of colonial rule, and these ranged from religion and region to class and caste. These were all inherited by the new country. In the initial years, the euphoria of formal decolonisation and charismatic leadership temporarily put all these problems on the backburner (though they did periodically surface in the forms of riots, movements, and agitations). However, as the excitement waned and unresolved realities took the centre stage, the country and its citizenry was beset by despondency and a consequent loss of faith in the vision of its leaders. The conception of the unified nation and sense of national identity were also questioned, as was the capability of the modern nation to adequately and fairly represent all sections of its populace. Dissenting voices gained ground, and the secular, democratic republic envisaged by the founding fathers of the constitution came to be interrogated. Religious, ethnic, regional, class and caste considerations vied for legitimacy/primacy with these ideals. The divergences between secular nationalist ideas and ideologies of initial times and emergent group identities led to greater plurality, as also to the rise of expediency and manipulation as logic.

The changing realities of the country find expression in all genres and across the various languages and regions of India and reflect this change in tenor. Writing back to colonisation was complemented by dissent against the existing realities of the nation state. This is seen most succinctly in the Indian novel. The idealism and optimism of integrative nationalism and national identity are reflected in the early novels and their realistic modes of representation, which critiqued yet connected to the reality of the country as it existed. As homogenised national identity was found to fall short and increasingly challenged in the latter part of the twentieth century, the novels of this period are characterised by skepticism and disillusionment, and become increasingly heterogeneous and fragmentary. Around this time, globalisation happened, and India aspired to reposition itself, economically and politically, as a global player.

The Indian novel has come a long way since its first days. Wrought in turn by colonisation of the country, independence, and the myriad developments that ensued within the country, it is in present times significantly impacted by political, social, and cultural changes occasioned by globalisation, economic liberalisation, and the concurrent refashioning of the idea of India. Both Indian novels in English and novels written in the bhashas (the languages of India) are affected by these global changes. The translation of bhasha novels into English is in significant part a manifestation of the impact of globalisation and the role played by the English language. This article focuses on the impact of globalisation on both these categories of the Indian novel. Within the framework of the stated concerns, trends are analysed and new directions are envisaged.

Let us begin with the Indian novel in English. The plurality of what constitutes literatures written in English today is in stark contrast to the times when it was synonymous with a particular geographical location. From American, Canadian, and Australian Literatures to the literatures of Asian and African countries, the thematic, cultural, social, and linguistic complexities of this body of literature defy all attempts at classification. Labels like Colonial Literature, Dominion Literature, and Commonwealth Literature intended to bring together the literature of Great Britain and English language literature from those parts of the globe which were impacted by England's colonial policies. Of these, the term Commonwealth Literature has had the widest currency. While some critics argue that it is an apolitical term used to designate literature produced in English from those parts of the world which were historically connected to Great Britain, others acknowledge that the historical and political implications of the term cannot be wished away.

Implicit in this debate as well as accruing from it are two positions: the universalist and the localist. The universalist view argues that all works written in English can be classified as different manifestations of a global phenomenon and ultimately move towards a multicultural formation both in terms of subject and readership, and should thus be studied under one rubric. The localist position assigns a premium to the place-value of a work of literature and its rootedness in a particular milieu, tradition, and culture. Works in English from the erstwhile colonies which call for a certain degree of familiarity with the context in which they are situated are cases in point. Works rooted in cultural specificities, for example in the folk traditions of a particular culture, cannot be fully understood if one is not familiar with them. The debate assumes greater significance in the present times of globalisation and supposed interconnectedness of cultures.

The debate about how the current body of writing in English is to be situated in a global perspective remains contentious in India too. Some academic bodies like the Indian chapter of ACLALS (The Association for Commonwealth Literature and Language Studies) continue to use the term Commonwealth. The other position is exemplified by authors such as Amitav Ghosh, who while withdrawing his novel *The Glass Palace* from the works shortlisted for the Commonwealth Writers' Prize a few years back, draws attention to what he calls the imperialism of categories. He points out that there are many other languages in which writers from the Commonwealth countries write, and privileging one language is unfair. He draws attention to the curious logic of his eligibility—he qualifies to contend for the prize only because he belongs to a country that was once ruled by Imperial Britain! The author's dissent has been interpreted by some as an act which helps him position himself and his works politically and with respect to the market.

While Ghosh's withdrawal from the shortlist draws attention to the debate on categories and nomenclature, the criticism of his stance extends the debate to the ways in which the production and reception of the novel and the author are viewed today. Apart from the localism/universalism binary, it brings in the dynamics of a globalised world reality where our ideas and aspirations are significantly impacted by marketing strategists and financial analysts of transnational corporate houses—a world where creative writing is seen as a lucrative industry that attracts privileged Euro-American investment and which is marketed like any other consumer product.

The novel represents reality; it is also published and sold. A look at the present-day marketing strategies for consumer goods abundantly reveals the inordinate attention being paid to the packaging and presentation of products. The moot question is the appeal of the product. The publishing industry is no exception to this global trend. Since the creative arts cannot be strategically promoted as products by agencies which market publishers, there are other ways in which this is done. The literary equivalent of the launch of a product and its marketing is the announcement of an astronomical advance to an author, the euphoric media hype which showcases an author during the pre-release functions, and the gala functions that are subsequently organised during the release of their books. These authors and books are carefully chosen, and often the run-ups to the launch focus on their USPs. What is also interesting is that in many of the cases, the authors are usually first-timers projected as rising stars on the literary horizon.

This is not a country-specific phenomenon, and can be seen happening across the globe. The publishing houses, media, and the author are often complicit in the whole enterprise. The mechanism that creates the hype around authors focuses more on extra-literary considerations as factors in the marketing of the novels. The old idea of a masterpiece written with single-minded devotion and acknowledged for its literary value is thus, oftener than not, passé, or incidental if not irrelevant. This process is repeated with each new book and each new novelist whose agent is competent enough to negotiate a lucrative contract with an established publishing house. This is not to say that literary merit is ignored. But publicity is commensurate with investment. We often have authorial reputations built up in the West which are at considerable variance with the reception of their works in India. And these are not discrete incidents. They fit into a larger pattern—a critical acknowledgement of a sudden 'coming of age' of novels written in English by Indian authors, resident and non-resident. That this coincides with the phase in which there is a sudden spurt in Indian novelists getting international literary awards and multinational publishing houses like Penguin and Picador setting up shop in India cannot be ignored.

Significant discrepancies between the authorial reputations built up in the west and reception in India, as in the case of authors, thus needs to be carefully looked into. This phenomenon has to be understood in terms of language first. That globalisation has led to English becoming increasingly important is an established fact. Those writing in English thus start with an initial advantage vis-à-vis the global readership. And Indian diasporic novelists who straddle multiple cultures through birth, parentage, work or choice are thus doubly advantaged.

The Indian novel in English is usually contested at two levels. Firstly, it is put in the dock for the choice of language and faces sentimentalised regionalist/nationalist ire, and includes all Indian novelists writing in English. Secondly, it is charged with being the product of globalisation, and governed by the demands of the market. Primarily, novelists with diasporic or multicultural affiliations are at the receiving end of these charges but resident authors are not entirely exempt.

English is now officially one of the languages of India as stated in the Indian Constitution, and thus as valid a choice as any other Indian language. And if the Indian novel as a genre, which was also shaped by the interaction between the West and India, is not contested, why the Indian novel in English? However, the global visibility of the Indian novel in English vis-à-vis novels written in the other Indian languages brings in issues of authenticity, native-ity and representativeness of the country's multi-lingual and multi-cultural reality.

The second charge seems to be much discussed, especially in the aftermath of the publication of Salman Rushdie's *Midnight's Children* in 1980 and the globalisation of the Indian economy in the decade following it, during which Rushdie and a whole new generation of writers started getting noticed in the West. This was a significant period for the Indian novel in English, in terms of the boom in the number of titles published, the sheer variety of the work and the attention Indian novelists received in terms of global reception, awards and advances. That the novelist, in turn, responded to these developments and the Indian novel developed accordingly is a corollary to this fact. The localist/universalist binary is helpful in understanding this development. Novels dealing with the specificities and nuanced localities of India would risk being unintelligible to the greater global audience. So there are novels which present simplified renderings of the complex Indian scenario, keeping in mind global intelligibility. Often, these works are well-received abroad, but appear crude and simplistic to Indian readers. This could account for diverse responses to the same work in India and abroad. Conversely, the novels which do not do away with the nuances of the Indian scene sometimes read like elementary introductions to the history, culture and society of the country. Often, this approach veers towards patronisation and exoticisation of the country. India sells. There are also novels which deal with recognisable historical markers on which stories are pegged so that they are easily relatable. A cosmopolitan audience and the economic realities are thus significant impetuses, and diasporic writers or writers with multicultural affiliations are better placed to understand/exploit these dynamics. This is evident in the profile of the Indian novel in English.

The debate about Indian novels in English is thus a debate about the relationship between India and English and also about the changing contours of what India and Indians mean in terms of existing realities. Indian novels written in English are privileged, the privilege being located in the language, awards and the advances, and the leverage these issues have in the consumerist dynamics of a globalised world. The privileged in this dynamics have greater market visibility and their cosmopolitanism makes them more visible in academic spaces too. They do not constitute the entire picture though, and their visibility and privileging on the global level should not be taken as constitutive of Indian realities in a global context.

The relation between Indian novels in English and novels written in the bhashas has always been acrimonious. The debate between the academic and the creative writer is best illustrated in the Meenakshi Mukherjee–Vikram Chandra debate about the authenticity of representation. Mukherjee's view that Indian novelists writing in English are downplaying local specificities to fashion out a 'pan-Indian' reality which is more comprehensible to the globalised world is dismissed by Chandra as a persistent yet misplaced intellectual 'anxiety about the anxiety of Indianness' of how 'third world cosmopolitans' are playing into the hands of an 'all-devouring and all-distorting West'. The contentions of Amit Chaudhuri, the radical nativist position of Bhalchandra Nemade or the dramatic rebuttals of Subodh Sarkar and Sitanshu Yashaschandra are about the place of bhasha writings in the canon of Indian literature and also about taking Indian novels and novelists to task. Disparaging comments by Salman Rushdie and V. S. Naipaul about bhasha literatures and running down Indian language authors holds up the other end of the debate. Rushdie and Naipaul are downright dismissive of bhasha writing. Rushdie and Elizabeth West equate Indian writing in English with Indian Literature, completely ignoring bhasha literatures while editing the *Vintage Book of Indian Writing 1947–1997*. Naipaul is similarly dismissive of bhasha authors. In his introduction to *The Picador Book of Modern Indian Literature*, Amit Chaudhuri challenges the privileging of Indian writing in English. Nemade describes English as a 'killer language' and his 'footwear' metaphor to describe English is frequently referred to. The arguments which privilege bhasha literature usually focus on the authentic-ity of the bhashas and the colonial taint of English, leading to the contention that the bhashas and bhasha users are better equipped to deal with their cultural specificities than those writing in English.

Novels written in the bhashas primarily draw upon shared linguistic and cultural realities of specific communities and cater to them. Circumscribed readership and limited visibility was a reality for bhasha novels and their writers. Global dynamics, however, continually blur boundaries as authors and readers situated in different cultures can simultaneously produce and receive works beyond geographically demarcated spaces. In acknowledgement of these realities or perhaps, fortuitously, around the time that multinational publishing houses set up shop in India, committed publishers and editors like Geeta Dharmarajan, Urvashi Butalia and Mini Krishnan took up the task of translating and editing bhasha literatures into English, making a significant impact on the market as well as academia. Globalisation and its consequences have thus been instrumental in novels in the bhashas reaching out to a wider readership that now also comprises people who read translations of these novels in other Indian languages, as well as the global reader who reads these works in English translation. This has helped balance the general global impression of Indian novels being synonymous with Indian novels in English, in general perception. Translations also enriched academic discourse on Indian novels and opened up more than one window into the heterogeneity of India.

That translation is as an essential aspect of reaching out to a larger readership is undeniable. Translation of novels from one bhasha to another, though problematic, is relatively less so, as the circulation is usually within the country and between language communities which are in interaction with each other. Translations into English bring in a few problems of their own. As there is no clear-cut roadmap about how these translations should address the larger readership engages with, bhasha novels in English translation, like Indian novels in English, also get caught in the local/universal binary. One approach is to keep in mind the potential global readership and simplify cultural nuances. This could lead to the translation rendering the work facile. The other approach is the culture-specific translation that attempts to retain the specificities of the text by detailing all that needs explanation, either within the body of the translated text or through footnotes and glosses. This could risk being incomprehensible because of complicated details or else lose out on readability by attempting to be too explanatory. The task becomes still more difficult when we take into account the diversity of readership—the global non-Indian English reader, the Indian reader diasporic/cosmopolitan reader, and the Indian reader belonging to a different language/region/culture, each reader having different expectations. The heterogeneity of readership and the complexities of the translation process make this a complex task. Considering the large number of bhashas in which novels are written and the bewildering diversity they portray, translators have an array of narratives from which to choose. This also draws attention to the issue of who is translated, who is left out, who translates and with what effect, and how much of that choice is related to the dynamics of the market, and how it affects academia or the idea of Indian literature.

Globalisation then has rendered the indigenous/foreign debate between the bhashas and English largely redundant. It is not the central issue it is sometimes made out to be. The hierarchy of global relations, transnational movement and multiculturalism, together with the contemporary realities of the market—the ruthlessness of competition, the reader as consumer and the calculated strategising of the market affect both the novelist and the translator. It also translates into greater volume and visibility for the novel, whether written in English or translated into English from the bhashas. Globalisation and its manifestations are here to stay and it difficult to expect the novelist or the translator to remain untouched. It is for the discerning readers, students, and critics to generate a discourse that will help keep things in perspective. It is this discourse which will elucidate whether or not the Indian novel will stake out new directions in terms of its writing and its translation.

We end with a conclusion that is quite apart from the dynamics of all these novels in English and in the bhashas which we have talked about. Various young writers such as Chetan Bhagat, Durjoy Dutta, Amish Tripathi, Ravinder Singh and Anuja Chauhan among others have all been part of a new phenomenon which characterises Indian fiction in English today. Their novels are all bestsellers which redefine authorship, they are not dependent upon publishers/agents/ translators to sell their books, they talk about Indian realities in a studiedly artless way that makes critics refer to them as simplistic, direct and low-brow, and yet they are setting trends, generating a whole new category of novels that have millions of readers, and have (for lack of a better word) democratised the publishing and reading of English novels in India, taking it to a plethora of readers like never before. Making a distinction on the basis of mass readership as opposed to quality in terms of production and reception and ignoring Chetan Bhagat and many writers who have followed this path would mean ignoring millions of readers who read them. Ignoring them would also mean not taking into account the dynamics of a transitioning India, which is the dominant backdrop and origin of most of these novels, and which this large readership which cuts across region, language, class and culture relates to. This development, going beyond the institutionalised production and reception of novels written in and translated into English, points to the emergence of a new literary paradigm that deals matter-of-factly with the Indian negotiation with globalisation and deserves serious consideration.

The most important feature of these new novels is their complete disregard for a global audience as well as the elite who were the key constituency of earlier Indian novels written and translated into English. Straddling class and urban-rural divides, these novels focus on bhasha speakers and those readers for whom English is an aspirational reality, and who relate to the language on a functional level. Some critics are of the view that this is commercialisation on an intra-national level. Popular culture, regional inflections and usages, and newer negotiations between English and global reality today have all contributed to shaping these novels. And there is no denying the fact that these novels have redefined interrelations between the novel form, English language and the bhashas and their negotiations with the market, opening up the possibilities of still newer formations in the Indian novel today.

About the Contributors

Abdullah Khan is a New Delhi-based writer and literary critic. His debut novel on Patna will be published soon.

Abhay Mohan Jha is a Champaran-based freelance journalist. He is also a farmer and lawyer.

Abinash Chaudhary is a New Delhi-based public policy professional. He has written on a range of subjects for some of the leading publications in India.

Aditya Mani Jha is a journalist and writer, currently working with *Business Line*. He has written poems, short stories and articles for many publications.

Anuraag works in advertising on communication strategy, and is currently with J. Walter Thompson.

Atul K. Thakur is a New Delhi-based public policy professional, management consultant, journalist and writer. He has previously edited *India Since 1947* (Niyogi Books, 2013). He has been a columnist for some of the leading publications in South Asia.

Banibrata Mahanta teaches English Literature at Banaras Hindu University, Varanasi. He is the author of *Joseph Conrad: The Gothic Imagination* (2006) and has published widely in national and international journals.

Chandrahas Choudhury is a New Delhi-based author, columnist, and literary critic. He is the author of the novel *Arzee the Dwarf* (2009), and is an active reviewer and columnist.

Daipayan Halder is a senior journalist and writer. He is currently Editor of the newspaper *DB Post*. His first book of non-fiction, *Blood Island: The Marichjhanpi Massacre*, will be published shortly.

Dhruva Jaishankar is a public policy professional. He is currently with the Brookings Institution's India Center in New Delhi, as a Fellow for Foreign Policy.

Jaithirth Rao is an Indian entrepreneur. He was the founder and former CEO of the software company MphasiS and is currently the Executive Chairman of Value & Budget Housing Corporation. He often writes for financial publications.

Jayati Ghosh is Professor of Economics at the Centre for Economic Studies and Planning, School of Social Sciences, Jawaharlal Nehru University, New Delhi. She is the author of several books and many scholarly articles, and is a regular columnist on economic issues for *Frontline* and *Business Line*.

Kajal Basu is a senior journalist and writer. Formerly he was the Editor of *Tehelka* magazine.

Mahima Kaul is with the Public Policy Division of Twitter. She was previously with the Cyber & Media Initiative at the Observer Research Foundation, New Delhi.

Manu Bhagavan is Professor of History at Hunter College and the Graduate Center, The City University of New York. He is the author or (co-)editor of 5 books, including *The Peacemakers: India and the Quest for One World* (2012).

Manu Joseph is a New Delhi-based writer, journalist, and former editor of *OPEN* magazine. A columnist for both international and Indian newspapers, his debut novel was *Serious Men* (2010).

Namrata Goswami is currently a Minerva Grantee (a grant awarded by the Office of the US Secretary of Defense Minerva Initiative). She regularly consults for the NATO Partnership for Peace Consortium 'Emerging Security

Challenges Working Group' and is a Senior Analyst and Subject Matter Expert with Wikistrat and Auburn University Futures Lab.

Namrata Rathore Mahanta is an Assistant Professor at the Department of English, Mahila Mahavidyalaya, Banaras Hindu University, Varanasi.

Omair Ahmad is an author, journalist, and columnist. He has written several books, including the novel *Jimmy the Terrorist* (2010).

Pallavi Rebbapragada is an author, journalist and columnist based in New Delhi.

Rajarshi Singh is a Consultant at the Pratham Education Foundation's research wing ASER Centre, New Delhi, India. He has a PhD in Computational Mechanics from Carnegie Mellon University, Pittsburgh.

Rajeev Bhattacharya is a Guwahati-based senior journalist and author. He has worked for several leading newspapers and was the founding executive editor *of Seven Sisters Post*. His most recent book is *Rendezvous with Rebels: Journey to Meet India's Most Wanted Men* (2014).

Rajeev Ranjan Chaturvedy is a Research Associate at the Institute of South Asian Studies, an autonomous research institute at the National University of Singapore.

Rajiv Jayaram is a New Delhi-based journalist who has written extensively for *The Financial Express.*

Ramachandra Guha is a leading social historian and public intellectual. He has written extensively on topics related to the environment, social change, politics, and cricket. He is the author of many books, including, most recently, *Democrats and Dissenters* (2016).

Rasheed Kidwai is a senior journalist and writer. He is currently Associate Editor of *The Telegraph*, Kolkata. A regular political commentator on television, radio, and in print, he is the author of a book based on the Congress party, *24 Akbar Road* (2010).

Reetika Khera is a development economist who teaches at IIT Delhi. She has edited *The Battle for Employment Guarantee* (2011).

Rini Barman is a New Delhi-based researcher and writer. Her articles have appeared in various publications.

Robin Jeffrey is Visiting Research Professor at the Institute of South Asian Studies, an autonomous research institute at the National University of Singapore, and Visiting Research Professor at the Asia Research Institute, Singapore.

Samir Saran is Vice President of the Cyber & Media Initiative at the Observer Research Foundation, New Delhi. He is also a columnist for leading publications in India and abroad.

Sandeep Dikshit was a member of the 14th and 15th Lok Sabhas, representing the East Delhi constituency. Previously he headed SANKET, a social development group that pioneered the world's first sub-national Human Development Report in 1996.

Shamya Dasgupta is an experienced sports journalist and is currently Senior Editor with *Wisden India*. He is the author of *Bhiwani Junction: The Untold Story of Boxing in India* (2012).

Shashi Tharoor is a two-time MP from Thiruvananthapuram, a former Union Minister of State and former Under Secretary-General of the United Nations. He is the author of many books, including, most recently, *An Era of Darkness: The British Empire in India* (2016).

Sopan Joshi is an environmentalist and a Research Fellow at Gandhi Peace Foundation, New Delhi. He was formerly, Managing Editor, *Down to Earth*. As a columnist, he writes for some of the leading publications in India.

Sukanya Natarajan is a Doctoral Candidate at the Center for the Study of Law and Governance in Jawaharlal Nehru University, New Delhi. She was formerly a Research Fellow at the Japan Center for Economic Research and Berlin School of Law and Economics.

Sunil Khilnani is a Professor of Politics and Director of the King's College London India Institute. He is the author of several books, including, most recently, *Incarnations: India in 50 Lives* (2016).

T.S.R. Subramanian is a former Cabinet Secretary of India. He has a Master's degree in Public Administration from Harvard University and is the author of several books, including, most recently, *India at Turning Point* (2014).

Tabish Khair is Associate Professor in the Department of English, University of Aarhus, Denmark. He is a poet, literary critic, and author of several books, including, most recently, *The New Xenophobia* (2016).

Udaya Narayana Singh is an author, academician, and linguist who has published several works in English, Maithili, and Bengali. He is currently Professor, Rabindra Bhavana, and Chair, Centre for Endangered Languages, Visva-Bharati, Santiniketan.

Vinod Rai is Chairman of Bank Board Bureau, India, and a Visiting Senior Research Fellow at the Institute of South Asian Studies, Singapore. A former Comptroller and Auditor General of India he is also the author of *Not Just an Accountant: The Diary of the Nation's Conscience Keeper* (2014).

Vivek Kaul is a senior journalist who is currently a regular columnist for firstpost.com and firstbiz.com. He is the author of the *Easy Money* trilogy of books (2013–15).

Wajahat Habibullah is a retired IAS officer who worked extensively in Kashmir. He was the first Chief Information Commissioner of India and thereafter Chairperson of the National Commission for Minorities. He is a prominent political analyst and the author of *My Kashmir: The Dying of the Light* (2014).

Acknowledgements

My first book was launched on 22 July 2013, with a panel discussion featuring eminent publice intellectuals and journalists, including the late B.G. Verghese. His inspiring words on that day sounded like a demand for a sequel. That is why this book is dedicated to him, as well as to my paternal grandparents late Upendra Thakur and late Gita Thakur, and my maternal grandfather late Bimlendra Lal Mishra.

I must express my immense gratitude to eminent historian Sunil Khilnani for his foreword. I heartily appreciate that he read all the essays and discussed them with me before putting forth his views. I greatly value the effort of all the contributors, who generously spared their thoughts, time and effort to make this book possible. I am humbled to get early endorsements for the book from leading thinker Pratap Bhanu Mehta, senior journalist Indrajit Hazra and academician and author Harsh V. Pant.

I recall with humility the good words on my books from Ramachandra Guha, Shashi Tharoor, Jean Drèze, K. Natwar Singh, Bimal Jalan, Prem Shankar Jha, Jagmohan, Pankaj Mishra, Amit Chaudhuri, Raghuram Rajan, Ashutosh Varshney, Christophe Jaffrelot, Shekhar Gupta, Raj Kamal Jha, Bibek Debroy, Yogendra Yadav, Siddharth Varadarajan, M.K. Venu, Siddhartha Gigoo, Hemender Sharma, T.T. Rammohan, N.N. Jha, Taj Hassan, Niranjan Sahoo, Vinay Sitapati, Kanishka Gupta, Prayaag Akbar, Santosh Goenka, Vivan Sharan, Raghav Priyadarshi and Rajesh Mehta. From Banaras, where I studied (at BHU), I acknowledge my enduring bond with Rakesh Singh of Harmony Book Shop at Assi Ghat, and Prof. Ram Kirti Shukla and Prof. Ashok Kaul. I am also indebted to this city—its institutions, common residents and scholars.

My sincere thanks to my publishers Bikash De Niyogi, Tultul Niyogi and Trisha De Niyogi for their invaluable support, as well as the Niyogi Books Editorial Director Nirmal Kanti Bhattacharjee and Senior Editor

K.E. Priyamvada.

In recent years, I have written extensively for Nepal's leading English newspaper. It has been a pleasure exchanging ideas with Akhilesh Upadhyay, Chief Editor of *The Kathmandu Post*, Sudhir Sharma, Chief Editor of *Kantipur* and Senior Editors Apekshya Shah, Sanjit Pradhananga, Kamal Dev Bhattarai and John Narayan Parajuli. For a long and active intellectual collaboration, my warmest thanks to Pranaya S.J.B. Rana, Madhukar S.J.B. Rana, Greta Rana, Bishal Thapa, Tirtha Raj Wagle, Bishal Dhakal and Jitendra Jha. I am also thankful to the editors at *The Pioneer* and other publications, who helped me evolve as a columnist.

I would like to acknowledge, with great fondness, my family members—without whose ever-present help and support I would not be where I am today. My heartfelt thanks to my maternal grandmother Vinita Mishra, my parents Dhrub Narayan Thakur and Baby Thakur, my brother Ashutosh Kumar Thakur and my wife Chitralekha Thakur. I heartily appreciate my uncle Bashishth Narayan Thakur and aunt Hema Thakur, as well as Kamal Kant Thakur, Arhula Jha, Hira Jha, Renu Jha, Manglesh Thakur, Dipesh Thakur, Rina Thakur, Archana Jha, Aditya Jha, Shashinath Jha, Anshumesh Jha, Ravindra Jha, Salil Jha, Basant Kumar Thakur, Arun Jha, Aradhana Thakur, Pooja Thakur, Prity Thakur, Ravi Ranjan Thakur, Prabhat Ranjan Thakur, Neha Jha, Ayush Jha, Anushka Thakur, Divija Thakur, Abhishek Jha, Avinash Jha, Priya Jha, Shashank Mishra, Tushar Mishra, Umang Mishra, Manjari Mishra and my infant nephew Siddharth Thakur, for making home delightful and familial bonds unbreakable.

I deeply appreciate your warmth and kind words on my writing: Anjani Mishra, Anil Mishra, Prabhat Mishra, Prafulla Mishra, Prashant Mishra, Manoj Jha, Mamta Jha, Jibachh Jha, Rekha Jha, Rashmi Ranjan Jha, Prabhat Ranjan Jha, Bhavesh Nandan Jha, T.N. Thakur, Prashant Thakur, Pankaj K. Choudhary, Padmanabh Mishra, Neeraj Jha, Umesh Pathak, Chandan Pandey, Saahil Juneja, Shrey Goyal, Sushil Mishra, Ramesh Ranjan, Gourinath, Taranand Viyogi, Krishnanand Mishra, Gaurav Kumar, Dilip Jha and Priyanka Aman.

This book is a sincere attempt to provide informed perspectives on various aspects of India, for readers who seek to understand the future course of our nation. My humble thanks, therefore, to all my readers who seek to engage with this ongoing discussion.

Praise for the previous book in this series
India Since 1947: Looking Back at a Modern Nation (2013)

'A collection of 30 incisive essays from India's leading scholars and young writers on topics as varied as politics, economy, cinema and literature.'

The Hindu

'Given India since 1947 is too broad a topic, the editor's efforts to thread his way through the country's history in a single volume has succeeded beyond measure.'

The Economic Times

'This is a serious book, meant for readers who have genuine concern for India in action and of its past as a nation since 1947. The beauty of broad canvas and the finest opinion on a large set of themes, make this volume worth possessing and keeping it in memory for a long time.'

IBN Live

India Since 1947: Looking Back at a Modern Nation is an anthology on modern India edited by Atul K Thakur, journalist and policy practitioner...The range of contributors in this volume appears to be quite diverse and impressive.

-The Times of India

'*India Since 1947* provides an interesting glimpse into India's past and provokes readers to think about their idea of India. The book will be an essential read for those striving to understand India through an Indian lens.'

India Quarterly

'An extraordinary compilation of essays that encompasses all constituting aspects of modern India, and touches upon a wide variety of subjects that provide immediate relevance for the present and the decades gone by.'

The Kathmandu Post (Nepal)

'In order to trace India's journey since the advent of its independence in 1947, there is a dire need of books written with a historical perspective...*India since 1947: Looking Back at a Modern Nation* is one such attempt and has come out as a very promising book.'

The Daily Star (Bangladesh)